J F K: ORDEAL IN AFRICA

JFK

ORDEAL IN AFRICA

Richard D. Mahoney

New York   Oxford
OXFORD UNIVERSITY PRESS
1983

Copyright © 1983, Oxford University Press, Inc.

Library of Congress Cataloging in Publication Data

Mahoney, Richard D.
  JFK: Ordeal in Africa

  Includes index.
    1. Africa—Foreign relations—United States.
  2. United States—Foreign relations—Africa.
  3. Africa—Foreign relations—1960–   .
  4. United States—Foreign relations—1961–1963.
  5. Kennedy, John F. (John Fitzgerald), 1917–1963.
  I. Title.
  DT38.7.M33   1983   327.7306   82–24685
  ISBN 0–19–503341–8

Printing (last digit): 9 8 7 6 5 4 3 2 1

Printed in the United States of America

To my mother and father

The conjectural element of foreign policy—the need to gear actions to an assessment that cannot be proved true when it is made—is never more crucial than in a revolutionary period. Then the old order is obviously disintegrating while the shape of its replacement is highly uncertain. Everything depends, therefore, on some conception of the future.

Henry A. Kissinger

Acknowledgments

This history is based primarily on declassified documents from the Kennedy White House (the National Security Files and the President's Office Files) which are housed in the John F. Kennedy Presidential Library in Dorchester, Massachusetts. It is also drawn from the Adlai E. Stevenson Papers at Princeton University, the Chester Bowles Papers at Yale University, the G. Mennen Williams Papers at the National Archives in Washington, D.C., and from the collection of transcribed telephone conversations between the President and senior officials in his administration that is not yet in the public domain.

To the archivists who work in the security vault at the Kennedy library (where I spent more than a year), I wish to pay special tribute. They processed what must have seemed an unending stream of declassification requests with unfailing humor and competence. I am certain that the library's namesake would be pleased with the way his documentary heritage is being handled. Megan F. Desnoyers, Suzanne K. Forbes, and senior archivist William W. Moss were particularly helpful all the way along.

Interviews comprise the other major source of this history. Two hundred and twenty-three principals—from former British prime ministers to Belgian mercenaries—shared their recollections with the author. The unknown scholar has little to offer the public men and women whose assistance he seeks. There is no assurance that the hours they take to answer his questions will ever be reflected in a favorable, or even recognized, historical verdict. That is why my sense of debt is especially great and my inability to mention all of these individuals particularly regrettable. Responsibility for this book is surely mine, but the story itself is truly theirs.

My sincere thanks to: Rajeshwar Dayal, George Ivan Smith, Thomas A. Cassilly, Jr., Martin F. Herz, Lewis Hoffacker, Frank C. Carlucci, G. McMurtrie Godley, Robert Rothschild, Frédéric Vandewalle, J. Wayne Fredericks, Samuel E. Belk III, Carl Kaysen, Ralph A. Dungan, Lord Home, Lord Harlech, Sir Robert Jackson, the late Sir Geoffrey de Freitas, Erica Powell, Michael Dei-Anang, Alberto Franco Nogueira, Pierre Salinger, Harris L. Wofford, Jr., Gerald J. Bender, and Karen B. Maloney.

A note on oral histories is in order. To diminish the factual slippage inherent in such exchanges, interviewing was done with the aid of White House, State Department, Central Intelligence Agency, and embassy documents from the period. To avoid the journalistic practice now employed by some scholars of citing or quoting from unnamed sources, I have identified the pertinent individuals in the endnotes. In cases where the respondents specifically requested anonymity, a numbered index of confidential sources is cited in the text. This index will be deposited along with the rest of my research files at the Kennedy library. It will be available for use by other scholars after a suitable period of time.

The reader should know that this history has built on the definitive scholarship of Catherine Hoskyns and Stephen R. Weissman on the Congo, Dennis Austin and W. Scott Thompson on Ghana, and John Marcum on Angola.

A special word of gratitude is due George W. Ball, who gave the author access to his valuable papers and to W. Averell Harriman, who was not only kind in answering all of my questions and in reading an early draft of the manuscript, but also in arranging other interviews on my behalf. A grant from the Shell Foundation financed my first year of research and travel. The School of Advanced International Studies financed a second year, thanks to the intercession of Riordan J.A. Roett.

My personal thanks to: Maurice W. Kelley for instilling an interest in the academic profession in the first place; Robert E. Osgood for guiding me in scholarly ways during the doctoral process; Witney Schneidman and Gerard Rice for their intellectual companionship; the James C. O'Neill family for kindly providing shelter in a time of need; David B. Kay and James D. Thayer for sparing the reader many a banal thought and ungrammatical phrase as a result of their painstaking work on the manuscript in its early stages; and John W. Warner, who brought the full force of his editorial gifts to bear on this narrative during its final year.

Susan Rabiner, my editor at Oxford University Press, was quick to spot some merit in the original manuscript and was firm in encouraging me to improve upon it. I also wish to thank Joaquin M. Duarte, Jr., who did everything he could to lighten my professional load during the final year of rewriting, and Jacques Lowe, who generously allowed the use of his dramatic photograph for the cover of this book.

My father, William P. Mahoney, Jr., attentively read each of the manuscript's five drafts with a generous spirit. His example sustains me. My mother, Alice D. Mahoney, was always sympathetic of my labors and was warmly appreciative of the final result. Without the devoted work of my aunt, Peggy M. Spaw, who spent hundreds of hours over the past two years helping me to recast the narrative and to rethink my judgments, this book would not have been written.

Phoenix, Arizona
August 18, 1983

R.D.M.

A NOTE TO THE READER

The account which follows features the Congo, Ghana, and Portuguese Angola. While there were other African countries that were also important to the United States during this period, I have selected these three countries because they received proportionally more of the President's attention.

To fellow students of American foreign policy, I offer an admission of bias from the outset: diplomacy is politics. Walter Lippmann described the political art as one involving "a complex of material circumstances, of historic deposit, of human passion. . . ." By reason of its human makeup, diplomacy would seem to elude the strict confines of conceptual frameworks or quantitative models.

The experience of the Kennedy administration in Africa at least attests to the truth of Lord Salisbury's observation that victories in diplomacy are won by "a series of microscopic advantages: a judicious suggestion here, an opportune civility there, a wise concession at one point and a far-sighted persistence at another. . . ." National interests, rather than men, may be the crucial ingredients in foreign policy, but it is the men who make the difference in protecting or undoing those interests abroad. As John Kenneth Galbraith remarked to President Kennedy, foreign policy reflects the "fundamental instincts of those who make it."

This history revolves around the men in power at the time—their "thoughts, fears, and hopes," as Kennedy once put it, in dealing with new and puzzling problems. In assessing the central character of that cast, Gibbon's description of the Byzantine general Belisarius may suggest a comparison: "His imperfections flowed from the contagion of the times; his virtues were his own."

Contents

The six provinces of the Congo as of July, 1960.

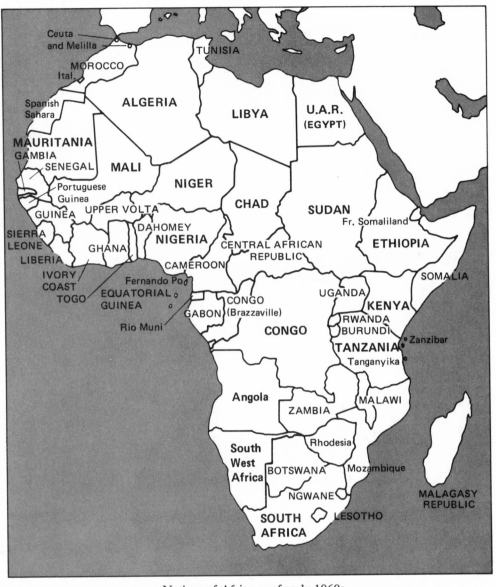

Nations of Africa as of early 1960s.

J F K: ORDEAL IN AFRICA

INTRODUCTION

Nationalism
and the Cold War

> .... The fundamental principle of this [peace] treaty is a
> principle never acknowledged before ... that the countries
> of the world belong to the people who live in them, and
> that they have a right to determine their own destiny and
> their own form of government and their own policy ...

Woodrow Wilson
(*September 1919*)

> It should be an obvious that we are not interested in seeing
> colonial empire administrations supplanted by [the] philos-
> ophy and political organizations emanating from and con-
> trolled by [the] Kremlin.

George C. Marshall
(*February 1947*)

World War II left the Western European powers battered and vulnerable
to a new scourge that was about to descend upon them—nationalism in
their overseas dominions. The experience of the war fundamentally altered
the expectations of colonial peoples. African students in the West demanded that the leaders of the allied powers live up to their war-time
declaration to "respect the right of all peoples to chose the form of government under which they will live." African soldiers, 250,000 of whom
had fought alongside British and Free French forces, believed that they
had fought for allied freedom in exchange for being granted their own.
One Nigerian Private, Theo Ayoola, might have spoken for all of them
when he wrote home in 1945: "We have been told what he fought for.
That is 'freedom.' We want freedom, nothing but freedom."[1]

National revolution in Africa and Asia coincided with another historic
development brought about by World War II—the emergence of the
United States and the Soviet Union as the two great powers in the postwar
world. Within weeks of the allied victory in Europe in May 1945, Soviet
and American cooperation began to give way to disagreement over the

political future of Eastern Europe. The relationship between the two worsened in the months that followed. Faced with Soviet pressure on Turkey and Iran, a communist insurgency in Greece, and Stalin's determination to maintain control over Eastern Europe, President Harry S Truman decided that he was "tired of babying" the Soviet Union. "Unless Russia is faced with an iron fist and strong language," he wrote his Secretary of State in January 1946, "another war is in the making."[2] The Cold War had begun.

At the time that Truman was taking steps to confront Russia with an "iron fist," twenty-nine-year-old John F. Kennedy was campaigning for the Democratic nomination in Massachusetts's Eleventh Congressional District. Kennedy had grown up in the internationalist tradition of Woodrow Wilson and Franklin Roosevelt. By the age of twenty-two, he had crossed the Atlantic more often than he had crossed the Mississippi. He had also privately taken strong exception to his father's preference, as U.S. ambassador to Great Britain, in the late 1930s, for keeping America out of the war at any cost.[3] Although he knew little about nationalist stirrings in Asia and Africa at the time he began his political career, John Kennedy had inherited a pronounced antipathy toward colonialism which, he claimed, had kept Ireland "in bondage for nearly a thousand years."[4]

During Kennedy's first two terms in the House (1947–51), the Cold War spread from Europe to Asia. With it grew the American public's sense of alarm about international communism. During his first term in the Senate (1953–59), anticolonial rebellion intensified in Africa. It was clear that Washington had to fashion a policy that would meet U.S. security concerns and yet address nationalist aspirations. But how?

The American dilemma was not new. In 1918, President Wilson had given vivid expression to America's desire to remain true to its anticolonial origins and to present a liberal alternative to Lenin's revolutionary Bolshevism. Yet Wilson had found at the Versailles Conference in 1919, as Roosevelt would in his talks with British Prime Minister Winston Churchill a generation later, that the Europeans were steadfast in their resistance to American pressure on the status of their colonial dependencies. The fact was, moreover, that in any definition of U.S. security, Europe had to come first.

As the bitterness of the Cold War deepened in the late 1940s, the U.S. grew more fearful, as Secretary of State George C. Marshall put it, that the European colonial empires would be supplanted by a far more threatening tyranny, the Kremlin. No one doubted that the Soviet Union intended to profit from the anticolonial turmoil. The question was, how strong was the nationalist impulse? Was it strong enough to sweep communism as well as colonialism before it? In Africa, at least, much of the answer had to do with the origins of the nationalist current. The men with whom John Kennedy would later have to deal were the heirs of that long struggle.

THE EUROPEAN CONQUEST

The European powers had carved up Africa in a fit of imperial rivalry at the end of the nineteenth century. "When I left the Foreign Office in 1880, nobody thought about Africa," Lord Salisbury remarked. "When I returned to it in 1885, the nations of Europe were almost quarreling with each other as to the various portions of Africa they could obtain."[5]

In many ways, Belgium's King Leopold II started the "scramble" by trying to set up a private empire for himself in the Congo in the late 1870s. Tensions mounted after Britain invaded and occupied Egypt in 1882, thereby nullifying France's claim to joint control over that country with the British, as well as upsetting the Anglo-French balance of power. Prince Otto von Bismarck entered the picture in 1883 by suddenly annexing to the German Empire the Cameroons, Togoland, and South-West Africa. Bismarck next invited the French government, still angry over its loss of Egypt, to join with him in a conference of all European powers to be held in Berlin to set the rules of the colonial game. The key agreement that emerged from the Berlin Conference of 1884–85 was that no European annexation of African territory would be valid unless there were "effective occupation."[6]

Africa's coastal peoples (many of whom had grown dependent on the Europeans in the course of the slave trade) generally fell quickly to the invaders. Effective occupation of the interior was another matter entirely. The warrior kingdoms of West and Central Africa resisted fiercely, despite the vastly superior firepower of the Europeans. French colonial forces did battle off and on for sixteen years against the Islamic revivalist Samori Touré in the deep interior of West Africa before finally defeating and capturing him in 1898. To the south, in the hinterland of the Gold Coast, the British fought three wars against the Ashanti before annexing their empire as a crown colony.[7]

Subversion was the other means of conquest. The rich and willful Cecil John Rhodes was asked by Queen Victoria to secure Central Africa for the British crown. Rhodes's Pioneer Column trekked into Matabeleland in 1890, giving assurances of peace and fruitful commerce. Ndebele King Lobengula, for his part, promised that he would give the settlers the mining concession that they wanted and would forbid his *impis* from

attacking the whites. "There is a wall around the word of a king," Lobengula said.

The word of the intruders was something else. Rhodes and his men
first sent settlers, then troops, and finally began to consort with the
Ndebele's enemy, the Shona. Lobengula knew what was coming. He
likened himself to a fly before a chameleon "that advances very slowly
and gently . . . until at last he darts out his tongue." When the Ndebele
finally went to war, they were slaughtered.[8]

To the north in Katanga, Leopold had already succeeded in subverting
the Bayeke. The Bayeke chief Msiri was murdered by one of Leopold's
agents and a suitably pliable successor was installed. The official account of
Leopold's seizure of the Congo overlooked such untidy events. Leopold's
court historian, Emile Banning, was moved to record: "The partition of
Africa on both sides of the Equator . . . was achieved peacefully, with
neither trouble nor jolts, and without any of the onerous and bloody conflicts which accompanied and noticeably impeded the colonization of the
two Americas . . . ."[9]

Meanwhile in Angola, Portugal was continuing its own "historic civilizing mission," as Premier António de Oliveira Salazar later described it.
Over the course of four hundred years, the Portuguese had colonized
Angola with the contents of their prisons. The *degredados* were described
by one observer in 1875 as "the choicest specimens of ruffians and whole-
sale murderers . . . [who] rob and cheat and in a few years become rich
and independent and even influential personages." The readiest victims of
the "civilizing mission" were, of course, the Africans.[10]

NATIONALIST STIRRINGS

Although the first years of the twentieth century, in one historian's phrase,
"glittered with the apparent splendor of colonial empires and clanked with
their accoutrements," there were scattered stirrings of resistance.[11] Britain's
West African Frontier Force was fully engaged in the conquest of Bornu
and the Fulani emirates of Nigeria until 1906.[12] The forest peoples of the
Ivory Coast and French Guinea and the desert tribes north of the Niger
continued to fight the French up to 1915, and, in some cases, beyond.

Among Africa's educated elite, there were efforts at political opposition. In the Gold Coast, the Aborigine Rights Protection Association successfully agitated against changes by the colonial government in the traditional land-tenure system. In 1900, thirty-two black delegates from Europe,
Africa, and the Americas met in London at the first Pan-Africanist
Congress. They framed an appeal to all nations of the world to liberate

the black man. A year later, a number of Angolans living in Lisbon published a protest accusing Portugal of having committed "an outrage against civilization" in Africa. The "century of nationalism" in Africa had begun.[13]

The great catalyst to African nationalism over the next fifty years was war in Europe. The end of World War I thrust Soviet Russia and the United States, each armed with a new and rival ideology, to the forefront of international relations. Each would contribute to the nationalist infection that would eventually spread throughout Europe's colonial dominions.

On January 8, 1918, President Woodrow Wilson presented to Congress his Fourteen Points plan for postwar peace. Point Five called for "a free, open-minded, and absolutely impartial adjustment of all colonial claims. . . ." Although it is doubtful that Wilson ever intended to apply his ideal of "self-determination" to anything but the colonies of defeated Germany, his Secretary of State, Robert Lansing, foresaw its effect in the rest of the colonized world. "Will it not breed discontent, disorder and rebellion? . . . The phrase is simply loaded with dynamite. It will raise hopes that can never be realized. It will, I fear, cost thousands of lives."[14]

At the Versailles Peace Conference the following year, Wilson proposed that defeated Germany's African colonies be made the common property of the League of Nations rather than partitioned among the victors. His British, French, and Japanese counterparts were disturbed by the radical nature of the American proposal, but ultimately agreed to hold the German territories under mandate from the League of Nations.[15] Wilson's trusteeship precedent, to be embodied more fully in the Charter of the United Nations, would pave the way to independence for Tanganyika, Togo, and the Cameroons.

The American call for self-determination registered immediately throughout the colonized world. J.E. Casely-Hayford of the Gold Coast cited Wilson's declaration in launching the Congress of West Africa in 1920. In Paris, a thirty-year-old Vietnamese named Nguyen Ai Quoc (later to be known as Ho Chi Minh) drew up an eight-point program for Vietnamese emancipation patterned after Wilson's Fourteen Points and tried to hand deliver it to Wilson at Versailles. He was shown the door.[16] Wilson's crusade was abandoned, however, when the Senate rejected the Versailles Treaty and declined to join the League. America turned inward.

In Russia, the Bolsheviks, propelled to power by the chaos caused by the war, dedicated themselves to the international projection of class struggle. At the Second Comintern Congress in 1920, Lenin dismissed

Wilson's liberal reformism and proposed a "linkage of Communist and national revolutions, with Russia as the bridge between the two."[17] Historian Arthur Link described the exchange as democracy's "first full-dress debate with international communism."[18] But Soviet Russia was soon consumed in its own turmoil. Not until well after the end of World War II would the Soviet Union and the United States move from ideological to political confrontation in the colonized world.

The African generation that had seen its kingdoms fall to European weaponry now began sending its sons to learn the white man's way. Most finished their educations in local missionary schools, but a few hundred made their way to Western universities in the 1930s. In their racial isolation, the African students looked to their heritage for support. Some, such as Jomo Kenyatta and Kofi Busia, set forth their pride in traditional African society in academic monographs.[19] Others, such as J.B. Danquah and Nnamdi Azikwe, used journalism as their medium of defiance when they returned home.[20] Still others, such as Léopold Sédar Senghor and Agostinho Neto, wrote poetry in European tongues to communicate their "négritude" across tribal and colonial boundaries. Jean-Paul Sartre called the poetic renaissance Black Orpheus—"the descent of the black man into himself."[21]

All of them dreamt and talked of liberation. Shortly after he arrived in New York in October 1935, Kwame Nkrumah wrote to a friend in the Gold Coast that "No African student who visits this country can return home without being determined to liberate Mother Africa from imperialist chains of exploitation."[22] There was a fever among them. "We worked all day and talked all night," Gold Coaster Michael Dei-Anang remembered.[23] They were looking for a creed, a set of slogans—Leninism, Wilsonianism, Fabianism—with which to set their colonies afire. The universities where they matriculated became hotbeds of anticolonial activism. "The first skirmishes in the struggle for political freedom," a Nigerian student said at the time, "are being fought today in the colleges of the United States."[24]

The century's second great cataclysm, World War II, shook the imperialist governments to their foundations and set the stage for political freedom in Africa. African students in the West saw that their hour was at hand. Kwame Nkrumah abandoned his studies in London and boarded a ship for home, determined to fulfill his vow to liberate Mother Africa. He formed his own party, fomented a nationwide strike against the colonial government, and landed in jail. Nationalists elsewhere in British East Africa followed suit. In colonies that had been heavily settled by whites, such as Algeria, Madagascar, and Kenya, nationalist agitation in the mid-

1940s was greeted with gunfire. Tens of thousands lost their lives in Algeria and Madagascar. The colonialists had sown the wind in the first half of the twentieth century; they would reap the whirlwind in the second half.

It was President Franklin D. Roosevelt who restored Wilson's vision to American foreign policy. The Atlantic Charter, which he signed with Prime Minister Winston Churchill in 1941, declared: "We respect the right of all peoples to choose the form of government under which they will live." Churchill subsequently informed the House of Commons that the declaration applied only to countries occupied by the Axis powers; that he had not become the king's first minister to preside over the dissolution of the British empire. Roosevelt, in turn, was quick to correct him: the declaration applied "to all humanity."[25] Throughout the war, Roosevelt prodded Churchill to plan for the liberation of India at the end of the war. He was even more emphatic regarding Indochina. "France had milked it for one hundred years," he wrote Secretary of State Cordell Hull. "The people of Indochina are entitled to something better."[26]

Roosevelt pushed for an extension of Wilson's trusteeship system. On April 10, 1945, just two days before his death, he approved the United Nations trusteeship plan that he had discussed with Stalin and Churchill at the Yalta summit conference.[27] Stalin had readily agreed to the plan, possibly detecting in American idealism the beginning of the end for the West in Asia and Africa. Churchill continued to have deep reservations about the proposal, fearing that it would open the floodgates of nationalism. Faced with Soviet-American agreement, however, he had had no choice but to go along with the idea.

The UN Charter, signed in San Francisco in July 1945, devoted three of its nineteen chapters to the advancement of colonial peoples. Key articles in the Charter enabled UN machinery to clear the path toward decolonization. Article 77 made provisions for trusteeship over dependent territories. Article 10 authorized the General Assembly to discuss and make recommendations on any questions within the scope of the Charter. Article 39 permitted the Security Council to employ forceful measures to maintain or restore international peace and security. In order to bring the Charter to signature, loopholes were left in key articles, but the political meaning of the Charter rang loud and clear to African nationalists: they now had a forum and, as Nkrumah liked to put it, a "protector." For Africa, the floodgates were beginning to inch open.

In Asia, the colonial powers were engulfed in the nationalist tide. India and Pakistan gained their independence from Great Britain in 1947. Nationalist movements in French Indochina and Dutch Indochina demanded to be freed as well. The only question was whether the colonial powers had the will and the means left to resist. Much depended on American foreign policy, which was about to change.

THE COLD WAR

Roosevelt had died confident that the "era of good feeling" between the U.S. and the Soviet Union would provide for an enduring peace after the war. At the Yalta summit in February 1945, Soviet concessions seemed to affirm Roosevelt's hope. Stalin accepted the American proposal that the veto in the UN Security Council be used only in enforcement disputes and not in peaceful settlements. He also agreed to hold free elections in Eastern Europe after the war and repeatedly expressed his hope for fifty years of peace and big-power cooperation. The inauguration of the United Nations four months later seemed to institutionalize such aspirations.

Such promise quickly faded after Roosevelt's death. Truman, initially disturbed about Soviet intentions in Eastern Europe, began to assume the worst in January 1946. The Soviet Union refused to withdraw the Red Army from Iran and demanded from Turkey both a naval base in the Dardanelles and joint control over the strait. From Moscow, George F. Kennan described the Russians as fanatical and neurotic—determined that the "internal harmony of our society be disrupted, our traditional way of life be destroyed, the international authority of our state be broken."[28] Winston Churchill declared in Fulton, Missouri, a month later that the Russians had lowered an "iron curtain" over Eastern Europe and now posed a "growing challenge and peril to Christian civilization," which could be held in check only by a "fraternal association of English-speaking peoples."[29]

Columnist Walter Lippmann regarded the Kennan message as the sort of overstatement that might lead to overreaction, even war. Churchill's ringing suggestion of a common front disturbed him even more. Lippmann reminded his readers that the "line of British imperial interest and the line of American vital interests are not to be regarded as identical."[30] He feared that Britain, in its weakened state, might maneuver an unwitting America into defending the British empire in the name of anticommunism.

When the British informed Washington in February 1947 that they could no longer afford to suppress the communist-led rebellion in Greece without American support, Lippmann detected a British imperial gambit to acquire "a transfusion of American power, based on our fear of Soviet Russia."[31] But President Truman saw only the Russian enemy at the gate. He convened a joint session of Congress and asked for $400 million to help the Greek and Turkish governments. "[T]otalitarian regimes imposed upon free peoples by direct or indirect aggression," Truman declared, "undermine the foundations of international peace and hence the security of the United States . . . We cannot allow changes in the *status quo* . . . by such methods as coercion, or by such subterfuges as political infiltration."[32] The Truman Doctrine was born.

Under Secretary of State Dean Acheson told congressional leaders to prepare for Armageddon. He explained to them why the American commitment had to be global. "Like apples in a barrel infected by one rotten one, the corruption of Greece would infect Iran and all to the East. It would also carry infection to Africa through Asia Minor and Egypt to Europe."[33] As set forth by Russian expert Kennan, the means by which to contain Soviet expansion into "every nook and cranny" was the "adroit and vigilant application of counterforce at a series of constantly shifting geographic and political points."[34] The strategy became known as containment.

To Lippmann, the containment strategy, as defined by Kennan, was nothing less than a "strategic monstrosity." It could only be attempted by "recruiting, subsidizing, and supporting a heterogeneous array of satellites, clients, dependents and puppets" all over the globe.[35] As necessary as he thought the NATO alliance was to the defense of Western Europe itself, Lippmann feared that America might become the defender of European colonialism overseas. The first instance of this defense of the imperial *status quo* occurred in Indochina.

During World War II, the U.S. had given military aid to anti-Japanese forces in Vietnam fighting under Ho Chi Minh. Although he was a communist, Ho was deeply grateful to President Roosevelt and repeatedly communicated his desire for close relations with the U.S. After the liberation of Indochina, the American military mission in Vietnam had flown a guard of honor of two fighter planes in Hanoi in celebration of the establishment of the Democratic Republic of Vietnam. The French were furious at this American display of "infantile anticolonialism," but saw the writing on the wall. In March 1946—a year before the proclamation of the Truman Doctrine—France agreed to grant Vietnam full autonomy within the Indochinese Federation.[36]

Within six months of the signature of the agreement, France betrayed its promise. The French government established a puppet regime in the south under Bao Dai, who had served as "emperor" during the Japanese occupation. French forces turned their artillery on Haiphong, killing 6,000 Vietnamese. Ho appealed for American intercession, but to no avail. In Washington, the single imperative of foreign policy was to contain communism; the anticolonialist tradition was put aside. Secretary of State Acheson subsequently denounced Ho as a "Commie" and as the "mortal enemy of native independence."[37] By 1951, the U.S. was paying 40 percent

of the cost of France's war against the Viet Minh, Ho's nationalist movement. As Lippmann had warned, America was becoming the praetorian of
European empire.

In the fall of 1951, Congressman Kennedy decided that he would make
a trip to Indochina and other areas of Asia and the Middle East "to get
some first-hand knowledge, some facts to bite on, to know how these people
regard us." As his brother Robert, who accompanied him on the trip, later
remembered, John Kennedy's experiences and observations during those
seven weeks would have "a very, very major" impact on his thinking.[38]

1

The Education
of John F. Kennedy

> I grew up in a community where the people were hardly a
> generation away from colonial rule. And I can claim the
> company of many historians in saying that the colonialism
> to which my immediate ancestors were subject was more
> sterile, oppressive and even cruel than that of India.
>
> John F. Kennedy
> to Jawaharlal Nehru
> (*January 1962*)

John Kennedy's first two terms as a Massachusetts congressman coincided with the descent of the U.S. into the Cold War. After their surprise defeat in the 1948 elections, the Republicans came back to Washington in January 1949 determined to find an issue with which to challenge Truman. The issue they seized upon was the defeat of Nationalist China by the communist forces of Mao. In the final months of Nationalist (Guomindang) rule on the mainland, the Truman administration decided to cut its losses in China by disengaging its support from the corrupt and hopeless regime of Chiang Kai-shek. For this, it was accused and convicted in Congress of having "lost" China to the Communists.[1]

At least initially, Congressman Kennedy shared the Republican view of what had gone wrong in Asia. On the floor of the House in January 1949, Kennedy charged that the White House and the State Department were to blame for the communist victories in China. "So concerned were our diplomats, the Lattimores and the Fairbanks, with the imperfection of the democratic system in China after 20 years of war and the tales of corruption in high places that they lost sight of our tremendous stake in a non-Communist China. This House must now assume the responsibility of preventing the onrushing tide of communism from engulfing all of Asia."[2]

In February 1950, the atmosphere in Washington turned ugly. Republican Senator Joseph R. McCarthy of Wisconsin, playing upon popular fear of communist penetration of the U.S. government after the conviction of Alger Hiss for perjury, claimed that he had uncovered the names of communists in the State Department. As Robert J. Donovan wrote, "Mao's victories and the suspicions aroused by the Hiss case and McCarthy's thunder created a perfect atmosphere for charges of a stupendous plot inside the Truman administration—a plot that enabled communism to triumph in the world with the help of conspiracy and treason in Washington."[3] In June 1950, North Korea invaded South Korea. All doubts about the wisdom of equating nationalist conflicts with the designs of international communism were swept away in the anticommunist furor.

KENNEDY IN ASIA

As the crises deepened in Korea and Indochina, involving both the United States and France in major land wars, Kennedy decided to go to Asia to see for himself. "It was men rather than scenery I sought," Kennedy remarked on the Mutual Broadcasting Network after his return, "and I talked with all types of them—with generals, such as Eisenhower and Collins and Ridgway, and de Lattre, the Commander-in-Chief of the French troops in Indochina, with prime ministers such as Ben Gurion and Nehru and Liaquat Ali Khan. . . ."[4] Kennedy also made unscheduled trips outside the capitals and later reported that he questioned everyone he could—"ministers and ambassadors and consuls and businessmen and also the man in the street." In Saigon, "he was met at the airport by what seemed half of the French army, ready to brief him . . . to prove to him how committed the natives were to the French type of freedom." But Kennedy soon jumped the traces, got the names of the best reporters in town, and showed up unannounced at their apartments looking so young that they had trouble believing he was really a congressman.[5]

After his return to the U.S., Kennedy voiced strong dissatisfaction with the conventional view of what was occurring in Asia. "This is an area of human conflict between civilizations striving to be born and those desperately trying to retain what they have held for so long." He told his listeners that he had visited several Asian countries "in which the fires of nationalism so long dormant have been kindled and are now ablaze . . . Here colonialism is not a topic for tea-talk discussion; it is the daily fare of millions of men. This is also an area of revolution, which manifests itself at times in bloody riots and assassinations, in bloody guerrilla war . . . and pitched battles and full-scale modern war."[6]

It was during his 1951 trip that Kennedy had his first direct encounter with a nonaligned government. He came away from his talks with Nehru and his ministers with a live-and-let-live attitude that would later characterize his administration's relations with Nkrumah, Nasser, and Sukarno. "Russia and America are nations [of] whose quarrels India wishes no part . . . she can neither be bribed or cajoled to join either our or the Russian camp," he observed in 1957. "She will deal and has dealt with Communism in her own way, but not in ours."

The communist threat in Indochina, however, was perceived differently by Kennedy in 1951, and this perception carried through his presidency. Although the war seemed to be going France's way in 1951, Kennedy was pessimistic about the prospects of winning by military force alone. For the U.S. to have allied itself with "the desperate effort of a French regime to hang on to the remnants of empire," without exacting in exchange political reform in Indochina was a serious mistake, he thought. He was confident that the war could be won if France conceded independence to the Vietnamese. Only then would they have a stake in defeating the communist insurgency. "To check the southern drive of Communism makes sense but not only through reliance on force of arms. The task is rather to build strong native non-Communist sentiment within these areas and rely on that as a spearhead of defense."

What was critical, Kennedy believed, was a vigorous diplomatic presence in the field. He remarked in his 1951 report that "One finds too many of our representatives toadying to the shorter aims of other Western nations, with no eagerness to understand the real hopes and desires of the people to which they are accredited." As President, Kennedy would express a similar thought in a letter to all chiefs of U.S. missions overseas: "The practice of modern diplomacy requires a close understanding not only of governments but also of people . . . Therefore, I hope that you will plan your work so that you may have the time to travel extensively outside the nation's capital."

After his election to the Senate in November 1952, Kennedy continued to study Indochina. Edmund A. Gullion, a Foreign Service officer in Saigon whom Kennedy had befriended on his trip to Indochina (and who later became Kennedy's ambassador to the Congo), conferred on occasion with the senator, as did Harvard Sinologist, John F. Fairbank. In May 1953, Kennedy addressed a letter to Secretary of State Dulles asking him forty-seven specific questions about American involvement in Indochina.[7]

Rising in the Senate on July 1, 1953, Kennedy reiterated his view that the Viet Minh insurgency could never be put down unless France offered independence to its colony in return for opposing the communist guerrilla action:

> . . . the war can never be won unless the people are won from sullen neutrality and open hostility to support it. And they never can be, unless

they are assured beyond a doubt that complete independence will be
theirs at . . . the war's end.[8]

He offered an amendment to the administration's military-aid bill making
continuing U.S. military support for the French war effort contingent on
French agreement to grant Indochinese independence. The Eisenhower
administration was opposed and, with the support of a number of Democratic senators, defeated the amendment by a vote of sixty-four to
seventeen.

In 1954, Kennedy renewed his effort to convince the Senate that the
U.S. should recognize the nationalist dimension of the Viet Minh in-
surgency. In a speech to the Cathedral Club in Brooklyn, New York,
Kennedy described Ho Chi Minh as a popular leader who had "influence
penetrating all groups of society because of his years of battle against
French colonialism." The rebels, communist or not, were seen as liberators,
Kennedy argued.[9]

The Eisenhower administration, however, had no interest in the sort
of political concession Kennedy was proposing. In January 1954, the
French (now with more than 200,000 casualties) had their backs to the
wall. The administration was considering emergency measures to relieve
a major French garrison of 15,000 men completely surrounded by the
Viet Minh at Dien Bien Phu.[10] Vice President Richard Nixon launched
what Richard Rovere called, "one of the boldest campaigns of political
suasion ever undertaken by an American statesman." Hundreds of congressmen, newspapermen, and radio and television personalities were
rounded up and sent to the State Department for the purpose of conversion
to the hard line.[11] Kennedy, for one, dissented emphatically, publicly demanding to know how "the new Dulles policy and its dependence upon
the threat of atomic retaliation will fare in these areas of guerrilla
warfare."[12]

On April 6, 1954, Kennedy delivered a long and forceful speech on
the Senate floor regarding Indochina policy. The United States could not
declare war on nationalism, he said.

> To pour money, material, and men into the jungles of Indochina with-
> out at least a remote prospect of victory would be dangerously futile.
> . . . no amount of American military assistance in Indochina can
> conquer an enemy which is everywhere and at the same time nowhere,
> "an enemy of the people" which has the sympathy and covert support
> of the people.

The next day, President Eisenhower stated that the U.S. would not
retreat from its commitments; to do so would trigger a domino effect of
communist takeovers in Southeast Asia.[13] To place the entire Southeast

Asian area under the protective embrace of containment, the U.S. subsequently formed a coalition of anticommunist states into the Southeast Asia Treaty Organization (SEATO).

At the Geneva Conference in the summer of 1954, the U.S. refused to associate itself with the Final Declaration of the parties regarding a negotiated settlement. France, Britain, the Viet Minh, and the rest of the communist powers approved the accord, which provided that the political future of Vietnam be resolved by national elections in 1956. Apparently anticipating that Ho Chi Minh would be the unquestioned victor, however, the new strongman in Saigon, Ngo Dinh Diem, blocked the elections.[14]

CRISIS IN THE MIDDLE EAST AND NORTH AFRICA

Although drained by the nationalist scourge, Britain and France had one high card left to play in their struggle against colonial insurgency— America's obsession with communism. Eisenhower and Dulles were aware of this and were not particularly happy about backing the colonialists in their eleventh hour, but the experiences of the U.S. in China and Indochina had left the Eisenhower administration deeply suspicious of the ultimate outcome of the nationalist struggle. "Precipitate action [for independence] would in fact not produce independence," Secretary Dulles declared, "but only a transition to a captivity far worse than the present dependence."[15] Further, they believed that political independence would produce "vacuums" that would invite Soviet aggression and the need for American intervention. No sooner had the Indochina crisis subsided somewhat than new trouble arose in the Middle East.

In early 1955, Great Britain moved to strengthen its military position in the Middle East and so as to isolate the regime of Egypt's Gamel Abdel Nasser and thereby slow the spread of radical Arab nationalism. Dulles saw the chance to replicate his SEATO treaty in a new setting; and in April he convinced the British to join with the pro-Western regimes in the area (Turkey, Iran, Iraq, and Pakistan) in forming the Baghdad Pact. Interpreting this as an antinationalist alliance, Nasser signed an arms deal with the Soviet Union. Another American rearguard action seemed to be in the offing.

With a presidential campaign already under way in the summer of 1956, the Democrats, sensitive as they were to Republican accusations that they had been "soft on communism," abstained from criticizing the Eisenhower foreign policy record. When Democratic foreign policy spokesman Dean Acheson did criticize the administration, he was often more bellicose than Dulles.

Kennedy, however, was moving in the opposite direction. He was increasingly disturbed by the automatic manner in which nationalist change was associated with international communism. During a campaign appearance for Adlai Stevenson in September 1956, Kennedy voiced his stiffest dissent to date on the subject of nationalism and American foreign policy. The crisis in the Middle East, he said, was caused not by communist subversion, as the administration was maintaining, but rather by

> the Afro-Asian revolution of nationalism, the revolt against colonialism, the determination of people to control their national destinies . . . In my opinion, the tragic failure of both Republican and Democratic administrations since World War II to comprehend the nature of this revolution, and its potentialities for good and evil, has reaped a bitter harvest today—and it is by rights and by necessity a major foreign policy campaign issue that has nothing to do with anti-Communism.[16]

At a time when nationalism was officially regarded as capable of creating "dangerous vacuums," Kennedy's position bordered on heresy. Stevenson's office specifically requested that the senator make no more foreign policy statements in any way associated with the campaign.[17]

The situation in the Middle East in the summer of 1956 was not yet hopeless. Nasser had requested Western financing for the construction of a dam across the Nile at Aswan. The Americans had tentatively agreed to provide the lion's share of the money, particularly after the Soviets had made a rival offer. When Nasser recognized the People's Republic of China in July 1956, however, the U.S. broke off talks on the Aswan Dam. Dulles explained the reasons for American withdrawal, saying "we do not want to give such aid if it merely supports governments which are subservient or sympathetic to international communism."[18]

A week later, Nasser nationalized the Suez Canal. The British were infuriated and prepared to invade Egypt in concert with the French and the Israelis. President Eisenhower, however, would tolerate no such intervention; invasion would violate international law.[19] Dulles was subsequently asked to assume the role of diplomatic middleman. The British and the French, however, rejected the American call for compromise and, in collusion with the Israelis, secretly launched an invasion of Egypt in the final week of October.

Eisenhower was infuriated when he learned of the invasion. He telephoned British Prime Minister Anthony Eden and proceeded to give him a tongue-lashing that reduced Eden to tears. The Americans (with Soviet support) then forced the British and French into a showdown at the UN. The Soviet Union threatened to attack the Europeans unless they withdrew. Humiliated and embittered, Britain and France withdrew their forces.[20]

After Suez, the President pledged to stop "armed aggression from any nation [in the Middle East] controlled by International Communism" by filling the Middle Eastern vacuum "before it is filled by Russia." The Eisenhower Doctrine came into full force in the Lebanese civil war in 1958. Despite ample evidence that the source of the fighting was a domestic power struggle, Eisenhower believed otherwise. "Behind everything," he later wrote, "was our deep-seated conviction that the Communists were principally responsible for the trouble."[21] This perception required the landing of 14,300 marines in July 1958 at the request of the Lebanese president, Camille Chamoun.

In Kennedy's mind, Eisenhower's preoccupation with communist designs and his penchant for military pacts and alliances left little room for diplomatic initiative. He attributed the "paralysis" of U.S. foreign policy to the fixation on Russia's capabilities, on Russia's diplomatic and economic initiatives, on Russia's seemingly greater flexibility and power to maneuver. "Less and less have we and our allies been concerned with our own capacities, our own positive objectives, and our own ability to reach new goals consonant with our own values and traditions."[22]

Kennedy objected not only to the Eisenhower policy, but the self-righteousness with which it was being carried out. Foreign policy was "being starved on a diet of negatives," Kennedy declared. He had doubts about the good-versus-evil approach to foreign policy and the public scolding of nations that refused to fall into Dulles's tidy division of the world into either American or Soviet camps. He found inappropriate Dulles's string of axioms: "godless Communism"; the "Soviet master plan"; the "liberation of enslaved peoples"; and the "immorality" of neutralism. "Public thinking is still being bullied by slogans which are either false in context or irrelevant to the new phase of competitive coexistence in which we live," Kennedy observed in 1957.[23] Quoting British historian Denis Brogan, he proposed that "we strike a balance between . . . the 'illusion of omnipotence' and a somber contemplation of the impossibility of absolute solutions."[24]

Early in 1957, Kennedy decided to make a major critique of the administration's position on France's colonial war in Algeria. By 1957, the French had committed over 500,000 troops to the effort to suppress the nationalist rebellion. Torture, atrocity, and terror on both sides had turned the pride of France's empire into a chamber of horrors. Mindful of France's humiliation at Suez, the Eisenhower administration had been maintaining a policy of strict silence on Algeria—at least until Kennedy's attack, which *The New York Times* called "the most comprehensive and outspoken arraignment of Western policy toward Algeria yet presented by an American in public office."[25]

THE ALGERIA SPEECH

On July 2, 1957, Kennedy accused the Eisenhower administration of courting disaster in Algeria. He charged that Eisenhower's policy of non-involvement in Africa and Asia was really made up of "tepid encouragement and moralizations to both sides, cautious neutrality on all the real issues, and a restatement of our obvious dependence upon our European friends, and our obvious dedication nevertheless to the principles of self-determination, and our obvious desire not to become involved." The result, Kennedy said, was that, "We have deceived ourselves into believing that we have thus pleased both sides and displeased no one . . . when, in truth, we have earned the suspicion of all."[26]

The previous decade had proven that the tide of nationalism in the Third World—from Indochina to India to Indonesia—was "irresistible," Kennedy declared. It was time for France to face the fact that Algeria had to be freed. When would the West learn, he asked, that colonies "are like fruit that cling to the tree only till they ripen?" Didn't the French debacle in Indochina, which ended at Dien Bien Phu, serve as a warning of what lay ahead for France in Algeria if something were not done?

> Did that tragic episode not teach us whether France likes it or not, admits it or not, or has our support or not, that their overseas territories are sooner or later, one by one, going to break free and look with suspicion on the Western nations who impeded their steps to independence? . . . [N]ationalism in Africa cannot be evaluated purely in terms of the historical and legal niceties argued by the French and thus far accepted by the State Department. National self-identification frequently takes place by quick combustion which the rain of repression simply cannot extinguish.

In the United States, a storm of protest greeted Kennedy's address on "Facing Facts on Algeria." President Eisenhower complained about "young men getting up and shouting about things."[27] Secretary Dulles commented acidly that if the senator wanted to tilt against colonialism, perhaps he might concentrate on the communist variety. Most prominent Democrats were equally scornful. Adlai Stevenson dismissed Kennedy's speech as "terrible." Dean Acheson described the speech as "foolish words that wound . . . a dispirited ally."[28]

In France, the speech provoked an even more furious outcry. Paris's largest daily, *Le Figaro*, remarked: "It is shameful that our business is so badly directed that we are forced to endure such idiocies." *U.S. News and World Report* noted that "An American has unified France—against himself!" Responding to Kennedy's speech, French President René Coty told the French Senate that France would "never negotiate with cutthroats since independence would give the 1,200,000 Europeans living in Algeria one alternative—leaving their homeland or living at the mercy of fanaticism." French Defense Minister André Morice publicly wondered whether Kennedy was "having nightmares." Talk of independence, Morice said, "will cost many more innocent lives."[29] Harvard historian Arthur M. Schlesinger, Jr. reported to Kennedy from Paris that summer that "Algeria is beginning to poison France."[30]

In Algeria itself, feeling among the European colonists against the speech ran so high that French authorities warned American newsmen and residents to stay off the streets to avoid reprisals. Two days after the speech a bomb exploded outside the American consulate in Algiers. The French Resident Minister in Algiers, Robert Lacoste, called the bomb "a Communist joke" and challenged Kennedy to come to Algeria. The senator declined.[31]

As Kennedy had clearly intended, the speech drew a great deal of press attention. Most of it, however, was unfavorable. Of the 138 editorials clipped by Kennedy's office, 90 opposed the speech and only 48 supported it.[32] The sentiments of *The New York Times* were typical: "It took courage —perhaps rashness—to present a case so critical of French politics . . . a situation like this requires the most delicate exercise of diplomacy and not a smashing public attack on the floor of the United States Senate."[33]

Taken aback by the virulence of official and editorial criticism, the senator telephoned his father. Had he made a costly political blunder? "You lucky mush," Joseph P. Kennedy replied, "You don't know it and neither does anyone else, but within a few months everyone is going to know just how right you were on Algeria."[34] Former governor of Connecticut Chester Bowles also reassured Kennedy: "These sniping editorials will quickly be forgotten. What will be remembered is the fact that you have offered a practical program that is squarely in line with our American interests, traditions, and principles."[35] The senator's wife, Jacqueline, ran into Acheson in New York's Penn Central Station and took the opportunity afforded by a delayed train to tell him off for criticizing her husband's speech.[36]

A week after his speech, Kennedy himself replied to his critics: "Of course, Algeria is a complicated problem. Of course, we should not assume full responsibility for that problem's solution in France's stead. And, of course, the Soviet Union is guilty of far worse examples of imperialism." But again Kennedy pointed to the perils of neutrality on the issue: France was paralyzed politically, decimated economically, and had stripped NATO

of its defense forces. Kennedy drew on a paragraph from a previous speech
on Indochina to conclude his reply:

> The sweep of nationalism is the most potent factor in foreign affairs
> today. We can resist it or ignore it but only for a little while; we can
> see it exploited by the Soviets with grave consequences; or we in this
> country can give it hope and leadership, and thus improve im-
> measurably our standing and our security.[37]

Practically no one in the American foreign-policy establishment regarded the Algeria speech as anything more than a partisan political blast
designed to attract attention. But foreign correspondents such as Alistair
Cooke of the *Manchester Guardian* and Henri Pierre of *Le Monde* recognized what their American counterparts had not—that Kennedy knew what
he was talking about on Third World issues. In a letter to the editor of
The New York Times, Pierre wrote: "Strangely enough, as a Frenchman
I feel that on the whole Mr. Kennedy is more to be commended than
blamed for his forthright, frank and provocative speech."[38] Although
Le Monde opposed Kennedy's call for Algerian independence, it identified
the senator as one of the few serious students of history in American
politics: "The most striking point of the speech of Mr. Kennedy is the
important documentation it revealed and his thorough knowledge of the
French milieu."[39]

For African visitors in Washington, Kennedy became the man to meet.
His dramatic speech on Algeria had coincided with the rush to independ-
ence in Black Africa. As President Léopold Sédar Senghor of Senegal told
Ambassador Philip M. Kaiser, there was never any doubt thereafter in
Africans' minds where Kennedy's sympathies lay.[40] President Moktar Ould
Daddah of Mauritania remembered how thrilled he had been as a student
in Paris to read the speech and how dramatic an impact it had made on all
Africans living in Paris.[41] Algerian guerrillas encamped on the thickly
forested slopes of the Atlas Mountains received the news with a sense of
amazement. An American correspondent who visited one camp later
related to the senator his surprise at being interviewed by weary, grimy
rebels on Kennedy's chances for the presidency.[42] Angolan nationalist
leader Holden Roberto traveled to Washington in 1959 to meet Kennedy
because of his "courageous position" on Algeria. "My vivid recollection
of the ideas you articulated made it possible for me to convey to my people
the warmest evidence of your sympathy and understanding for their
plight," Roberto wrote the President in 1962.[43]

And so they came to Room 362 of the Senate Office Building: Mongi
Slim (Tunisian ambassador to the U.S. and later president of the UN
General Assembly); J.G.N. Strauss Q.C. (former leader of the opposition

in South Africa); Holden Roberto (Angolan nationalist organizer); Tom Mboya (prominent Kenyan labor leader); Daniel Chapman (Ghanaian ambassador to the U.S. and to the UN); and A.K. Chanderli (the representative of the Algerian government-in-exile and later foreign minister).[44]

Every time the senator returned to his Senate office from a campaign swing on the road to the presidency, there always seemed to be an African visitor or two waiting to see him. Kennedy, curious as ever, welcomed a chat and usually ended up comparing political notes. He told Mongi Slim that "a rapid, friendly decolonization . . . would be the means of stopping the cold war's extension to Africa," and then questioned him as to how Algerian independence might be most effectively achieved.[45] The senator's assistant on African affairs, Winifred Armstrong, spent much of her time locating housing for African visitors in segregated Washington.[46] Kennedy's correspondence continued with Africanists such as W. Arthur Lewis, the West Indian economist who was then advising Prime Minister Kwame Nkrumah of Ghana.

Developments in North Africa in 1958 seemed to vindicate Kennedy's demand a year earlier for action by the U.S. When France bombed a town in Tunisia, leaving 68 dead, the UN Security Council went into emergency debate. Tunisian Ambassador Slim went to Kennedy's office and found the senator depressed and angry.[47] Those who had pretended, Kennedy told the press, that Algeria was solely France's concern "are now witnessing in the Tunisian tragedy the ominous results of this barren policy."[48]

Eisenhower, in a closed briefing for selected congressmen, predictably reaffirmed his policy of "non-involvement." But Secretary Dulles privately informed Kennedy that America could no longer afford a neutral position on Algeria; he confided that he had used Kennedy's speech to advantage in putting quiet heat on the French.[49] CBS radio news analyst Eric Sevareid observed in his broadcast that Kennedy had been prescient: "When Senator Kennedy a year ago advocated outright independence for Algeria, he was heavily criticized; were he making the same speech today, the response would pretty surely be different in considerable degree."[50]

In France, there was violent disagreement among the politicians in Paris and the generals in Algeria over the prosecution of the war. In May 1958, units of the French army revolted and threatened a coup d'état against the government in Paris. The government quickly capitulated and the Fourth Republic was over. The erstwhile savior of France, General Charles de Gaulle, emerged from his self-imposed exile at Colombey-les-Deux-Églises to head the new government in Paris. One Frenchman, Hilaire du Berrier, accused Kennedy of being partly responsible for the army putsch: "Your speech of July 2, 1957, had much to do with the army movement in Algeria today . . . I gather from my letter from M. Jacques Soustelle."[51]

KENNEDY AND THE LIBERALS

Kennedy was not alone in his criticism of Eisenhower policy in Africa and Asia. Prominent liberals such as Bowles and Stevenson had argued for a change in American policy and indeed had more firsthand exposure to the Third World than their younger colleague had. The difference between Kennedy and the liberals was one of approach. Kennedy's outlook was fatalistic. To him, decolonization was an inevitable process in which the U.S. had no choice but to participate. Bowles and Stevenson, on the other hand, depicted decolonization in moral terms. They related Asian and African nationalism to America's own ideals.

Bowles's book *Africa's Challenge to America* was eloquent in its endorsement of African independence; but unlike Kennedy's speech on Algeria, it made no specific recommendation regarding American policy.[52] Stevenson traveled to Africa twice, once in 1955 and again in 1957, both times as a corporate drummer for Reynolds Metals. Stevenson endorsed the principle of African self-determination but, perhaps in deference to his promotional status, avoided public association with particular nationalist movements.[53]

Responding to Kennedy's Algeria speech, Stevenson was not supportive: "I think there has been enough preaching to the French. Algeria is a French problem." He privately assured French Premier Guy Mollet that there would be no change in U.S. policy.[54] In contrast to Kennedy's provocative position, Stevenson's statements about decolonization had a practiced and predictable ring. In May 1960, Stevenson published an article on Africa in *Harper's*, which emphasized that the African relationship was a matter of moral calling: "And so we must see that more than economic interest, more than social influence, more than political balance are at stake in Africa. What is being tested is, in the last analysis, the moral capacities of our society."[55]

Had Bowles or Stevenson given the Algeria speech, it would have been filled with talk of American principles and of the prospects of a future democracy in Algeria. Yet Kennedy's reading of the Algerian situation, as the title of the speech suggested, had simply to do with facing facts. His recommendation of independence for Algeria was carefully tailored to what was practical for the United States. Kennedy doubted the exemplary value of American free enterprise to African development. Accordingly, his commentary often contained a strong dose of skepticism in it, which sometimes put him at odds with his liberal colleagues. Regarding aid, he wrote in October 1957:

> Old liberal bromides have no appeal to nations which seek a quick transition to industrialization and who admire the disciplined attack which Communism seems to make upon the problems of economic modernization and redistribution. The more immediately persuasive experiences of China and Russia probably approximate what lies ahead for states such as Indonesia and Egypt.[56]

The difference of emphasis between Kennedy and the liberals—already evident in the late '50s—would break into an open split in the first year of the Kennedy administration.

Kennedy, to be sure, had never counted himself among the liberals in the Senate and on major votes had rarely stood with them. For the liberals, the great issue of conscience during the fifties was McCarthyism. During the four-year battle on Capitol Hill between Senator Joseph McCarthy and his liberal opponents, Kennedy had stood clear of the fight, apparently for reasons less philosophical than personal (his brother Robert did work for McCarthy and his father was a friend).[57] On the other important issue on the liberal agenda, civil rights, Kennedy's record was indifferent at best. As the 1960 presidential campaign drew near, the senator solicited Dixiecrat support and backed even further away from civil rights legislation. "Still hearing good things about you and your future," one southern governor confided to Kennedy before one vote.

Among such Senate liberals as Joseph S. Clark, Hubert H. Humphrey, and Herbert H. Lehman, it was not surprising that Kennedy was suspect on a number of issues for his fence-sitting and truancy. His 1956 Pulitzer Prize-winning *Profiles in Courage* allayed some suspicion by associating its author—at least literarily—with issues of conscience. But the attitude of the day toward Kennedy was: "More Courage, Less Profile."[58]

Kennedy's Algeria speech, however, caused the liberals to take a second look. "My heartiest congratulations to you, Jack, for having the courage to speak out on the bankruptcy of our African policy," wrote Chester Bowles, the liberals' shadow secretary of state.[59] It succeeded not only in "rattling the windows of the White House"—as *Time* put it—but also in amazing the liberal group.[60] For those who had not paid attention to Kennedy's previous statements on Third World crises, the speech was unexpected. The senator's aide, Ralph A. Dungan, later described the speech as, in part, a bid to attract support from the party's liberal leadership.[61] Stevenson and Lehman saw the angle Kennedy was playing and became all the more dubious of his credentials as a liberal.

Other prominent liberals, however, were highly impressed. On the basis of the Algerian speech and several others later published in *A Strategy for Peace*, Michigan Governor G. Mennen Williams decided to throw his pivotal support to Kennedy for the Democratic nomination in the 1960 election. Senator Humphrey declared that Kennedy had performed "a service to the cause of freedom." Senator Clark helped Kennedy draft a resolution based on the speech. Gilbert Harrison, the editor and publisher of *The New Republic*, sent his congratulations. Kennedy took the opportunity to invite Harrison to his office for a chat. Walter Reuther, the president of the United Auto Workers, called the address "brilliant." "Your speech will hasten the day of independence," predicted Supreme Court Justice William O. Douglas. The eminent socialist Norman Thomas joined Protestant theologian Reinhold Niebuhr and three others in an open letter of support to *The New York Times*.[62]

To some, one bold speech on foreign policy did not make up for years of inaction on the critical issues before the Senate. "With your compassion for the Algerian, where is your compassion for the Mississippian whose murderers go free?" one constituent inquired. "I suggest you are not counting on the French vote for you to be President whereas the white Southern vote may make you such . . . Why else have you given such a sorry and disgraceful performance on *civil rights*."[63] Such communications, however, were rare, particularly since the American Committee on Africa had already sent out 10,000 letters and postcards soliciting support for "this refreshing and courageous example of statesmanship."[64]

Faced with the liberal rally to Kennedy, Stevenson tried belatedly to climb aboard the Algeria bandwagon. His law partner and longtime political collaborator, William McCormick Blair, Jr., tried to paper over the breach between the two by writing Theodore Sorensen: "Some people seemed to assume that Adlai was taking issue with Jack which, of course, he was not. *Time* Magazine is misleading people again."[65] Sorensen coolly replied: "Let me assure you that no one in this office was unduly disturbed by any quotations, real or fictional, by Governor Stevenson . . . Nor are we disturbed over the fact that such disagreement exists, as I gather from various sources it does. You were neither the first, nor the last to join that particular parade."[66]

Three years later, the roles were reversed; this time Kennedy was the supplicant seeking a rapprochement with Stevenson. His purpose was to secure Stevenson's endorsement for his 1960 presidential bid. Kennedy's first go-between was Professor Schlesinger, who urged Stevenson to come out for Kennedy: "[I]t will give him [Kennedy] a sense of indebtedness to the liberals," Schlesinger argued. "If, on the other hand, he is eventually nominated as the candidate of the eastern bosses and the southerners . . . it will saddle him as candidate and President with tacit obligations to the more hopeless elements in the party."[67] Kennedy also asked his chief adviser on African issues Barbara Ward, who was also personally close to Stevenson, to go to Libertyville to prevail on the governor to withdraw in favor of Kennedy. She did, but the answer she got from Stevenson was that he would not withdraw: "Kennedy stands for nothing," Stevenson told her.[68]

The other woman who knew Stevenson's political heart was Eleanor Roosevelt, so Kennedy went hat in hand to Hyde Park. The meeting did not go well. Kennedy later wrote Mrs. Roosevelt to assure her that, "I intend to work in close association with Adlai and Chester Bowles." Kennedy said that he was going to appoint Adlai as the head of his foreign-policy strategy team. "I told him that this was not enough," Mrs. Roosevelt wrote a friend. She wanted proof of close cooperation—references and quotations from Adlai's speeches in Kennedy's remarks. She wanted them to share the same platform to show that "their philosophies were similar."[69]

The Kennedys, particularly Robert, whom Stevenson called the "Black Prince," would remember Stevenson's dilatory and obstructive behavior before the Democratic convention in 1960. These old differences would have much to do with the later frustration of Adlai Stevenson as ambassador to the United Nations during the Kennedy Administration.

After the Algeria speech, Bowles and Williams urged Kennedy to join the Democratic Advisory Council on Foreign Policy. In doing so, they hoped he would join their running battle against DAC Chairman Dean Acheson and his former lieutenant from the Truman administration, Vice Chairman Paul H. Nitze. Acheson had been using the DAC forum not only to criticize the Eisenhower administration but also to belittle the "special pleaders"—those "in favor of freedom for Algeria."[70] Jonathan B. Bingham (who would become one of Kennedy's ambassadors to the UN in 1961) wanted the senator to help dump Acheson—"His present bitterness and rigidity, his obsession with nothing but power concepts, make him in my book the wrong person to head the Council's foreign policy committee."[71] Despite his recently acquired liberal imprimatur, Kennedy had no intention of institutionally associating himself with the liberals, and declined the invitation.

It was the perfect prologue to what was to come later (with many of the same *dramatis personae*)—Kennedy, drawn by temperament to Eastern hardliners like Acheson and McGeorge Bundy, but intellectually more at home with liberals such as Bowles and Stevenson, ultimately electing to find his own way between the two camps.

PRESIDENTIAL POLITICS

In May 1959, the Senate Foreign Relations Committee established a sub-committee on Africa. Kennedy was the natural choice to head it and assumed the position with a private appeal to British Africanist Barbara Ward: "If, from your vantage, you know of any material which I could read or you have any ideas which you feel deserve attention over here, I hope you will send them to me. In this area it is so difficult to get expert advice that any counsel from you will be doubly appreciated."[72]

Kennedy originally planned to sponsor a series of private consultations before holding subcommittee hearings. Despite these good intentions, how-ever, the subcommittee became a casualty of presidential politicking. As the race for the Democratic nomination drew closer, Kennedy spent less and less time in the Senate and virtually none at all in committee meetings. After only one hastily organized session in which Ward briefed the senators, the African subcommittee under Kennedy's stewardship—as Vice President Richard M. Nixon charged several times during the 1960 cam-paign—closed its doors before it ever opened them.[73]

During 1959 and 1960, Kennedy made thirteen prepared speeches on Africa. Most of the drafting was done by Harris L. Wofford, Jr., a brilliant thirty-four year-old attorney who had edited the first report of the U.S. Commission on Civil Rights to the President and Congress in 1959. What these speeches may have lacked by way of analytical content in comparison with earlier Kennedy speeches, they made up in sharper and more dramatic phrasing. "Call it nationalism, call it anti-colonialism, call it what you will . . . Africa is going through a revolution. The word is out—and spreading like wildfire in nearly 1,000 languages and dialects—that it is no longer necessary to remain forever poor or forever in bondage."[74]

Kennedy proposed the establishment of a multinational African Educa-tional Development Fund to "plan the long-range educational needs of Africa in order to help establish the school systems and universities which would eventually allow Africa to educate its own people." The fund would finance the sending of Western agronomists, engineers, and tech-nicians to assist in African development. African students—"the future leaders of Africa"—would be provided with scholarships to come to the U.S. to study. In this proposal were the seeds of Kennedy's Peace Corps.[75]

A frequent target in Kennedy's remarks was the Republican heir apparent, Vice President Nixon, who had become something of an African specialist himself after a four-week tour of the continent in 1957. Kennedy took exception to Nixon's alleged Cold War fixation on Africa, particularly the Vice President's remark that in Africa the United States had to commit itself to "winning men's minds." Kennedy claimed that the people of Africa were *more interested in development than they are in doctrine. They are more interested in achieving a decent standard of living than in following the standards of either East or West* (Kennedy's emphasis)."[76]

The Kennedy-Nixon exchange on African relations had begun shortly after the Algeria speech. Kennedy had reserved a special salvo for Nixon in his remarks: "Instead of recognizing that Algeria is the greatest unsolved problem of western diplomacy in North Africa today, our special emissary to that area this year, the distinguished Vice President, failed even to mention this issue in his report."[77]

The battle was joined. Nixon told Washington columnist Drew Pearson that he was "burned up," that on a flight to Plymouth, Massachusetts, a week before Kennedy's speech, he (Nixon) had told several newspapermen that, "All hell was going to break loose in that French part of North Africa unless the United States persuaded the French to grant some form of independence." Nixon said he was surprised "when early last week mimeographed copies of young Jack Kennedy's speech on Algeria were distributed to the press." According to Nixon, Kennedy's speech outlined the same ideas that Nixon himself had expressed to newsmen. Nixon told Pearson that he wasn't accusing the Boston newspapermen of leaking his ideas to their fellow Bostonian, but that he suspected it.[78]

Nixon's claim that Kennedy had somehow pirated his own critique of the Eisenhower administration Algerian policy might have been hard to believe, but more of the same was in the offing. The Vice-President told selected Washington newsmen that the White House was seething over what it regarded as "a brashly political" move to embarrass the administration. He claimed that Kennedy's remarks could "dangerously encourage the Algerians to further excesses in their revolt against French rule." According to Nixon: "Ike and his staff held a full-fledged policy meeting to pool their thinking on the 'whys underlying Kennedy's damaging fishing in troubled waters.' "[79]

It hardly took a White House staff meeting to determine what game Kennedy was playing, and Nixon's allegations only made Eisenhower and Nixon look worse. Alistair Cooke thought the White House was playing into Kennedy's hands:

> Kennedy's gratuitous but bold pamphlet on Algeria could be trusted to do two things: to astound the French and infuriate the White House. Ergo, the Senator's shadowy figure is suddenly spotlighted in Europe. At home he has made himself the Democrat whom the President must "do something about," the one presidential hopeful the Republicans will delight to scorn. It is a form of running martyrdom that Senators Humphrey and Johnson may come to envy.[80]

Five months after the Algeria speech, *Time* published its first cover story on Kennedy. It was called, "Man Out Front."[81]

Kennedy succeeded in capturing the Democratic nomination, but still faced an uphill battle. He was far behind Nixon in the polls. Liberal support from his own party had effectively disintegrated. Although Kennedy considered his choice of Lyndon B. Johnson as his running mate to have been a necessary concession to the South, it had touched off a revolt among liberals already disaffected by Kennedy's defeat of Humphrey and Stevenson for the nomination. Black support had evaporated.

Schlesinger wrote Kennedy in August that "There has been a disastrous emotional letdown since L.A. Why? Partly Lyndon . . . partly the awkward handling of the civil rights issue," but mostly because liberals feel "they are not wanted. The apathy, the qualms and the pique of American liberals constitute Nixon's great secret weapon." They were the "enthusiasts," the ones who would take to the street and get out the vote for Kennedy, and he had lost them. "I think you should exploit one of your strongest assets—i.e., that you are far more liberal than Nixon," Schlesinger wrote. "Adlai Stevenson can bring you more electoral votes than Lyndon Johnson can. . . . Once the issue-minded Democrats catch fire, then the campaign will gather steam. To develop enthusiasm we have no choice but to give the enthusiasts something to believe in."[82]

The problem was, of course, that despite Kennedy's well-cultivated image as a fresh, political face, his Senate record on liberal issues was weak and, in the case of civil rights, particularly so. Virtually the only claim to liberal fame that Kennedy had was his record of bold statements on African policy. In a memorandum to the senator in preparation for his debate with Vice-President Nixon, speechwriter Richard Goodwin proposed that Kennedy go to his strongest suit in his opening remarks: ". . . American foreign policy has reached a crossroads . . . a moment of crisis in which the new nations of Africa and Asia are on the razor edge of their decision whether to turn to the East or West." Goodwin emphasized that "Africa would be a timely and dramatic point of reference" where "the [Eisenhower] administration has ignored the needs and aspirations of these young countries and has failed to match Soviet efforts in that part of the world."[83]

Kennedy's handling of the Africa issue in the 1960 campaign—his pitch to the liberal and black vote—was a minor classic in political exploitation of foreign policy. In three months of campaigning, Kennedy made reference to Africa 479 times in his speeches. An exchange between Kennedy and Nixon in their fourth debate was typical:

> KENNEDY: I have seen us ignore Africa. When Guinea became independent, the Soviet ambassador showed up that very day.

> We did not recognize them for nearly two months. The
> American ambassador did not show up for nearly eight
> months. If there's one thing Africa needs it's technical
> assistance and yet last year we gave them less than 5 per-
> cent of all the technical assistance that we distributed
> around the world.

NIXON: Let's look at Africa. Twenty new countries in Africa
        during the course of this administration. Not one of them
        selected a Communist government.[84]

Kennedy had found an issue with which to put the Eisenhower administration on the defensive. Three days after the debate, Assistant Secretary
of State for African Affairs Joseph Satterthwaite gave a full-length defense
of the administration's African policy.

Except for his eleventh-hour appeal for the release of Dr. Martin
Luther King from jail, Kennedy offered little in the way of concrete
programs to black Americans during the campaign. Instead, he made
constant references to relations with Africa. The strategy was to use
concern for Africa as a means of wooing American blacks without alienating Southern whites. Before a predominantly black audience in downtown
Los Angeles, Kennedy asked: "Do you know the most important new
area of the world is Africa? It controls one-fourth of all the votes in the
General Assembly. I am the chairman of the Subcommittee on Africa of
the Senate Foreign Relations Committee. Do you know how many Negroes
we have in our State Department Foreign Service out of 6,000? Twenty-
six. Do you know how many Federal judges there are, Federal District
judges? Zero out of 220. We can do better. We can do better."[85]

In August, to illustrate his concern about Africa and to sharpen his
attack on the Republican administration, Kennedy asked two-time ambassador to the Soviet Union and former governor of New York Averell
Harriman to go to Africa on a fact-finding tour. Harriman agreed and
visited eight African states on his tour, cabling periodic reports to the
candidate. Kennedy quoted from these reports in his campaign remarks,
particularly those regarding American policy in the Congo crisis and the
strained relations between the U.S. and the newly independent countries
of Ghana and Guinea.[86] Kennedy himself hired a helicopter to fly from
Los Angeles to Disneyland for a highly publicized visit with Guinean
President Ahmed Sékou Touré. At the meeting, Sékou Touré warmly
congratulated Kennedy on his support for Algerian independence.[87]

In his campaign speeches. Kennedy repeatedly stressed the need to
bring African students to the U.S. for university training. In August 1960,
he got an unexpected chance to make good on his proposal at the expense
of the Eisenhower administration. The African-American Students Founda-

tion (AASF) raised more than one million dollars in 1960 to provide scholarships for students from seven East African colonies. Tuition money in hand, the foundation asked the State Department on two different occasions to finance the transportation of the students to the U.S. Both requests were refused.[88]

When Kennedy learned of the State Department's refusal to help, he invited Kenyan labor leader Tom Mboya (who had flown to the United States to appeal the decision) to come to Hyannis Port to see what could be done. On July 26, they discussed the matter. Since the State Department would not provide the money, Kennedy offered to provide $100,000 from the Joseph P. Kennedy Foundation to charter a plane. The AASF accepted Kennedy's offer and his one condition—that no public announcement be made.

The Nixon campaign office learned of the Mboya-Kennedy deal and successfully urged the State Department to offer $100,000 for the airlift. Republican Senator Hugh Scott was called upon to do the dirty work. He told the Senate that since the department's offer, "the long arm of the family of the Junior Senator from Massachusetts had reached out and attempted to pluck this project away from the U.S. Government." He expressed surprise at the decision of the AASF but said he could "understand the pressures brought by the Kennedy people and their anxiety to take over the functions of the Government in advance of the election."

At the conclusion of Scott's remarks, Kennedy shot to his feet and angrily called the allegations "the most unfair, distorted and malignant attack I have heard in 14 years in politics." He then detailed his own association with the airlift:

> . . . the Kennedy Foundation went into this quite reluctantly. Mr. Mboya came to see us and asked for help when the Federal Government had turned it down. We felt something ought to be done. To waste 250 scholarships in this country . . . to disappoint 250 students who hoped to come to this country, it certainly seemed to me would be most unfortunate, and so we went ahead.

The chairman of the Senate Foreign Relations Committee, J. William Fulbright, remarked to the press that Scott's speech was "an outrageous distortion of the facts. If it is true that the State Department was pressured into allocating funds, it was an unacceptable interference with the orderly conduct of foreign policy by the State Department for partisan political purposes." Clearly embarrassed, the State Department spokesman issued one explanation that the AASF characterized as "patently incorrect" and a second, amended version that Fulbright described as revealing the department's "deplorable" willingness to be used as a political tool by the Nixon campaign organization.

The controversy brought Kennedy a windfall of favorable press attention and provided him with excellent ammunition on the campaign trail.
During the month-long flap, Nixon's lead in the national polls fell by four
points. To counter Kennedy, the Vice President resurrected a 1952 campaign theme—"the liberation of the enslaved peoples of Eastern Europe."
In the final days of the campaign, Nixon pledged that he would "go to
Eastern Europe." He solemnly promised that, if elected, he would also
send Presidents Hoover, Truman, and Eisenhower to Eastern Europe as
emissaries of liberty "to carry the idea of freedom."[89]

GREAT EXPECTATIONS

Around their early morning campfires, Algerian Front de Libération Nationale (FLN) guerrillas listened on a wireless to the presidential returns
coming in from the United States. During the election vigil—as Algerian
Premier Ben Bella related to President Kennedy in 1963—there was
cheering throughout the camp when Kennedy had pulled ahead, but when
Nixon began to overtake him, there was cursing.[90]

Traveling through black Africa a month after the election, Senator
Frank Church witnessed something similar. "Whenever our presence became known, eager crowds would gather to shout, 'Kennedy, Kennedy.'
The word had spread through Africa that the newly elected president of
the United States had, as a senator in 1957, spoken up for Algeria in her
war for independence against France. For the first time, our country
was being identified, Arab and Black alike, with legitimate African
aspirations."[91]

The self-styled leader of Black Africa, President Nkrumah of Ghana,
also remembered Kennedy's "courageous and realistic policy of Algeria
for the Algerians." Nkrumah wrote to the newly elected President in
January 1961 that he looked forward to "complete kinship" with him in
the years to come. Nkrumah appealed to Kennedy to save the life of
Premier Patrice Lumumba of the Congo, who had been overthrown and
imprisoned by his American- and Belgian-supported opponents and who
was in danger of being murdered by them.[92]

Another African, this one a washing man named Kweku Anyani of
Cape Coast, Ghana, also wrote the new American President: "We of
Africa have our fingers crossed for you."[93]

The issue of Africa had served Kennedy well. It had forced the
Republicans onto the defensive in foreign policy and had provided him
a surrogate for the explosive subject of civil rights. Now Africa waited
to see if Kennedy would live up to his promise.

2

Eisenhower's Legacy

> We dare not accept new elections in the Congo . . .
> We dare not accept the convocation of the Parliament . . .
> We dare not even see Lumumba included in a coalition
> government for fear that he could come to dominate the
> cabinet. For a country that subscribes to the democratic
> creed, this is a remarkable predicament.
>
> Martin F. Herz
> *State Department Congo Desk*
> (*January 1961*)

In the summer of 1960, the Cold War spread into Black Africa. Like the headlong lunge of the European powers some seventy-five years earlier, the Soviet-American scramble had more to do with Great Power rivalry than with any special interest in the area. The mood on both sides that summer was ugly. "It has a terrible similarity to 1914," British Prime Minister Harold Macmillan noted in his diary.[1] When the Congo fell into anarchy within a week of achieving its independence in July, the super-powers—first Russia, then the U.S.—went in for the kill. Macmillan, like many others, feared the worst: "Now [the] Congo may play the role of Serbia. Except for the terror of nuclear power on both sides, we might easily slide into the 1914 situation."

THE AMERICAN RESPONSE TO AFRICAN INDEPENDENCE

Until 1960, the Eisenhower administration's response to African independence was essentially defensive. Anticolonial zeal was frowned upon; the legacy of Wilson and Roosevelt, as well as the precedent of Philippine independence, was put aside. When the American representative on the United Nations Visiting Mission to Tanganyika endorsed the request for a twenty-five-year timetable for Tanganyikan independence, he was forced by Washington to reverse his rash move.[2] (Tanganyika became independent six years later.)

Official caution was rooted in the fear that nationalist upheaval in Africa would open the door to communist subversion, as had allegedly happened in Southeast Asia and in the Middle East. After touring six African countries in 1957, Vice President Nixon reported to the President that Africa was the new area of conflict "between the forces of freedom and international communism."[3]

In 1957, at least, the Kremlin entertained no such illusion. There were no significant communist parties on the continent after 1950, when the South African Communist Party was banned. The Kremlin viewed African nationalist movements as "bourgeois" and thoroughly unproletarian. Although the very emancipation of the colonies struck a blow at the "imperialist" world, as Lenin had predicted, an official statement of Soviet policy as late as 1961 indicated that the Soviets expected the West to stay in control of the "bourgeois states": "In the majority of states that achieved independence as a result of forced constitutional concessions on the part of the colonizers, the imperialists have succeeded to this day in retaining their commanding positions in economic, political, and military affairs."[4] The Kremlin could only hope to capitalize on Western mistakes.

The Europeans, of course, gave the communists credit for every outbreak of anticolonial discontent. With Washington's prevailing assumption of a vast communist design, the Americans took the Europeans at their word. Even after the African rush to nationhood was well under way, the administration gave only grudging endorsement to independence. As Assistant Secretary of State C. Burke Elbrick informed the Senate Foreign Relations Committee in 1958: "Premature independence and irresponsible nationalism may present grave dangers to dependent peoples."[5]

In his memoirs, President Eisenhower likened the arrival of independence in Africa to a "destructive hurricane." Given his background, it was not surprising that the President's fundamental point of reference in foreign policy was European relations.[6] During his service as Supreme Commander of NATO forces, Eisenhower had established a close rapport with many of the leaders of Europe and accordingly viewed the proper American role in Africa's transition from colonialism as one that supported the European powers.

The disastrous misunderstanding among the allies at Suez in 1956 only made the President more conscious of the delicacy and sensitivity of the task the Europeans faced and may well have been an important factor in his decision to remain silent during France's agony in Algeria. On a visit to Lisbon, Eisenhower hailed Portugal's "contribution to civilization" and listened "sympathetically and respectfully" to Dr. Salazar's appeal for American recognition of Portugal's stake in Africa. "We are united in a common cause," declared Eisenhower, and the Portuguese were reassured.[7]

While Eisenhower's deference to the European powers may have contributed to the unity of NATO, it also had the effect of frustrating the development of U.S.-African relations. When newly independent African governments asked the U.S. for economic and military assistance, Washington's practice was to demur unless the former colonial power agreed to the request.

Guinea became independent in 1958, after trade-union nationalist Sékou Touré orchestrated an overwhelming electoral "non" to France's offer of community status. The French had pulled out in a fit of pique, taking all administrative records and stripping their colonial offices—even ripping phones out of the wall. A desperate Sékou Touré appealed to the United States for economic aid. Out of deference to its affronted ally, however, Washington ignored the request. The U.S. did not send an ambassador to Guinea until nine months after the rebel colony announced its independence.[8] When Sékou Touré sent another request to Eisenhower for a small amount of military aid, Washington again did not answer. The State Department initially claimed that it had never received the letter, but later admitted that "an irregular request did arrive."[9]

Czechoslovakia, a leading distributor of Soviet weaponry, subsequently made an unconditional arms offer to Guinea, which Sékou Touré accepted. By 1960, there were more than 1,500 Soviet and Eastern European technicians in Guinea, and Sékou Touré and Khrushchev were in close touch on the Congo crisis. In press stories, Eisenhower administration officials identified Sékou Touré as another communist "dupe." The Guinean President angrily responded to the charge, telling a reporter for *The New York Times*: "If you insist Guinea is Communist, that settles it."[10]

THE CONGO CRISIS: JULY 1960

On June 30, 1960, Belgium granted its giant colony independence, despite the fact that the Congolese were totally unprepared for the tasks of self-government. At the time of independence, less than twenty Congolese had received a higher education. The Congo's civil service was exclusively staffed at the middle and upper levels by Belgians. The Congolese economy remained under Belgian tutelage while military command of the army, the Force Publique, was entirely white.[11]

The Belgian gamble—*le pari belge*—was to transfer the trappings of power to the Congo while maintaining de facto control over the new state. When there was restlessness among African troops a few days after independence, the Belgian military commander, General Emile Janssens, assembled the soldiers at Camp Léopold II and wrote on a blackboard: *Avant Indépendance = Après Indépendance* (Before Independence = After Independence).[12] The Congolese troops rebelled, attacked Europeans, and pillaged property. The Belgian Government responded by airlifting paratroopers into the Congo. At the week's end, hundreds of Congolese had lost their lives. The Congolese Government addressed an urgent appeal to the United States to send 3,000 American troops to restore order in the newly independent Congo. The Eisenhower administration, however, declined the request for troops, suggesting instead that the Congo look to the United Nations for help.[13]

Congolese President Joseph Kasavubu joined Premier Patrice Lumumba in sending a message to United Nations Secretary-General Dag Hammarskjold asking for military assistance. After two days of deliberations, the UN Security Council adopted a resolution that called on Belgium to remove its troops from the Congo. The peacekeeping mandate authorized the Secretary-General "to take the necessary steps in consultation with the Government of the Republic of the Congo, to provide the Government with such military assistance as may be necessary . . ." In the Security Council, the United States did not vote with its European allies but with the Soviet Union in favor of the peacekeeping operation, which would become "the most controversial in the history of the United Nations."[14]

UN military intervention in the Congo satisfied the Eisenhower administration's primary goal in the Congo: to prevent the Soviet Union from taking advantage of political chaos in the strategically located and resource-rich country.[15] Multilateral cooperation would contain communist subversion more effectively than unilateral American intervention, which might invite Soviet retaliation. During the first weeks of the crisis, the United States transported more than 10,000 UN troops by land and sea from their home countries to the Congo.

For the Soviet Union, the UN operation appeared equally advantageous since the Security Council mandate authorized the eviction of the Belgians and the restoration of order by predominantly African and Asian troop contingents. Within hours of the passage of the UN resolution, Soviet transport planes were airlifting Ghanaian and Guinean soldiers to the Congo. Lumumba and Kasavubu appealed to Premier Khrushchev to "watch hourly" over the situation. In reply, Khrushchev promised "any assistance."[16]

Belgium's military intervention in the Congo, ostensibly intended to protect its 85,000 nationals living there, soon went far beyond that. A few days after the crisis began, the Belgium government financially and militarily abetted in the secession of the Congo's richest province, Katanga, whose mining complex was owned and operated by the Belgian company, Union Minière du Haut Katanga.[17] Katanga's secession brought the Congo to the brink of civil war. The U.S. embassy in Léopoldville reported that elsewhere in the Congo Belgian troops had been unnecessarily brutal in achieving their military objectives. They were "completely irrational and in many cases behaved worse than the worst Congolese."[18]

An enraged Lumumba declared that the Congo was "at war" with

Belgium and blamed the U.S. for not criticizing, much less restraining, its ally. "We will take aid from the devil or anyone else as long as they get the Belgian troops out," he warned on July 20. "If no Western nation helps us, why can we not call on other nations?"[19] Broadcasts over Radio Congo turned violently anti-Belgian; Soviet planes began flying in food supplies. The American embassy repeatedly alerted Washington to the fact that the withdrawal of Belgian troops was "the central, all-pervading issue occupying all Congolese minds" and warned prophetically that, "If the UN did not get them out, the Congo would get someone who would."[20]

But Washington remained convinced that it was Lumumba—not the Belgian troops—who was responsible for the disorder. Lumumba's fury at the Belgians was not, Washington believed, a reaction to their brutality but rather the result of his own communist associations. At a National Security Council meeting on July 21, 1960, CIA Director Allen Dulles described the Premier's background as "harrowing." It was safe to go on the assumption, Dulles said, that Lumumba had been "bought by the Communists."[21]

Lumumba, however, had not given up on the Americans. During the last week in July, he made a three-day visit to Washington. To the "disgust" of the Belgian press, Lumumba slept in the same bed in Blair House that *le Roi des Belgas* had used during a prior visit to Washington. The Premier conferred at length with Secretary of State Christian A. Herter. Twice during their talk Lumumba asked for American help in getting Belgian troops out of the Congo. Herter was noncommittal. Lumumba warned that if the U.S. continued to support Belgium's position, there would be a rupture in U.S.-Congo relations. The Premier repeated this warning in a meeting with Under Secretary of State C. Douglas Dillon again to no avail.[22]

Lumumba was "acutely disappointed" by his reception in Washington.[23] He had not seen President Eisenhower, who had remained in Newport, Rhode Island, for the duration of the visit. What talks he had had with senior Administration officials had left him little hope for U.S. support of the Congo's position.

American officials, for their part, had been suspicious of Lumumba's true intentions to begin with. Their suspicion turned into outright antagonism when they learned about his "disgusting" personal comportment in the course of his visit to segregated Washington.

During the first weeks of the Congo crisis, reports of the rape of white women were widely featured in the American press. According to a State Department memorandum, these reports became the "continuing preoccupation" of the White House and the State Department.[24]

Belgian Foreign Minister Pierre Wigny fueled the atmosphere by providing the Security Council with detailed and lurid "first-hand" reports of rape. "Madame O. said: 'I did not give in, I resisted, but they pulled out my pubic hair and stuffed it in my mouth for me to swallow. I was raped by several soldiers . . . Then they brutally pushed a rough object into my vagina and afterwards wrenched it out.' "[25] These reports became items of such passionate discussion in the State Department that one Foreign Service Officer felt obliged to remind his superior in writing that "The UN did not go into the Congo to save white women from being raped."[26]

While he was in Washington, Lumumba further contributed to the prevalent sense of racial outrage by asking the State Department's Congo desk officer, Thomas A. Cassilly, Jr., to provide him with a female companion. What exactly did the Premier have in mind? asked the surprised Cassilly. *"Une blanche blonde,"* Lumumba replied. Cassilly reported the request to his superiors, who turned the matter over to the CIA. A suitable woman was procured, but before she could be delivered to the Premier, the hostess of Blair House found out about the arrangement and forbade any such activity in the President's guest quarters. The CIA then arranged a more discreet meeting-place, but by this time the story had reached the White House.[27] Ambassador Timberlake arrived in Washington a week later with "verified" reports of the rape of Belgian women.

After conferring with Lumumba and receiving information regarding his personal habits, senior officials such as Under Secretary Dillon, were convinced that Lumumba was "just not a rational being." During the meeting Lumumba had stared at the ceiling, had mumbled incoherently to himself, and had, at points, broken into unrelated discourse. "You had the feeling that he was a person that was gripped by this fervor that I can only describe as messianic . . ." Dillon recalled.[28] The Americans also believed that Lumumba, who smoked hemp, was a "drug addict". They were equally persuaded that he was a man incapable of controlling himself. He had insulted President Eisenhower's good friend, Belgian King Baudoin, at independence ceremonies. *"Nous ne sommes plus vos macaques!"* (We are no longer your monkeys), Lumumba had declared.

> We have known ironies, insults, and blows which we had to undergo morning, noon, and night because we were Negroes . . . Who will forget the rifle fire from which so many of our brothers perished, or the jails into which were brutally thrown those who did not wish to submit to a regime of injustice, suppression, and exploitation?[29]

The Americans saw Lumumba as a man of violence and interpreted his every action accordingly. While in Washington, he had caused alarm by asking for a gun: "On m'a promis une arme." (As it happened, it was the CIA's own Lawrence Devlin in Léopoldville who had suggested to Lumumba that he ask for one.)[30] Likewise, Lumumba got the blame when an American Air Force crew was beaten by a group of Congolese soldiers, who had mistaken them for Belgians. U.S. Ambassador Clare H. Timberlake observed that the incident should remove "any lingering trace of the fiction that we are dealing with a civilized people."[31]

On the last day of his visit in Washington, Lumumba administered the coup de grâce to his already dubious reputation in the eyes of the Americans. In an interview with the Soviet news agency, Tass, he expressed "deepest gratitude" to the Soviet people and personally to Nikita Khrushchev for flying food supplies to the Congo.[32] The interview was indiscreetly timed, but got the message across to the U.S. If this did not suffice to alert officials in Washington, then a priority message from Léopoldville should have done so. A prominent Congolese politician, Joseph Ileo, had told the American mission that if Lumumba returned "empty-handed" from the U.S., that is, without at least some promise or commitment, he would turn to the Soviet Union.[33] Two weeks before his visit to Washington, Lumumba had given the UN commander an ultimatum to get the Belgian troops out or "regretfully we may be obliged to call upon the Soviet Union to intervene."[34]

On August 1, President Eisenhower presided over a National Security Council meeting at the summer White House in Newport, Rhode Island. At the meeting, the NSC concluded that the United States should be prepared "at any time to take appropriate military action to prevent or defeat Soviet military intervention in the Congo."[35]

SOVIET INTERVENTION AND AMERICAN RETALIATION: AUGUST 1960

When he returned to Léopoldville, Lumumba accepted Khrushchev's standing offer of military assistance. By mid-August, eleven twin-engined Ilyushin 18 planes with Soviet crews had arrived in the Congo. With them had come more than 100 Soviet and Eastern European technicians, as well as nearly 100 trucks with spare parts. The CIA station in Léopoldville cabled a flash message to CIA headquarters on August 18: "Congo [is] experiencing [a] classic Communist effort [to] takeover [the] government. There may be little time left in which [to] take action to avoid another Cuba."[36]

The White House hastily called a meeting of the National Security Council. At the NSC meeting that same afternoon discussion centered on Lumumba. ". . . we were talking of one man forcing us out of the Congo," President Eisenhower declared, "of Lumumba supported by the Soviets."[37] The tenor of Eisenhower's remarks about Lumumba was strong enough for two officials at the meeting to conclude that the President had authorized Lumumba's assassination. Robert H. Johnson, an executive member of the National Security Council, recalled "my sense of that moment quite clearly because the President's statement came as a great shock to me." Eisenhower's Special Assistant for National Security Affairs, Gordon Gray, later told the Special Group (in charge of covert operations) that his "Associates" (a euphemism for the President) had expressed "extremely strong feelings on the necessity for very straightforward action" against Lumumba. The implication was that removal from office was not enough. Accordingly, the Special Group agreed not to rule out "any particular kind of activity which might contribute to getting rid of Lumumba."

The next day, August 19, CIA Director Allen Dulles sent a cable to CIA Station Chief Lawrence Devlin in which he stressed that, in the view of "high quarters here", Lumumba's "removal must be an urgent and prime objective." Devlin was given still "wider authority . . . including more aggressive action" than he had been given before in order to remove Lumumba.[38] Shortly after Dulles' cable to Léopoldville, CIA scientists began preparing a deadly poison (composed of anthrax and other toxic viruses indigenous to the tropics) that was to be put into Lumumba's food. This "first aid kit" was flown to Léopoldville in September.[39]

In retrospect, the decision to assassinate Lumumba seems puzzling. There is no evidence of any calculation by the White House that the Congo was of long-term interest to the U.S. Soviet intervention was certainly cause for concern, but hardly for panic. By the time the Soviet planes and crews arrived in Léopoldville, a UN army of 10,000 had already been assembled to keep the peace. Under these circumstances, the possibility that 100 Soviet and Czech technicians could pull off a "classic communist takeover" was remote, to say the least. Why, then, the decision to assassinate Lumumba? The answer has to do with human overreaction; in particular, overreaction by an administration fed up with Russian threats and ready to believe on the most superficial of evidence that Patrice Lumumba was a "Soviet instrument."

In the summer of 1960, the Cold War was at its iciest. "The Congo affair on top of everything else," columnist I. F. Stone wrote, "gives the world the atmosphere of a bar-room on the verge of a brawl."[40] The United States had suffered a series of stunning setbacks abroad: the loss of Cuba; the expansion of the communist insurgency in Laos; the cancellation of the President's trip to Japan because of leftist riots; the U-2 incident; and most disturbingly, the bitter confrontation between Eisenhower and Khrushchev at their summit meeting in Paris in May 1960.

EISENHOWER'S ROAD TO THE CONGO CRISIS

In September 1959, nine months before the confrontation at Paris, Khrushchev and Eisenhower adjourned their meeting at Camp David in a mood of goodwill. In his televised farewell address to the American people, the Soviet Premier elected not to discuss what he called "the old boring arguments of the Cold War period." President Eisenhower agreed to negotiate a test ban treaty with the Russians and accepted Khrushchev's invitation to visit the Soviet Union the following summer. Historian Louis Halle declared that the Cold War was over.[41]

Three months later, Eisenhower "began to reexamine the image of America across the world" and discovered that he "did not much like what he saw." The legacy of Secretary Dulles (who had died of cancer in May 1959) was a negative one. For all his energy and high purpose, Dulles had acted as the adversary of compromise.[42] His practice of "brinksmanship"—going to the brink of war in order to force concessions from communist opponents—had frustrated Eisenhower's preference for self-restraint. Now Eisenhower was on his own, and he greatly wanted peace: ". . . in the long run, there is nothing but war—if we give up all hope of a peaceful solution."[43]

A month before the Paris summit, the prospects for a test ban treaty with the Russians appeared to be excellent. Two weeks before the summit, however, a U.S. high-altitude reconnaissance plane was shot down over the Soviet Union and its pilot, Francis Gary Powers, was captured. Instead of denying responsibility for the U-2 flight (as Khrushchev virtually invited Eisenhower to do), the President tried to justify it. Walter Lippmann commented, "*To avow* that we intend to violate Soviet sovereignty . . . makes it impossible for the Soviet government to play down this particular incident . . ."[44] (emphasis his) The President then chose not to break the news of his suspension of U-2 flights over Russia until he met with Khrushchev in Paris.

In the interim, however, the Russians fumed. At a news conference before the summit meeting, Khrushchev furiously denounced Eisenhower as a "thief" and demanded an apology. At the summit meeting, he told Eisenhower that his invitation to visit the Soviet Union had been withdrawn. When Eisenhower replied that he would not apologize for the incident, Khrushchev stood up and walked out of the conference chamber.

The entire experience left the President furious at the Russians and bitterly resigned to the hopelessness of achieving peace in what remained of his presidency. In July 1960, he told his science adviser, George Kistiatowsky, that "he saw nothing worthwhile left for him to do now until the end of his presidency."[45] It was in this somber setting that

Lumumba showed up in Washington and impressed certain administration officials that he posed a dire threat to American interests.

AN ASSESSMENT OF LUMUMBA

For all his observed and reported inadequacies, Lumumba was recognized by the Americans as a gifted politician and a mesmerizing orator. To Dillon, Lumumba's oratorical skill was itself cause for fright:

> He had this tremendous ability to stir up a crowd or a group. And if he could have gotten out (of prison) and started to talk to a battalion of the Congolese Army, he probably would have had them in the palm of his hand in five minutes.[46]

Both his admirers and antagonists seemed to agree on at least one fact: that Lumumba was a genuine nationalist, fanatical in his opposition to foreign control of the Congo and, unlike his Congolese contemporaries, cared for something more than his own remuneration.[47] "We shall show the whole world," Lumumba promised at independence ceremonies, "what the black man can do when he is allowed to work in freedom and we shall make the Congo a shining example for the whole of Africa."[48]

English Africanist Catherine Hoskyns observed that as an administrator, Lumumba was "entirely dominant." Most of the ministers in his government respected "his brilliance, his capacity for hard work, and his ability to get results. Most were afraid of him and few could stand up to him in argument."[49] One who feared him was President Joseph Kasavubu, who had been the Belgians' choice for Premier. The first news Washington received from Léopoldville about its assassination conspiracy concerned Kasavubu. When anti-Lumumba leaders approached him with a plan to assassinate the Premier, he told them simply that there was no one "of sufficient stature to replace Lumumba."[50]

Three weeks after the Soviet move into the Congo, W. Averell Harriman, on his fact-finding tour for Senator Kennedy, spent an hour with Lumumba. There were few American diplomats as experienced in negotiating with communists or as hardbitten professionally as Harriman. Yet his reading of Lumumba was essentially neutral; he saw no reason to doubt Lumumba's explanation of the Russian presence. The Congolese Premier told Harriman that "Communist dictatorship was as bad as colonialism" and that he wished to steer a policy of neutralism between East and West. The former Governor reported to Senator Kennedy that Lumumba had insisted that he was not a Communist but wanted to use the Russians. Kasavubu, he had charged, was controlled by the Belgians. As a sovereign nation, Harriman reported Lumumba as arguing, the Congo had the right to receive aid from whomever it wished.[51]

Even after his appeals for aid had been turned down in Washington, Lumumba continued to seek private channels of American aid. He signed an agreement in New York with the Phelps-Stokes Fund, a philanthropic and education fund, for the recruitment of American blacks to serve without cost to the Congo government. The agreement was never implemented because of Washington's stricture against bilateral aid. Lumumba had also granted a multi-million dollar financial and managerial concession in the Congo to L. Edgar Detwiler, an American entrepreneur of questionable standing, despite the protests of the African and communist missions in Léopoldville.[52]

Although his broadcast attacks against Belgium grew increasingly bitter as time went on, Lumumba never denounced the U.S. over the radio. On the very day that Eisenhower said the words that Allen Dulles took to authorize assassination, Lumumba addressed the Congolese people over the radio: "We know that the U.S. understands us and we are pleased to see the U.S. position in bringing about international peace . . . If the Congolese place their confidence in the U.S., which is a great friend, they will find themselves rewarded."[53] On August 23, in another radio speech, Lumumba announced his intention to send 300 students to the United States. Meanwhile, CIA scientists were preparing a deadly poison to be sent to Léopoldville for the purpose of assassinating him.[54]

The Eisenhower administration had reason to know better. Although CIA Director Dulles had described Lumumba as having a "harrowing background" at a National Security Council meeting, the fact was that prior to independence, Lumumba had been the unofficial *American* candidate for Premier.[55] As Martin F. Herz, a Congo expert in the African Bureau concluded, Lumumba was "most susceptible to the influence or control from Kwame Nkrumah and to a lesser extent, Nehru, Sékou Touré, Nasser, Keita and perhaps Sukarno and Tito, not Khrushchev."[56]

Dulles, nonetheless, found it "safe to go on the assumption that Lumumba had been bought by the Communists," neglecting to add that Lumumba had also received money under the table from the Belgians, in particular from Union Minière.[57] The fact that Lumumba traveled first to Washington in search of aid (and never, in any case, to Moscow) might have also given President Eisenhower and his subordinates cause to reconsider their extreme assessment of the man.

But the mood of the President—a normally serene and equable man— was intemperate and even bitter that summer. At times in meetings on the Congo, he made little sense. When Under Secretary Dillon, for example, raised the issue of what to do if Lumumba expelled the UN from the Congo (as he was legally entitled to do), Eisenhower was emphatic in reply: "We should keep the UN in the Congo even if we had to ask for Europeans to do it." This was, of course, effectively impossible, given Hammarskjold's dependence on the Afro-Asian powers in the peacekeeping operation as well as the Soviet Union's right to exercise its veto on any new mandate resolution from the Security Council. Dillon saw the impossibility of the proposal. He informed the President that, as much as the State Department agreed with his feelings, Ambassador Lodge believed that if the Congolese Central Government told the UN to leave because of its inaction in dealing with the Belgians, it would have to leave. Lodge was "wrong", Eisenhower replied. The U.S. should keep the UN in the Congo "even if such action was used by the Soviets as a basis for starting a fight."[58] From the standpoint of the United Nations, of course, this presumption was neither legally nor politically supportable.

As historian Townsend Hoopes put it, the administration, in its final months, "ran steadily down like a tired clock, its energies spent, its coherence blurred."[59] No considered profile of Lumumba ever emerged from the NSC deliberations or from communications to the field, but rather an assortment of negative labels that descriptively ascended over time. At first, Lumumba was "radical" politically. Then, by some leap of perception, he became a "dangerous Marxist." His acceptance of Soviet aid revealed him as a "Soviet instrument" according to Eisenhower and endowed him with a "harrowing background" according to Dulles. The CIA favored the analogy of Cuba, which by a single caricature obscured a multitude of Congolese realities. (As Justice Holmes once observed, "The minute a phrase becomes current, it becomes an apology for not thinking accurately to the end of the sentence."[60])

SHOWDOWN IN LÉOPOLDVILLE

Lumumba's break with the United Nations set the stage for the fatal event. Hammarskjold had consistently refused to order the UN force to invade Katanga as Lumumba wished, or to accede to the Premier's request that UN troops be placed at his command. As a result, Lumumba (reportedly with Soviet encouragement) informed Hammarskjold that the Congo had lost its confidence in the Secretary-General and called for direct military action by the African and Asian contingents to end the secession.[61] He implied that the Secretary-General was conspiring with the Belgians and that the UN would be expelled. Hammarskjold was deeply stung; he privately characterized Lumumba as an "incipient dictator." When reports reached New York that Lumumba's soldiers had arrested UN officials, Hammarskjold advised the U.S. ambassador to the UN that a "showdown" was approaching. Lumumba had to be "broken."[62]

Lumumba's decision to break with the UN was the critical blunder of his brief career. By dealing with the UN, he had enhanced his standing with his own people and had given African and Asian governments the opportunity to support him. Without the UN, however, that recognition and support were lost. By inviting the Soviet Union to intervene, Lumumba became a pawn—and ultimately a victim—of the Cold War.

In Léopoldville, the rival powers and their operatives maneuvered to strengthen their positions. The Soviet Union stepped up its assistance. Ghana, Guinea, and Egypt also distributed money for Lumumba's cause. The Premier himself turned increasingly to his leftist advisers, principally Madame Blouin, Andrew Djin, and Serge Michel. Much was made of the claim that these advisers were communists or at least pro-Soviet, but this seems doubtful.[63] By late August, "It was clear that the Belgians were organizing Abako [Kasavubu's political movement, which was based in Léopoldville] and other elements to overthrow Lumumba and that Lumumba was prepared to fight back dirty."[64]

Working in concert with Belgian agents, the CIA pumped more money into the effort to topple Lumumba. Dulles approved a $100,000 disbursement for political operations in August alone. The total budget for "large-scale . . . paramilitary support to anti-Lumumba elements" was probably several times higher.[65] With virtually a carte blanche from Washington, the CIA station, which had "bloomed into a virtual embassy and miniature war department," could not help but become the senior partner in the U.S. mission in the Congo.[66] Station Chief Devlin was instructed to keep State Department representatives in the dark about certain covert operations. This increased the CIA's leverage over its diplomatic counterpart.[67]

It was during this period that the CIA station recruited the Congolese leaders (later known as the "Binza Group") who would become the building blocks of American policy. President Kasavubu, Foreign Minister Justin Bomboko, Sûreté Chief Victor Nendaka, Commissioner for Finance Albert Ndele, and Colonel Joseph Mobutu (who had already been recruited by the Belgian Sûreté in Brussels in 1959) were all drawn under the wing of the CIA.[68]

On September 5, 1960, President Kasavubu announced over the radio that he was dismissing Premier Lumumba. Lumumba in turn dismissed Kasavubu in another radio broadcast a few hours later. Under Article 22 of the Loi Fondamentale, Kasavubu was clearly within his constitutional rights in dismissing his Premier. The more important question was whether he could prevail over Lumumba in the political contest that was bound to ensue.

Had the UN not intervened, Lumumba would probably have prevailed in the struggle for power because of his majority in Parliament and control of most units of the army. But the Secretary-General's special representative, Andrew Cordier, an American, ordered all airports to be closed to all but UN traffic. He later justified his action as having been necessary to prevent civil war. In so doing, however, he also prevented Lumumba from airlifting his troops via Soviet Ilyushins from Katanga, where they were fighting, to the capital city.[69] Another UN official went down to Radio Congo and had the radio crystal removed.[70] A cordon of UN troops prevented Lumumba from entering the radio station to make a broadcast. Meanwhile, his opponent Kasavubu was broadcasting speeches from across the river in Brazzaville.[71]

It is virtually certain that the U.S. played a central role in Lumumba's dismissal. More than a week before Kasavubu acted, anti-Lumumba leaders (who were in contact with the CIA) approached the Congolese President with a plan to assassinate Lumumba. Although Kasavubu refused to subscribe to the plot, he was undoubtedly aware of the depth of American antipathy for Lumumba. Andrew Tully claims that CIA men reminded Kasavubu that "it was within his realm of responsibility to depose Lumumba and form a new government." Ten days before the dismissal, the U.S. Special Group in Washington (the interagency covert operations oversight group) discussed means to get rid of Lumumba constitutionally.[72]

But Lumumba was not so easily defeated. On September 7, he appeared in the lower house of the Congolese Parliament. Ambassador Timberlake reported:

> At his very best, Lumumba then devastated the points raised by the opposition . . . He made Kasavubu look ridiculous. He attacked the UN saying the country was not really free if arms, airports, and radio facilities were controlled by the UN. How could the UN justify this interference if it refused to liberate Katanga? . . . He had turned to the Russians for planes only when Belgium supplied planes to Tshombe and after both the UN and the U.S. had abandoned him by failing to furnish transportation.[74]

Lumumba's counterattack was made all the more persuasive by his "goon squads," which threatened and beat his opponents. On September 8, the lower house voted overwhelmingly to reinstate him. The next day, the Senate—supposedly an anti-Lumumba bastion—followed suit.

Alarmed at Lumumba's comeback and the prospect of an airlift of Soviet troops, the White House ordered a U.S. naval task force (then touring African waters) to head toward the Congo. Included in the task force were two destroyers, two amphibious vessels with landing craft and 500 Marines. The attack carrier, the U.S.S. Wasp, had already been positioned near the mouth of the Congo River.[74] The signal to Moscow was unmistakable. The White House continued to press the CIA for "vigorous action" against Lumumba. CIA Director Dulles believed that even out of the government, Lumumba would be a threat. His "talents and dynamism appear overriding factors in reestablishing his position each time it seems half lost," the director cabled Léopoldville.[75]

In Léopoldville, the West tried once again to bring down Lumumba. On September 12, Colonel Mobutu, who had previously played no role in the struggle for power and who had taken refuge in UN quarters from his own mutinous troops, announced a temporary military takeover to neutralize the disputants. He gave the Soviets and their allies forty-eight hours to leave. This coup was reportedly the brainchild of American and Belgian intelligence agents. CIA Station Chief Devlin, for example, wired CIA headquarters on the day after the coup that he was serving as "adviser" to the Congolese effort to "eliminate" Lumumba. At an NSC meeting on September 21, with Eisenhower present, Dulles argued that the military takeover was not enough. "Mobutu appears to be the effective power in the Congo for the moment but Lumumba was not yet disposed of and remained a grave danger as long as he was not yet disposed of."[76]

The coup, which had dislodged the Russians and their allies, provided some reprieve for Eisenhower's hardline policy, at least until Lumumba could be finally disposed of. But it also created another problem. Under the terms of the Security Council resolution, Hammarskjold's commitment was to the constitutional government of the Congo, which Mobutu had now overthrown. Without a legal government in power, the UN might have to withdraw. The Afro-Asian governments, moreover, who were providing some 80 percent of the troops in the UN's 12,000-man army, were predominantly committed to Lumumba.

On September 13th, Harriman wired Kennedy:

> I believe our best hope is in the strongest support by the Security Council for the continued backing of Hammarskjold . . . and insistence that the Russians and Belgians or others stop giving aid outside the United Nations. It is of the very highest importance that African opinion be exerted . . .

Nkrumah was being difficult, Harriman reported, but he could be dealt with. Once independent, Nigeria would oppose the Soviet intervention in the Congo. Former French Africa, with the exception of Guinea, would oppose communist designs. Tunisian President Habib Bourguiba, whose influence with the West Africans was considerable, could be counted on to support a moderate position. Harriman concluded: "I doubt that Khrushchev, when he addresses the Assembly, will wish to face strong United Nations opposition to his actions in the Congo."[77]

SHOWDOWN AT THE UN

Faced with dissension among UN members and an illegitimate regime in power in Léopoldville, which the UN command could not legally recognize, Hammarskjold called a special session of the General Assembly. Despite his personal distaste for Lumumba, the Secretary-General was now convinced that unless the deposed Premier were restored to some position of power, the UN might have to withdraw. Hammarskjold appealed to the Americans to encourage Kasavubu to compromise "without putting money in his pocket."[78]

There was no better time for the United States to attempt Hammarskjold's suggested reconciliation with Lumumba than in late September 1960. Lumumba was out of power, surrounded by a protective cordon of UN guards; Mobutu was in power, beholden to his American and Belgian patrons. The Soviets were gone. Most of the African and Asian powers, which previously had demanded Lumumba's outright restoration as premier, were willing now to tolerate the establishment of a coalition regime in which he would share power. In short, a "return to legality" seemed politically and diplomatically propitious.

Washington, however, would accept nothing short of Lumumba's elimination. There would be no fence mending with his African supporters or renewed backing of Hammarskjold, as Harriman had proposed. Khrushchev himself then enroute to New York for the UN Special Session, could not have devised a more disastrous American position.

The first round at the UN Special Session went to the U.S. On September 19, the General Assembly voted 70–0, with the Soviet Union and its allies abstaining, to prohibit all military assistance to the Congo except through the UN. A Soviet resolution censuring the Secretary-General for assisting the colonialists and calling for the removal of the entire UN Command was overwhelmingly rejected. The judgment against the Soviet Union was devastating. The *Christian Science Monitor* observed: "Perhaps not since Poland refused to return all the way into the Soviet satellite sheep-pen has Moscow encountered such a setback."[79]

Three days later, on September 22, Eisenhower took the podium and proposed a plan for the military protection and economic development of Africa under the UN. He pledged noninterference in the internal affairs of African countries. The response from African delegates was favorable, even though Eisenhower had proposed no specific solution to the power struggle in Léopoldville.[80]

Eisenhower then conferred with Lumumba's chief African supporter, Ghanaian President Kwame Nkrumah. Ghana had been the first power to come to the aid of the Lumumba government with troops. In addition to their large military contingent, the Ghanaians had maintained an active and influential diplomatic mission in Léopoldville since three weeks before the Congo's independence. From July through September, Nkrumah had remained in close contact with Lumumba, who consciously modeled himself after his Ghanaian mentor. In August 1960, the two leaders had signed a secret agreement politically uniting their countries.[81]

At his meeting with Eisenhower and Secretary of State Herter, Nkrumah remarked that he had not accepted an appointment with Khrushchev the previous day because he had wanted to talk to Eisenhower first.[82] Nkrumah's major objective was to reach some sort of understanding with the American President regarding the leadership crisis in the Congo, but Eisenhower preferred to reminisce about his days as Supreme Allied Commander. During the war, he told Nkrumah, he had led "such varied forces as the British, the French, and the underground Belgian and Netherlands forces. From this he learned that peoples differing widely from each other could get along together and he wished that everyone could have a similar experience." He told Nkrumah that as he arrived at the UN building that morning, the crowds had shouted, "Give 'em hell, Ike, give 'em hell." "But what do we gain by giving them hell?" he asked Nkrumah, who by this time was looking at him blankly.[83]

Nkrumah brought the Congo up again and pressed for U.S. support for the UN operation. Eisenhower responded positively, noting that in his speech he had been careful not to place the problem on a bipolar basis. "Our policy is to solve problems through the UN even when we ourselves would prefer them worked out in another way."[84]

Summit meetings may consist of such euphemisms, but Nkrumah most surely suspected that Eisenhower's assurance was outright fiction. Through his informants in Léopoldville, Nkrumah was aware that American CIA agents were working with the Belgians to subvert Lumumba's government. He also suspected that Mobutu had been bought off by the Belgians. In the aftermath of the Kasavubu-Mobutu coup, two of Nkrumah's personal emissaries in the Congo had been expelled.[85] It was not surprising that Nkrumah left his meeting with Eisenhower "heartily dissatisfied" with the American's assurances about working through the UN.[86]

The next day Nkrumah addressed the General Assembly and sharply attacked the Western role in the Congo. He charged that "imperialist intrigue, stark and naked, was desperately at work" to prevent a reconciliation between President Kasavubu and Premier Lumumba.[87] In response, Secretary Herter remarked to newsmen, in a statement cleared by the White House, that "Nkrumah was definitely moving toward the Soviet bloc." Nkrumah then countered by accusing "the nations of the West as being fanatically anti-communist," but privately suggested to American industrialist Edgar Kaiser that he was willing to explain his position to Herter in person.[88]

Kaiser's assistant, Chad Calhoun, telephoned the U.S. mission to set up a meeting: "It's only a few floors between Nkrumah on the 24th floor of the Waldorf and Herter on the 35th. Just phone him and he'll run right up those steps." Herter refused; instead, he sent Assistant Secretary of State Joseph Satterthwaite to Nkrumah's suite. Incensed, Nkrumah refused to see him and accepted Khrushchev's invitation to spend the weekend at the Soviet's villa on Long Island.[89] The *Washington Post* observed: "Nkrumah's eminence gained through martyrdom last week." A Ghanaian schoolteacher in Accra told *The New York Times* correspondent: "Of course the Communists are gaining in Ghana. After all, they have all of the West working for them."[90] The American ambassador to Ghana, Wilson Flake, was called home for good.

On campaign stops, candidate Kennedy began to ask what had gone wrong in Ghana:

> Why did the people of Ghana and the leadership decide, even with a great tradition of being tied to the British . . . why have they . . . suddenly begun to tie their policies to that of the Soviet Union? It is not chaos. It is not a military seizure of power like Cuba. Yet, Mr. Herter said 3 weeks ago that Ghana is supporting the foreign policy of the Soviet Union. What made Nkrumah, who studied in Pennsylvania, who went to, I believe, Lincoln College, what made him decide . . . that the Soviet Union had more to offer him than the West?[91]

Part of the answer was mediocre diplomacy in Accra. The assignment of Ambassador Flake had been curious: a southerner, his previous post had been as deputy chief of mission in South Africa, hardly ideal training. Nkrumah found him uninformed—no match for his sophisticated Soviet counterpart who had arrived in 1959.[92]

In the Congo, the story was much the same. Ambassador Timberlake —as one senior colleague put it—was in way over his head. His French was halting. He seemed alternately puzzled and infuriated by the inhospitable Congolese, whom he described in a cable as "primitive people" who could only respond to "simple stimuli."[93] After the Russian intervention, Timberlake proposed that the U.S. give Kasavubu a "plush" plane that would make Lumumba's Ilyushin look like a "Model T Ford." Such a gift could become "an important key in the formation of the new government if Lumumba is overthrown." The department turned down the proposal.[94]

Timberlake's colleague in Brussels, William Burden, was a wealthy Republican socialite whose largesse in the '56 presidential campaign had gotten him his ambassadorship. Burden's approach to the Congo crisis

consisted of taking the Belgians at their word. In October 1960, he reported to Washington that the allegation that Belgium was trying to
separate Katanga from the rest of the Congo was "false"—this at a time
when the Belgian government was supplying military aid to Katanga and
contemplating formal recognition of the secessionist province.[95]

Ambassadorial incompetence had been one of Kennedy's continual
complaints against the Eisenhower administration. "We are going to have
to be better represented. We are going to have to have the best Americans
we can get to speak for our country abroad," he told a crowd three days
before the presidential election. "Too many ambassadors have been chosen
who are ill-equipped and ill-briefed. Campaign contributions have been
regarded as a substitute for experience. Men who lack compassion for the
needy here in the United States were sent abroad to represent us in
countries which were marked by disease and poverty and illiteracy and
ignorance, and they did not identify us with those causes and the fight
against them."[96]

ILLEGITIMACY AND CONSPIRACY

Lack of ambassadorial leadership in Léopoldville gave the CIA Station
unbridled rein. Station Chief Devlin notified Washington that although
the Kasavubu-Mobutu regime was "weakening under" foreign pressure to
bring about a reconciliation with Lumumba, he was still giving the assassination plan the "highest priority." Ambassador Timberlake remained
ignorant of the entire conspiracy.[97]

Hammarskjold's special representative in the Congo, Rajeshwar Dayal,
however, refused to recognize the Mobutu regime, which the United
States was trying to legitimize. When Mobutu's troops arrested Lumumba's
deputy, Antoine Gizenga, Dayal secured his release. In early October,
Mobutu served a warrant for Lumumba's arrest. Dayal, with Ham-
marskjold's backing, refused to remove the UN guard protecting Lumumba.
Mobutu then issued an ultimatum to the UN with Timberlake's support.
Kasavubu accused the UN of "conniving at crimes."[98]

The CIA station was meanwhile trying to carry out the plan to
assassinate Lumumba. The poison, along with "rubber gloves, a mask,
and a syringe," had arrived in Léopoldville in late September, but CIA
agents could not gain access to Lumumba's house because of the UN
guard. Two professional criminals with records of service for the CIA
(codenamed QJ/WIN and WI/ROGUE) were flown into Léopoldville
from Europe. Agent QJ/WIN's assignment was to "pierce both Congolese
and UN guards" to gain access to Lumumba. Agent WI/ROGUE asked
QJ/WIN in December to join him in "an execution squad." Arms were

delivered to at least one of Lumumba's opponents, a Congolese senator, for purposes of assassination.[99]

The embassy reported that despite the ambassador's efforts to bring together Tshombe, Kasavubu, and other pro-Western leaders, the anti-Lumumba coalition simply did not have enough votes to survive a vote of confidence in the Parliament. "Lumumba is the central problem. There is always the danger that no matter how firm the opposition lines up, Lumumba's oratory plus threats can turn it into a victory for himself."[100] Mobutu and his troops were the only barrier to Lumumba's return to power. Timberlake reported, "I would not like to see them emasculated." The State Department agreed—a coalition government would be "disastrous."[101]

Much of the Third World, however, continued to resist American policy and to support Lumumba. When eight African and Asian countries tried to seat the Central Government's (i.e., Lumumba's) delegation in the General Assembly, the U.S., according to a secret State Department report, advised Kasavubu to appoint a delegation and fly it to New York. After a bitter debate, Kasavubu's delegation prevailed in the credentials dispute and was seated. *Le Monde*, citing U.S. pressure on the Latin American representatives, called the vote "a success of the big American stick."[102]

The U.S., though, paid a high price for the victory. The vote drove a deep wedge between the West and the Africans. Every major troop contributor sided with the Soviet Union in opposing the seating of the Kasavubu delegation. Senator Wayne Morse, who was serving as an American delegate to the UN at the time, described the delegation exercise as a "terrible mistake" that forfeited African trust in the United States. "You can buy your Kasavubus, you can buy a few stooges in Katanga," Morse told the Senate Foreign Relations Committee, "but it is only temporary, and you are building on quicksand."[103] By forcing the credentials issue, the U.S. and other Western powers may have driven a nail into Lumumba's political coffin, but their action also gave his followers no choice but to secede. At the end of November, they set up a rival government in Stanleyville. There were now, at least nominally, four governments in the Congo.[104]

THE KATANGA CONNECTION

Profiting from the political struggle in Léopoldville, secessionist leader Moise Tshombe moved ahead in consolidating the Katanga secession. Belgium sent the regime a 7-to-9-ton shipment of military materiel in September.[105] Belgian officers, later to be augmented by French mercenaries, trained the Katangan gendarmerie as an independent fighting force. Union Minière continued to operate its vast mining complex and to provide the wherewithal for the secessionist regime. The financial effect on the rest of the Congo was unmistakable: without Katanga, the Congo was economically stillborn.

In August, with the permission of the State Department, Michel Struelens, a Belgian civil servant, opened an office in New York called Katanga Information Services. What Struelens sought from the U.S. government was de facto recognition of Katanga's sovereignty.[106] Had the U.S. opposed the Belgian buildup in Katanga and discouraged Struelens's entry, there is little doubt that the secession (which would bedevil the UN and the U.S. for the next two and one-half years) would not have been as durable as it turned out to be. But as one historian wrote, the diplomacy of the West during this period was "short-sighted and unscrupulous."[107]

With the specter of Lumumba—whether in or out of power—shadowing their every deliberation, American officials regarded pro-Western Katanga as their ace-in-the-hole. Washington decided that it could not risk alienating virtually all Black Africa by recognizing Katanga officially, however much as it would have liked to. The State Department, nonetheless, advised several posts: ". . . . should other states recognize Katanga, it is possible the U.S. might reconsider its position."[108] Under Secretary Dillon's attitude was: "Don't close the door on Katanga."[109] Ambassador Timberlake urged at one point that Katanga be permitted political independence.[110] Under Secretary of State for Political Affairs Livingston Merchant looked on the secession, according to one Foreign Service Officer in the African Bureau, "with all the objectivity of a large stockholder in Union Minière."[111]

One American scholar on the Congo believed that the Eisenhower administration's attachment to Katanga stemmed in good part from its belief in the virtues of big business: "A tender regard for corporate profit-making and the benefits of social stability was consistent with the interests of Belgian investors, settlers, and civil servants in the Congo." Senior American officials had business ties to the Congo. Dillon's family firm, for example, had made a $15 million loan to the Belgian Congo in 1958. Robert Murphy, the "grand old man of the Foreign Service" who had represented the U.S. at independence ceremonies in Léopoldville and who subsequently was an influential adviser on Congo policy, was openly pro-Belgian. He also served during this period as director of Morgan Guaranty International, the "traditional fiscal agent in the U.S. for the Belgian Congo government." Another vigorous partisan of the Belgian position was the American ambassador in Brussels, William Burden. During his ambassadorship, Burden maintained a directorship in American Metal Climax, a company whose Rhodesian copper interests were to make it "a leading corporate defender of the conservative order in Katanga."[112]

CONFRONTING THE UN

The final, and perhaps inevitable, act of Eisenhower's Congo policy was confrontation with the UN itself. In his first report to the Secretary-General, Special Representative Dayal stated that "a single government of conciliation" was not possible without reconvening Parliament and bringing the Armée Nationale Congolaise (ANC) under control. Both requirements were anathema to the Americans. Reconvening Parliament might mean Lumumba's return to power. Controlling the ANC might possibly cause the downfall of Mobutu. Dayal's second report took direct aim at Mobutu. It described him as a usurper of political power and called his troops "rabble . . . the principal fomenter of lawlessness." The report went on to state that Mobutu's takeover had coincided with the systematic return of the Belgians to the Congo.[113]

Mobutu retaliated by arresting UN personnel. His troops hijacked forty UN trucks and stole supplies. Dayal, in turn refused to meet with any of Mobutu's commissioners and told a correspondent for *The New York Times* (in an interview that was never printed) that the U.S. was financing Mobutu. The UN Special Representative let it be known that he believed that Mobutu's effort to arrest Lumumba was "just a trick to assassinate Lumumba."[114]

In a series of notes to the Belgian government, Hammarskjold continued to insist that Belgium stop sending military and political advisory personnel to the Congo, and that it immediately withdraw those already there. The Belgians were incensed. Foreign Minister Pierre Wigny called Hammarskjold's demands "stupid even for the UN," and said the entire UN operation was a "failure."

At the urging of Ambassadors Timberlake and Burden, Washington moved against the UN. On November 4, the State Department Press Officer expressed "every confidence in the good faith of Belgium" and said the U.S. government found parts of Dayal's report unacceptable. Charles Bohlen, the Soviet expert who was then directing U.S. policy at the UN, was instructed to set Hammarskjold straight. "Accompanied by [U.S. Ambassador James J.] Wadsworth, he infuriated Hammarskjold with peremptory demands and pointed reminders that the U.S. was being asked to foot most of the bill for the Congo operation."[115]

On November 27, Lumumba escaped his confinement and attempted to flee to Stanleyville, where many of his loyalists had gathered. The CIA was aware of Lumumba's escape plan nearly two weeks before it occurred and had been studying "several plans of action." The station worked with Mobutu and his Belgian advisers to block possible escape routes. Had Lumumba proceeded directly to Stanleyville, he would probably have succeeded in evading his antagonists. But he insisted on stopping the convoy to greet friends and to address supporters along the way. This gave Mobutu time to locate his whereabouts. On December 1, he was captured near a river crossing in Kasai Province and was transferred to a prison at the Thysville army camp two days later.[116]

News of Lumumba's arrest and imprisonment occasioned anger and disillusionment among the Africans. It led to a complete breakdown of relations between the UN command and Mobutu's forces. The most serious consequence of all was that Antoine Gizenga's regime in Stanleyville became viable as a result of Lumumba's imprisonment. Gizenga's political ability paled in comparison to Lumumba's. (Nkrumah dismissed him as "that hopeless man.")[117] But with Lumumba in jail, African and Communist countries extended diplomatic recognition and, in some cases, military aid to the new Lumumbist regime.

U.S. Ambassador Wadsworth defended Mobutu's action before the Security Council. Lumumba, he said, was "a threat to the security of the state." Indian Defense Minister Krishna Menon responded by pointing out that there had been no due process, no recourse to the courts, and no consultation with the Congolese Parliament concerning Lumumba's arrest and imprisonment.[118]

Hammarskjold was blamed for the failure of the UN force to prevent Mobutu from arresting Lumumba. The Soviet ambassador fulminated against what he called the NATO-supported, Hammarskjold-abetted, Belgian plot to use Mobutu's "fascist gangs." African and Asian delegates began to express support for Khrushchev's troika plan to abolish the Secretary-General's office and replace it with a triumvirate (one member each from the western, socialist, and neutral blocs).[119]

Six pro-Lumumba governments announced their intention to withdraw their contingents from the UN force. This would mean withdrawal of 5,680 troops—more than one-third of the entire peacekeeping army.[120] The continued participation of the large Ghanaian contingent was doubtful. Hammarskjold darkly predicted that if the UN were forced to pull out there would be open civil war in the Congo:

> If and when that were to happen, the world would be facing a confused Spanish war situation, with fighting going on all over the prostrate body of the Congo and pursued for nebulous and conflicting aims. Could such a situation be contained? And if not contained, how would it influence peace and war in the world?[124]

On December 25, 1961, Gizenga's Lumumbist troops invaded Kivu Province, taking the capital Bukavu and arresting the pro-Mobutu governor. With Belgian encouragement and logistical support, Mobutu tried to retake Bukavu by airlifting his troops to Usumbura, the capital of the Belgian-administered territory of Ruanda-Urundi. The operation was a total disaster and Mobutu subsequently went into hiding.[122]

For the second time in a month, Bohlen and Wadsworth were instructed to see Hammarskjold. The State Department's instructions had the ring of an ultimatum. The Americans demanded that the Secretary-General remove Dayal, that Kasavubu receive the UN's all-out support, that Guinean and other "unreliable" troop contingents be withdrawn and replaced by "more reliable" troops (possibly from Latin America) and finally that the UN Command stop Gizenga's troop movements and respect Tshombe's "legitimate" right of defense. Hammarskjold refused. He referred to what had happened in Lebanon and what was happening in Laos, "reflecting his deep-seated distrust of U.S. intelligence activities in these situations and giving further indications that [the U.S. was] similarly involved in the Congo."[123]

A few days later, a story was leaked ("dictated," Hammarskjold thought) to *The New York Times*. Washington officials were reportedly "becoming increasingly uneasy over the trend in the Congo and the performance of the UN there." Dayal was described as "hostile to the Kasavubu administration and to western influence." Hammarskjold was described as being "under such heavy pressure from the Communist and Afro-Asian powers that he has been unable or unwilling to correct the situation." Secretary Herter called the Secretary-General and apologized.[124]

The situation in the Congo was changing hourly. Lumumba's return to power—once seemingly impossible—now appeared probable. Joseph Kasongo, the President of the Chambre des Députés, told an embassy officer that the only solution was to release Lumumba.[125] A correspondent for the London *Daily Telegraph* wrote on January 19 that, "Support for him [Lumumba] has grown throughout the country since his capture by the forces of Colonel Mobutu." Even in Tshombe's capital of Elisabethville, the regime was obliged to arrest 1,000 suspected Lumumbists.[126]

A week before the Kennedy administration took office, there was a mutiny at Camp Hardy where Lumumba was being held. The CIA station reported that the mutiny would "almost certainly . . . bring about [Lumumba's] return to power." Congolese officers were assaulted and their wives raped by the mutineers who threatened to release Lumumba. Kasavubu, Mobutu, and Justin Bomboko, the Foreign Minister, were greatly alarmed since the Thysville garrison had been considered the most secure in the country. Troops loyal to Lumumba massed on the Orientale-Equateur border. The CIA station predicted that the government might fall "within a few days," and Devlin discussed emergency measures with his protégés, the Binza boys.[127]

The CIA station proposed that, in addition to ridding itself once and for all of Lumumba, the Kasavubu-Mobutu regime follow Katanga's example and recruit large numbers of white officers to put some backbone into the ANC. Ambassador Timberlake, whose diplomatic role had previously been little more than a fig leaf for the CIA operation, objected when he learned of this plan. He cabled home that this "will not cure the disease from which Mobutu's army is suffering but will simply provide expensive aspirin tablets to reduce fevers temporarily." The "plain fact" was that Mobutu's soldiers had no will to fight and Kasavubu and his associates had little will to govern. They were neither legitimate nor popular and the imprisoned Lumumba—whatever his transgressions—was both. The embassy recognized that even in jail Lumumba was "the largest single factor in Congolese politics."[128]

3

Lumumba's House

Should we help Lumumba?

Kennedy to Harriman
(*November 1960*)

On Wednesday, November 9, 1960, John Kennedy learned at his home in Hyannis Port that he had been narrowly elected President. Later that day, Patrice Lumumba, confined to his house in Léopoldville by two rings of UN and Congolese (ANC) soldiers, sent him a long telegram of congratulations.[1]

In the telegram, which was smuggled out of Lumumba's house by Moroccan messengers, the deposed premier spoke of his admiration of Kennedy's support for African independence and urged Kennedy to act immediately through the UN to restore peace in the Congo.

Several days later, Averell Harriman flew down to Palm Beach, Florida, to give the President-elect his impressions of the Congo crisis. Harriman remembered that Kennedy was concerned about one thing: "Should we help Lumumba?" Harriman said that he was not sure we could help him, even if we wanted to.[2] In the two months that followed, Kennedy found himself surrounded by world leaders—Khrushchev, Nehru, Nkrumah, Hammarskjold, Baudoin—demanding that he take action regarding Lumumba's fate.

ESCAPE AND ARREST

The premier's residence, where Lumumba was confined, was situated on a bluff overlooking the River Congo along the palm-lined Boulevard Albert Ier in Léopoldville's most manicured *quartier*. "*La Résidence Tilkens*," with its ivory facade and two-tiers of ochre-tiled roof framing the arched porch on the second floor, was an elegant remnant of the days when King Léopold II owned the Congo "in his person and in perpetuity." It was in this house that Lumumba had drafted his thundering dismissal of King Baudoin during independence ceremonies. It was also in this house that

Lumumba had prepared his fateful appeal to the UN to intervene with troops. Then, one month later, he had broken his appointment (and his government's relations) with Secretary-General Hammarskjold, who had come to the house to meet with him. The two would never meet again.[3]

Ever since Lumumba had officially moved into the Premier's residence in June 1960, it had seemed that he—and the country—had been enveloped in crisis: first, the rebellions and the provincial secessions, then the intervention of the UN and the Soviet Union, and finally his own disputed dismissal. It was to this house on September 11, 1960, that the military police had come to place Lumumba under arrest, but soldiers faithful to Lumumba immediately set him free after the intercession of ANC General Victor Lundula.

Later Sûrété Chief Nendaka had procured a warrant for his arrest, but Mobutu would not send his soldiers into the house: "I have no intention of letting my soldiers be killed for Lumumba." Another antagonist, Etienne Tshisekedi, who had close ties to the Americans and Belgians, had proposed that water and electricity to the house be cut off, but this too was never done.[4]

Four times during September and October, Lumumba had "escaped" confinement to rally supporters and to give speeches before large and cheering crowds. The Kasavubu-Mobutu regime had responded with an ultimatum to the UN, which they blamed for Lumumba's sorties: "The ANC is ready to do battle with the UN in order to arrest Patrice Lumumba."[5] Mobutu, again, did not have the stomach to act.

Outside the inner ring of blue-helmeted UN soldiers surrounding the house and the second ring of Mobutu's paracommandos, there was a third presence: the CIA's small squad of assassins trying to "pierce both Congolese and UN guards" to reach "the target."

POSSIBILITY USE COMMANDO TYPE GROUP FOR ABDUCTION EITHER VIA ASSAULT ON HOUSE UP CLIFF FROM RIVER OR, MORE PROBABLY, IF ATTEMPTS ANOTHER BREAKOUT INTO TOWN . . .[6]

Lumumba, however, eluded his would-be assassins by securing himself in the house with his wife and children. He dismissed most of his servants, "so entry by this means seems remote," Devlin reported to headquarters.[7] The CIA's "hunting season" was further frustrated by the inability of agents to establish an "observation post" near the house, possibly for the purpose of positioning a sniper.[8]

In late October, Lumumba smuggled three of his children out of the house and had them secreted aboard a plane bound for Cairo.[9] His wife Pauline left the house in early November for Switzerland to give birth to a daughter who died several days later. As the body was being shipped to Lumumbist stronghold Stanleyville, Lumumba made plans to break out. By means of a UN phone, he alerted his collaborator, Thomas Kanza, to the plan of escape. Kanza appealed to him to stay in the house. Lumumba replied: "One of us must sacrifice himself if the Congolese people are to understand and accept the ideal we are fighting for."[10]

They were waiting for him. "[A] decision on breakout will probably be made shortly . . . station has several possible assets to use in event of breakout and studying several plans of action," Devlin cabled headquarters.[11] On the night of November 27, during a tropical storm, Lumumba escaped. He picked up his wife and son Roland at the Guinean embassy and, with several followers, fled east toward Stanleyville. When President Nkrumah of Ghana heard the news, he shook his head: "O impetuous man."[12]

The CIA worked with Mobutu and Sûreté Chief Nendaka "to get the roads blocked and troops alerted [to block] possible escape route."[13] Three days after his escape from Léopoldville, Lumumba was arrested at Mweka, near Port Francqui. He was beaten with rifle butts by ANC soldiers and flown back to Léopoldville. He was then taken before Mobutu who, according to the Associated Press, "with folded arms, calmly watched the soldiers slap and abuse the prisoner . . ."[14] Hammarskjold's Special Representative Dayal vigorously protested the treatment of Lumumba and reported that the prisoner had suffered serious injuries.[15]

Kasavubu advised Hammarskjold: "Please regard this question, as I and the entire country do, as a domestic matter." During the Security Council debate concerning the arrest, U.S. Ambassador Lodge reiterated Kasavubu's position.[16] An outraged Nkrumah blamed Hammarskjold for having done nothing to stop the arrest: "Do you, Your Excellency, not see the bitter irony in the fact that the Government and Parliament which invited the United Nations to assist with the restoration of law and order have been forced to the wall by the systematic use of violence before the very eyes of the United Nations High Command?"[17]

Lumumba's followers continued to believe that if their imprisoned leader could remain alive until January 20, 1961, when Kennedy took the presidential oath, he might escape execution.[18] Gizenga sent a message to the President-elect in mid-December 1960 appealing for support. Lumumba's former minister delegate to the UN, Thomas Kanza, visited with Mrs. Roosevelt, whom he found encouraging. Nkrumah wrote Adlai Stevenson, his former guest in Accra, to urge him also to help before it was too late.[19]

Lumumba himself seemed less hopeful. He wrote his wife a final letter,

which was smuggled out of prison: "I write you these words without know-
ing whether they will ever reach you, or when they will reach you, and
whether I will still be alive when you read them."[20]

THE PRESIDENTIAL TRANSITION

On the day before his inauguration, Kennedy met with Eisenhower to
discuss foreign policy problems. On each crisis, Eisenhower urged Kennedy
to continue the hard line. He advised him not to rule out the possibility of
unilateral military intervention to save Laos from the communists.[21]
Regarding Cuba, Eisenhower said that it had been "the policy of this
government" to aid the anti-Castro guerrillas "to the utmost." (As if to
put the finishing touches on Kennedy's Cuban inheritance, Eisenhower
had severed diplomatic relations with Cuba only seventeen days before
he left the White House. He then told his staff that he wanted the Cuban
exiles to set up a government-in-exile. "I'd like to see recognition accorded
promptly. If possible, before January 20."[22])

The Eisenhower administration also made eleventh-hour efforts to tie
its successor's hands in Africa. Kennedy's sharp attacks on the Eisenhower
record in Africa before and during the campaign has aroused antipathy
in the Washington foreign policy community. The Eisenhower men tried
to rush through the appointments of six senior State Department officials
as ambassadors to the new African countries in late December 1960.
Chester Bowles and Robert Kennedy, representing the transition team,
succeeded in blocking the effort.[23]

Nowhere was the Eisenhower record more vulnerable to exposure than
in the Congo. The American plot to kill Lumumba was caught up in a
web of secrets and alliances that could not, under any circumstances, be
permitted to unravel.

The Eisenhower men remembered how Kennedy had demanded
freedom for Algeria. They knew of Kennedy's personal acquaintance with
African nationalists whom they had shunned. He had said in November
1960 that the U.S. had failed in the Congo. The transition team was
anticipating "major changes" in policy.[24] To those in their final days in
power, such "changes" could mean leaks, exposure, ruined careers—
"another China."[25]

During the week preceding Kennedy's inauguration, CIA Station Chief
Devlin's communications from Léopoldville took on an ominous tone.
Mobutu's moment of elation in December, after having caught Lumumba,
had given way to what Devlin described as "a spirit of defeat."[26] Mutinies
broke out among the ANC rank and file at Thysville. At Camp Hardy,
where Lumumba was imprisoned, soldiers beat up and jailed their own

officers. Lumumba's followers managed to smuggle out a recorded message from Lumumba to the Congolese people: "In our good fortune as in bad, I will always remain at your side. It is with you that I have fought to liberate this country . . ."[27]

Both the embassy and the CIA station believed that the government could fall "within a few days." Devlin's cable to Director Dulles on January 13—well timed to edify the new President—sounded more like a policy statement from Washington than an intelligence communication from the field:

REFUSAL TAKE DRASTIC STEPS AT THIS TIME WILL LEAD TO DEFEAT OF [UNITED STATES] POLICY IN CONGO.[28]

As Kasavubu, Mobutu, Nendaka, and the other "Binza boys" met under emergency conditions to decide what to do with Lumumba, Kennedy's appointees received final briefings on the eve of their assuming office. Regarding the Congo, one of them later wrote: "[T]o a new American administration committed to vigor in foreign policy and to sympathy with the emerging nations, history could hardly have devised a more baffling and frustrating test."[29]

During his first week in office, Kennedy requested a full-scale review of U.S. Congo policy and, in particular, recommendations for action regarding Lumumba. Secretary of State Dean Rusk's directive to the Congo Task Force (an interagency group of senior officials) reflected the President's wish for thoroughness: "Take the ceiling off your imaginations." In the words of one participant, the discussions that followed involved "a literally agonizing balance of risks."[30] The Eisenhower holdovers—Dulles, Bissell, and Dillon—waited uneasily for what would emerge.

The new President found himself under pressure from all sides regarding Lumumba. Nkrumah sent a 2,000-word letter to Kennedy setting forth the African position and criticizing past U.S. policy in angry terms. "What are we to think when we find in the Congo the U.S. supporting . . . a military dictatorship of a brutal and ineffectual type" that had imprisoned its Prime Minister "under disgusting and degrading conditions?" Lumumba's murder, Nkrumah warned, would have "the most serious effect" on Africa's relations with the United States. "Time is running short. I am absolutely certain that if you were to personally intervene to secure the release of Mr. Lumumba, this would in fact be significant, and I would like to make as strong as possible a personal appeal to you to do this."[31] In reply, Kennedy said that the situation "concerns me as much as it does you" and expressed his hope that together he and Nkrumah could work out some solution.[32]

A letter from King Baudoin also found its way to the President's desk.[33]

Baudoin warned Kennedy that Lumumba's release would mean a communist takeover in the Congo. Contrary signals were meanwhile coming in from New York. Ambassador Stevenson reported that Hammarskjold was urging him to work for the release of Lumumba, whom the Secretary-General had characterized as "a man of authority, shrewd, able, one to reckon with." In his discussions with Stevenson, Hammarskjold had accused Ambassador Timberlake of having "pleaded for the arrest of Lumumba" and told Stevenson that he (Hammarskjold) had made successive appeals on January 19th and 20th to President Kasavubu asking him to treat the prisoners humanely.[34]

Like Nkrumah, Nehru was infuriated by the West's role in undermining Lumumba. "Mobutu's forces have behaved scandalously. Shocking treatment meted out to Lumumba and others has also aroused deep resentment," he wrote Hammarskjold in January 1961.[35] The Eisenhower administration had tried to force Hammarskjold to withdraw his Special Representative Dayal (an old friend of Nehru and one of India's leading diplomats) from the Congo on the grounds that Dayal was pro-Lumumba and committed to the disbanding of the Kasavubu-Mobutu regime. Dayal's decision to throw up the protective UN cordon around Lumumba's house in October had incensed Kasavubu and his collaborators and had frustrated the CIA's attempt to get at Lumumba.[36] Nehru warned Hammarskjold that unless Lumumba were released and the activities of foreign agents curtailed, India would not send the 5,000 troops that Hammarskjold desperately needed to sustain the peacekeeping operation.

To dramatize the dangers of continued American intransigence, Hammarskjold showed Stevenson the communications from Nehru. In the course of a three-hour meeting with Stevenson on January 25, the Secretary-General proposed that the U.S. immediately take three steps: make a quiet, direct approach to Khrushchev (who had threatened to intervene again in the Congo) for a Cold War truce, undertake a "strenuous diplomatic effort" to prevent the antagonistic powers (Belgium, France, and the radical Afro-Asian nations) from forcing the UN out of the Congo, and avoid backing the Kasavubu-Mobutu regime to the point of excluding the possibility of compromise.[37]

At the first meeting of the Kennedy cabinet, Stevenson repeated the Hammarskjold proposal.[38] In his State of the Union address a few days later, the President promised to stand behind the UN: "We shall continue to support the heroic efforts of the United Nations to restore peace and order . . . efforts which are now endangered by mounting tensions, unsolved problems, and decreasing support from many member states."[39] As Hammarskjold had proposed, Kennedy sent messages to the Third World leaders who were contemplating a withdrawal of their contingents because of foreign subversion and the plight of Lumumba. "African independence must be genuine independence, not just a cover for some form of continuing control from the outside, . . ." Kennedy wrote Nehru.[40]

Stevenson was charged with the duty of approaching Soviet Ambassador Zorin to discuss a "truce." He told Zorin that "speaking personally"—diplomatic language to make it clear that he was not speaking under official instruction—he believed that the United States would favor early establishment of constitutional government.[41]

Did this mean the release and restoration of Lumumba? Timberlake, who was home for consultations, thought that it did and was shocked by the appearance of an American "sell-out" to the Russians. Others were disturbed that Stevenson had not cleared the démarche through the usual State Department channels. Timberlake telephoned CIA Director Allen Dulles and Joint Chiefs of Staff Chairman Lyman Lemnitzer to alert them to this unexpected move by the new administration.[42] Hammarskjold predicted to Dayal that a backlash in Washington was likely: "This simple victory for realism receives of course comments that Washington has made concessions to the Soviets."[43]

THE KENNEDY PLAN

On February 1, the Congo Task Force submitted its policy proposals to the President.[44] The Task Force recommended that the UN be given the right through the Security Council to use force to bring Congolese military factions under control and to cut off outside assistance. This proposal represented a sharp break from past U.S. policy, which had favored a toothless UN presence in the Congo in which UN forces were little more than a fig-leaf for the exercise of American and Belgian power. Under the new plan, which incorporated most of Hammarskjold's recommendations, the armies of Gizenga, Mobutu and Tshombe, as well as the Belgian complements of advisory personnel to the last two, stood to be subdued by the UN. Regarding Moscow, the Task Force recommended that the U.S. "work in favor of accommodation on the basis of neither the East nor the West filling the vacuum in the Congo."[45]

The President approved the new policy—soon to be known as the "Kennedy Plan"—on February 2. Over the next few days he sent letters to several leaders, including de Gaulle, Nkrumah, and Nehru. He asked the French President to support the American effort to broaden the UN mandate. De Gaulle, whose government was informally assisting Katanga, refused.[46] In his message to Nkrumah, Kennedy expressed reservations about the release of Lumumba and the reconvening of Parliament—Nkrumah's chief demands. He did assure the Ghanaian President, however, that the United States would press for "a broadly based government which would probably have to be federal in character, but with secession banned."[47] He invited Nkrumah to fly down from New York after his appearance at the UN General Assembly for an unofficial visit. Nkrumah agreed.

A few days before he received Kennedy's message, Nehru had rejected Hammarskjold's second request for a battalion of Indian troops. He had suggested that the Secretary-General first approach the Americans: ". . . if the drift is to be stopped and total chaos prevented, the help of the friendly and powerful countries who are the allies of Belgium should be definitely enlisted for the evacuation of the Belgians . . . Since Kasavubu survives by their blessings, it would be possible for them, if they so desire, to bring necessary pressure on him or withdraw their support completely."[48] The Kennedy Plan provided for those measures.

With Kennedy's personal assurance that the U.S. would follow through in the Security Council with its proposals, Nehru privately informed the Secretary-General that India would send 5,000 troops to the Congo.[49] Two years later, this would be regarded as a major turning point in the resolution of the Congo crisis.

Stevenson's work in selling the plan to the nonaligned powers at the UN was highly successful. The Russians were reportedly shocked at the turnaround in African and Asian sentiment. Soviet Ambassador Zorin paid a visit to Stevenson's office on February 9 and told him that he found some measure of agreement between their governments on three points: the withdrawal of Belgium, the convening of Parliament, and the release of political prisoners.[50]

RELEASING LUMUMBA

But what about Lumumba? Was he to be saved under Kennedy's plan? Or was the political price of ransoming him too high? Perhaps sensing that Lumumba's fate might be sealed before Kennedy was even inaugurated, Governor G. Mennen Williams (who had been named Assistant Secretary of State for African Affairs) summoned a Belgian diplomat two days before the inauguration for an informal communication—that Lumumba not be "liquidated."[51] Stevenson recommended Lumumba's release or, at the least, his protection from further harm. The African Bureau at State, under the vigorous leadership of Williams and his deputy, Wayne Fredericks, began laying the bureaucratic groundwork for a change in policy. One memorandum argued that in view of Eisenhower's association with Belgium, which had aided the Katangese secession, Lumumba's disenchantment with the West was hardly surprising: "It would have been to any leader who wished to keep his country unified."[52] Even Timberlake admitted in testimony before the Senate Foreign Relations Committee that "the sad fact is that there is not anybody down there outside Lumumba who has got the kind of energy and drive and imagination which would let him be Prime Minister."[53]

Senator Wayne Morse said that the peoples of Africa and Asia were asking the United States: "What happened to your professed support for self-determination?" According to Morse, the answer they got was that America supported representative rule only when it served America's interest. "When our people are in power we are satisfied. But we will not allow the African people to determine for themselves who their own leaders would be. That was why we had to remove Lumumba from power."[54] A memorandum from the Bureau of Intelligence and Research at the State Department recommended that the U.S. not exclude completely Lumumba's possible participation in a new government.[55]

But these stirrings of dissent among the newcomers were not enough to neutralize the prevailing phobia about Lumumba within the established centers of power in Washington. The CIA's vested interest in protecting its clients in Leopoldville was deep. Top agency officials such as Allen Dulles, Richard Bissell, and Bronson Tweedy had authorized and organized the assassination attempts against Lumumba. There could be no going back for personal, as much as official, reasons. Dulles met with President Kennedy about the Congo on January 26.[56]

Devlin had reported on January 14—six days before Kennedy took office—that Lumumba was to be delivered into the hands of his most hated enemies in Bakwanga.[57] According to another source, it was Devlin's "forceful intercession" with Kasavubu and others that brought about the transfer. Devlin has denied this, but one CIA officer, Paul Sakwa, remembered that Devlin subsequently "took credit" for the assassination.[58] The CIA base chief in Elisabethville, Mr. Doyle, provided a touch of levity in the otherwise grim proceedings:

THANKS FOR PATRICE. IF WE HAD KNOWN HE WAS COMING, WE WOULD HAVE BAKED A SNAKE.[59]

In the White House, caution was the order of the day. The new administration was facing other crises of equal or greater magnitude: Kennedy was contemplating putting 10,000 Marines on alert—as he later did—for possible intervention in Laos; the invasion of the Cuban exiles that would end disastrously in the Bay of Pigs in April was in the planning stages; and Khrushchev, by declaring on January 6 that the allied position in West Berlin was "especially vulnerable," had reignited that Cold War tinderbox. At least in the view of Dulles and other Eisenhower holdovers, the release of Lumumba would result in a communist takeover and one more breach in the containment wall.[60]

During his first two weeks in office, Kennedy was still feeling his way on the Congo. He conferred with Barbara Ward, who encouraged him to ignore Foggy Bottom and to listen to Hammarskjold.[61] He also visited with his younger brother, Edward M. Kennedy, who had recently returned from a fact-finding tour of the Congo and other African countries. The younger Kennedy recommended that Lumumba be released from prison, and then proceeded to disseminate a memorandum of the conversation within the government implicitly associating the President with this position. There were complaints. The special assistant for National Security Affairs, McGeorge Bundy, took the matter to the President who laughed and said, "Ted seems to have his own policy on Lumumba."[62]

The President's only definitive statement on Lumumba's release came in a letter to Nkrumah: *before* any political prisoners would be released, the U.S. believed that the Congolese armed forces would have to be brought under control and a new government established.[63] This was mere temporizing, since Lumumba's imprisonment was the central cause of the breakdown in order and the collapse of constitutional government. Nonetheless, the U.S. ambassadors in New Delhi and Lagos were instructed by Secretary Rusk to tell the Indian and Nigerian Prime Ministers "orally but not in any written memorandum . . . that in view of Lumumba's past record of irresponsibility as Prime Minister we would view with grave concern his return to the position."[64]

And what of protecting the imprisoned Lumumba from further harm? Washington would only commit itself to a request for "decent treatment" for *all* political prisoners in the Congo.[65] The Kennedy administration washed its hands of the matter.

Governor Williams went up to Capitol Hill to explain the administration's position. Williams clearly doubted the duty he had been given and his testimony showed it. Lumumba was dangerous, he explained to the senators. "You lock him up like a Houdini and somehow he winds up running the show . . ." There were "dilemmas within dilemmas" in the U.S. position: "We want self-determination but we do not want a coalition government . . . We want to have them call a parliament but we do not want Lumumba there . . ."[66]

Ambassador Timberlake, for some reason, was still worried that the Kennedy plan would bring Lumumba back. He believed, furthermore, that the Kennedy men had deliberately bypassed the CIA and the Defense

Department in formulating the new policy. With Timberlake in attendance, Congo meetings during the administration's first two weeks had a sieve-like quality to them.[67] Leaks about the "dangerous consequences" of the Kennedy plan were soon front-page features.

The *Washington Post* (in a story that was picked up internationally) reported erroneously on February 3 that the administration favored "disarming" all Congolese armed forces. The *New York Herald-Tribune's* correspondent on the Congo, Marguerite Higgins, wrote that the Kennedy policy would place Lumumba in a coalition government, a move that was not remotely contemplated by the administration.[68] This called for another reluctant trip to Capitol Hill: "We do not feel Lumumba should be released," Williams told the Senate Foreign Relations Committee behind closed doors.[69] In the words of a State Department memorandum, Agence France-Presse "almost immediately muddied the waters with the French-speaking Africans by disseminating highly tendentious versions of what the U.S. was proposing." USIA Director Edward R. Murrow pointed out in a meeting on February 6 that the effect of the leaks and misrepresentations was crippling.[70]

THE MURDER OF LUMUMBA

In the Congo, the effect of erroneous press reports was even more damaging. The Kasavubu-Mobutu regime began to consider the Kennedy administration a threat to its very survival. The Kennedy plan was seen as evidence of "a new and unexpected solidarity with the Casablanca powers . . . " (the radical nonaligned African governments that supported Lumumba).[71] The Léopoldville regime turned on the American embassy with sudden vehemence. The embassy received calls from "friends" suggesting that it would be unwise for Americans to be on the streets after dark.[72] ANC troops were put on alert. In early February, Mobutu announced that before being disarmed his troops would do battle against the UN, a threat he carried out two weeks later.[73]

The CIA station in Léopoldville bore much responsibility for the rupture. It had opposed any political solution to the power struggle and, worse, had fortified the resolve of Kasavubu and Mobutu, Nendaka, and the rest to use violence against others to save themselves. During the first two weeks of January, as the inauguration of the Kennedy administration drew near, Devlin had spoken of the need to take "drastic steps" before it was too late. The irony was that despite the Kennedy administration's efforts in Washington and New York to find a workable fomula for peace in the Congo, Devlin and his associates (with a virtual carte blanche from

CIA headquarters and unlimited funds on which to draw) had more influence over the course of events in the Congo than had their nominal superiors in the White House and the State Department.

The effect was tragic: reports that the incoming administration planned to liberate the imprisoned Lumumba on the one hand, and the CIA's deadly urgings on the other, acted like a closing vice on the desperate men in Léopoldville. On January 17, they put Lumumba and two of his leading supporters aboard a plane bound for Bakwanga, Kasai, the home territory of Lumumba's tribal enemy, "King" Albert Kalonji. When it was learned enroute that there were UN troops at the Bakwanga airport, the plane was redirected to Elisabethville. Lumumba and the other two prisoners were beaten repeatedly during the flight. The sight of the brutality caused the Belgian radio operator to vomit, and the crew locked themselves in the cockpit. Shortly after arriving in Elisabethville, the prisoners were executed, probably at the order of Katangese authorities. In Léopoldville the house that Lumumba had lived in was looted by Mobutu's soldiers.[74]

White House photographer Jacques Lowe caught Kennedy, horror-struck with head in hand, receiving the first news by telephone a full four weeks later on February 13th.[75] All the anguished searching for a way around Lumumba had been for naught. Forty-eight hours before Kennedy had even taken the presidential oath, Lumumba was already dead.

Lumumba's antagonists could now breathe more easily. They had finally freed themselves of his debilitating presence. But they were to find, as were their American and Belgian patrons, that his absence would haunt Congolese politics. As one of Lumumba's hated enemies, Katangese Foreign Minister Evariste Kimba, remarked to an American diplomat, "only Lumumba might have been big enough to govern the Congo." Who was there to replace him?[76]

Five years later, after seizing power, General Mobutu proclaimed Lumumba a national hero: "Glory and honor to that illustrious Congolese, that great African, the first martyr of our economic independence . . . "[77] Rumor had it among the people that Mobutu had had Lumumba's body disinterred from its shallow grave in Elisabethville and flown to Leopoldville where it was then dissolved in acid.[78] Mobutu announced that a statue of Lumumba would be erected in his heroic memory.[79] Even those who had delivered Lumumba to his murderers wanted his magic back. Jean-Paul Sartre wrote: "Lumumba alive and a captive is a symbol of the shame and rage of an entire continent . . . Once dead, Lumumba ceases to be an individual and becomes all of Africa, with its will toward unity, its dissensions, its discord, its strength and its impotence."[80]

In the aftermath of the execution, the CIA was privately exultant.

"Stinky" (the agency's nickname for Lumumba) had finally been eliminated.[81] Fourteen years later under the glare of a congressional investigation, the CIA turned penitent. Agency officials involved in the plot tried
to minimize their role in so far as the documentary record would permit.
"The fate of Lumumba in the end was purely an African event," former
CIA Africa Division Chief Bronson Tweedy testified.[82] John Stockwell, a
CIA agent who had served in the Congo from 1965 to 1969, concluded
otherwise: "Eventually he was killed, not by our poisons, but beaten to
death, apparently by men who had agency cryptonyms and received agency
salaries."[83] Whichever conclusion lies closer to the truth, there can be
little doubt that the CIA—though not the actual assassin—was a moving
force behind the murder.

The Kennedy plan, paradoxically, may also have contributed to
Lumumba's execution, or so the State Department secretly concluded in
March 1961: " . . . the murder of Lumumba was quite possibly triggered
by the new U.S. approach which involved U.S. advocacy of the freeing of
all Congolese political prisoners . . . [It] was thus—as [were] so many
other developments in the Congo crisis—a perfectly logical distasteful
political event."[84]

News of Lumumba's death shook the world. Headlines in New York
announced "FIGHTING AT UN OVER LUMUMBA, 'MURDERER' CRIES BY
BRAWLING NEGROES"; in London, "COMMONS IN UPROAR OVER MURDER OF
MR. LUMUMBA"; in Cairo, AFRICANS STORM CAIRO'S DIPLOMATIC QUARTER,
PALL OF SMOKE OVER NILE"; in Lagos, "CROWDS WITH STONES DEMON-
STRATE AND ATTACK EUROPEANS."[85]

Philip Deane of *The Observer* described the scene at the UN: "In
small, private wakes for Patrice Lumumba, the Afro-Asian delegates . . .
swallow their drinks as if there were a bitter taste in their mouths . . . They
may not have all felt much concern for Lumumba alive and active; but
out of the buried corpse has arisen a powerful new spectre . . . that could
destroy the world organization itself."[86] Most believed that the UN was
responsible and Hammarskjold was deeply shaken. He cabled Dayal:
"Here the battle goes on and there have never been any hands more
covered with blood than mine according to those who, for reasons of their
own, remember that this is Easter time."[87] Militant African regimes pointed
to the event as proof that the neocolonialist West would use any means—
even murder—to subvert African independence. Belgian embassies in
several African capitals were sacked and burned.

The U.S. did not escape recrimination. Guinean President Sékou
Touré wrote Kennedy a scathing letter, which the President with great
anger took as an accusation of personal responsibility for the death.[88]
Nkrumah, with his voice breaking, told the Ghanaian people that the U.S.

and other Western countries had to answer for "conniving at a brutal and savage colonial war . . . Alas, the architects of this murder are many."[89] The U.S. embassy grounds in Accra were invaded by a crowd and the chancery was damaged.

On February 15, Ghana, Guinea, the United Arab Republic, and the People's Republic of China recognized Gizenga's government in Stanleyville. The next week, Mali, Morocco, Cuba, the Algerian government-in-exile, and several Eastern European countries followed suit. Nkrumah's invitation to Soviet President L.I. Brezhnev to visit Accra reflected neutral Africa's turn to the East.[90]

In the United States, the news of Lumumba's murder provoked racial riots. During an address by Ambassador Stevenson before the Security Council, a demonstration led by American blacks began in the visitors gallery. It quickly turned into a riot in which eighteen UN guards, two newsmen, and two protestors were injured. Outside of the UN building, fights between whites and blacks broke out. A large protest march into Times Square was halted by mounted police.[91]

One prominent black journalist charged that the U.S. was "morally responsible for the creation of a monster"—namely, a dictatorship whose method of governing was murder.[92] James Reston wrote: "We are beginning to see a confluence of the world struggle for freedom in Black Africa and the struggle for equal rights in the Negro communities in America." Reston described it as "an event of momentous importance" whose effect the United States was only beginning to feel.[93]

Aimé Césaire, the Martiniquais poet and apostle of négritude, wrote that for all of Lumumba's flaws, one would remember "his prodigious vitality, his extraordinary faith, his love for his people, his courage and his patriotism . . . one may not approve of all the political acts of Patrice Lumumba. No doubt he made mistakes . . . [but] at least his heart never flinched."[94]

All hope of a Soviet-American truce on the Congo was swept away by the wave of Soviet denunciations of the Secretary-General and the West in the wake of Lumumba's murder. The Soviet government called Hammarskjold the "organizer" of the murder.[95] A Soviet-American confrontation over the troika plan (to replace the Secretary-General with a triumvirate) now seemed certain.

Moscow issued a statement on February 14 pledging to give "all possible help and support to the Congolese people and its lawful Government." Press reports shortly thereafter indicated that Stanleyville was receiving arms shipments from the Soviet Union. Was massive assistance next?

From a hideaway office in the Secretariat building on the afternoon of February 15th, Ambassador Stevenson telephoned President Kennedy, who was to hold a nationally televised press conference that night.[96] He recommended that the President open with a tough statement on the Congo warning against unilateral intervention and strongly supporting the UN. That evening Kennedy told the nation that he was "seriously concerned at what appears to be the threat of unilateral intervention" in the Congo and warned: "There should be no misunderstanding of the position of the United States if any government is really planning to take so dangerous and irresponsible a step." Massive, unilateral intervention by any country, the President said, would bring with it "risks of war." He denounced the "purported recognition of Congolese factions as so-called governments" and said that the only legitimate government was that of President Kasavubu—a remark that infuriated both Sékou Touré and Nkrumah and touched off a heated exchange of letters between Kennedy and the Ghanaian President.[97]

Kennedy's warning reflected the central preoccupation of every American president since World War II—containment of the Soviet Union. As Nkrumah had argued, however, the connection between Soviet imperialism and violent change in Africa and Asia was usually tenuous or nonexistent. Nationalism, not communism, was the explosive cause of turmoil, and this fact was consistently ignored by the United States. Washington confused the unconditional demand for rights with communist subversion.

Certainly, the Eisenhower administration's antagonism toward Lumumba was based on the belief that he was a "Soviet instrument." The Kennedy administration had initially seemed more inclined to assess the Congolese upheaval on its internal merits, rather than on a cold war basis. For this reason, it had sought a deal with Moscow based on mutual restraint in the Congo. Soviet statements in the aftermath of Lumumba's death to aid his successor Gizenga, however, stimulated the American containment reflex. The Congo accordingly became a test case of the Kennedy administration's will to deter the Soviet Union and to preserve credibility among "friends," no matter how illegitimate these friends might be, or how extraneous the Congo was to U.S. national security.[98]

Emergency measures followed. Governor Williams flew to Khartoum to obtain a formal guarantee (in return for the promise of American aid) that the Government of Sudan would continue to bar the transit of supplies to Stanleyville. Egyptian President Nasser, who had given support to Lumumba, was put on notice that the U.S. would view with gravity intervention on behalf of Gizenga.[99] At the Pentagon, contingency plans for limited war were drawn up. They provided for the dispatch of 80,000 troops by air or sea. Task Force 88, a group of five U.S. naval vessels, appeared off the Congo, ostensibly for "good will." (Kennedy would later come to regret this move).[100]

The CIA dusted off its plans—for the second time—to have Mobutu attack Gizenga's forces in Orientale Province. Another member of the agency's camarilla, Sûreté Chief Nendaka, moved swiftly against the Lumumbists in Léopoldville unleashing what the UN Special Representative Dayal called "a new wave of terror." Mobutu dispatched six Lumumbist leaders to Bakwanga where they were executed.[101]

Lumumba's wife returned to Léopoldville from Luluabourg to claim her husband's body and their possessions from the house on Boulevard Albert Ier. She came, in the Bantu tradition of mourning, with bare breasts and a shaved head. ANC soldiers were occupying the house and denied her entry. They beat her two-year-old son Roland. She sought refuge with Dayal who found her "the picture of sorrow and despair."[102] Dayal arranged for a UN plane to take them back to Lumumba's secessionist stronghold in Stanleyville. The normally phlegmatic Kasavubu exploded at this gesture of civility toward the wife and son of his murdered adversary. He called for military mobilization against UN forces. Elements of the ANC were reported to be contemplating an armed assault on Dayal's residence on the banks of the River Congo. It was evident that Hammarskjold's Special Representative stood to lose his life if he remained in Léopoldville.[103]

Dayal formally requested that Tshombe send the remains of Lumumba and the other murdered men back to Léopoldville. Tshombe refused: "According to Bantu tradition, it is formally forbidden to unearth—be it for several seconds—a body which is covered with earth because the deceased would thereby be gravely affected and his soul would haunt those surviving him."[104]

A NEW UN MANDATE

The Security Council convened on February 17, 1961, in an atmosphere marked by Soviet bluster and African fury. As the spokesman for the West, the U.S. was under attack. The meeting was, therefore, a test of the American capacity for restraint, particularly in the wake of Kennedy's grim warning to the Kremlin.

The resolution submitted to the Security Council by three African and Asian powers raised the most disturbing apparitions for the U.S.: the UN peace-keeping force under the command of personnel from nonaligned countries would be permitted the "use of force, if necessary, in the last resort"; Belgian and other foreign military personnel would be expelled from the Congo; the Congolese Parliament would be reconvened;

and there would be an immediate investigation into the deaths of Lumumba and his colleagues.[105]

Secretary Rusk objected to the proposed resolution. The European Bureau believed that Stevenson should be instructed to use the veto, or, at least, to abstain. The Assistant Secretary of State for European Affairs, Foy Kohler, raised the ready specter of Soviet intervention. He argued that the U.S. should preserve full leverage of unilateral action.[106]

The African Bureau, under the direction of the administration's pre-eminent Africanist, Wayne Fredericks, whose counsel even the supercilious Bundy sought, countered that the subverter of peace in the Congo was not the Soviet Union but Belgium. The U.S. had to tell the Belgian government to get its military and political advisors out of the Congo immediately, Fredericks argued. Only then could the UN deal forcefully with the central cause of the crisis—the secession of Katanga. The failure of the Eisenhower administration to recognize that fact had "ruined" its policy.[107]

Assistant National Security Advisor Walt W. Rostow—normally no advocate of the soft line—maintained that the Congo was no place for the direct application of American power. He wrote Bundy two days after the announcement of Lumumba's death:

> It is time for each political leader to pause and ask himself this question: are my policies designed to achieve the unity and independence of the Congo, and the welfare of its people; or are they designed to achieve narrow political advantage? . . . The lesson of these tragic months is simple: if the struggle for power persists, the people will suffer, and the cause of peace will be endangered . . . This is a game where none can win and all are certain to lose.[108]

Stevenson, whose standing in the White House was at its height during the first months of Kennedy's presidency, stuck to his belief that "the only way to keep the cold war out of the Congo is to keep the UN in the Congo." After a series of meetings with his African counterparts, Stevenson expressed his confidence that the Afro-Asian resolution could be softened. He recommended that the President send "urgent dispatches . . . at the highest level to the governments of India, Nigeria, and Liberia" to encourage moderation.[109]

Kennedy once again sided with Stevenson, even though he was piqued by the ambassador's habit of making policy in New York, sending instructions down to Washington, and, worst of all, getting front-page coverage the next morning in *The New York Times*. Kennedy introduced himself at one Congo meeting as "the ambassador's special representative in the White House." Assistant Secretary Harlan Cleveland was called on to mediate "the rift between the President's ego and Stevenson's vanity." Solution came in the form of a daily memo from Cleveland for the

President's bedtime reading on what Stevenson was doing in New York. This did not restore the locus of Congo policymaking to the White House, but at least it put Kennedy a few hours ahead of *The New York Times*.[110]

Consistent with Stevenson's suggestion, the President sent lengthy messages to the chiefs of state of India, Liberia and Nigeria to solicit support for three U.S. amendments to the draft resolution. Kennedy's attempt to blunt the cutting edge of the Afro-Asian resolution failed completely. Ambassador Stevenson fared no better before the UN Security Council. He introduced three amendments to the resolution before the council: first, that there be specific reference to the Secretary-General; second, that the UN should exclude not only foreign personnel (the Belgians) but also foreign arms shipments (to Stanleyville); and third that all "peaceful measures" be employed by the UN before force was resorted to. Soviet Ambassador Zorin promptly vetoed the first two amendments, and sensing total opposition from the nonpermanent members of the Council, Stevenson withdrew the third.[111]

Stevenson then telephoned the President to request his authorization to vote affirmatively despite the extremity of the resolution.[112] Personal differences notwithstanding, Kennedy admired Stevenson's forensic grace and consummate parliamentary skill. "Adlai's got an iron ass and, my God, in the job he's got the nerve of a burglar," the President remarked to a visitor during this period.[113] Kennedy gave the go-ahead and, at 4:20 A.M. on the morning of February 20, the Security Council (with France and the Soviet Union abstaining) approved the Afro-Asian resolution.

In the Congo, the news that the Security Council resolution had passed touched off a revolt against the UN. Kasavubu, whose power stood to be stripped away by the Security Council's directive to reconvene Parliament, declared over the radio that the UN had "betrayed" the Congo. He made an impassioned appeal to the ANC to "arise and go forward" to do battle against UN forces. Mobutu, whose troops, according to the terms of the resolution, were to be brought under the discipline and control of the UN, arrested sixty UN civilian workers and a week later seized the port of Matadi, killing two UN soldiers.[114]

By endorsing the Security Council resolution, the Kennedy administration put itself in a delicate position. Backing the UN peacekeeping operation meant backing away from the Kasavubu-Mobutu regime. The danger in such a move was that it might enable Gizenga and his communist supporters to seize power. However overwrought, the warnings of Timberlake, Devlin, and some of the more siege minded in Washington were compelling: "The Communists will have a field day."[115]

The reconvening of Parliament was also risky. The Parliament had always been a Lumumbist stronghold. Unlike their Russian adversaries, the Americans had no candidate for the premiership. If the Parliament resumed its functions and elected a new government (which the UN legally needed to carry out its mandate), Gizenga was the odds-on favorite to be elected to Lumumba's former post. Such a development meant almost certain civil war.

The array of personalities in the Congo also discouraged an American-supported return to popular rule. Timberlake's cables had a defiant tone to them: "I understand the confusion among sincere and honest government leaders over what should be done in [the] Congo." We could not, however, "permit ourselves to join in panic." The UN, he said, had moved "measurably closer to the Soviet Line" and for that reason had to be bypassed.[116] The CIA Station simply ignored Washington's diplomatic initiatives and continued its efforts at "king-making" in Léopoldville.[117]

At the other end of the spectrum were Hammarskjold and Dayal, both of whom were furious at the Belgians and contemptuous of Kasavubu and Mobutu. Their stance was too close to that of the Afro-Asians for the Kennedy administration's comfort, for neither Hammarskjold nor Dayal could be relied on to neutralize the ANC or to reconvene Parliament in ways favorable to the U.S. and Belgium. This made implementation of the Security Council mandate a matter of serious risk.[118]

THE COALITION STRATEGY

Six weeks went by as the administration's Congo Task Force (and the diverse bureaucratic interests it embodied) deliberated. In mid-April 1961, the group recommended that the U.S. support the reconvening of Parliament and accept the formation of a government of national unity with Lumumbist elements in it. As Secretary Rusk explained to the President, a coalition government seemed to be the only alternative to civil war:

> . . . we considered that the risks of Gizengist inclusion in the Government in a minority position and controlling no politically sensitive ministries would be less of a risk than leaving Gizenga in his Orientale redoubt where he is a standing invitation to Communist penetration and where his isolation tends to drive him closer to the Soviet bloc.[119]

Kennedy approved the Task Force's recommendation. The Congo thereby became a test case of the administration's coalition-regime approach to Soviet containment. The essence of Kennedy's perception, which he had voiced during the fifties—was that "by making national independence the crucial question [we] invite[d] the neutrals to find a common interest with us in resisting communist expansion."[120] By drawing both right and left into a regime with strong nationalist orientation, Kennedy believed that coalition government could serve as a buffer to communist subversion.[121]

The tactical dimension was critical to the administration's strategy. Diplomatic pressure to fuse the factions into a coalition was combined with covert pressure to prevent any slippage to the left. In the Congo, this meant that while Parliament would be allowed to reconvene, its choice of a new government would be "shepherded covertly."[122] Two years later, the contradiction in this approach would become fully evident.

The administration's first order of business in carrying out the new policy was to neutralize Gizenga and to find a sufficiently attractive pro-Western alternative. The second order of business was to prevent the U.S. mission in Léopoldville from obstructing a return to popular rule. The third—and in many ways the most difficult—was to remove Dayal, control Hammarskjold, and prevail on UN officials in the Congo to use their influence to bring about a victory by pro-Western elements at the antici-pated parliamentary conclave.

Fortunately for the West, by April 1961 Gizenga's secessionist regime was in the process of disintegration. As a result of a dispute between Moscow and Cairo, the irregular flow of military and economic aid to Gizenga had all but ceased. Nasser's agents in Stanleyville had stolen Soviet documents destined for Gizenga, apparently, in order apparently to find out what the Soviet embassy in Cairo was up to.[123]

The CIA also had a hand in disrupting the relationship between Stanleyville and its foreign supporters. American agents reportedly seized $3 million worth of European currency from one of Gizenga's agents in Khartoum.[124] The American vice consul in Stanleyville, David K. Grinwis, was meanwhile bribing several of Gizenga's collaborators. Despite Devlin's excitement with the communist possibilities in Stanleyville, U.S. Consul Thomas A. Cassilly, Jr. reported to the embassy that the Lumumbists were Marxist in greeting only.[125]

Gizenga, whose chief claim to power was that he wore Lumumba's mantle, had none of the ambition or ability of his redoubtable mentor. He was a cowardly and languid man who rarely ventured out of the governor's mansion, where he spent most of his time cavorting with his so-called *garde féminine* and receiving aphrodisiac injections from a quack Yemeni doctor.[126]

In late April, the U.S. got the break it had been waiting for. The commander of Stanleyville's 5,000-man army, General Victor Lundula, concluded an agreement with General Mobutu in which he recognized Mobutu as military commander-in-chief.[127] In Washington, the Task Force recommended that "the rapprochement of the Léopoldville and Stanley-ville regimes must be clinched by follow-up action . . . The UN should leave no stone unturned to fill the present void created by USSR inability to get material aid to Gizenga."[128]

During this period, the American mission identified Cyrille Adoula, a forty-year-old labor leader, as a promising challenger to Gizenga for the premiership. Adoula was sufficiently pro-Western to suit the Americans. He was the former Secretary-General of the Congolese chapter of the Belgian socialist trade union movement as well as a personal friend and close collaborator of Irving Brown, the AFL-CIO's chief representative in Europe and Africa.[129] Adoula's nationalist pedigree was also substantial. Along with Lumumba, he was co-founder of the Mouvement National Congolais. During the first months of 1961, he had tried to mediate the rift between Gizenga and Kasavubu and Mobutu. Unlike most of his Congolese counterparts with Belgian or American ties, he had emerged from the Lumumba murder with relatively clean hands. Rusk described the self-effacing Adoula as "the strongest and most attractive of the moderate Congolese leaders." Governor Williams exuberantly announced to Sir Roy Welensky, prime minister of Rhodesia, that "Adoula had been America's choice from the start."[130]

REMOVING TIMBERLAKE AND DAYAL

For Ambassador Timberlake, blocking a return to popular rule had become something of a holy calling. Kennedy was soon shocked into the recognition that his policy would go nowhere unless there were a change of command in Léopoldville. At 10:10 P.M. on March 5, Ambassador Timberlake requested that U.S. Naval Task Force 88 reverse its course and proceed slowly north toward the Congo "because of uncertainty as to the outcome of developments in Leopoldville."[131] The Task Force was made up of five vessels with an amphibious attack capability of 500 marines, six helicopters, tanks and landing craft to move the troops from ship to shore. The commander of the Task Force complied with Timberlake's request and later received authorization to proceed toward the Congo from the Commander-in-Chief of the Atlantic fleet. The action was taken without the knowledge of the President, the Secretary of State, or any other high-ranking official in the White House or the State Department.

Thanks to a leak, *The New York Times* the next day drew attention to the Task Force's crucial change of course. Kennedy was in a "state of rage" over the unauthorized military maneuver.[132] He sent a memorandum

to the Secretary of State and the Secretary of Defense: "Did Ambassador
Timberlake notify the Department before he requested the Admiral to
turn around his ships? Did the Admiral notify the Navy Department
before he acceded to the request?" The President observed: "In view of the
importance that this decision has been given it seems that we should take
action in the future to have the opportunity to review these decisions
before they are finalized."[133] The White House investigation found that
"None of the actions were (sic) taken pursuant to consultations in the
Defense or State Departments . . . A decision with serious foreign policy
implications was made by persons at the field level without any prior
consultation with Washington."[134]

The President was scheduled to discuss the Congo with his top advisers
on March 3. Before the meeting, NSC Staff Director Bromley K. Smith
sent Bundy a lengthy cable from Timberlake with the comment: "Even
though this dispatch was summarized in the Top Secret summary, you
will find the full text of unusual interest."[135] The President was shown the
dispatch and was appalled. The message was overwrought and, at points,
incomprehensible.

> I have probably been more discouraged than anyone else by the fact
> that the moderates have repeatedly inflicted serious wounds on their
> internal and external corpus (which their enemies have promptly en-
> larged), while their friends have shuddered in genuine horror at such
> apparent sadism while groaning at the senseless profligacy with which
> they treat their all too slender assets. Of course, Lumumbists are no
> better but they have fared better lately because they have shot lesser
> game . . .[136]

Timberlake's outright opposition to the administration's original
Congo plan had won him few friends among the incoming Kennedy team.
Under Secretary of State Bowles had a particular animus against Timberlake
on the basis of a disagreement dating back to their service together in
India in the early fifties.[137] Now there was evidence that the ambassador
was not entirely in control of himself, much less of the situation in the
Congo. At the White House meeting, the President decided that Timber-
lake should again be called home—this time for good.[138]

Timberlake's unauthorized summons of Task Force 88 was not the
only instance of insubordinate action by the U.S. mission in the Congo.
In February 1961, Seven Seas Airlines, a private American corporation,
flew three Fouga Magisters (French jet trainers) to Katanga. The planes
were flown to Katanga via Malta by a Boeing C-97 Stratocruiser, reportedly the property of the Vice President of Seven Seas. The American
company, according to two sources, was under contract with the CIA

and had previously delivered weapons and military supplies to Katanga by flying from Luxembourg to Elisabethville via Brazzaville.[139] Seven Seas had also shipped UN supplies and, as a result, had free passage over African territories.

According to one former CIA official, the agency's purpose in arming pro-Western Katanga was to build up a fall-back regime if the government in Leopoldville fell to the Lumumbists.[140] This practice was expressly contrary to U.S. policy and in direct violation of the UN Security Council resolutions.

The story of the shipment of the Fougas could hardly have broken at a more inopportune time—a few days after news of Lumumba's murder while the UN Security Council was meeting. Nkrumah was one of several African and Asian leaders who was upset at the illegal shipment. He wrote to Kennedy and inquired: "How does it come about that three allies in the North Atlantic Treaty Organization (the United States, Belgium, and France) are involved in sending military aircraft to Katanga in flagrant disregard of the Security Council resolution? . . ."

> To put it bluntly, it is hard for us to believe that your Intelligence Services did not know, in advance, that an American aircraft would be used for carrying the planes or that the American aircraft company in question would have ever made the flight if it had been warned by the United States Government of the serious consequences of so doing.[141]

Kennedy was highly embarrassed by the revelation. He explained to Nkrumah that "the United States Government did not, in fact, learn of this shipment in sufficient time to prevent a transaction which took place entirely outside the borders of the United States." The President pointed out that Ambassador Stevenson had said that the United States "deplores in the strongest terms" the delivery of the aircraft.[142] Stevenson's remarks, Nkrumah observed, "entirely miss the point . . . African opinion is deeply shocked by what seems to us to be the almost casual way in which the matter is treated in the United States."[143]

The Department of State announced on March 30 that the Department of Commerce had formally prohibited "the transportation of certain military and para-military items by the United States registered vessels or aircraft from any points of origin to destinations in the Congo. . . "[144] In May, the President sent out a letter to all American ambassadors informing them that they were the sole source of authority for all activities of American agencies in the countries to which they were accredited. This included the Central Intelligence Agency.[145]

Hammarskjold wrote Stevenson on March 12: "We are now facing a crucial and, indeed, in some respects more dangerous phase in the Congo operation."[146] The army and police in Leopoldville had unleashed their fury on UN personnel. The port of Matadi was still under siege. Hammarskjold accused the Western missions in Léopoldville of kindling "the fires of misunderstanding, suspicion, and fear." In a veiled reference to Timberlake and Devlin, Hammerskjold said that there were those who was fostering "the vain belief that this is a moment at which the Congo might afford a break with the UN. I would, through you, wish to appeal to your government to give urgent instructions to your representatives in Leopoldville to use energetically all their influence in the same direction, in support of the UN."[147]

At the center of this imbroglio was Rajeshwar Dayal, Hammarskjold's Special Representative in the Congo. The Kasavubu-Mobutu regime warned that it would step up its military campaign against the UN unless "the communist Dayal" (who had refused to recognize the regime's legitimacy) were withdrawn. The Western missions in Léopoldville endorsed his dismissal. The Belgians and the British blamed Dayal for having caused the fighting between Mobutu's troops and the UN contingents. Timberlake thought the dispute had racial origins: "I can state categorically that dark skin is not an asset in Congolese eyes. They are more apt to accept white in view of their experience."[148] Nehru was equally obdurate: India would not send one of its promised 4,700 troops to the Congo unless Dayal stayed.

Hammarskjold, caught in one more Congo crossfire, refused to move. The tall, slender Indian was something of an alter ego for the Secretary-General. There was a monkish quality to both men—in manner, aloof and ascetic; in mind, privately consumed with spiritual questions and publicly engaged in their defense. In an interview with Edward R. Murrow, Hammarskjold had spoken at intense length about "the writings of the great mediaeval mystics for whom 'self-surrender' had been the way to self-realization, and who in 'singleness of mind' and 'inwardness' had found the strength to say yes to every demand . . . 'Love'—that much misused and misinterpreted word—for them simply meant an overflowing of strength . . . "[149] He sharply told Stevenson that the "over the table" attacks on him by the Russians were no worse that the "under the table" attacks on Dayal by the West.[150] Dayal would stay.

The fate of Dayal was directly connected to U.S. policy in the Congo. In April, the administration had decided that Parliament should be reconvened to form a government of national unity. In order to shepherd the formation of such a government, the U.S. needed the support and the imprimatur of the UN. It was clear that Dayal would never give it, just as he had never recognized the existing regime. This concern was reflected in a State Department policy paper: if the U.S. was to support a return to popular rule, "We must intensify our efforts to prevent the return of Dayal, by direct representations with Nehru."[151]

Not everyone in the administration concurred with this recommendation. Bowles, who knew and respected Dayal, had strong reservations about pushing for his removal. The issue was discussed at a White House meeting on the Congo on March 3. Kennedy said that if any progress were to be made in resolving the crisis, we first had to "sweep house." Dayal would have to go.[152] Rusk flew to New Delhi in late March to ask Nehru to accept Dayal's recall. Stevenson was instructed to obtain Hammarskjold's concession.

Rusk had his work cut out for him. The Indian Prime Minister resented the attacks on Dayal. So long as Nehru refused to send the troop contingent to the Congo, India held the Security Council mandate hostage. In his meeting with Nehru, Rusk said that "the principal source of the difficulty had been an uncertain UN mandate, under which the Secretary-General had not felt himself able to adopt clear UN policies in the Congo and to give his civilian and military representatives clear guidelines about UN objectives." It was not surprising, Rusk remarked, that "tempers had worn thin, . . . " that "impatience and frustration had led to remarks which might have been later regretted." Perhaps "Mr. Dayal's patience has been exhausted," Rusk suggested. Perhaps the Prime Minister "might wish to suggest someone else."[153]

Nehru had nothing to suggest—only the public announcement on April 3 that he was "entirely opposed" to Dayal's removal. The fact that 3,000 Gurkhas arrived the same day in Elisabethville could not help but increase Nehru's bargaining power. The message from New Delhi a few days later was even more explicit: " . . . if Dayal does not return to his Congo post . . . India may have to reconsider the use of its troops there."[154]

Stevenson fared no better with Hammarskjold. When he was ushered into the Secretary-General's office on March 20, he found Hammarskjold "in a great rage" over the front-page story in *The New York Times* that reported that the Secretary-General planned to "defy" Kasavubu and keep Dayal in Léopoldville "as long as possigle." Hammarskjold had just finished venting his anger on Orville Dryfoos, the publisher of *The New York Times*. He told Stevenson that any action in relation to Dayal might be construed as bowing to American pressure. "Nehru had become personally involved and Hammarskjold's own prestige was at stake." And who would replace Dayal, the Secretary-General asked Stevenson? There were very few UN officials equally qualified or available. Stevenson, however, did not budge. He later told Cleveland that he "really laid it on the line hard." Dayal had to go. The President wanted it that way.[155]

The White House showed no signs of yielding. The rising chorus from Capitol Hill—little of it informed—had the administration worried. Senator Fulbright, citing stories written by Joseph Alsop and Marguerite Higgins, said Dayal had "really been playing the Communist game." The *Washington Post* came out with a cartoon by Herblock showing Dayal in a jeep blazing the trail for Khrushchev in the Congo, who was following in a bulldozer.[156]

Hammarskjold made repeated appeals to Kasavubu to reconsider his government's position on Dayal. Kasavubu responded with threats of violence and said he would not be responsible for Dayal's safety if he returned and would tear up the armistice agreement with the UN if he did.[157] Faced with no choice, Hammarskjold made an offer to the Americans and the British: he would recall Dayal and convince Nehru to go along if the U.S. and the U.K. would agree to withdraw their own ambassadors from Léopoldville.[158]

The Kennedy administration—eager to be rid of Timberlake anyway—quickly agreed to the swap on condition that it be kept absolutely secret. The Macmillan government, at first resistant, later consented to the exchange. The Secretary-General then sent a message to Nehru expressing his "feelings of revulsion" for the decision he had to take.[159] Nehru regretfully agreed.

Dayal took it silently—"altogether worthy of a stoic," Conor Cruise O'Brien observed.[160] Dayal explained to Bowles why he had refused for so long to resign: "[I]t would have weakened the Organization and would have done violence to the Charter . . . "[161]

The task fell to Governor Williams to inform Timberlake in early May that he deserved "a well-earned rest" and that after he went on leave he would not be returning to the Congo. A leaked medical report claimed that Timberlake had health problems. Senator Thomas Dodd charged that the report was contrived. In Senate hearings several months later, Dodd insisted that Nehru had exacted Timberlake's removal in exchange for Dayal's recall. Williams was constrained to reply that this was "absolutely incorrect," that there had been "absolutely no deal . . . no linkage."[162]

The swap marked a turning point in American policy. From the Kennedy administration's point of view, Timberlake's departure was long overdue. When he left in June 1961 a serious obstacle to a moderate and conciliatory line in Leopoldville had been removed. With Dayal out of the way, the U.S. mission in the Congo could proceed with its plan to bring about the establishment of an anticommunist coalition government under circumstances of its choosing and control. The U.S. had also succeeded in pushing Hammarskjold into a corner. Dayal's fate prefigured the Western showdown with Hammarskjold in September 1961, when the Secretary-General would make his final try for peace in the Congo.

Dayal's successor was Dr. Sture Linner, a Swedish scholar who had been involved in an expatriate mining interest in Liberia and who was acquainted with Hammarskjold's brother. The Americans were very high on Linner. One senior official described him as "a natural candidate for the 1961 Nobel Peace Prize."[163] There was little doubt that Linner's objectives closely paralleled those of the U.S. mission. His relationship with the new American Chargé d'Affaires, G. McMurtrie Godley—with whom he maintained "virtually day-to-day and hour-to-hour communications"—was described as "extremely close." Gullion reported to the President at one point that Linner was "highly cooperative with us," and indeed "pro-United States in outlook."[164] Linner's UN colleagues found him to be a malleable man who was no match for his energetic and scheming deputy, the Tunisian Mahmoud Khiary.[165] Together they were soon to play key roles in bringing a pro-Western government to power in the Congo.

THE LOUVANIUM CONFERENCE

With the Soviet Union temporarily displaced, Gizenga's star fading and Adoula's rising, and Dayal recalled, Washington moved to reconvene Parliament. In mid-July, parliamentary delegations began arriving at Louvanium University on the outskirts of Léopoldville. A battalion of UN troops moved into the area and sealed off the campus to insure security and to prevent compromising contact with outside influences. An electric fence was erected around the site of the conference and entry was limited to a single gate guarded by UN soldiers. UN officials made frequent reference to this *cordon sanitaire* as insuring a just and genuine result from the Congo's only democratic body.[166]

Sixty Lumumbist parliamentarians from Orientale and Kivu provinces attended the Louvanium conference. Their participation brought the number of representatives in attendance to 188 out of 221 elected to the original Parliament. Tshombe did not respond to the UN appeal to send his eight delegates from Katanga to Louvanium.

Washington went to work to persuade its European allies to back the Louvanium conference. The Belgian government was asked to intercede with Tshombe. Bowles suggested that the President invite Belgian Foreign Minister Paul-Henri Spaak to Washington to discuss his "fresh approach to the Congo."[167] Kennedy stopped in Paris on May 31 (en route to Vienna to confer with Khrushchev) to see President de Gaulle. At their meeting, Kennedy told de Gaulle that at the instigation of the United States, the UN Secretary-General was "setting up" a government in the Congo (a revealing choice of words if de Gaulle's account is accurate). Kennedy said he needed French support. De Gaulle "declined to have anything to do with the operation."[168]

A week after his return from Europe, Kennedy discussed with senior White House and CIA officials a proposal approved by the State Department for covert action at Louvanium.[169] At the conference, African, Soviet, and American agents were soon engaged in hot competition to influence the composition of the new government.[170] At least two weeks before the meeting of Parliament, UN mediators Linner and Khiary were advancing Adoula's candidacy. Khiary showed Conor Cruise O'Brien an envelope on which was written "the core of the government he hoped to see elected: Prime Minister Adoula; Vice Premiers Gizenga, Sendwe, Bolikango."[171] With the collaboration of Linner and Khiary, the Americans were confident that their man would win.

Washington was shocked to learn on July 26 that Gizenga's representatives (the Bloc Nationaliste) were prevailing. They had won thirteen out of fourteen parliamentary posts. Although the moderates (the Bloc Nationale Democrate) had won the presidency of the Senate, they had lost the far more important presidency of the Chamber to the Lumumbists. Contrary to Rusk's assurance to the President, it seemed probable that Gizenga, not Adoula, would be designated premier.[172]

Kennedy, in evident alarm, sent a message to Rusk, who himself was "very nervous about what might be going on behind those closed doors."[173] CIA Director Dulles was alerted. Rusk dispatched an urgent message to U.S. Chargé Godley in Leopoldville. Gizenga's designation as premier was unacceptable. It would be regarded as a serious reverse for the West and a communist advance. Rusk authorized Godley to use all means to stop it.[174]

Washington's reaction to the predicament at Louvanium pointed up a telling feature of the Kennedy administration's approach to crises elsewhere in the developing world. Initially, the administration worked to neutralize the disputants and to achieve a political settlement. However, once the prospect that a radical nationalist should take power—even democratically—emerged, the problem suddenly took on global proportions as a threat to U.S. national security and was dealt with accordingly. Shortly after Rusk's emergency directive to the field to stop a Gizenga victory at all costs, the State Department mounted an eleventh-hour mission to Katanga to persuade Tshombe and his parliamentarians to fly to Louvanium to tip the balance in Adoula's favor. The effort failed.[175]

Devlin and his colleagues had meanwhile located an underground sewage tunnel leading into the sequestered conclave and began passing money destined for key legislators.[176] On the inside, Khiary and his Swiss *homme de main* used the money to bribe the parliamentarians.[177] Kasavubu made several crucial visits to the conference (according to Williams, these visits "saved the bacon"), and Albert Ndele, the governor of the Bank of the Congo and one of the CIA's "Binza boys," was "deeply involved during the final session."[178] Mobutu warned that the army would intervene if a "unity Premier" was not endorsed. The fall-back position of the U.S. was that if Gizenga became prime minister, Mobutu, Nendaka, Ndele and the rest would seize power.[179]

Gizenga protested that the failure of the Congolese army to be withdrawn from the Léopoldville area and the frequent visits to Louvanium by Kasavubu and UN officials violated the conditions for the meeting of Parliament.[180] Linner and Khiary were undeterred. They, like the Americans, wanted their verdict and feared that a Lumumbist takeover would mean the end of the UN Congo operation. In the end, "Russian, Czech, Egyptian and Ghanaian agents were simply outbid [by the CIA] where they could not be outmaneuvered."[181]

Wearied by their isolation, fearful of another Mobutu coup, and finally undone by bribery, the Lumumbists struck a deal: they would support Adoula as premier in exchange for half the ministries in his new government.[182] On August 1, President Kasavubu designated Adoula *formateur*. After choosing his cabinet, Adoula received an overwhelming vote of confidence.

There was a moment of euphoria in Washington. A relieved Rusk told the Senate Foreign Relations Committee in closed session: "We were very gratified through direct contacts we were able to establish, as well as through some effort on the part of certain UN officials, that Adoula managed to come out of this as prime minister . . . " The Secretary of State credited the UN's "closely coordinated activities" with the U.S. mission for "this significant success over Gizenga."[183] The official version of what happened at Louvanium—one repeated time and again by American and UN officials in the months that followed—was somewhat different. It was "an act of faith in the democratic process," George Ball declared in a major speech on the Congo.[184]

For those in the new administration, who had already faced humiliation in Cuba, sharp disappointment in Vienna, and frustration with the lingering impasse in Laos, the news from the Congo was especially welcome. "You should know," Walt Rostow wrote the President, "that there is optimism all over town that the Congo situation is on the way toward solution . . . we could be witnessing the most encouraging development since you became President." It was nothing less than a political breakthrough, Rusk reported to Kennedy. "The second Soviet defeat in the Congo."[185]

Adoula moved into the premier's residence a few weeks after his election. He told aides that he disliked the house. The air in it was bad. He complained that the night mists coming off the river were affecting his sleep.[186] The New York Times correspondent in the Congo, David Halberstam, reported that among the people the premier's residence was still called "Lumumba's house."[187]

4

Engagement in Katanga

[I]s there someone
In the depths of my being
Waiting for permission
To pull the trigger?

Dag Hammarskjold
(*June 18, 1961*)

The savagery of the Cold War might never have spread to Central Africa had it not been for the secession of Katanga—the Congo's alien within. Katanga's secession deprived the newly-independent Congo of half of its national revenue and brought the country to the brink of civil war. It also figured directly in the death of the two men most capable of restoring unity to the troubled country—Patrice Lumumba and Dag Hammarskjold.

ORIGINS

Modern Katanga was conceived in a deal between two of the great imperialists of the nineteenth century, Léopold II, King of the Belgians, and Cecil John Rhodes, British empire builder. Beginning in 1876, the Belgian monarch tried to secure his claim to the vast Congo basin in Central Africa. Rebuffed in his attempts to find favor for his African scheme in Europe, Léopold set upon the hapless Chester A. Arthur, President of the United States. Arthur willingly succumbed for nothing: he rallied the Congress and gave a ringing endorsement to the King's scramble for African real estate. Bismarck was more discriminating in judging Léopold's overture: "Schwindel."[1]

Rhodes was meanwhile pushing northward from the Cape Colony, blackmailing the Boers and annihilating African tribes in the land that would later bear his name.[2] In 1890, the so-called "Colossus of Africa" dispatched expeditions into a territory fabled for its mineral riches—Katanga, which was controlled by the fierce Bayeke tribe. One of Rhodes's so-called apostles, Harry Johnston, warned British Prime Minister Lord Salisbury about making any concessions to the scheming Belgian King.

Léopold, he wrote, "has by many a hook and crook, by many a wile and intrigue . . . created a fine little empire for Belgium. But why his enterprise should be viewed by *us* with indulgence . . . I cannot conceive." (emphasis in original.)[3]

When Léopold learned of Rhodes's move into Katanga, he appealed to his cousin Queen Victoria to restrain her singularly enterprising subject, but to little avail. Desperate to stop Rhodes, the King raised mercenary forces of his own to seize Katanga. The Bayeke chief Msiri resisted Belgian intrusion. One of Léopold's agents murdered him and a suitably pliant successor was installed. Léopold—a man whose greed was surpassed only by his improvidence—then found himself in control of Katanga's riches without the means to exploit them. Rhodes did have the means and a deal was struck. Katanga was thereby begotten.

At first, "l'affaire Katanga" went well. In 1894, the imperial powers established a border between Katanga and the British protectorate later known as Rhodesia. In 1900, Rhodes's mining giant, Tanganyika Concessions, Ltd. was given a monopoly on mineral prospecting in Katanga, while the King kept 60 percent of the profits through his own corporate dependent, the Comité Special du Katanga.[4] At the turn of the century, the arrangement seemed to be the very model of imperial cooperation.

Then Rhodes died in 1902 and with him his dream of a British imperial road from the Cape of Good Hope to the Nile delta. Thanks to the Casement report and other humanitarian accounts emanating from the Congo, the western world stumbled on to Léopold's private chamber of horrors. Hundreds of thousands of African laborers had been mutilated, murdered, or driven to starvation during the King's "prolonged raid for [the] plunder" of ivory and rubber in the Congo.[5]

Novelist Joseph Conrad, then plying the River Congo, described the consequences of the Belgian system of forced labor: "They [the African laborers] were dying slowly—it was very clear. They were not enemies, they were not criminals, they were nothing earthly now—nothing but black shadows of disease and starvation, lying confusedly in the greenish gloom."[6] The other imperial powers, particularly Britain, were embarrassed: God may have intended—as John Ruskin had put it—that the white race should seize Africa's "fruitful waste ground," but Leopold had gone too far.[7] American President Theodore Roosevelt demanded an international conference on the Congo. The Belgian Parliament insisted that Leopold turn the Congo over to the Belgian state. As the Parliament debated the annexation treaty, Léopold—a veritable master of corporate machination—stashed away his Congolese jewel, Katanga, through a clever scheme with his British partner, Tanganyika Concessions.[8]

In 1906, Léopold's representatives and Rhodes's successors created the

Union Minière du Haut Katanga and conceded to this offspring a monopoly on mining in upper Katanga. Tanganyika Concessions and the Belgian conglomerate Société Générale split ownership of share capital in Union Minière and divided up its board of directors between themselves.[9]

Léopold died a year after the Belgian Parliament took away his Congo "Free State." But Katanga—the bastard child of Léopold and Rhodes—lived on and flourished under the guardianship of Union Minière. For the next fifty years, Union Minière's Belgian, British, and French stockholders (120,000 of them in 1961) enjoyed something of the touch of Midas. Katanga's mineral lode—largely situated only a few feet below the surface—became one of the richest in the world. In 1960, the province produced more than 60 percent of the world's cobalt. It ranked fifth in the world in copper production. Zinc, manganese, gold, silver, iron, germanium, and cadmium were also mined. The single uranium mine at Shinkolobwe enabled the United States to construct the atomic bomb in 1943.[10]

Union Minière, however, did more than extract ore from Katanga to enrich Europe. It also built the most extensive hydro-electric scheme in colonial Africa and constructed a grid of rail lines linked to the Atlantic by Tanganyika Concessions's Benguela Railway. Union Minière's $3 billion investment, to be sure, remained in the hands of the 30,000 whites (1959) who inhabited Katanga's cool highlands, but the Katangese native benefitted in social status and standard of living as well. Tshombe's well-heeled background as playboy and sometime businessman exemplified the degree of status attainable in colonial Katanga.

The rest of the colonial Congo, however, languished in brutality and ignorance. Léopold's inhumane labor practices continued under a more benevolent guise. Belgium trained the colonial army to prey upon the populace. In stationing native troops, the colonialists took care to pit tribe against tribe. As Léopold had once explained, "wars do not necessarily mean the ruin of regions in which they rage." Irish nationalist Roger Casement—who collaborated with Conrad in exposing Léopold's brutal rule—wrote in his diary: "I *saw* those hunted women clutching their children and flying panic-stricken to the bush; the blood flowing from those quivering black bodies as the hippopotamus hide whip struck and struck again; the savage soldiery rushing hither and thither among the burning villages; the ghastly tally of severed hands."[11] Educational policy consisted of the premeditated tethering of the African. *Evolué* (evolved) status allowed a handful of Africans access to the white world. The rest the Belgians referred to as "*macaques*" (monkeys).[12]

Belgium's hasty grant of independence to the Congo in July 1960 did nothing to resolve seventy years of colonial mismanagement. Behind the independence charade—the so-called *pari belge* (the Belgian gamble)—

was the calculation in Société Générale's boardroom to hold on to Léopold's lost realm while granting the Africans only the trappings of power.

THE KATANGA SECESSION

In Katanga, fully six months before independence, there was serious talk of secession among white settlers and the black politicians they financially supported. In the manner of Rhodes, Prime Minister Roy Welensky of the Federation of Rhodesia and Nyasaland offered to join Katanga to his white-ruled territory. This time, however, Union Minière and the white *ultras* wanted to cut their own deal.[13]

The mining company found a suitable in-house partner in Moise Tshombe. A week after Belgium had freed the Congo, Tshombe made the declaration the whites were waiting for: "May God protect independent Katanga!" To Herman Robiliart, president of Union Minière, this made good sense and he proposed that the new self-proclaimed Katangese President be given the equivalent of honorary white status for his services. Tshombe was flown to Brussels in December 1960 and decorated by King Baudoin for "valor and loyalty"—much as King Léopold II had decorated his imperial agent Le Marinel in 1894. Even for Ambassador Timberlake, the spectacle of this unseemly pairing was too much: "It makes me physically ill," he cabled Washington.[14]

Katangese independence—contrary to widespread impression—was not based solely upon Union Minière's profit and Tshombe's greed. The special legacy of Katanga's precolonial imperium (under both the Lunda and Bayeke ascendancies) also figured into the peculiar symbiosis of white and black in Elisabethville.

The secession of 1960 revived the century-old Lunda desire to restore its empire over Katanga. The Lunda ascendance from the sixteenth to the nineteenth centuries had been characterized by the partial conquest of the older Baluba empire—an ancient rivalry that was soon to figure into the UN's struggle with Tshombe. As son-in-law of the Lunda paramount chief, Mwata Yamvo, Tshombe made much of his putative right of succession—however attenuated by blood and history. In order to win over the Baluba in North Katanga, who were loyal to the Central Government, Tshombe decided to recognize Albert Kalonji's secessionist "Mining State of Kasai" in whose territory the other half of the Baluba tribe lived. Behind the Kalonji secession was the Belgian diamond mining company controlled by Société Générale, Forminière.[15]

In North Katanga, a violent groundswell of Baluba resistance greeted the news of Kalonji's sell-out and the prospect of Lunda domination. A

Belgian journalist reported: "The whole Baluba countryside is mobilized, it seems, for a sort of holy war. 'Pirogues' [dugout canoes] filled with armed youth descend the river. The attackers are drugged with hemp, but they appear to follow very clear tactical orders, attacking convoys from the rear . . ."[16] Soon there were reports of atrocities of the most hideous nature against black and white alike.

Tshombe, in good Lunda fashion, unleashed his mercenary-led gendarmes, who slaughtered the Baluba with equally unsparing ferocity. The UN was eventually forced to intervene and establish a refugee camp whose population came to number 45,000 to save the Baluba from extermination.[17] Neocolonial ambitions in the Congo of both the black and white varieties had touched off new tribal bloodletting.

THE AMERICAN POSITION ON KATANGA

Before the fall of 1961, the U.S. had remained largely ignorant of the complex drama of Katangese independence. To the Eisenhower administration, Belgian paternity over the province, while not ideal, at least meant that there were no communists or rampaging black men in Katanga as there supposedly were elsewhere in the Congo. Tshombe played this perception for all it was worth. He told U.S. diplomats that he was really *"un américain manqué,"* that he had played football as a youngster in an American missionary school, and was a practicing Methodist.[18] Other Congolese nationalists, Tshombe would say, were not as truthworthy as he; Lumumba, Gizenga, and Adoula were pictured as closet communists. Mobutu, Kasavubu, and Bomboko were cast as native walk-ons—*des bantoues simples.* To illustrate the meaning of Katangese independence, Tshombe fell on his knees before Ambassador Timberlake and asked him if he (Timberlake) wanted to see Tshombe in this position before "the nonentity Kasavubua," "the inexperienced Mobutu," or "the snippet Bomboko?" "I prefer death," Tshombe concluded.[19] Such impassioned poses took their toll on several well-intentioned U.S. senators and dignitaries who, while searching for a way out of the Congo thicket on behalf of their government, crossed Tshombe's carefully laid path.

Liberals in the Kennedy administration thought that they suffered no such delusions about Tshombe and the nature of his secession. Governor Williams identified him as an opportunist. Katangese "independence" was merely a matter of money. The prevailing view was that Katanga would not fight to preserve such a sham. A year later, however, after two bloody assaults by the UN army, Katanga was still holding out. Washington's strategy had not penetrated the reality of tribal power in Katanga. In appraising Tshombe, they were looking at the wrong mask.

The incarnation of Katanga's traditional state of separatism and a major reason for its durability was not Tshombe so much as Godefroid Munongo, grandson of Msiri, the Bayeke chief shot by the Belgians in 1891. David Halberstam described him as a "sinister looking man [who] exuded an aura of intrigue . . . proud of his heritage, ruthless and instinctively drawn to power." It was Munongo who made the secession a matter of war. Munongo told Belgian Major Guy Wéber that he dreamt of the restoration of the Bayeke empire and spoke of the blood that would flow in its renaissance.[20] He had named his own son Msiri, regularly consulted the Bayeke fetish, and reportedly participated in the dismemberment of enemies. He hated the Belgians (his father had died in a Belgian jail) but he hated less familiar intruders even more. In July 1960, when Katanga broke away from the Congo, Munongo lay in wait for whoever would try to stop it. First to come was Lumumba and then Hammarskjold.

To Lumumba, the secession had been intolerable—it "tore the heart out of Congolese nationhood."[21] Over half of the Central Government's revenue and foreign-exchange earnings were lost. The secession also ignited tribal and regional separatism elsewhere in the Congo. Diamond-rich south Kasai seceded a month after Tshombe's declaration of independence and aligned itself with Katanga. Lumumba was determined to bring Tshombe, Munongo, Kalonji, and the rest of the pretenders to heel. His efforts to do so cost him his premiership and subsequently his life.

Separatism in the Congo opened the door to a more sophisticated form of savagery—the Cold War. In August 1960, Lumumba asked Hammarskjold to allow him use of UN planes in order to suppress the secessions in Kasai and Katanga provinces. The Secretary-General refused on the grounds of noninterference in the Congo's internal affairs. Lumumba then appealed to Khrushchev, who immediately dispatched 17 Ilyushin transport planes to the Congo to ferry the Central Government troops to Kasai.[22]

It was this that drew the deadly attention of the White House: Lumumba was no longer an unruly nationalist; he was now a "Soviet instrument." In American eyes, Katangese independence assumed a new proportion: Tshombe became a potential anticommunist strongman and Katanga the West's ace-in-the-hole until Lumumba could finally be eliminated.

HAMMARSKJOLD'S POLICY ON KATANGA

By the time Kennedy took office, Hammarskjold was having second thoughts about his hostile opinion of Lumumba. He spoke to Stevenson of Lumumba's gifts, his courage, and the need to bring about his release from prison.[23] It was too late, however; Lumumba had already been delivered into the Munongo's hands. It was Msiri's grandson Munongo and one of his white mercenaries who consummated the independence of Katanga by bayonetting and shooting Lumumba—a man who had fought for much of what Msiri had died for.[24]

After Lumumba's death in early 1961, the Security Council directed the UN to do what Lumumba had tried and failed to do: to expel foreign personnel from the Congo. This time Hammarskjold elected to back the Lumumba position to use forceful measures to bring about Tshombe's capitulation. In so doing, Hammarskjold needed the full support of the United States and this became a problem.

Both Hammarskjold and Kennedy—as much as any Westerners in their time—were identified with the cause of African independence. The disagreement that emerged had less to do with differences over UN objectives in the Congo than with each man's unwillingness to compromise his own authority by accommodating the other. During the February 1961 Security Council meeting, Stevenson's strong adherence to the Hammarskjold line had prevailed over whatever reservations the President and the rest of his advisors might have had. After February, however, as Hammarskjold began implementing the terms of the Security Council resolution, American doubts about unconditional support for the UN operation hardened. Thanks in good part to American duress, Dayal lost his post in May and this was a blow to Hammarskjold. In July at Louvanium, direct American intervention resurrected Adoula at the eleventh hour, in violation of the UN's pledge of neutrality. Had the Secretary-General known of Linner's part in the CIA's brisk exercise in *machtpolitik*, he would, no doubt, have been doubly galled.[25]

Hammarskjold's resistance to U.S. influence of the peacekeeping operation seemed to grow in proportion to his dependence on U.S. financial support. (In April, the U.S. made a pledge of $77.5 million to bail out the nearly bankrupt UN; by May, the U.S. Air Force airlift of UN troops and supplies to the Congo was equal in size to the Berlin airlift of 1948.)[26] In private communications with Stevenson, Hammarskjold repeatedly pointed out that however much the U.S. paid the piper, it still could not call the tune. He remarked in a speech in August 1961 that the UN had to serve the interests of all nations and not become the pawn of the most powerful. The Secretary-General held no more fundamental view of his office than this. He would admit that the UN was "a feeble creation of men's hands;" it was only faith in "this human dream" that gave it reality.[27]

Kennedy, to be sure, had a stronger interest in the diplomatic possibilities of the UN than Eisenhower had, but his view of the UN fell far short of Stevenson's identification of the organization as "the last, best hope of mankind." Kennedy saw the UN as a vehicle through which to frustrate Soviet activity in the Congo. His modus operandi was to endorse the UN's objectives without necessarily adhering to them—to exert control over the Congo operation without accepting responsibility for the consequences.[28] Bundy (probably echoing the President's sentiments) pointedly advised Stevenson on one occasion to avoid swallowing the Hammarskjold line so uncritically.[29] The Americans, in short, were wary of Hammarskjold's bold instinct for action. Columnist Walter Lippmann, a Kennedy intimate, gave a sense of Washington's ambivalence toward Hammarskjold: "Never before, and perhaps never again, has any man used the intense art of diplomacy for such unconventional and such novel experiments."[30]

The irony in the American wariness was that the U.S. had no readier champion against the Soviet Union than Hammarskjold. The Russians certainly realized this; they often pointed to the fact that all three of the Secretary-General's top advisors—Ralph Bunche, Andrew Cordier, and Heinz Weischoff—were Americans. Had the Kennedy men forgotten what had happened the previous September when Khrushchev, in sneering terms, had told the General Assembly that the Secretary-General "has always served the interests of the U.S. and other monopoly capitalists." Hammarskjold had coldly replied: "It is not the Soviet Union or, indeed, any other big powers who need the UN for their protection; it is all the others. In this sense the Organization is first of all *their* Organization, and I deeply believe in the wisdom with which they will be able to use it and guide it. I shall remain in my post . . ." Khrushchev's angry pounding of his desk was drowned out by the hail of applause from the rest of the Assembly. Hammarskjold left the hall to a standing ovation.[31]

The Europeans also seemed unaware that the Secretary-General was their best insurance against Soviet intrusion into the decolonization process. Their relations with Hammarskjold in the summer of 1961 were even more contentious than Washington's. For reasons altogether different from those of the Russians, they wanted to be rid of him. He was the *décolonisateur*, the arch meddler. De Gaulle's disdain for Hammarskjold's "holy road" of peacekeeping was complete. When France invaded Tunisia in July 1961, Hammarskjold's attempt at mediation was met with a French rebuff.[32] Even the internationalist Paul-Henri Spaak, the new foreign minister of Belgium who had once served as president of the UN General Assembly, regarded the Swede as "power-hungry and dangerous."[33] In Britain, the Tory leadership still blamed Hammarskjold for having brought the Eden government to its knees at Suez five years earlier.[34]

The UN operation in the Congo was in some ways a reprise of the Suez drama, with Europeans again making a final fling at the preservation of empire. This time Lumumba was in the role of Nasser—the mercurial nationalist engaged in the violation of European property. The Belgian intervention of the previous July was reminiscent of the Anglo-French-Israeli invasion of Egypt. Hammarskjold was again assailed from both sides. Again in his isolation, his sense of mission carried him through. "Pray that your loneliness may spur you into finding something to live for, great enough to die for," he had once written.[35]

There was the same sense of fatalism in 1961 as before—that there was no turning back from a course once taken. During the crisis in the Middle East in 1956, he had written to his old friend and aide, the Australian George Ivan Smith (soon himself to undertake an assignment in Katanga), about "other and greater forces, partly unknown and inscrutable to us which seem to have taken over . . . Curious with the feeling of fate which we had so strongly in the region—from which even now I cannot get away—fate requiring the sacrifice of unreserved engagement, but somehow bowing to such engagement."[36]

Hammarskjold used the French word "engagement" in the sense Camus had—to express the standard of courage that he thought was required of those who aspired to greatness. The literal English translation of Hammarskjold's "engagement" may be "commitment" but the implications intended are far larger. They are to be found throughout Hammarskjold's journal—"defiance," "sacrifice," "surrender to duty," "fulfillment in death" —as they are in Camus's writings.

Hammarskjold found camaraderie in combat of the sort Camus had once described: "Tense faces, brotherhood in danger, the strong pure friendship of men for men, these are the true riches because they cannot last."[37] The diplomats sent by Hammarskjold to the Congo tended to be men in his likeness: highly literate with a proven will to be independent. Gustavo Duran, then serving in Stanleyville, was an American whose service as a Republican general during the Spanish Civil War had drawn the abusive attention of Joseph McCarthy and later calculated expressions of uneasiness from Eisenhower's State Department. (Like Hammarskjold, Duran was given to stinging deprecation. Asked if Gizenga was a communist, he replied: "Communist? No. Gizenga is a constipated sacristan."[38])

To head the mission in Tshombe's secessionist capital of Elisabethville, Hammarskjold chose a man with whom he was not acquainted personally: Conor Cruise O'Brien, an Irish diplomat and writer who was known at the UN for his biting wit and his unavenged hostility toward colonialism. With O'Brien's capacity for self-dramatization and Khiary's already demonstrated instinct for action, Hammarskjold had on his hands the makings of a fight with the Katangese.[39]

Under the terms of the February resolution, the UN's objective was to bring about the expulsion of the 500 to 600 foreign advisory personnel in Katanga who were thought to be the backbone of the secession. Hammarskjold's strategy was to confront Tshombe with decisive military superiority and to force him, on that basis, to accept a negotiated capitulation. In August 1961, Hammarskjold ordered a battalion of Indian troops to join the UN's other contingents in south Katanga. Norwegian Colonel Bjorn Egge compiled a list of 512 white military personnel serving Tshombe, and O'Brien—initially with Hammarskjold's full authorization— began the dangerous process of effecting their expulsion.[40]

THE BATTLE FOR KATANGA: ROUND I

Katanga was meanwhile celebrating its first year of independence. Buoyed by Union Minière's royalty payments, the secessionists were recruiting mercenaries and stockpiling arms. Munongo indicated that he was sympathetic to at least part of the UN mandate: he wanted the Belgian army officers then serving in Katanga dismissed in favor of a more bloodthirsty species of white—French counterguerrilla veterans of the Indochina and Algeria wars. By early summer of 1961, he had assembled his band of so-called *affreux* (the terrible ones). One of them, who had recently returned from slaughtering Baluba, remarked to a journalist: "In Indochina and Korea, it was war. Here it is mutual carnage . . ."[41]

Rhodesia's support proved critical to Katanga's claim of sovereignty. Welensky secretly provided Tshombe with fighter aircraft and Tanganyika Concessions' Benguela Railway became an important conduit of arms shipments into Katanga. When O'Brien used UN troops to arrest and expel a political advisor to Tshombe, Munongo retaliated by arresting and expelling the Belgian consul, whom he accused of consorting with the UN. By late August, the situation had turned ugly and certain UN units—most notably India's—were spoiling for an order to have at Munongo's mercenaries.[42]

Military action by the UN, however, seemed risky. The UN was nearly bankrupt. Lumumba's murder had poisoned collaboration between Africa and the West, which was critical to a continuation of the operation. The Europeans were still angry at both the fact and the precedent of UN intervention into postcolonial affairs. The Belgian ambassador complained to Secretary Rusk about his government's "shock" at a message from Hammarskjold in which he had demanded (using the word "immediately" twelve times) that Belgium remove its 250 officers from Katanga.[43]

The Soviet Union, still furious at Hammarskjold, was hoping to push through its troika proposal to replace him at the General Assembly meeting in September. In letters to Nehru, Nasser, Nkrumah, and Sukarno,

Chairman Khrushchev had identified Hammarskjold as the "chief assassin" of Lumumba.[44] UN Congo chief Sture Linner told Ambassador MacArthur that the UN desperately needed "a success in Katanga before the General Assembly met in September" to blunt the Soviet vendetta.[45] In his journal, Hammarskjold wrote:

> Again a bow is drawn,
> Again an arrow flies
> —and misses . . .
>
> What have I to fear
> If their arrows hit
> If their arrows kill,
> What is there in that
> To cry about? [46]

The public Hammarskjold, however, was not so resigned to the martyrdom that haunted him in his private moments. "Assez de ces tergiversations!" (Enough of this indecision) he snapped at the new U.S. ambassador to the Congo.[47] He flew to Geneva to prevail upon Foreign Minister Spaak to order the withdrawal of the Belgian officers and advisory personnel from Katanga. Spaak's reception was frosty, but he did agree to order the repatriation of Belgian personnel. By August, Belgium had essentially complied with the Security Council's wishes.[48]

In Elisabethville, O'Brien tightened the vise on Tshombe who, after agreeing to the UN plan for the withdrawal of his mercenaries, equivocated. In the early hours of August 28, UN units blockaded Munongo's residence, occupied the post office and radio station, and began arresting the mercenaries. During the following two days, 338 were captured; 104 remained. The Belgian consul, acting on his own accord, succeeded in sidetracking the operation by convincing O'Brien that those who remained could be deported peacefully. The British Government—its old animus aroused—delivered a stern protest to Hammarskjold. From Rhodesia, Welensky denounced the UN action and pledged his support for Katanga. With comfort from friends such as these, Tshombe and his ministers decided to keep their remaining mercenaries and to stick it out.[49]

The situation quickly deteriorated. Tshombe put his gendarmes on alert. Munongo organized violent anti-UN demonstrations in the streets of Elisabethville and then attempted to abduct O'Brien's deputy on September 10. The UN deadline for the repatriation of the remaining mercenaries came and went. In Léopoldville, Khiary procured arrest warrants from the central government for Tshombe and his ministers and delivered them to O'Brien on September 11. When Tshombe refused to agree to fly to Léopoldville to meet with Hammarskjold (due to arrive there the next morning), Khiary gave O'Brien the go-ahead for the planned military putsch, code-named "Morthor," the Hindi word for smash.

At 4 A.M. the next day, Indian and Swedish units converged on the post office, the radio station, and the residences of Tshombe and his ministers. This time the mercenary-led gendarme units were ready. Heavy fighting broke out. For the next eight days, there were pitched battles in the streets of Elisabethville. Much of the time UN forces were pinned down by sniper and mortar fire from residential areas. There were several hundred casualties, many of them civilian.

Katangese forces captured a company of 191 Irish troops. A single Fouga Magister jet (nicknamed the "Lone Ranger") piloted by a Belgian mercenary wrought havoc on UN forces for the better part of six days, strafing troop positions and truck convoys, destroying seven UN transport planes on the ground and preventing the UN from flying reinforcements and supplies to Elisabethville. Wayne Fredericks, who had once worked for the Strategic Air Command, was incredulous: "I always believed in air power, but I never thought I'd see the day when one plane would stop the United States and the whole United Nations."

Tshombe and Munongo escaped the UN dragnet. (O'Brien later claimed that the British consul had helped Tshombe to escape.) From Rhodesia, Tshombe announced that at least 1,000 had been killed in Katanga. Rhodesian Prime Minister Welensky called the UN action a serious threat to the Rhodesian Federation and ordered troops and aircraft to move up to the border. Reports of atrocities by Indian troops (such as firing on Red Cross vehicles and executing prisoners) made headlines in newspapers around the world. International attention focused on whether the Secretary-General had ordered the UN action in Katanga.

The United States was caught completely by surprise by the UN military move. UN Under Secretary-General Bunche cabled Hammarskjold (who was in Léopoldville trying to arrange a cease-fire) that President Kennedy and Secretary Rusk were "extremely upset" that there had been no consultation with the U.S. government. Rusk had urged that Hammarskjold bring Adoula and Tshombe together and warned that American support would evaporate "if the Gizenga line was to become predominant" (i.e., if the UN tried to re-integrate Katanga forcibly).[50]

Hammarskjold was infuriated by this "extraordinary demarche." The United States had not objected to the expulsion of the Belgian officers on August 28. What, he asked, had they done since then to bring Tshombe to his senses? "It is better," he instructed Bunche to tell Rusk, "for the UN to lose the support of the U.S. because it is faithful to law and principles than to survive as an agent whose activities are geared to political purposes never avowed or laid down by the major organs of the

UN . . . It is nice to hear these parties urge 'most strongly' that we do everything in our power to bring Adoula and Tshombe together after having gone, on our side, to the extreme point in that direction without any noticeable support at the crucial stages from those who complain."

INDECISION IN WASHINGTON

Those who were complaining did not simply do so out of surprise at the fighting. Support at the crucial stages from the U.S. was impossible as long as the Kennedy administration continued to waver in its commitments. The President would not make up his mind. Rusk's approach to the Congo, as Schlesinger put it, was to think about it as little as possible. He seemed transfixed by the "Gizenga danger" (much as his predecessor had been by the "Lumumbist threat") and largely ignored the menace posed by Katanga. Deputy Assistant Secretary Fredericks had done his best to exorcise the prevailing image of Gizenga as a communist operative. He had tried to impress upon Rusk in a long meeting in the Secretary's office that Gizenga had neither the capacity nor the discipline to take orders from Moscow. The point was apparently lost on Rusk who remarked in parting: "I know those agrarian reformers. I dealt with them in China."[51]

But even on China, the reality of nationalism had escaped Rusk. During his tenure as Assistant Secretary for Far Eastern Affairs, his China hands had impressed upon him that the Chinese were unhappy with Moscow. But Rusk had stuck to slogans, declaring after the communist takeover that Mao's China was merely "a colonial Russian government, a Slavic Manchukuo on a large scale." In 1961, he was still providing the President with Cold War boilerplate on the Congo and a variety of other issues. He was a man who mastered process but not substance—"the good staff man who never should have been general." Rusk would often start National Security Council meetings with a lucid summary of the problem and then for the duration of the meeting say nothing on the merits on the courses of action available. This frustrated the President, and Ambassador Galbraith knew his audience when he wrote Kennedy in September 1961: "The problem with Dean Rusk is that he thinks that just because foreign policy was bad under Truman and Eisenhower, it should at least be mediocre under Kennedy."[52]

Congo analysis by the NSC staff was not much better. Rostow, who had drawn apparent inspiration from the rush of events in Katanga, began producing memoranda of a downright fanciful sort. "[T]here still exists the possibility that Tshombe's Army may revolt, moving against the 20,000 Belgians in Elisabethville," he informed the President on August 4th.[53] When the September fighting broke out in Katanga, Under Secretary Ball called Rostow to ask for guidance regarding the U.S. position. Rostow told Ball that he had a plan. The Congo would be transformed into a "dramatic six months enterprise," he said, with German involvement "up to their ears."[54] The Germans presumably knew nothing of this, having ended their involvement in Africa some forty years earlier.

The British and the French were quick to capitalize on American befuddlement. British Foreign Secretary Lord Home and French Foreign Minister Maurice Couve de Murville conferred with Secretary Rusk on September 14. Home convinced Rusk that their governments should approach Hammarskjold to bring about a cease fire—an entirely superfluous exercise since the Secretary-General was already in the Congo trying to do just that. Nonetheless, the next day, the British special envoy Lord Lansdowne and Ambassador Gullion asked Hammarskjold to remain in the Congo as long as hostilities continued to show the "seriousness with which the responsibilities of the Secretary-General under UN resolutions are being carried out."[55] Hammarskjold was piqued. "I assume that the same seriousness thus supposedly demonstrated is considered by the distinguished Foreign Ministers and the President to apply also to the terms of the [UN] resolutions themselves," he cabled Bunche.

The leverage of the Western powers was then exerted on Hammarskjold in the most direct way. With the UN forces in desperate need of fighter and transport aircraft to protect and strengthen their military positions, Bunche made urgent requests for planes from Ethiopia, Sweden, and India. Ethiopia responded at once but the request for overflight clearance from the British encountered "determined procrastination." Hammarskjold had also asked the U.S. for transport planes to fly reinforcements from Stanleyville to Elisabethville. He learned on the 16th, however, that the American planes had been recalled "by higher authority" from Kano (Nigeria) while actually en route to the Congo. Hammarskjold commented to Bunche that it was "a sad reminder of our experience after Bizerte" (in reference to his July 1961 attempt to get U.S. help in flying three Tunisian battalions serving in the Congo back to the Tunisian city of Bizerte, which had been invaded and was being occupied by France.)[56]

While the Western press excoriated Hammarskjold for waging war, most of the Afro-Asian governments exhorted him to finish Tshombe off. Hammarskjold struck a balance between these positions: he ordered limited reinforcements to be sent to Katanga to right the tactical balance, but instructed O'Brien to seek an immediate and unconditional cease-fire with Tshombe. He cabled O'Brien that he would fly to Ndola, Rhodesia, to meet personally with Tshombe. O'Brien was "horrified" by the instruction since it had the look of capitulation with Welensky in the role of mediator.[57] The decision must have been equally unpalatable to Hammarskjold, but mounting Western opposition left him little choice—at stake was the survival of the UN peacekeeping operation. O'Brien later wrote that the "diplomatic propellant" of Hammarskjold's final odyssey had been the Western demand that the Secretary-General personally intercede to stop the fighting in Elisabethville.[58]

THE DEATH OF HAMMARSKJOLD

Hammarskjold may have sensed, as he had before, that in Léopold's Congo the "feeling of fate" was everywhere. Behind each of the antagonists there loomed the ghost of a larger figure: behind Welensky, there was Rhodes; behind Baudoin, Léopold; behind Munongo, Msiri; behind Gizenga, Lumumba. On the afternoon of September 17, Hammarskjold and his party left Léopoldville by plane, skirted Katanga for fear of the marauding Fouga, and descended in the darkness toward the last remnant of Rhodes's empire of White Africa.[59] Shortly before the *Albertina* was to land at Ndola, Rhodesia, it crashed, mortally injuring all aboard.

Kennedy received the news in the Oval Office on Monday morning. (U.S. Air Force Attaché Colonel Ben Matlick had been the first to reach the scene of the crash.) Throughout Africa and Asia, there was widespread suspicion of foul play. Bullets were reported to have been found in the bodies of the victims. Many believed that Tshombe's Fouga had shot down the *Albertina*. There were indeed grounds for suspicion. British Rhodesian authorities, for example, had neglected to launch a search for fifteen hours. Three weeks after the crash, Welensky's secret communication to Tshombe asking him to tell his pilots to be more "discreet" in their use of Kipushi and Ndola airports had an inculpatory ring to it: "I must be seen to be behaving correctly if I am to help you."[60]

After receiving the news, Stevenson, Assistant Secretaries Williams and Cleveland and their Deputies Fredericks and Woodruff Wallner recommended that U.S. fighter aircraft be dispatched to Katanga to support the UN forces. The Joint Chiefs of Staff was called into emergency session and recommended that eight aircraft be sent to Katanga to seek out and destroy the Fouga Magister jets. "Full latitude" would be given to the fighter commander. Secretary Rusk concurred with this order and sent the consensus recommendation to the President.[61]

Kennedy, however, had doubts about U.S. military intervention. His experts had promised him his success at the Bay of Pigs. In Laos his generals had talked of the advisability of a nuclear air strike.[62] The military's primary instinct was always to escalate, Kennedy remarked to Carl Kaysen.[63] That was why the White House had little faith in Pentagon recommendations.

Kennedy accordingly ruled that the U.S. would send no jets to the Congo unless the UN were unable to find another country to do so. If the fighter planes were sent, they were only to be used to "support and defend" U.S. and UN transport planes, not to seek out and destroy the Fougas. In the end, no fighter planes were sent to the Congo.

On September 24, the President flew up to New York to address the opening session of the General Assembly, which Irish Ambassador Frederick Boland had convened "in the shadow of an immense tragedy." A tired-looking Kennedy told the delegates: "Let us here resolve that Dag Hammarskjold did not live or die in vain." Hammarskjold's cause would remain "at the top of our agenda."

One UN official reacted bitterly to the sudden stiffening of Western resolve: "It has taken Hammarskjold's death to get the cooperation we needed from the British and American Governments to carry out an operation largely designed . . . to remove from Central Africa a standing invitation to the Russians and others to meddle and intervene . . ."[65]

The Soviet Union had lost no time in trying to take advantage of the atmosphere of shock at the UN and the state of disarray in Western policy. After it became apparent that the troika idea had no chance of passing in the General Assembly, the Kremlin (through the intercession of Indian Defense Minister Krishna Menon) urged Acting Secretary-General U Thant to accept Russian military aid to end the Katangese secession once and for all.[66] Thant—the Burmese diplomat whom Hammarskjold had described as being "too weak" to succeed Dayal in the Congo—refused, but the threat was clear.[67]

Leadership based on nothing more than self-interest was no longer enough. Two days prior to Hammarskjold's death, the Kennedy administration had refused to send USAF transport planes to Katanga. The day after his death, however, there had been a rush to dispatch an attack squadron of American jets to the fighting. Such expediency led to a policy without rational moorings.

THE TURNING POINT

Kennedy had to make a choice: either pick up the fallen standard of Hammarskjold's leadership of the peacekeeping operation, or fall back into the more familiar role as leader of the North Atlantic Alliance, accepting the European view of the Congo crisis and allowing Hammarskjold's "great adventure" to fail. With Hammarskjold in power, the U.S. had been able to avoid committing itself to either position and to straddle the European-African rift. Hammarskjold had occupied the stormy center drawing fire from both sides. Now, by force of circumstance, Kennedy was impelled to choose whether or not to take his place. In either case, the Soviet threat could not be ignored. The major question was how to contain it—either through alliance with Europe or through cooperation with the states of Africa and Asia. Could Kennedy buy enough time to develop a long-term African solution, or would he revert to Cold War tactics?

The rift between the Third World and the West had never been wider. The British were in a slow boil about the September fighting in Katanga. In Brussels, Spaak sat silently atop the pyre of Belgian public opinion, which held the UN accountable for Belgian civilian casualties. In Africa and Asia, Hammarskjold's death—like Lumumba's—revived the specter of a Western conspiracy to abort African independence. The sentiments of the *Indian Express* were typical: "Never even during Suez have Britain's hands been so bloodstained as they are now." Nkrumah's warning to Kennedy was particularly pertinent: "I am absolutely convinced that unless this crisis can be resolved by cooperation between the African states and the Western powers, fatal damage will be done to the relations between Africa and the United States and the Western world."[68]

Divisions within the administration over Katanga ran along the lines of the European-African split. Without policy guidance from the White House, Congo discussions at the State Department took on a kennel-like quality. Ambassador Stevenson, Governor Williams, Assistant Secretary Cleveland, and the rest of the "Africa Firsters" lobbied for a UN military build-up aided by units of the U.S. Air Force. Williams continued to send memoranda in all directions reiterating what came to be known as the "AF Theorem": separatism would bring civil war to the Congo, which would bring communist subversion; ergo, Katanga had to be subdued.[69]

Williams's counterpart in the European Bureau, William R. Tyler, thought that this was exactly why pro-Western Katanga should not be snuffed out by the UN army. From Brussels, Ambassador Douglas MacArthur II, whose manner of dealing with equals and superiors alike was reminiscent of his imperious uncle and namesake, appraised the idea of a UN military build-up as the height of foolishness. Spaak, he cabled, could simply not stand for another round of fighting.[70]

Secretary Rusk continued to observe strict personal neutrality on the Congo question. As Lippmann had warned President-elect Kennedy in December 1960, Rusk was a "profound conformist" with a thorough incapacity to "deviate from what he considered the official line."[71] Rostow's exuberance had already given both the President and Bundy more than enough reason to wonder about the value of his analysis. Under Secretary Bowles, who did know something about the Congo, was hardly more helpful. When Ambassador Gullion dropped by Bowles's office for a final visit before leaving for the Congo, the Under Secretary described the location of the Ambassador's residence in Léopoldville—"right on a bluff overlooking the Amazon."[72]

Typically, Kennedy did not tip his hand on Congo policy until faced with the political consequences of inaction. In late September a small but disconcerting rebellion broke out on Capitol Hill. Senators Russell, Dodd and Thurmond (Democrats) as well as Dirksen, Hickenlooper, and Goldwater (Republicans) had begun tolling the bell of anticommunist Katanga. Senator Dodd, a key supporter of the President's domestic program, threatened to make the "lying Irish playboy" O'Brien and his "communist deputy" Michel Tombelaine his "star witnesses" in a Senate Internal Security Subcommittee investigation.[73]

The President was already at work trying to shore up his right political flank. (Joseph Kraft later wrote that Kennedy's political motto might have been: "No enemies to the right.") In July 1961, for reasons unrelated to Congo matters, the President had contemplated ousting Bowles as Under Secretary. After the September tragedy in the Congo, the President privately decided to follow through and cut Bowles loose. The real problem at Foggy Bottom was Rusk, but he was not as expendable as Bowles, whose style, it was said, conflicted with that of the President.[74]

NEW LEADERSHIP AND A NEW POLICY

The presidential nod went to George W. Ball, who would become Kennedy's "Commander-in-Chief for Congo Affairs."[75] Ball was unique in important ways: he was as articulate as any of Kennedy's academics, trusted by the Foggy Bottom pros, and he proved intuitive enough to comprehend the inscrutable Rusk. Above all, Ball was independent— Bundy said *too* independent.[76] When the President sarcastically asked at a National Security Council meeting which "bright soul" had decided to send Nkrumah such a warm letter (committing the U.S., in effect, to heavy loan participation in the Volta River Project), Ball replied: "You did."[77] In 1961, Ball began his in-house dissent against Vietnam policy. It was not received kindly. He warned the President that unless something were done now, he would have a half million troops in Vietnam by the end of the decade. Kennedy replied: "George, you're crazier than hell."[78]

But the President had similar fears as Ball and once likened military intervention to taking a drink: "The effect wears off and you have to take another."[79] In Vietnam, one sip of the military solution would lead to another. In the Congo, Kennedy had already passed up the first drink once and would do so again.

The turning point for the Kennedy administration in both crises had come in the third week of September. On the same day that Hammarskjold had been killed, a provincial governor in Vietnam had been beheaded by the Viet Cong. As Diem's forces began giving ground, "All hell broke loose" in Washington.[80] It was clear that the administration could no longer afford to "preserve options." It was a time for choice. Kennedy's predisposition on both questions was evident in the men he turned to for advice. To map out strategy on the Congo, he asked George Ball to take charge. To assess the situation in Vietnam, he asked General Maxwell Taylor and Walt Rostow to go to Saigon. Ball recommended diplomatic action; Taylor and Rostow, military intervention. In the months that followed, Kennedy would send several thousand men to solve the crisis in Vietnam. In the Congo, he would send one man to seek a diplomatic solution.

Ball's memorandum of September 24 argued forcefully that the only course for the United States in the Congo would be to take charge of the peacekeeping operation and to bring an end to the Katangese secession.[81] Military intervention had to be kept strictly multinational under UN auspices. Over the long term, Ball wrote, the antidote to civil war and Soviet intervention was the preservation of Adoula's coalition regime. He predicted, however, that Adoula's coalition would not survive unless Katanga were reintegrated, and for this to happen, the U.S. had to support the UN operation even if it involved military hostilities.

Ball proposed that the U.S. take three steps to strengthen its diplomatic hand in the crisis. First, there should be an immediate build-up of UN fighting power (primarily airstrike capacity) to destroy Tshombe's assurance of his own military superiority and to impress upon him the futility of trying to hold out. Second, the U.S. had to protect Adoula's government of national unity as the moderate alternative to civil war between left and right. Third, the U.S. had to strike at the foreign sources—both financial and political—of Katanga's strength and intercede with the British and Belgian governments to do the same.

The Ball memorandum was pouched to Hyannis Port on September 24 and was approved by the President without a change. By late November, Kennedy had assembled a new foreign policy team. Ball took over Bowles's position as second in command at State. To replace Rostow (who went to State to head the Policy Planning Staff) as Bundy's deputy, the President chose Carl Kaysen, an MIT economist with a prosecutor's instinct for the facts. Backing Kaysen at the White House on Congo matters was Samuel E. Belk III, a former Eisenhower NSC staffer and aide to Allen Dulles. Special Assistant Ralph Dungan continued to act as the President's eyes and ears on Congo developments as well as his intramural fireman on a host of other issues.

Kennedy's selection of Edmund Gullion as ambassador was of singular consequence to Congo policy. In the President's view, Gullion was *sans pareil* among his Third World ambassadors—his best and brightest. There was no ambassador in the New Frontier whose access to the Oval Office was more secure than his.

The acquaintance had begun in the late forties when Secretary Acheson had asked Gullion to help a young congressman from Massachusetts with a speech on foreign policy. They had met again in 1951 in Saigon, where Gullion was serving as political counselor to the American mission. Gullion's characterization of the French position as hopeless clearly made a strong impression on Kennedy who, in a radio address after his return to the U.S., categorically dismissed the prospects for survival for the French empire in Asia. For his first Senate speech on Indochina in 1954, Kennedy had drawn heavily from a secret briefing Gullion had given to the Council on Foreign Relations in New York. Kennedy had concluded —as had Gullion—that a military victory in Vietnam was impossible without exerting control over the political forces at play.[82]

Gullion had subsequently been fingered by his superiors for supposedly having provided Kennedy with ammunition for his attack on the Eisenhower administration's policy. He was pulled off the Vietnam desk (and participation in the peace talks then beginning in Geneva) and—as Kennedy put it—placed "in the deep freeze."[83] In 1961, Gullion was serving as acting head of the U.S. Disarmament Agency (later Arms Control and Disarmament Agency) when the President asked him to go to the Congo.

In a very real sense, the Congo became a testing ground of the views shared by Kennedy and Gullion on the purpose of American power in the Third World. As Kennedy remarked over the phone one day, if the U.S. could support the process of change—"allow each country to find its own way"—it could prevent the spread of the Cold War and improve its own security.[84] Both Kennedy and Gullion believed that the United States had to have a larger purpose in the Third World than the containment of communism. If the U.S. did not, it would fall into the trap of resisting change. Nationalist movements would seek Soviet help and use violent methods to secure power. Moderate forces would either collapse, or be swept to the left or right. By resisting change, the U.S. would concede the strategic advantage to the Soviet Union.

The alternative to a policy based solely on resistance was one based on neutralizing the process of radicalization by forging a coalition at the center. This was what Kennedy and Gullion would try to achieve in the Congo. Both thought that America's own national experience was relevant to the Congo's ordeal in nation building. When British Prime Minister Harold Macmillan wrote the President asking why the U.S. was so set against allowing Katanga financial and military autonomy, Kennedy replied, "In our own national history, our experience with non-federalism and federalism demonstrates that if a compact of government is to endure, it must provide the central authority with at least the power to tax, and the exclusive power to raise armies. We could not argue with the Congolese to the contrary."[85] Gullion, a Kentuckian who had grown up amid stories of the Civil War, saw the Congo crisis in the light of America's great testing—that "the house divided against itself could not stand."[86] Accordingly, he was disinclined to accept anything less than complete Congolese reunification.

Administration officials agreed that American credibility on the issue of decolonization in Africa was at stake in the Congo. As Ball commented to the President, the communist countries had been exploiting "the contention that the UN would not challenge white colonial interests in Katanga because of the hypocritical nature of the Western position. With our support the UN can and must show that we mean what we say where colonial interests are involved."[87]

The challenge in the Congo, Kennedy once remarked, was "making things stick in a place where everything falls apart."[88] Half of the ministerial positions in the Adoula regime were held by Lumumba's former lieutenants, who were both a serious threat to Adoula's position and yet a necessary part of the government of national unity. Gullion's marching orders required artful execution; he had to keep Adoula in power, but at the same time keep the Lumumbists (chiefly, Gizenga and Gbenye) on their stools in Léopoldville. With Lumumba's skeleton in the Western closet and the energetic Mr. Devlin still operating, this was no easy task.

Hammarskjold had warned the Americans about avoiding the temptation to bankroll Adoula's government with a large military and economic aid program. That would be the "kiss of death" for Adoula among rival Congolese nationalists, he had predicted.[89] Compromise at the center also meant avoiding another temptation to which the Eisenhower administration had readily succumbed—purging the Lumumbists in the name of anti-communism. This approach, of course, was precisely what the U.S. Congress and the European allies demanded of the administration before they would accept Adoula.

More than anything else, Kennedy's coalition strategy depended on the capacities and good fortune of Adoula, whose very political vulnerability had made him the acceptable choice to both left and right at Louvanium. Could Adoula, in Kennedy's words, "command popular support as against the military . . . carry out social and economic reform . . . get a modus vivendi among all forces prepared to commit themselves to democracy . . ."?[90] Adoula, a sober and modest man, had none of

Lumumba's mass appeal. He did not control key units of the army as did Mobutu. Unlike the Lumumbists in his government, Adoula had no tribal backing, and in the balkanized Congo this was a serious deficiency. After visiting Adoula in Léopoldville, U.S. Ambassador to the General Assembly Philip M. Klutznick reported that he was "haunted by the strange feeling that the Adoula government may be the 'Kerensky government' of the [Congo] revolution . . ."[91]

Gullion was nonetheless convinced that it could be done. Intrigue-ridden Léopoldville was hardly unfamiliar for the new ambassador, who had been chargé in Saigon during the latter months of France's "dirty war" and who had also served as acting chief of mission in Athens and Helsinki when those cities were overrun by the Nazis. Having dealt with paramilitary operations before, Gullion instinctively brought Devlin to heel.

The events of September had swept away the American pretense that there was an easy way out of the Congo mess. Hammarskjold's death had had a cathartic effect on Washington. The policy review and personnel shake-up were not the only signs of new resolution. The President also decided in November to ask the Congress to allocate $100 million to rescue the UN from outright bankruptcy. Senator Hubert Humphrey warned administration officials that such a request would imperil the entire foreign assistance bill. It would prove to be the President's toughest foreign policy fight on Capitol Hill.

Thanks to Belgian propagandist Michel Struelens, Katanga had mean-while found her apostle in Washington—Connecticut Senator Thomas Dodd, who scheduled hearings on the "loss" of the Congo to communism and who denounced the State Department with energetic regularity. He wrote Stevenson that the department's "blind determination" to back the UN in Katanga could only end in tragedy, and released the letter to the press before it had even gotten to Stevenson.[92] (In White House circles, it was said that when Tshombe wrote his memoirs, he would title them: *Dodd is My Co-Pilot.*) Progressive on most domestic issues, Dodd had a history of alliances with right-wing clients overseas. Two earlier anti-communist champions of his were Trujillo and Castillo Armas. What made the senator a problem for the administration was his position as a ranking member of the President's party and his ready use of anticommunist histrionics.[93]

FIRST TEST OF THE COALITION STRATEGY

Before Kennedy's policy could take effect, war broke out again in the Congo. Under enormous pressure from the Parliament to make good on his promise to subdue Tshombe, Adoula unleashed two ANC battalions with predictably disastrous results. Katangese aircraft bombed the invading troops, routing them completely. Adoula was in serious trouble.

The UN asked the U.S. to issue a public statement of support for possible UN military action against the offending Katangese aircraft. Kennedy disagreed: if the action was really necessary, he remarked to Ball, then let the UN air force go ahead and attack the planes. A statement from Washington would give the appearance that the U.S. was authorizing the action and might lock the U.S. into support for the military actions that followed. He voiced another reservation: "We don't want to completely crush Tshombe until we know who will inherit this."[94]

The President's reluctance to "crush Tshombe" reflected a contradiction in his coalition strategy, which would later emerge full blown: if the center could not hold, then the right had to be strengthened. Such hedging might have made perfect tactical sense but its effect was to weaken the center. As Adoula stumbled, the Kennedy administration readied the safety catch—a seizure of power by the Binza boys.

The President, in any case, had reason to be worried in November. Gizenga had gone into open rebellion and had reestablished his secessionist regime in Stanleyville. After the Central Government's military humiliation in Kasai, "it became increasingly clear that not only Orientale but also parts of Kivu and Kasai [provinces] were beginning to look to Gizenga rather than Adoula for leadership."[95] The coalition on which the U.S. had based so much was breaking apart. Aerial shipments of arms and supplies from communist and radical governments to Stanleyville resumed. Eleven Italian airmen serving the UN were murdered by Gizenga's troops. The U.S. consul in Stanleyville, Thomas Cassilly, was seized and beaten before a crowd of several thousand. On hand to record the event was a photographer from the Tass news agency. In classic Congolese fashion, a letter was given to Cassilly—after his beating and imprisonment—informing him that he was *persona non grata*.[96] Within the Adoula regime, Lumumbist Interior Minister Christophe Gbeyne began flexing his muscles. He mobilized militant bands of Lumumbist youth and was reported to be forming his own corps of security personnel to undercut pro-Western Sûreté Chief Nendaka. One informed observer predicted that a Lumumbist takeover was only days away.[97]

In an atmosphere of alarm, the administration discussed possible courses of action to save Adoula and to stop the Lumumbists. At a White House meeting, the President was moved to jot down, "must act before the USSR does."[98] Kennedy asked the State Department to investigate what turned out to be a purely fantastic report that the UN was transporting Gizenga's troops to Kivu and that a contingent of UN officials, led by the enterprising Conor O'Brien, had flown to Albertville to greet Gizenga's troops. ("Is that guy still in the Congo?" Kennedy asked Ball.)[99] Rusk, who had never seen much merit in the coalition regime in any case, wanted Gizenga militarily "liquidated." He informed the President, "We believe Adoula could now move openly and forcefully against Gizenga and yet hold the other radicals with him."[100] Adoula clearly thought otherwise; he flew to Kivu in December for discussions with his rebellious Vice Premier.

Gullion continued to counsel patience and restraint. In mid-November, there was a minor political breakthrough that gave the Adoula coalition a new lease on life. Cléophas Kamitatu, a leading Lumumbist and co-founder (along with Gizenga) of the *Parti Solidaire Africain*, shifted his crucial support to Adoula, conclusively parting company with Gizenga. Gullion, who had helped orchestrate the move, then arranged a leader grant tour of the U.S. for Kamitatu in mid-December. Kamitatu returned from the U.S. "favorably impressed."[101]

With Kamitatu at Adoula's side, Gbenye made no play for power. When Gizenga subsequently attempted to fuse the *Parti Solidaire Africain* (PSA) and the *Mouvement National Congolais* (Lumumba) into one national party, Gbenye and fellow Lumumbist Joseph Kasongo broke publicly with him. Without support from fellow Lumumbists in Léopold-ville, Gizenga could make mischief in the hinterland but he could not take power in the capital. The Kennedy strategy of co-opting the Congolese left had survived the first round.

THE BATTLE FOR KATANGA: ROUND II

The primary threat to the survival of the Adoula regime, however, came not from the left but from Tshombe. It had been Adoula's inability to end the Katanga secession that had led to Gizenga's defection. With Tshombe in Geneva (where he was recuperating from his last bout with the UN) and Munongo contemplating a pre-emptive attack on Albertville, the drift toward civil war was undeniable. Over Ball's objections. Kennedy asked Ambassador Harriman, who was also in Geneva at the Laos peace talks, to approach Tshombe and to try to talk some sense into him. The major result of these discussions with Tshombe was Harriman's conversion to Katanga's cause.[102]

The President himself made little headway with fellow heads of state on the Katanga question. Tory attachment to Katanga had effectively tied British Prime Minister Macmillan's hands. The most he could offer Kennedy was nominal support for the UN operation accompanied by a persistent refusal to contribute in any affirmative way to its purpose.[103]

Indian Prime Minister Nehru visited Washington in early November. Under Secretary Bowles thought that this visit might provide an opportune chance for the President to work out an understanding with Nehru on the military aspects of the UN operation. Kennedy was not so sure. He told columnist Arthur Krock, off the record, that he believed that Nehru's UN policy was "animated by a wish to assure the help of Russia in staving off China," which was threatening India over the province of Kashmir.[104] Kennedy doubted therefore that Nehru could be relied upon in the Congo.

The leader upon whom Kennedy found that he could rely was, ironically, Belgian Foreign Minister Spaak. Spaak's visit to Washington in November marked the beginning of intimate diplomatic collaboration between the U.S. and Belgium on the Congo. When they met, Kennedy recalled his trip to Brussels in 1939 when he had read about Belgium's brilliant young prime minister (Spaak himself). The meeting went well, and Spaak came away impressed by Kennedy's "amiability and gentility" in taking the Belgian position into account.[105]

A few days after his Washington visit, the Foreign Minister announced that his government would confiscate the passport of any Belgian national serving in Katanga's armed forces. He recalled Belgian Consul-General Créner, who had resisted UN efforts to remove foreign military and political advisors from Katanga, and replaced him with Colonel Frédéric Vandewalle, who proved to be somewhat more supportive of the new policy. Later in November, the Belgian government secretly informed the U.S. mission in Brussels that if Tshombe did not make a major concession in two weeks (by the end of the first week in December), Belgium would withdraw its 500 remaining technicians from Katanga.[106] As the sacking of the Belgian consulate in Elisabethville in August had indicated, Spaak was running serious risks in confronting Tshombe.

Spaak's skillful and courageous management of Belgium's Congo policy not only gave the UN a new lease on its peacekeeping operation, but also strengthened Kennedy's resolve. The first public test of the administration's willingness to pick up where Hammarskjold had left off came at the Security Council meeting in mid-November. Spurred on by the Soviets, the militant Afro-Asian states introduced a resolution that would mandate military force to end the secession. This, Rusk wrote the President on November 11, would be a "pyrrhic victory" for both the Congo and the UN. Katanga might be re-integrated but it would be an "economic wreck."[107]

On the eve of the Security Council meeting, Tshombe sent Kennedy an enticing wire reminding him that "force should not be used where negotiations are still possible. It is a fact that I maintain my offer to meet with Mr. Adoula."[108] Unfortunately for Tshombe, receipt of this communication coincided with the release of the UN commission's report of its investigation into Lumumba's death. The report concluded, among other things, that Tshombe could have been present at the murder. Kennedy telephoned Cleveland to ask him how "hard" the commission's evidence was on this point, indicating perhaps that the President was still trying to size up the man who had so impressed Harriman in Geneva.[109]

The Security Council convened in a stormy atmosphere reminiscent of earlier Congo meetings. The Soviet Union resorted to its usual tactic of trying to drive a wedge between the African states and the Western powers by vetoing two U.S. amendments to the Security Council resolution. Without these moderating amendments, the Europeans refused to support a resolution authorizing the use of force. Foreign Minister Spaak appealed to Washington to dissociate itself from the resolution and to abstain. Stevenson, however, achieved an informal entente with the Africans concerning the use of force and persuaded Kennedy to let him cast an affirmative vote. On November 24, the U.S., with its allies abstaining, joined the majority in authorizing the UN to use "a requisite measure of force, if necessary" to deport the mercenaries and foreign advisory personnel from Katanga.[110]

Tshombe labeled the resolution an act of war and announced that he would scorch the earth and use poisoned arrows to repel the UN invaders. Later that week, with the visiting Senator Dodd at his side, Tshombe toured the mining centers of Jadotville and Kolwezi evoking a "tremendous popular response" and being greeted by "delirious throngs" of blacks and whites—or so Dodd reported to the President.[111] In Elisabethville, mercenary-led units of gendarmes began surrounding UN positions and digging in.

Anticipating the outbreak of more fighting, the UN command quickly built up its forces in Katanga via U.S. Air Force Globemasters. Kennedy approved a plan to retrain and rearm the ANC "with the implicit objective of giving the Central Government enough power to crush Tshombe's military forces." The CIA station in Léopoldville was given the green light to neutralize Adoula's adversaries, either by buying them off or by purging them. To shore up the Adoula regime, the U.S. funneled considerable amounts of aid through the UN.[112]

Gullion flew back to Washington in the first week of December for consultations about the situation in Katanga. He met with the President and recommended that if fighting broke out, UN forces should be allowed to "proceed." Did that mean that the "wrap should be taken off the UN?" the President asked. Gullion said yes, and Kennedy nodded his head in silent affirmation: the U.S. would stand behind the UN.[113] Hammarskjold had gotten his way.

On the evening of November 28, Katangese paratroopers burst into a private home in Elisabethville where Senator Dodd was being feted. They abducted UN representatives Brian Urquhart and George Ivan Smith. U.S. Consul Lewis Hoffacker, who had just pulled up to the house as the paratroopers were taking their captives away, bravely intervened and rescued Ivan Smith but failed to secure the release of Urquhart.[114]

UN troops were put on alert and began patrolling Elisabethville in armored personnel carriers. Gurkha Colonel S.S. Maitra informed Katangese authorities at the American consulate (where Hoffacker was trying to arrange Urquhart's release) that if the UN official were not freed within forty-five minutes, he would assault Tshombe's presidential palace, even if it cost the life of every man in his battalion. At Hoffacker's urging, General Raja countermanded this ultimatum.[115] Early the next morning, Urquhart was released in badly beaten condition.

The Katangese continued to engage in hostile acts. A Gurkha patrol was ambushed and two of its soldiers were killed. Eleven UN personnel were kidnapped on December 3 and Katangese troops blockaded the road between UN headquarters and the airport. Secretary-General U Thant warned that these roadblocks threatened UN security and communications and, as a matter of self-defense, had to be removed. When this demand was ignored and UN authorities spotted a large concrete tank (the so-called Mammouth built in one of the Union Minière's factories) heading toward the airport crossroads, Ivan Smith gave the order to attack. Gurkha troops stormed the roadblocks and heavy fighting broke out.[116]

Gullion and Williams flew to New York on December 6 to join Stevenson for a strategy meeting with the Secretary-General. Washington wanted to be sure that this time the UN had a firm military plan of action. Thant told the Americans that the UN would defend its positions and, if attacked by Katangese forces, would retaliate. Gullion considered this insufficient: the UN should take the offensive and seize communication centers and power stations. He asked Thant if the UN would be ready to provide temporary administration of Katanga.[117] Stevenson told a group of reporters that the U.S. fully supported the UN action and would provide up to twenty-one additional transport planes to carry troops to Elisabethville. In retaliation, the Katangese government put Consul Hoffacker under house arrest.

On December 6, UN jets strafed Katangese positions and destroyed several planes on the ground, including the infamous Fouga that had wrought so much damage in the September fighting. U.S. Air Force C-124s continued to fly sorties airlifting 900 UN troops from Léopoldville to Elisabethville as well as six anti-aircraft guns, five Swedish armored cars, and other equipment.[118]

On the ground, the fighting grew vicious. Under the direction of a French mercenary, Colonel Faulques, Katangese gendarmes used civilian

homes, factory installations, church steeples, and even hospitals to direct
fire at UN troops. The UN, in turn, began shelling schools, hospitals, and
Union Minière facilities—targets that were supposedly off limits. As the
civilian casualties mounted, UN troops soon found themselves fighting the
enraged white-settler community as well. In one battle for a downtown
underpass, over 100 European civilians fought alongside Katangese gendarmes despite strafing by UN jets and a full-scale assault by Swedish
troops. An extreme settler group—*Le Mouvement Pour l'Indépendance
et Résistance*—threatened to poison the UN water supply.[119]

Civilians—innocent and otherwise—became fair game for some UN
units. Concerning charges of rape by UN soldiers, Colonel Maitra remarked to Hoffacker that they weren't excessive "when one considers the
number of frustrated Afro-Asian soldiers here." Although it was the
Indians who were most often accused of brutality, the CIA matter-of-factly
reported that the Ethiopians were the "most effective" of the UN troops:
"They employ ferocious battle tactics which include execution of Katangans
and White mercenaries immediately after capture."[120] Haile Selassie's
contribution to the peacekeeping force came in the form of a "penal
battalion" made up of criminals who had been released from prison to
serve in the Congo.

When the Ethiopians killed three Red Cross workers, Ivan Smith
(who himself had nearly been shot by the rabble) accused Tshombe's
white mercenaries of having painted Red Cross insignia on vehicles that
were being used for military purposes. A secret investigation into the incident by three pathologists revealed otherwise; the Ethiopians had shot the
Red Cross personnel in cold blood, put their bodies in a Red Cross
vehicle that they then blew up with a bazooka round. Fortunately for the
UN, the report did not leak out. Never one to miss out on a propaganda
opportunity, Tshombe posthumously awarded the three Red Cross workers
(G. Olivet, S. Smeding, and N. Vroonen) the title of "Commanders of the
Katangese Order of Merit."[121]

President Kennedy was soon on the receiving end of European outrage over UN atrocities in Katanga. Spaak sent the President copies of the
formal protests he had made to U Thant. Chairman of the Board of Union
Minière Jules Cousin sent a bitter message to Kennedy saying that he had
personally witnessed "the indiscriminate killing and wounding of innocent
people" and that because of these "veritable murders by the hired killers
of the United Nations," he was returning to Kennedy the U.S. Freedom
Medal awarded him in 1946.[122] Even the normally unflappable Lord Home
was incensed. The UN, he said, was "sowing the seeds of its own
destruction."[123]

The President remarked to Bundy that the UN had better reassert control over its forces "quick." Bundy, in turn, told Ball that the President wanted that sentiment "to be put tough" to U Thant. Kennedy then telephoned Gullion to reiterate that our "objective" was limited and should not be exceeded.[124]

When Secretary Rusk arrived in Paris on December 11 for the NATO foreign ministers' conference, he found the allies furious over the fact that the U.S. had not consulted with them before giving U Thant the green light. Home wanted an immediate cease-fire. He put Rusk on notice that the U.K. was going to suspend the delivery of the 1000-lb. bombs it had promised UN forces until it was assured that U Thant was in control of the situation. If the fighting continued, Britain might withdraw its support altogether. Spaak joined Home in proposing the introduction of a Security Council resolution calling for a cease-fire, even if it caused a Soviet veto. The French government announced that henceforth it would bar overflight of its African colonies by planes carrying troops or supplies to UN forces in the Congo.[125]

Taken aback by the outpouring, Rusk telephoned Washington for guidance. He told Ball that the U.S. "should not accept responsibility for all that the UN was doing in the Congo." Macmillan was in serious political trouble. He was facing a motion of censure in the House of Commons. His Tory backbenchers were up in arms at the Prime Minister's announcement that Her Majesty's government would deliver the bombs for UN forces. Home had told Rusk that the issue was so explosive that it might cause the government to fall.

Ball informed Rusk that the UN offensive was only to be directed at certain key points. Rusk suggested that a cease-fire announcement be made during the offensive, but Ball disagreed.

The President then got on the line and pointedly suggested to Rusk that "some of our friends should use their influence with Tshombe." Perhaps a telephone call to Macmillan might help, Kennedy said, particularly if he mentioned the Volta Dam decision for good measure. Rusk reiterated his concern about the outcome of the parliamentary debate: "[i]t could really topple the government . . . Macmillan might have to say some pretty extreme things." Kennedy said he understood that; the purpose of the UN military operation was to get Tshombe to negotiate. The President's position was confirmed in a telegram to Rusk: the U.S. would support the UN's limited military operation and there would be no cease-fire until talks between Adoula and Tshombe began.[126]

That evening (December 13) the President dined alone with British Ambassador David Ormsby Gore, a personal friend. Ormsby Gore repeated what Rusk had said; if there were no announcement of an immediate cease-fire in Katanga, Macmillan could lose the vote of confidence.

He needed every vote. After dinner Kennedy telephoned Stevenson and instructed him to tell U Thant that the reconciliation process between Tshombe and Adoula should begin immediately.[127] Talks should accompany the UN military operation. Stevenson protested, but the President was insistent. The Secretary-General then dispatched a message to the British Prime Minister that said that Bunche was doing his best to bring about a negotiated solution.

At the close of the protracted Commons debate the next day ("the most heated since Suez," according to one correspondent) Macmillan read U Thant's letter, which he disingenuously represented as a friendly response to his government's call for an immediate and unconditional cease-fire. Labor party spokesman Harold Wilson remarked that the government was not really concerned with a cease-fire in the Congo, but only about a cease-fire with the extremist rebels in the Conservative party. Although a dozen right-wing Conservatives abstained from supporting Macmillan, the government won the vote by a comfortable margin. One progressive Tory member said at the day's end: "This government just rapes easy."[128] Kennedy called Ormsby Gore and asked, with a note of sarcasm, whether he thought all the effort of the previous evening had been worth it.[129]

Ambassador Stevenson made no effort to conceal his unhappiness with the President. He complained to Ball that it was "hard for him [Stevenson] to run this thing and not to run it." Most of the time he was not consulted. He wasn't even sure who was running things and implied that the President was buckling under congressional pressure.

When Bundy learned of Stevenson's complaints, he told Ball that if Adlai had any doubts about policy he should call the President directly.[130] Stevenson's complaints, however, had less to do with policy doubts than with unhappiness over his own diminishing influence on Congo decision making. As Kennedy's grasp of the crisis became increasingly sure, Stevenson found himself at the receiving end of decisions, no longer at the initiating end as he had been in the first months of 1961. It was not a change to which he adjusted easily.

The outcry in Europe and the persistent reports of UN atrocities provided ammunition for the administration's critics. Home from the NATO meeting, Rusk entered another shooting gallery. At a Senate Foreign Relations Committee briefing, Senators Frank J. Lausche and Bourke B. Hickenlooper repeatedly interrupted the Secretary. Lausche asked "whether we have the right to go in any place and tell people what they shall do domestically?" Hickenlooper wondered whether it was wise "to force the Katangans to subject themselves to the control of individuals who had hardly jumped out of trees yet?" Senator Hubert Humphrey thought that the administration had conspicuously failed to make its case to the public.

If the State Department did nothing in the face of the "deluge" of Katangese propaganda, he warned Rusk, "your chances of being the first man on the moon are better than being able to win this argument." The UN would be "crucified on this cross of the Congo with Mr. Tshombe emerging as a patron saint, which he ain't, to put it in the vernacular."[131]

As Humphrey had recognized, the administration was indeed losing the propaganda battle because of its indifferent effort to educate the American public about the merits of the UN mandate. Struelens had meanwhile gathered a small column of opinion molders. "Katanga is the Hungary of 1961" announced a full-page advertisement signed by well-known conservative senators, writers, and professors in *The New York Times*. The "American Committee for Aid to the Katangan Freedom Fighters" drew on the lists of the Committee of One Million and the Young Americans for Freedom to foster the cause.[132]

The State Department responded in a wooden manner to the well-orchestrated outpouring of Katangese propaganda that played up Katanga's anticommunist, underdog themes. When the department announced that Adoula was just as much an anticommunist as Tshombe, the Katangese President sent an open telegram to Rusk reminding him that Adoula called himself a neutralist, as had Fidel Castro, "as long as it was a question of obtaining American aid to establish his regime." Tshombe suggested that the Secretary explain to the American people what communists like Gizenga and Gbenye were doing in Adoula's government.[133] This message was prominently featured in the American press.

The President—supremely cautious about employing the Bully Pulpit —asked Ball to make the administration's case to the public. On December 19 in a speech in Los Angeles, Ball invoked the most unexceptionable article of faith in American foreign policy—the threat of international communism. The Soviet Union wanted to acquire "an asset without price —a base of operations in the heart of Africa from which to spread its tentacles . . . " The result, Ball declared, might be a direct confrontation that could "blow the flames of a brush-fire conflict into a horrible firestorm of nuclear devastation . . . our main objectives in central Africa would be drowned in blood . . . "

Kennedy was impressed with the speech but *The New York Times* was not; it ignored the address until Ball telephoned publisher Orvil E. Dryfoos and actually scolded him about the oversight. When Bundy found out that *Time* was going to put Tshombe on its cover, he unsuccessfully tried to discourage it.[134] The fact was that Katanga's struggle for independence made good copy; the administration's support for the UN's uncertain mandate and the shaky Adoula regime did not.

The President had more luck in neutralizing critics than in creating a popular consensus in favor of his Congo policy. He sent CIA director John McCone (who had also served as chairman of the Atomic Energy Commission under Eisenhower) down to Gettysburg for a visit with the former President. Eisenhower issued a statement a few days later in support of the Kennedy administration. Under Secretary George C. McGhee, who had already traveled down to Georgia to talk fellow Southerner Senator Richard Russell out of joining forces with Senator Dodd, interceded with the Republican leadership with unusual success. The notable exception was former Vice President Nixon, who brusquely told McGhee not even to try.[135]

As the fighting in Katanga entered its second week, the political fallout became intolerable for Washington. In eight days, there had been more than 700 casualties, many of them civilian. The Europeans were outraged. The American public was puzzled by the apparition of war being waged by an organization dedicated to the preservation of peace. In a quandary, the President called in his advisors on December 14 to discuss the situation.

MEDIATION AT KITONA

Before the administration could decide on a definite plan of action, the White House received on its open channel a message from Tshombe to the President: "I request your good offices as a broadminded and Christian man for the purpose of appointing a capable negotiator and putting a stop immediately to the useless bloodshed."[136] Gullion warned Washington that Tshombe's message was probably a ruse that should be ignored. Stevenson concurred, but the President was intrigued by the possibility of using the message to lure Tshombe to the conference table to negotiate with Premier Adoula. He cabled back saying that he was urgently exploring the possibilities. He then ordered a U.S. naval force in South African waters to head toward the Congo as a possible point of rendezvous for the parties.[137]

Kennedy's new course banked all on success. If Tshombe backed off and went public with Kennedy's secret communication, the UN and the Central Government would be greatly embarrassed. When an AP story datelined Brazzaville claimed that Tshombe was in direct contact with Kennedy, the administration feared that it had made just such a miscalculation.[138]

Ball typically advocated action: the United States should take complete responsibility for mediation by replacing Bunche with Gullion as mediator, and by having the UN arrange a forty-eight-hour truce. Stevenson was shocked. What Ball was recommending was tantamount to "taking over the United Nations" and asking the Secretary-General "to relinquish his responsibilities." Furthermore, the idea of a forty-eight-hour truce was foolhardy. The administration was about to make "a great, great mistake." Stevenson dictated an alternative message from Kennedy to Tshombe over the phone to Ball, who took it over to the White House.

The President saw merit in Stevenson's objections and altered his strategy accordingly.[139] The truce would be conditional on Tshombe's agreement to negotiate. This offer would be communicated secretly to the Katangese leader. Instead of a completely American operation, the mediation would be a joint U.S.-UN venture in which both Gullion and Bunche would participate. With this settled, the President spoke with Gullion by means of a military short-wave hook-up. He told the ambassador that the objective was to press for negotiations while the UN finished up its offensive. To put the full prestige of his office behind the reconciliation effort, Kennedy dispatched the presidential airplane *Columbine* to the Congo.[140]

The old-boy network was activated. At Bundy's request, Admiral Alan G. Kirk (an American business representative of several large Belgian corporate interests and Bundy's former naval commanding officer) telephoned the President of Union Minière, Herman Robiliart, on the evening of the fourteenth and asked him to use "every possible pressure to persuade Tshombe to go with Ed Gullion to meet Adoula." Robiliart (whose industrial facilities in Elisabethville had been stormed only the previous afternoon by the marauding Ethiopians) readily agreed to do so.[141]

Kennedy cabled Tshombe on December 16 advising him that all was ready and urging him to proceed to Kitona (a former Belgian air base) "within a matter of hours." Hoffacker was instructed to inform Tshombe orally that the UN would cease all operations as soon as he left for Kitona. The American consul delivered the message to Tshombe while UN jets were strafing around his palace.[142] The Katangese president immediately accepted Kennedy's offer and promised to meet Gullion at Ndola for the flight to Kitona.

It was now up to Gullion to get the disputants together. By this time, it was the leaders of the Central Government, however, who wanted no part of the talks. President Kasavubu accused Gullion of a sell-out. Adoula himself could not be reached since he was in Kivu province some 1,200 miles from Léopoldville. When Kennedy heard of Kasavubu's opposition, he got back in touch with Gullion over the short-wave hook-up and gave him instructions on what to say to Kasavubu and Adoula: first, that the appeal had come from Tshombe, not President Kennedy; second, that the military operations were continuing in Katanga; third, that the U.S. fully supported the UN; and fourth, that there would be no change in any aspect of U.S. policy unless Tshombe showed reason.[143]

This proved to be enough assurance for Kasavubu—particularly after Gullion compared his role in the crisis to "le grand Lincoln"—but Adoula was another matter. After he returned to the capital, the premier summoned Gullion and angrily told him that the U.S. was trying to force him to meet a traitor on equal ground. Gullion made no headway despite three hours of discussion and was forced to report to Washington that the effort had stalled.[144]

When Kennedy learned of this, he sent Gullion a message: "Do not let GOC (government of the Congo) delay us" and sent word to Ball that Adoula "be obliged" to respond.[145] Gullion then went back to Adoula. He took him to task, reminding him that the U.S. had backed both his government and the UN operation "at great strain on our friendships and alliances," and that President Kennedy had put his prestige on the line. Gullion warned the premier that if he did not go to the meeting he might lose American support. Finally, Adoula relented. A few hours later on the morning of December 18, Gullion, his Deputy Chief of Mission G. McMurtrie Godley, the U.S. Information Service director Fitzhugh Green, and a small contingent of marines boarded the *Columbine* to fly to Ndola to pick up Tshombe. Adoula proceeded directly to Kitona.

Tshombe, accompanied by the American and British consuls, met the American party at the Queen Elizabeth guest house near Ndola and immediately employed "some last-minute blackmail." He would not board the plane, he told Gullion, without the assurance of a general truce. The agreed-upon condition was a cease-fire, Gullion pointed out. The alternative—if Tshombe elected to return to Elisabethville—was a UN military take-over. Tshombe and his advisors would later charge that this "capitulation or oblivion" alternative constituted duress, but after several more hours of stalling. Tshombe boarded the *Columbine*, climbed into Mamie Eisenhower's old bunk, and slept until shortly before the *Columbine* landed at Kitona.[146]

The State Department sent the American team a twenty-one-point set of instructions for a prospective Adoula-Tshombe agreement. Gullion and the UN team, which had arrived from Léopoldville, reduced this to eight points. After initially registering agreement in principle on most of the eight points in the draft agreement, Tshombe suddenly declared that he had no power to negotiate without first consulting his government. Adoula lost his temper and the mediators intervened to separate the two groups. Gullion gave a stiff talk to both men while Bunche and Khiary put the draft agreement into more palatable language. Nevertheless, by midnight, negotiations had broken down completely. The planes were warmed up and the baggage stowed as the two groups stalked to their cars with Gullion running after them trying to salvage something in the form of a final communiqué. He and Bunche managed to get Adoula and Tshombe back into the former hospital that was serving as the negotiating center. The meetings resumed, but again reached an impasse. Finally, Khiary came up with the idea of including Tshombe's demand to consult with his government in a separate letter of transmittal to Bunche. Under great pressure from Gullion, Adoula accepted this formula.

At 2:30 A.M., the two leaders signed the eight-point declaration in which Tshombe recognized the *loi fondamentale* (the Congolese Constitution) and pledged to place his gendarmerie under the authority of President Kasavubu as well as to participate in the Congolese Parliament. The secession—at least legally—was over. Gullion returned to Léopoldville and telephoned the good news to President Kennedy, who was in Bermuda for talks with Prime Minister Macmillan. Then the ambassador went to bed for the first time in four days.[147]

Washington was highly gratified. Ball cabled the President and the Secretary that "[S]uch a complete capitulation by Tshombe goes far beyond our expectations." Gullion wrote the President that the accord signed at Kitona vindicated the "bold line" that the administration had taken, even if it had strained traditional friendships and alliances.[148] Kennedy remarked to Ambassador Ormsby Gore, "Maybe they *aren't* paying me too much."[149]

Ten years before, Kennedy had returned home from Asia with the simple perception that America could provide leadership in the Third World through a creative diplomatic presence based on the potential use of military power. Gullion thought the accord signed at Kitona affirmed that perception:

> Your initiative in exploiting the peace feeler from Mr. Tshombe (which he himself may have only regarded as a psychological warfare move) made possible the suspension of force at just the right moment for bringing together Mr. Adoula and Mr. Tshombe. Out of that meeting, and in no small part owing to the Administration's guidance and influence with the United Nations, has come an agreement which promises reunification and an end to the fighting.[150]

BACK TO SQUARE ONE

But even as Guillion was writing this dispatch, Tshombe, now out of American clutches, was busy backing out of the agreement. There was to be no "reunification and end to the fighting," just one more play at peace orchestrated by outsiders and repudiated by the Katangese. It was back to square one. With the UN now bankrupt, Katanga once again on the loose, and Lumumba's followers in revolt, Kennedy was soon asking the same question that Hammarskjold had asked: How much more could be sacrificed—in lives, money, and international respect—for peace in the Congo?

To Hammarskjold, resolution of the crisis had been worth any sacrifice. He had led his "posse of neutrals" into the Congo not only to keep the peace, but also to vindicate a precedent he had set elsewhere—one based on the principles of the UN Charter instead of on the balance of power. In the end there had been no turning back.

Kennedy did not see the Congo as a 'great adventure' but as an unwanted burden. Unlike Hammarskjold, he had no taste for engagement, just a well-developed sensitivity to political risk. Until Hammarskjold's death, Kennedy had carefully straddled the fence in the Congo. The presence of the UN had excused him from having to choose whether or not to defend the Congo from the Russians. It had allowed him to continue to preserve options. Of course, Kennedy had come to the presidency as a man of recognized promise. But for all his prescient words in the Senate about the meaning of nationalism, and despite the brave talk in his first weeks in the White House, the record in 1961 showed that he had been little more than a practitioner of wait-and-see diplomacy.

The irony of Hammarskjold's death was that it had impelled the uncertain Kennedy to do what the Secretary-General had tried and failed to do—to bring the Europeans back into the peacekeeping alliance and to force a showdown with Tshombe. The larger purpose of Kennedy's diplomacy had then emerged: to build a durable political center around the Adoula coalition. The signature of the Kitona accord—a tribute to Kenendy's skill in combining the threat of war with an offer for peace—seemed to vindicate the initiatives the President had taken. For a brief moment in December 1961, it seemed that the center would hold.

But in 1962, the center collapsed. Adoula's coalition unraveled and Tshombe never seemed stronger. Britain and France defected from the UN operation. The Congress balked at the President's request to refinance the UN. On the first anniversary of Hammarskjold's death, the UN and Katangese armies were headed for another bloody and inconclusive exchange. Within the administration, the two leading policy makers began pulling in opposite directions. Gullion demanded that Tshombe be crushed militarily. Ball called for disengagement—a "policy kill"—and advised the White House that Gullion be "cut down to size." Some wanted withdrawal, others demanded outright military intervention by the U.S. The President held repeated meetings, but they produced nothing. Amid what he called the "dark and tangled stretches of decision making," Kennedy took his own measure of engagement in the Congo. The choice, he wrote, was "as difficult and as complex as any in the entire range of our foreign policy operations."[151]

5

A Little Sense of Pride

> You were firm in your determination that the Katanga secession be ended. At the same time you sought to prove to the world that every possible peaceful means of solution was tried before forceful means were applied.
>
> McGhee to Kennedy
> (*January 22, 1963*)

"It is essential that you drive home to the British and Belgian Governments our determination to achieve an integrated Congo," Kennedy wrote his ambassador in London in 1962.[1] The President blamed the Europeans for having allowed Tshombe to back out of the Kitona agreement.

After the December 1961 fighting, the British and the Belgians emphatically made clear their opposition to any further UN military action in Katanga. Sensing correctly that without European backing the UN military threat was so much bluff, Tshombe had then backed out of the Kitona agreement. Union Minière's payments to the secessionist regime had subsequently allowed Tshombe to begin re-equipping his army. To Kennedy's astonishment, the British government had continued to do nothing to stop the Rhodesian Federation from shipping arms into Katanga and taking out copper.

The White House was meanwhile trying to convince Congress to purchase $100 million worth of bonds to bail out the bankrupt UN. The Democratic leadership on Capitol Hill wanted no part of the proposed appropriation. The Republicans sensed the possibility of a major legislative defeat for the administration. Kennedy found it galling that at the very time he was trying to justify the UN's borrowing of $10 million a month to finance the Congo operation, Union Minière was providing Tshombe with an equivalent amount, enabling him to hold out. He asked his ambassador to the Court of St. James's, David K. E. Bruce, to impress on the British and Belgian governments once and for all "failure to achieve a viable solution will almost certainly result in catastrophe for the commercial enterprises in the Congo."

BRUSSELS

Foreign Minister Spaak fully appreciated the danger in the stalemate, but there were limits to what he alone could do. Spaak had already warned Tshombe to stop his "dilatory tactics," and had unsuccessfully urged several Swiss banks to close out their Katangese accounts.[2] What the Lefèvre-Spaak Government could not survive politically was another UN military campaign in Katanga. The hundreds of Belgian civilians killed and wounded by UN troops had triggered a popular uproar in Belgium. In the Belgian Parliament, Spaak was under constant attack and was obliged to move in public under a heavy police guard. His political adversaries openly encouraged Tshombe to continue the secession. Rector Marcel Dubuisson of the Université de Liège informed Tshombe of a conversation he had had with King Baudoin: *"En bref, on vous espère longtemps encore dans la capitale du cuivre."* (In short, it is hoped you will stay for a long time in the copper capital.)[3] If the UN forced a military showdown with Tshombe, the Lefèvre-Spaak government would risk a rupture with the settler community of the sort that had toppled the French government in 1958 during the Algerian war.

Kennedy tacitly agreed to keep the UN army on the leash if Spaak would help convince Union Minière to stop its payments of royalties, taxes, and dividends to Katanga. The Americans felt that the Belgian government, which owned 23.8 percent of the voting shares in Union Minière, was in a position to bring about a change in company policy.

At the time of Congolese independence, Brussels was to have transferred its 23.8 percent share in Union Minière to the Government of the Congo. In the disorder that followed independence, however, the transfer was never made and Union Minière began paying the dividends owed to the Central Government to the Tshombe regime. Washington wanted the Belgian government to act as "custodian of the Congo portfolio" by voting its shares to change Union Minière policy and ultimately by transferring ownership of the entire portfolio to the government of the Congo.[4]

There were problems with the American proposal. In the first place, the Congo owned Belgium money, and Brussels made it clear that there would be no transfer of the stock in Union Minière until the two governments reached an agreement on the repayment of the debts (the so-called *contentieux*). Spaak also pointed out to American officials that Tanganyika Concessions, Société Générale, and the Compagnie du Katanga together controlled over 40 percent of the voting shares in Union Minière; it was therefore unlikely that the Belgian government could change company policy with a 23.8 percent voting share. Nonetheless, the Belgian government did agree to vote the shares it controlled in accordance with the wishes of the Central Government.

The Kennedy administration then approached Union Minière directly with the proposal that the company put the royalties, taxes, and dividends belonging to the Government of the Congo into escrow.[5] McGeorge Bundy asked his former commanding officer in the Pacific, Admiral Alan Kirk, to go to Brussels to explain the American proposal to the presidents of Union Minière and Société Générale, Herman Robiliart and Max Nokin. The Admiral's talks in Brussels yielded practically nothing in the way of concessions. Robiliart told Kirk that Union Minière had $3 billion invested in Katanga and that economic pressure on Tshombe would cause the expropriation or even the destruction of the installations by the Katangese.[6]

Douglas MacArthur II, the U.S. ambassador in Brussels, then "applied the blowtorch"—as he put it—to the corporate leadership of Union Minière. Robiliart and Nokin likened their position to that of the Belgian populace during the Nazi occupation. MacArthur agreed that the analogy was a good one and reminded them of the fate of collaborationists after the war. "Vague talking and half-hearted gestures" would no longer do, he insisted. After three disputatious hours, Robiliart and Nokin relented on the escrow proposal (to set aside 75 percent of the taxes Union Minière was paying Katanga as well as a percentage of the dividend and royalty payments) and agreed to telex Tshombe to urge him to agree to a division of revenues with the central government.[7]

Three months later, Union Minière informed the central government that it intended "eventually" to ship all its output from Katanga to the Congolese port of Matadi as soon as the Route Nationale was transport worthy and the Lubilash bridge was repaired. The difficulty with this good intention was that the Route Nationale, which encompassed over 2,000 miles of ancient railway and treacherous channels in the River Congo, had hardly changed much since the days when Joseph Conrad had used this passage on his trip into the interior.[8] As Premier Adoula observed to President Kennedy at their meeting in February, Union Minière could be relied on to play both sides of the fence until either the central government or the Tshombe regime triumphed.[9]

American pressure on Union Minière, nonetheless, seemed to have some effect on its payments to Katanga. In January 1962, the company suspended scheduled dividend payments because of damage to its installations. In May, after declaring a dividend of $19.8 million, Union Minière authorities announced that the payment had been indefinitely suspended. Overall during 1962, Union Minière's direct payments to Katanga decreased by 25 percent. This loss of revenue was a serious setback to

Tshombe who had already run up a debt of 400 million francs from previous arms purchases.[10]

What the Kennedy administration wanted from the British was some tough talk to their Rhodesian prime minister and Katanga's silent partner—Sir Roy Welensky. The UN had solid evidence that Rhodesia was providing arms to Katanga. Didn't Her Majesty's government control the federation's foreign relations? Rusk asked British ambassador to the U.S. Ormsby Gore. It did, Ormsby Gore replied, observing, rather lamely he later thought, that if London gave direct orders to Salisbury, this would lead to "tremendous rows" in Parliament.[11] The British government did procure an invitation for Secretary-General Thant to visit Rhodesia to examine the border situation, but when Welensky refused to allow UN observers to enter the federation, the Secretary-General rejected the invitation.[12]

The UN continued to accuse Rhodesia of shipping arms into Katanga and Welensky continued to issue fervent denials. The British were indignant at the very suggestion of Sir Roy's complicity. "We could not conceive of his denials being insincere," a British embassy official in Washington told Wayne Fredericks. However, Gullion reported from Léopoldville that Welensky was still pursuing "intense discussions" with the Katangese on the subject of Rhodesian-Katangese unification.[13]

Despite such reports, the President remained confident that he could turn the British around on Katanga. There were reasons for his confidence. Britain had a good record in managing the transition to independence in its colonies. Kennedy admired Macmillan as a statesman and hoped to convince him that stability in Central Africa depended on a unified Congo.

With this in mind, the President had gone to the Bermuda summit in December 1961 carrying a comuniqué to which he hoped Macmillan would subscribe. Although the communiqué went no further than to endorse the principles signed at Kitona, Macmillan wanted no part of it. He told Kennedy that regardless of Tshombe's "indecent dealings" with white mercenaries and Belgian business, he remained the West's best bulwark against communism in the Congo.[14]

The President's optimism about the prospect of British broadmindedness had failed to take into account a simple reality: the Tories liked Tshombe. He was prowhite, anticommunist, and dedicated to the preservation of European property, "not such a bad chap." Ambassador Ormsby Gore told Stevenson. The fact that a score or so of Macmillan's backbenchers had a piece of Léopold's nest egg heightened the attraction. No one in the Conservative government had forgotten the UN's role in

Suez five years earlier. British Foreign Secretary Lord Home would inform
Rusk that UN intervention in the decolonization process had to be
stopped.[15]

Rebuffed in their efforts to persuade the British to support the UN,
the Americans were determined at least to keep them neutral. Otherwise,
the UN's cause in Katanga was doomed. It was for this reason that
Stevenson visited Macmillan in March and received assurances from him
that, despite his government's reservations about the UN Congo operation,
Britain would continue to pay its assessed share of UN peacekeeping
costs. With the Soviet Union and France refusing to contribute to the
operation, Britain's provision of $500,000 per month was felt to be
essential.

As the Americans were soon to discover, however, there was more
appearance than substance to Macmillan's promise. In April, the Prime
Minister's Private Secretary confidentially disclosed that there could be
an open split between the two countries over Congo policy. He reported
that Macmillan believed that if Adoula gained the upper hand over
Tshombe, he would move rapidly toward the Soviet bloc. For this reason,
Tshombe's position had to be preserved as long as the British retained
responsibility in the Rhodesias. Otherwise, Adoula would be free to
support subversive attacks from the Congo against whites in the federation.[16]

Stevenson found the inconsistency between this report and Macmillan's
previous representation "weird." Kennedy was also puzzled.[17] There
could be no denying the credibility of the source. The only permissible
conclusion was that the British were equivocating—"assuming the ostrich
position," Ambassador Ormsby Gore told Bundy.[18] If the British government were to break with the U.S. over the Congo, the UN operation
would effectively be paralyzed. At Kennedy's urgent request, Macmillan
agreed to host tripartite talks with the U.S. and Belgium.

The President asked his ambassador in London, David Bruce, to head
the U.S. delegation. The British, Bundy told Ball, "will do more for Bruce
than they will for anyone else."[19] The U.S. planned to asked Belgium and
Britain to support the UN "even at the risk of hostilities" and proposed
that Léopoldville receive at least 50 percent of Katanga's revenue and
take command of its gendarmerie.

The talks opened on May 15, 1962 and for the next three days of
discussions, the Americans and the British were at loggerheads. The
British negotiator, Lord Dundee, had repeatedly declared that the UN
was not fit to fight a "colonial war," whatever that meant. British Ambassador Ormsby Gore had previously warned the White House about
Dundee, whom he described as a "fool" to be disregarded. Bruce could

only agree: the British were "sleeping dogs." The talks, in the end, were a "complete failure."[20]

The White House was fed up. "So much for a united front," Carl Kaysen said. "The heart of the matter," Bundy commented to the President, "is that Tshombe will never negotiate unless there is the possibility of the use of force against him. Thus if we were to accept the British position against the use of force the position becomes impossible."[21]

A few days after the tripartite talks, Macmillan sent Kennedy a message trying to justify the British position. The President's response was cool. The United States, he wrote, had no argument with the need for a federal constitution in the Congo. But Katangese automony could not be so great as to lead to a "resurgence of secession and outbreak of civil war backed by the great powers . . . It is not enough that an autonomous Katanga pay tribute to Léopoldville . . . secession in any guise is no longer possible."[22]

In response to Macmillan's complaint that the U.S. favored another military operation against Tshombe, the President pointed out: "[w]e have never, of course, contemplated an offensive military initiative by the UN." Regarding Macmillan's reference to the "awkward situation" that might arise in the Security Council if Britain opposed another resolution supported by the U.S., Kennedy responded tersely: "[o]ur powers to prevent this development are limited." The U.S., he continued, had already informed both Adoula and the UN chief of operations in the Congo, Robert Gardiner, that it was prepared to give "full support to the UN mediatory effort even at the risk of hostilities."

Kennedy reserved his sharpest commentary for Macmillan's complaint that Premier Adoula was behaving "unreasonably" and was pushing the country toward civil war. "We have told him [Adoula] that he ought to be patient, even beyond the expectations of most reasonable men. We have argued with him strenuously . . . and he has become more, not less, reasonable." However, should negotiations fail, he warned Macmillan, "Mr. Adoula will no longer heed or be free to follow the counsels of restraint . . . the Chief of the Congolese Government will be obliged to reassert his authority."

British doubts about Adoula struck a nerve in the White House. The administration had based its Congo policy on Adoula's political survival and was making its case to the Congress for UN funding by singing his praises: Adoula, they had argued, meant moderate nationalism and containment of Soviet subversion. In Senate testimony, Ball asked to go off the record to reiterate that the Congolese premier was not only dependable— he was "ours."[23] Though Hammarskjold had warned the Americans about clinging too closely to Adoula, with Gizenga in rebellion and Tshombe still holding out, it was hard to stay neutral. It seemed that the only way to keep the coalition regime intact and to silence the critics was to strengthen Adoula through direct support.

LÉOPOLDVILLE

As early as November 1961, the CIA had begun spending large sums of money to organize popular support for Adoula (particularly with labor and youth groups) and to improve his security apparatus. The agency had brought in several Cubans in exile to fly Congolese Air Force DC-3s.[24] Such assistance was neither supervised nor sanctioned by the UN. Although Secretary Rusk thought this unwise, the CIA Africa Division had been insistent. Due to the strong endorsement of the African Bureau at State, the White House had gone along with the idea.

Reporting from Léopoldville, *The New York Times* correspondent Halberstam thought that Adoula had better watch his step. By becoming too dependent on the Americans, he was losing touch with nationalist sentiment in the Congo. Gullion, to the contrary, believed that it was time for Adoula to get tough. After Kitona in December 1961 he wrote Kennedy that the moderates were now in a "position with UN support to turn on Gizenga to dislocate the plans of the Communist bloc."[25] However much such action frustrated communist designs, it proved to be the beginning of the end for the Adoula coalition.

In late December 1961, Adoula sent ANC units to Orientale to arrest Gizenga and to disband his regime. When fighting broke out between Adoula's forces and those of Gizenga in Stanleyville, Ambassador Stevenson asked Secretary-General Thant to send in UN troops to secure Stanleyville and overthrow Gizenga. Thant could hardly refuse, since the U.S. government had militarily backed the UN December action in Katanga on the condition that UN forces would subsequently help to bring about Gizenga's defeat. The Secretary-General pledged "all possible assistance." UN troops subsequently joined Central Government units in arresting Gizenga and capturing 300 of his gendarmes. The Vice Premier was then flown to Léopoldville under UN guard.[26]

Adoula now faced the ticklish problem of what to do with Gizenga. Despite Gizenga's treasonable activities, the Léopoldville regime still suffered from the stigma of having delivered Lumumba to his executioners. It could not afford another death, even of the "accidental" sort. When Adoula indicated that he might rehabilitate Gizenga, Washington cabled Gullion that "under no circumstances" should Adoula drop the charges.[27] The dilemma, however, remained: jailing Gizenga would give the opposition a rallying point; execution would turn him into another Lumumba.

Moscow was meanwhile getting maximum propaganda mileage out of

Gizenga's imprisonment. On January 24, *Pravda* accused the U.S. of giving Nendaka, the "organizer of the Lumumba murder," a "blank check" to dispose of Gizenga. On January 28, it reported that an assassination conspiracy had been agreed upon. Two of Gizenga's former wives made a well-publicized appeal to Yugoslavia's Tito to save their spouse.[28] Stevenson reported from New York that the Secretary-General was worried that Nendaka might execute Gizenga. Stevenson urged that he be kept alive "because if he were killed the Russians would have a great asset." There was also the prospect that Soviet Ambassador Zorin would call a Security Council meeting on the Congo in order to draw international attention to Gizenga's plight.[29]

The embassy had an idea. Gizenga would be made to "disappear to Cairo." (This was at a time when the agency was believed to be capable of arranging anything.) Adoula reportedly "jumped" at the idea. How was the disappearing act to be accomplished? Washington asked. Gizenga would be transferred to some remote part of the northern Congo, whence he would make his "escape," the embassy replied. Deputy Assistant Secretary Fredericks liked none of this. It evoked a distinctly unpleasant reminiscence. He could just see Gizenga somehow ending up in Munongo's eager hands. "Gizenga's death by violence would have the most unfortunate repercussions . . . We do not want to be tagged with the results," a wary State Department cabled the embassy. The plan was rejected.[30]

At a loss over what to do, Adoula ordered that Gizenga be confined to Mobutu's paracommando camp. Gullion was fearful of a "long Lumumba-like captivity" under Mobutu's brutish and singularly ineffectual authority. He urged Adoula to give Gizenga what little due process was available in the Congo by asking Parliament to remove Gizenga's immunity from prosecution. Adoula refused: it would open up a Pandora's Box since there were grounds for stripping immunity from dozens of others within that body. On January 30 Gizenga was transferred to a prison on the island of Bula-Bemba in the mouth of the River Congo.[31]

The arrest and imprisonment of Gizenga had a paradoxical effect on Adoula's political fortunes. On the one hand, he had finally subdued his most serious rival and had removed the lingering threat that Gizenga posed to the Central Government. On the other hand, Gizenga's imprisonment weakened the coalition regime by reducing its Lumumbist base of support. The government was now heavily weighted in favor of conservative elements, thus eroding its standing in Parliament.

Washington, however, had little interest in the fine points of Congolese politics. The President had his own parliamentary problems. The UN bond bill was off to a shaky start in the Senate Foreign Relations Committee. The Katangese cause was being picked up across the country. To neutralize

hostile commentary, the White House proposed that Adoula be brought to
the U.S. for political display.

With the Gizenga affair barely resolved, UN officials were concerned
about the timing of a visit. Indian Chargé Rahman warned Adoula that
it could prove to be a "fatal error." Gullion dismissed such "Cassandras"
and promised to bring Interior Minister Gbenye along as "insurance."[32]
No sooner did Adoula accept Kennedy's invitation, however, than the
lower house of the Congolese Parliament voted thirty-seven to thirty-seven
on a motion to request the release of Gizenga. This made Rusk very edgy.
Not to worry, Williams assured the Secretary, "Mobutu would be on guard
to prevent any Gizenga coup."[33]

WASHINGTON

The trip was on. Gullion requested that the administration roll out the
red carpet for Adoula, whose "vanity if not excessive is well developed."
Adoula arrived in New York on February 2 and was given a welcome
befitting a Churchill. Stevenson hosted a stag dinner at the Waldorf Astoria
with prominent political, business and foundation figures in attendance.
Mrs. Roosevelt received Adoula at her residence. The Premier was
escorted to high mass at St. Patrick's Cathedral where he and his wife
were blessed by Cardinal Spellman.[34] Such honors, columnist Arthur Krock
thought, proved that Adoula had become "the embodiment of several
reassuring symbols."[35] To keep the visit nonaligned, a brief session with
Soviet Ambassador Zorin was arranged.

In his speech to the General Assembly, Adoula paid tribute to "our
national hero Patrice Lumumba" (the only point at which he received
sustained applause) and criticized Belgium. In Washington, touchy
officials were nettled by a joking reference Adoula made to his "friend
and colleague Antoine [Gizenga]." Gullion warned him about such remarks, particularly since an audience with arch-anticommunist George
Meany had been arranged. Distressed, Adoula said his sarcasm had mis-
carried.[36]

The White House visit was a distinct success. President Kennedy
liked Adoula's candor and his evident familiarity with American history.
Recognizing a painting of Andrew Jackson in a gallery of presidential
portraits in the White House, Adoula remarked to Kennedy how much
he admired Jackson. Impressed, Kennedy quoted Jackson in his toast to
Adoula: "Our federal union; it must be preserved." Kennedy said that the
challenges of the Congo would have overwhelmed "a lesser man, a lesser
Government." Adoula replied that he was no "superman" but only a
common man duty-bound.[37]

Adoula's performance on Capitol Hill won praise from even the most confirmed detractors of the administration's policy. Senator George D. Aiken, no lover of the Congo operation, told Rusk that despite his previous doubts about Adoula, he was now "100 percent behind him."[38] With sentiments such as these ringing in their ears, administration officials put the final touches on their campaign to sell the UN bond bill to Congress the following week.

As a result of the Washington visit, Kennedy and Adoula began a personal correspondence. Two months after the visit, Kennedy would write:

> These three months have been trying for us. I am searching for an agreement to end the armaments race and you are searching for an agreement to reunite your country . . . You may be assured that we will spare no effort in bringing about this end.[39]

Adoula, an intensely emotional man, was buoyed by such messages, while the skeptical Kennedy was reassured about the chances he was taking in the Congo.

The $100 million bond appropriation to maintain the peacekeeping operation was pending before Congress. The fanfare of the Adoula visit was calculated to raise the right issues in the minds of key congressmen. In the meantime, Tshombe had devised his own strategy to encircle Congress with an outraged American public. He too would come to the United States. There would be interviews, rallies, and speeches sponsored by the American Committee for Aid to Katanga Freedom Fighters. When Tshombe went public with his request for a visa to visit the U.S., the White House decided to postpone action on the bond bill.[40]

With a *Time* cover story under his belt, Tshombe had no problem procuring invitations from *Meet the Press* and the National Press Club. His American agent, Michel Struelens, had already scheduled a mass rally at Madison Square Garden. Tshombe would share the stage with American presidential aspirant Barry M. Goldwater. "If Katanga can hold out till '64," a Goldwater aide told Struelens, "that could be our issue against Kennedy."[41] Fellow Democrat Dodd did not help the President and his bond bill when he formally invited Tshombe to testify before his Senate Subcommittee. To make matters worse, Adoula announced that he would be visiting the Soviet Union the following summer.

All of this must have pleased Kennedy's old family friend Arthur Krock, who correctly sensed a growing split within the administration over the merits of admitting Tshombe. Governor Williams ran up the red flag. Tshombe's presence in the U.S. "would play into the hands of the Communists," he argued, by undercutting Adoula.[42] Gullion's objection was more compelling. The central government would consider the admission of Tshombe "a calculated and offensive trick . . . an unfriendly gesture."[43] Stevenson concurred.

Legal adviser Abram Chayes did not. He argued that screening foreign visitors for political reasons violated free speech. Senator Lausche seemed to have the same general idea in mind when he asked Williams: "If Khrushchev's son-in-law Adzuhbei got a visa to visit the U.S., why couldn't Tshombe?"[44] The American Civil Liberties Union found a rare ally in the Young Americans for Freedom, which had sued in federal court for an injunction to prevent the State Department's denying Tshombe a visa.[45]

Gullion and several State Department officials went to see the President in the first week of February 1962 about the visa question. Kennedy asked if he had to give Tshombe a visa. Chayes said no. "Then I won't," Kennedy concluded.[46] The State Department subsequently announced that "temporarily" Tshombe would be given no visa since he had no Congolese passport. Tshombe was "enraged" and railed against the State Department, which he said was in the grip of "voracious financiers" seeking control of Katanga's riches. A month later Gullion reported that Tshombe was still in a state of "virtual frenzy" over being denied the visa.[47]

The President took a good deal of heat at home. Krock accused the administration of "evasion" and denying Tshombe his right to be heard. Kennedy subsequently offered a deal to his father's old friend, who was a mainstay of the Metropolitan Club, notorious for its continued exclusion of blacks: "I'll give Tshombe a visa and Arthur can give him dinner at the Metropolitan Club."[48]

Unfortunately for the UN bond bill, the visa denial did nothing to lower the temperature of public opinion. Michel Struelens was getting national attention with a countercampaign to liberate Katanga. The administration decided to postpone the introduction of the bond bill until Struelens could be silenced.

Struelens reported $240,000 as foreign agent expenditures between 1960 and 1962. In addition to this, the Katangese were funneling money into the U.S. and other Western countries from a small Swiss bank they had purchased in Geneva.[49] The Committee of One Million (originally formed to prevent U.S. recognition of the People's Republic of China) took up Katanga's cause, as did the John Birch Society. Although former President Eisenhower, ever the good soldier, supported his successor, other prominent Republicans jumped on the Katanga bandwagon. Richard Nixon dismissed the UN bond issue as "a carelessly designed financial scheme" and Herbert Hoover lent his name to pro-Katanga statements.[50]

Struelens ran ads in everything from *The New York Times* to black radio stations, depicting Katanga as the assailed David holding out against the assembled UN giant. The State Department played along in witless fashion by expressing "deep concern" about Struelens's "string of myths" and generally assisting the Belgian in his search for copy. The *Chicago Daily News* suggested, "[I]f one Belgian press man can outwit the combined brains of the whole corps of State Department publicists—including Rowan—Uncle Sam had better hire the Belgian and fire the Washington crew."[51]

The department did not learn quickly. Upon hearing rumors that Struelens was involved in an attempt to buy Costa Rican diplomatic recognition for Katanga, a department spokesman announced that these were grounds for his deportation. Unfortunately, the FBI's investigation into the alleged bribery attempt was inconclusive. When Dodd got wind of this bit of news, he scheduled a hearing on the affair. Ball disgustedly told Assistant Secretary of State for Congressional Affairs Fred Dutton that the department had been "very stupid . . . we will look sick because we have nothing on this fellow."[52]

When he was not sowing discontent in the U.S., Struelens was sending tendentious advice to Tshombe. He repeatedly enjoined Tshombe to avoid any commitments in his continuing talks with Adoula, to sign nothing, and to hold out until the Americans gave up on the UN.[53] Belgian Foreign Minister Spaak informed Washington that Tshombe would never take U.S. policy seriously unless Struelens were expelled. When the administration pointed out that under American law Struelens had committed no crime, Spaak responded that under Belgian law neither had Union Minière. How could the U.S. expect the Belgian government to take a tough stand against one of its largest companies, he asked, when the U.S. government refused to move against one noisy Belgian with a guest visa?[54]

Since deportation on political grounds was out of the question, the administration went digging for a little dirt. Attorney General Robert F. Kennedy authorized the FBI to tap Struelens's telephone.[55] State Department officials received daily reports of his communications with Tshombe. On at least one occasion, FBI agents broke into his office on Park Avenue. Struelens registered protests about FBI harassment with Senator Dodd.[56]

The administration's purpose in doing "a little discreet surveillance" was to compile enough evidence that Struelens had violated the rules governing his foreign-agent status so as to deport him. The FBI believed that it had uncovered sufficient material to do so by August 1962, but since the collection of the evidence had an unconstitutional coloration, the White House chose to shelve it. Struelens, it was decided, would be "kept on ice" until the bond bill cleared Congress. Then he would be "thrown out" of the country.[57]

The White House strategy on the bond bill was to sneak it through Congress. "Do you think we could get a quorum on Easter morning?" Kennedy dryly asked Ball.[58] Low profile was the order of the day. The UN was told to stay out of the news. Under Secretary-General Ralph Bunche assured Stevenson that even if the Katangese threw up roadblocks around UN positions, there would be no military response. Governor Williams was advised to lie low on the administration's Portuguese Africa policy. After appearances on the hill by Cleveland and Stevenson to promote the bond bill, Bundy reported the prevailing reaction as, "We love the UN, the Administration, but we don't love the way Harlan and Adlai talk to us." Cleveland and Stevenson subsequently left town and spent the duration of the week in New York.[59]

The soft sell did nothing to pacify the Republican opposition and may have cost the administration critical support from Democratic friends. In a major speech, Senate Majority Leader Mike Mansfield blasted the administration for its attachment to the UN, which he described as a center that exacerbated international problems instead of solving them. Senator Henry (Scoop) Jackson started a running fight with Stevenson over the UN's "disproportionate" role in U.S. foreign policy.[60] Even Walter Lippmann felt pessimistic enough to title his March 27 column, "The Sickness of the UN."[61]

Divisions within the administration over the wisdom of bailing out the UN weakened congressional support in the President's own party. Vice President Lyndon Johnson, whose disdain for the UN would surface later, "silently admired" Tshombe and was of no help on the bond bill.[62] Treasury Secretary Douglas Dillon, who had no use for the administration's Congo policy in any case, informed Cleveland that the UN's financial practices were profligate and indefensible. After a Congo meeting in the White House, Ball felt constrained to take Dillon aside for an "unhappy little talk" about the basics of Congo policy.[63]

With such discontent in the ranks, it was not surprising that the bond bill barely lurched through the Senate suffering dismemberment along the way. The Foreign Relations Committee decided that only $25 million would be purchased outright instead of $100 million; the rest would be purchased on a matching basis with annual payments of interest and principal deducted from regular U.S. contributions to the UN. As for the manner in which the amended bill was reported to the entire Senate, columnist Rowland Evans likened it to a "crash-landing." The President was forced to make a series of calls at the eleventh hour—particularly one to Senator George D. Aiken—to save the bill from defeat on the floor. After Senate passage, Kennedy observed that the entire experience was a classic exercise in how not to deal with Congress.[64]

The approach used in the House was more assiduous. During committee hearings the bill was widely endorsed and was reported out of committee only when assured of passage on the floor. The full House adopted the bill by a vote of 257 to 134. Despite the detours and the mangled nature of the final product, passage of the UN bond bill was the President's finest foreign policy victory on Capitol Hill to date. Elsewhere in the Western world, the bond issue fared less well, but the Americans had done their part.

ELISABETHVILLE

Tshombe was biding his time in Elisabethville. He knew that the UN was still in serious financial trouble and that the Europeans were still opposed to the UN operation. The whole drama surrounding the passage of the bond bill had revealed to him the fact of American hesitancy. Tshombe was playing a waiting game. To keep the UN army at bay, he had permitted negotiations with the central government to continue. Whenever there had been the slightest prospect of a firm agreement, however, he had resorted to his usual tricks—feigning sickness to avoid meeting Adoula, or resurrecting his claim of legal incapacity to bind his government.[65]

The entire charade had only confirmed what Gullion had long since concluded and what O'Brien had described so tellingly—that Tshombe's word was worthless:

Neither statements of fact nor written engagements could be relied on; no contradiction, no detected lie, caused Mr. Tshombe the slightest embarrassment. If caught out in some piece of duplicity—on political prisoners, refugees, mercenaries or anything else—he would show absent-mindedness tinged, I sometimes imagined, with a personal compassion for the naivete of anyone who supposed he would tell the truth, if he could derive the slightest advantage from telling anything else.[66]

Seven months of stalling had given the secessionists needed time to build up their military forces. By mid-summer 1962, Tshombe had equipped his gendarmes with new weaponry and had added nine aircraft (including three jets) to his air force. Munongo had assembled a contingent of 400 white mercenaries.[67] Katanga was again ready for war.

Adoula was meanwhile in desperate shape politically. His opponents in Léopoldville accused him of being an American puppet for refusing to invade Katanga. His purge of the Lumumbists in March 1962 had backfired badly. The Parliament, still a bastion of Lumumbism, had almost forced the Premier from office. Gullion's constant ministrations and Kennedy's personal messages were losing their effect. In a scene reminiscent of Lumumba's break with the UN, Adoula informed UN officials that either the UN agreed to use its planes to transport his troops to North Katanga, or it would be expelled.[68]

The State Department's Bureau of Intelligence and Research (INR) estimated that an attempted ANC invasion of Katanga would result in "No decisive military solution . . . but rather a civil war of uncertain duration and certain destructiveness." There would be a complete relapse into anarchy and another prime opportunity for the Soviet Union to intervene.[69]

The celebration of Katanga's second anniversary of independence in July 1962 put the match to the fuse. Tshombe moved 2,000 of his gendarmes into the center of Elisabethville to march in the independence day parade. The UN set up a checkpoint on the outskirts of Elisabethville to monitor the marching troops. During the military parade, Munongo sent a mob of 10,000 Katangese women and children armed with broomsticks to storm the UN checkpoint. At first, the Indian major of the Rajputana Rifles offered tea to the women. Then, upon seeing his troops being pounded with brooms, he observed: "They are doing to us exactly what we did to the British." He finally decided to order his troops to retaliate; a short time later, one woman and two children lay dead.[70]

Munongo called for war and UN tanks began patrolling downtown Elisabethville. There was a volley of accusations and counteraccusations between the UN and the Katangese. Spaak sent word to the Belgian consul in Elisabethville to prepare immediately for the evacuation of all Belgian women and children. President Kennedy described the situation at a news conference as "very, very serious."[71]

SANCTIONS AND SECOND THOUGHTS

The President conferred the next day with Gullion, Cleveland, and Williams. Gullion reported that unless something drastic were done about Katanga, Mobutu might attempt a military coup to prevent the Lumumbists from seizing power. Cleveland and Williams recommended that the administration draft a proposal for a graduated series of economic and political sanctions on Katanga to be considered by the UN.[72] They argued that, without sanctions, there was no hope for a negotiated solution.

Kennedy approved a sanctions program and Stevenson subsequently went to see Thant and Bunche to brief them on the U.S. "Proposal for National Reconciliation." Under its terms, Tshombe would be given ten days in which to undertake irreversible commitments to re-unify Katanga. If he rejected the proposal or delayed in its implementation, he would face an international boycott followed by an economic blockade.[73] The Secretary-General agreed to put the UN's imprimatur on the proposal, which came to be referred to as the "U Thant Plan." The administration then approached Spaak in confidence and secured his endorsement of the effort.

Confronted with a joint Belgian-American endorsement, the British government fell into line. Lord Home informed Washington that although he considered sanctions to be a "profound mistake," he would "press Tshombe hard" to accept the U Thant Plan. By August 28, all of the Atlantic allies except France had signed on to the plan, which had already been strongly approved by the African and Asian Congo Advisory Council. *Pravda*, of course, labeled this the "collusion of gangsters," but it was the first time in two years of UN peacekeeping that the leading states of the West and the moderate states of Asia and Africa had been in agreement on Congo policy.[74]

Elisabethville's reaction was predictably defiant: *"Le Plan U Thant a du Bluff!"* declared the *Echo du Katanga*.[75] Tshombe barely bothered to acknowledge the existence of the plan, and with good reason. The CIA reported that, with 20 aircraft and 500 mercenaries, the Katangese were fully capable of launching a surprise attack against the UN. By late September, they had completed work on new runways, camouflaged aircraft shelters, and underground fuel tanks.[76]

Within a month of the promulgation of the plan, the British began to back away from the idea of sanctions. They were convinced that Tshombe would fight before giving in, and that war could spread to Rhodesia. Lord Home flew to Washington in late September to inform the Americans that Britain wanted out. In a meeting with Home, Kennedy pointed out that only a unified West could "shove" Tshombe into an agreement. Home replied that the British government would not support forceful action, repeating a line that Americans had heard before: "Welensky might be driven to some folly of his own. He might reach an armed merger with Tshombe."[77]

Kennedy was furious. When he heard that Home had told Tshombe that the British would never support sanctions against Katanga, he ordered Assistant Secretary of State William R. Tyler to summon Ambassador Ormsby Gore and to "chew him out"—unprecedented treatment for the President's friend and close collaborator.[78] Ball observed that Home was not really being difficult: "All he wants to do is to mobilize America behind *his* foreign policy." (emphasis Ball's.)[79]

The truth was, however, that the Kennedy administration was having second thoughts about its own policy. The President feared that sanctions would only stiffen Katangese resistance, particularly given the British retreat. With the midterm congressional elections coming up, Kennedy's foreign policy men—Bundy, Kaysen, Dungan, and Schlesinger—saw a political tar baby in the making. Every country was entitled to its own War of the Roses, Schlesinger recalled someone as saying.[80]

Roger Hilsman, the director of INR and a man whose judgment the President trusted, submitted a skeptical estimate of the "intense and risky pressures" contemplated under the plan. Katanga was only one of the many existing threats to Congolese unity, he argued.[81] Ralph Dungan (in all probability speaking for the President) called Ball and advised him to freeze movement on the sanctions plan. He told him to instruct the African Bureau, and particularly "Soapy" Williams, to restrain themselves: "Every damn time I pick up the paper I see one more step taken . . ."[82]

A highly critical account of the UN Katanga operation entitled *Rebels, Mercenaries, and Dividends* soon became required reading at the White House. Its author, Smith Hempstone, was the African correspondent for the *Chicago Daily News* and a self-described Republican who had voted for Kennedy in 1960, thus sharing that dual affiliation with McGeorge Bundy and Robert McNamara. The book carried a simple message: that Katanga had always functioned as a separate state—both before and after the advent of the white man.[83]

Tshombe's Belgian advisers sensed American discomfort and drafted a letter from Tshombe to President Eisenhower (meant, of course, for his successor) setting forth a detailed defense of Katangese autonomy. Tshombe wrote that any solution had to take into account the basic fact that the Congo was a large and backward country whose inhabitants were illiterate and attached before all else to their tribes. He wondered whether this was adequately appreciated by outsiders: "Perhaps the diplomatic offices—concerned before everything else with international political balances and power relations—have not sufficiently considered the psychological base of authority in the African milieu."[84] The real dispute, Tshombe argued, was not between Léopoldville and Elisabethville, but between Léopoldville and the rest of the Congo. As heir to the colonial regime, the central government wanted a centralist system. But the fact was that it simply could not govern, no matter who was in power.

As if to confirm Tshombe's point, there were reports that Adoula was again in danger of being cast out of power by the Lumumbists. The premier was stalling on negotiations with Tshombe for a new constitution because the price of compromise on Katanga would be his head in Parliament. Ball was discouraged. Adoula had "fallen apart on us." Maybe

Tshombe was right—no one could govern the Congo.[85] Kennedy circulated Halberstam's final dispatch from the Congo:

> What has been decisively and incontestably proved in the Congo over the last 25 months—at the estimated price of $10,000,000 a month—is that if the Congo problem is given enough time and cash and effort and thought, it will not go away . . . Similarly, there are corollary rules: Moise Tshombe, if given enough time, will demand more time . . .[86]

Frustration with other crises in the Third World during the summer of 1962 had only added to the administration's doubts about U.S. policy in the Congo. Cuba was heating up again. Five thousand Soviet specialists on the island were engaged in a form of military construction that the CIA could only characterize as "something new and different." The Alliance for Progress, Kennedy's multimillion dollar aid partnership with the states of Latin America, barely begun, was already showing signs of strain. In July 1962, the Peruvian military seized power and Washington promptly suspended diplomatic relations. About Vietnam, Kennedy was troubled more often than not. Despite roseate reports from his subordinates ("Every quantitative measure we have," Secretary McNamara reported after a trip to Vietnam, "shows we're winning this war."), he had no confidence in a military solution.[87]

At Congo meetings, the President also expressed continuing doubts about the advisability of using military force to end the secession. Because of India's border war with China, there was now the possibility that India would withdraw its Congo contingent—the largest in the operation. The President wondered how the UN army could still be a credible fighting force if this were to happen.[88]

There were also doubts about the UN's political aptitude. Ball thought that the proposed 220-article federal constitution for the Congo drafted by UN legal experts was the height of absurdity. The U.S. Constitution had only 15 articles, he observed. The idea that a "primitive state" should have 220 was unthinkable. The State Department's legal adviser, Abram Chayes, attributed the document's length to the instincts of the UN's civil legists "who couldn't think of anything less than 500 pages as involving a binding obligation." Chayes predicted that Tshombe could negotiate for fifty years without ever showing bad faith.[89] This, of course, was exactly what Tshombe and his advisers had in mind.

When Tshombe sent word from Geneva asking to meet secretly with Harriman, Kennedy was in favor of postponing the sanctions plan altogether and trying another round of American mediation. Both Harriman and Ball could meet with Tshombe, the President mused, one for love and the other for truce.[90] The African Bureau loudly objected to the idea and it was dropped.

The President was clearly toying with the idea of pulling out, but nothing more. U.S. involvement in the UN operation was deep and long standing. After Kitona, Kennedy's international prestige was tied to the process of negotiating a settlement. On Capitol Hill, the President had fought for six months to get his bond bill passed. In Europe, he had made repeated personal efforts to prevail on the allies to stay hitched. These were not the sort of commitments that could be quickly or easily undone. But Kennedy—the consummate pragmatist as always—did want a way out of the Congo if disaster struck. George Ball was ready to find one.

Ball's idea was to find a constitutional solution that would create a loose Congolese confederation in which Adoula would be preserved and Tshombe would be allowed to play a national role. To achieve this, he told Bundy, there would have to be "direct [American] mediation by a new set of people."[91] What this meant in simple fact was disengagement by the United States.

The Under Secretary had his work cut out for him in trying to derail established policy. For administration liberals like Stevenson, Bowles, and Williams, backing the UN in the Congo was an article of faith. They considered Congo policy their domain—the one area of foreign policy where their influence with the President was determinative. Bowles's demotion the previous November had only sharpened this feeling. In pushing for disengagement, Ball faced a compelling political fact: Stevenson, Bowles, and Williams were all former governors of major states. If they elected to go public with contrary views, matters could become messy. The President could not permit the alienation of his liberal wing. The White House accordingly made it clear that Ball could proceed with his dissent, but that the burden of proof was his.[92]

Ball knew that a major change in Congo policy was impossible so long as Gullion's position remained unchallenged. Given the ambassador's relationship with the President, no one, not even the Secretary of State, had ever been able to stop Gullion from getting his way. Among senior administration officials, Gullion was an unpopular man. Harriman, for one, took exception to his highhanded manner of dealing with men who were supposed to be his superiors. In conversations with the White House staff, Ball began lining up opponents to Gullion. The ambassador, he announced to Kaysen, was acting "hysterically." Gullion's determination to subdue Katanga had taken on the quality of a "religious war," with Tshombe in the role of the "anti-Christ."[93]

Ball then moved to shake up Williams's African Bureau—the bastion of the pro-UN policy. He instructed Williams to replace that "totally negative" Congo desk officer, Frank Carlucci, as well as the "fanatical" Sheldon Vance, who headed the Office of Central African Affairs.[94]

Williams reluctantly complied by transferring Vance, but brought in an even more formidable person to replace him, G. McMurtrie Godley, Gullion's deputy chief of mission in Léopoldville. Godley was a bear-sized man of prodigious energy who had a habit of speaking his mind. He was the man who had enjoined the nervous Rusk during the Louvanium Conference to calm down and live with the results.[95] Bundy thought him "unruly" but Williams got his way. Carlucci—a small man of pokerfaced demeanor—remained as desk officer, despite Ball's order. While Williams swung a pro-UN broadsword in speeches throughtout the country, his deputy Wayne Fredericks did the épée work on the inside. When Rusk began suggesting that there was a need to reconsider Congo commitments, Fredericks sharply informed him: "If we don't have a Congo policy, we don't have an African policy."[96]

The seventh floor of the State Department soon faced an insurgency of sorts from the fourth floor. Along with two other young Foreign Service Officers, Charles Whitehouse and Alan Ford, Carlucci drafted weekly "horror papers" depicting the apocalypse facing the U.S. in the Congo if the UN operation failed. Ball angrily described these effusions as "a lot of mush." He told Bundy that the attitude in the African Bureau was that "we have to play the major role in every effort, we have to beautify the greens . . ."[97] Ball instructed Williams that henceforth every Capitol Hill briefing and every press communication had to be cleared upstairs. At one point, the Under Secretary vowed that he never wanted to see any two of the "Godley gang" serving again in the same place at the same time. (None of them ever did, but something of their singleminded spirit remained. As ambassador in Lisbon in 1974, Carlucci faced down Secretary of State Kissinger over the issue of U.S. covert intervention in the Portuguese turmoil. Mac Godley had meanwhile moved off to another front and was running the CIA's secret war in Laos.)

With Stevenson and Bowles alerted and the African Bureau mobilized against him, Ball faced an uphill battle even though he had the sympathy of the White House. What he needed was a devil's advocate, someone from the field with sufficient standing and enough hard evidence to say that our policy was wrong, that Gullion was obsessed with the eradication of Tshombe, that there was a way out.

The U.S. consul in Elisabethville, Lewis Hoffacker, had always harbored doubts about the UN campaign against Tshombe. He had witnessed the atrocities committed by both sides, and was deeply opposed to a military solution. After expressing strong reservations about the hard line, Hoffacker was pulled out of Elisabethville by Gullion and "buried" in Léopoldville.[98] Somehow Kennedy got wind of the transfer (possibly he had been tipped off by Dodd) and telephoned Ball to ask why Hoffacker

had been removed from Elisabethville. Ball investigated and, after deter-
mining what happened, ordered Hoffacker home.[99] The prosecutor had
found his star witness.

Ball arranged for Hoffacker to meet with the key men in the administration—McGhee, Dungan, Kaysen, and finally the President himself. No
record was made of the meetings but it can be presumed that Hoffacker
repeated the critique he had made earlier: American diplomacy had not
been even-handed; Gullion had treated Tshombe roughly at Kitona and
Tshombe's hatred for Gullion was now almost pathological; Gullion was
so committed to keeping Adoula in power (an objective that necessitated
bringing Katanga to its knees) that he blocked the making of concessions
to Tshombe.[100]

Hoffacker's listeners were impressed. No peacenik, he was a decorated
veteran of World War II and had shown extraordinary courage and restraint in the volatile atmosphere in Elisabethville. Ball tried to keep the
lid on the entire exercise in order to protect Hoffacker's career, which,
he feared, might be destroyed for his having gone over the heads of his
immediate superiors.[101]

The President wanted Senator Dodd to help the administration restore
relations with Tshombe. He invited the senator over to the Oval Office.
At the meeting, Kennedy gently alluded to "some people spending a lot of
money." That was encouragement enough for Dodd, who then agreed to
put his signature to a letter urging Tshombe to re-integrate without delay
and emphasizing that President Kennedy did not want to destroy him.
Hoffacker was charged with hand-delivering Dodd's letter to Tshombe.[102]

Gullion wanted none of it. He remarked that his whole effort was about
to be "perverted" by the administration's attempt to appease Dodd and
Tshombe. The ambassador's new man in Elisabethville, Jonathan Dean,
tried to stop Hoffacker from delivering Dodd's letter to Tshombe. Hearing
this, Rusk summoned Godley and stiffly enquired: "Does our ambassador
understand our policy?" "What do you think?" Godley replied.[103]

The African Bureau then went for its trump card—Gullion's relationship with Kennedy. The ambassador telephoned Ball via the military short
wave hook-up: the Hoffacker mission was "inappropriate" unless the
President had personally concurred in it.[104] Ball tried to be conciliatory:
"We are not trying to dictate policy. We do feel that he [Hoffacker] can
bring to you a sense of the situation here . . ." Gullion was insistent: the
President had to concur or the mission was inappropriate. There was no
need for the President's concurrence, Ball replied. It was his suggestion.
Ball then moved in for the "policy kill." He next proposed that the
President send a special emissary to the Congo—someone "cold and tough-

Secretary of State Dean Rusk

Under Secretary of State for Political
Affairs W. Averell Harriman

Assistant Secretary of State for
African Affairs G. Mennen Williams

Deputy Assistant Secretary of State
for African Affairs Wayne Fredericks

Attorney General Robert F. Kennedy

National Security Advisor
McGeorge Bundy

Senator Thomas Dodd.
Hartford Courant

U.S. Ambassador to the United
Nations Adlai Stevenson.
United Nations Photo

Prime Minister Patrice Lumumba and Secretary-General Dag
Hammarskjöld in New York, September 5, 1960. *United Nations Photo*

Ambassador Gullion and Premier Adoula with secessionist Moise
Tshombe in the middle, at the Kitona Conference, December 20, 1961.
United Nations Photo

JFK welcomes Congolese Premier Adoula to the White House,
February 5, 1962. *John F. Kennedy Library*

Tanganyikan President Julius Nyerere on a state visit, July 15, 1963.
John F. Kennedy Library

JFK and Harold Macmillan, Prime Minister of Great Britain,
April 5, 1961. *John F. Kennedy Library*

JFK bids goodbye to Belgian Foreign Minister Paul-Henri Spaak
after their discussion on the Congo, November 27, 1962.
John F. Kennedy Library

General Mobutu visits the Oval Office, May 31, 1963.
John F. Kennedy Library

JFK waiting to address the United Nations General Assembly shortly
after the death of Hammarskjöld, September 25, 1961.

John F. Kennedy Library

United Nations forces fire on Katangese mercenaries during
December 1961 fighting. *United Nations Photo*

Premier Antonio de Oliveira Salazar of Portugal, 1964.
United Press International Photo

Ambassador Mahoney asks Nkrumah to refuse refueling rights in Ghana for Soviet bombers during the Cuban Missile Crisis, October 30, 1962.

JFK and Under Secretary George Ball at a Cabinet meeting.

Alberto Franco Nogueira and JFK meeting during the Cuban Missile Crisis, October 24, 1962.

minded" to put Gullion in his place. "We are going downhill very fast," he warned the President.

Kennedy was worried about the prospect of a foreign policy fiasco on the eve of the congressional elections: "If there is a setback by Adoula, the UN, or the beginning of military action, it would come as a shock, and no one will understand what we have been doing."[105] Senator Dodd, temporarily back in the White House's good graces after his letter to Tshombe, recommended that the President send Under Secretary of State for Political Affairs George C. McGhee to the Congo to review the situation. McGhee was favorably regarded by the Katangese after he had publicly scolded Governor Williams for berating Katanga's propaganda campaign in the U.S.

The choice of McGhee was expedient for everyone in Washington. For the President, the McGhee mission could prepare the public for what he described as the "grim eventualities that may be coming up." It could bolster the administration's claim that it had explored every possibility for peaceful re-integration. The Belgian Embassy in Washington noted that in the past Kennedy had used the Texas millionaire to sell administration policy to right-wing Democrats.[106] For Ball, the mission would "cut Gullion down to size" and shift U.S. policy in the direction of disengagement. Senator Dodd saw similar possibilities.

THE McGHEE MISSION

In late September 1962, Under Secretary McGhee left for the Congo. From the UN's standpoint, his arrival could not have come at a worse time. The Katangese had shot down a UN reconnaissance plane the week before. Two days prior to McGhee's arrival, a UN soldier had stepped on a land mine planted near the Elisabethville airport, leaving two dead and four wounded.

When McGhee's plane touched down at Elisabethville airport, a broadly grinning Tshombe was waiting to greet him. There could be little doubt that the U Thant Plan was finished. Gullion's credibility with both Adoula and Tshombe was also seriously undermined; Tshombe used the visit to insult Gullion publicly. A large banner over the motorcade route through downtown Elisabethville declared:

WELCOME MR. McGHEE
A BAS GULLION ENNEMI DU KATANGA
(Down With Gullion Enemy of Katanga)

In his toast to McGhee at the welcoming banquet, Tshombe noted: *"Je crâche dans le visage du raciste Gullion."* (I spit in the face of the racist

Gullion.) McGhee made no attempt to defend the ambassador, fearing that this would jeopardize the success of his trip. Gullion was deeply stung.[107]

McGhee told Tshombe at their first meeting that President Kennedy "recognizes your leader qualities . . . and wants you to face a larger stage." The communists were trying to intervene again in the Congo and start a civil war, he warned. Tshombe then delivered the tried and true litany of his own struggle against communism. It was he who had subscribed to Bishop Booth's warning in 1946 at a Methodist conference that Africa was ripe for communist infiltration. It was he who had warned a doubting State Department that Lumumba was a communist. It was he who had called for a federal constitution two years before independence. For all this, he had been abused and his country subjected to violence. Anticommunist America had marked a proven anticommunist leader for destruction. Meanwhile, Adoula was opening the door to the communists by inviting Ghana and Egypt to send troops to the Congo. "Remember what I tell you," Tshombe declared to McGhee, "you Americans are working for the establishment of communism."[108]

McGhee was impressed. You are the "father of federalism," he told Tshombe. Tshombe conceded that this could be so and compared himself to Lincoln. McGhee joked that it was obvious that "President Tshombe" could prevail easily over President Kasavubu in a political race. Regarding his relationship with Union Minière, Tshombe blithely declared that he received no favors from the company and was in no way obligated to it. McGhee reported to Washington, "This is generally confirmed here."

Tshombe had made another convert. He showed McGhee a "most confidential" document signed by himself and Vital Moanda, president of Kongo Central Province, dated August 1962, in which the two leaders agreed to a federal constitution. McGhee sent this along to Secretary Rusk as "proof" of Tshombe's influence and intentions. Gullion hotly denounced the document as "self-incriminating," proof of Tshombe's "clandestine intrigue" to set up a series of "tribal fiefs" in order to take over the Congo.[109]

Ball, who must have been gratified to see Gullion on the defensive, added insult to injury by dismissing the ambassador's contention of a subversive plot. Tshombe's deal represented "diligence but not necessarily venality," he advised Gullion. The Founding Fathers had done the same thing in Philadelphia in 1787. Bribery by Tshombe was not a "totally unfamiliar phenomenon of political life even in the more evolved areas of the world."[110]

McGhee did obtain several promises from Tshombe during his visit, but they all proved evanescent. Tshombe had pledged to make a symbolic payment of $2 million in foreign exchange to the central government, but subsequently refused to pay up. The Lublilash bridge was reopened as promised and Katanga shipped two carloads of copper to Matadi, but refused to make further shipments. The "standstill" agreement for a cease-fire in North Katanga, which McGhee had been instrumental in bringing about, broke down in mid-October when mercenary-flown Katangese planes bombed ANC forces.[111]

What few concessions McGhee obtained were far outweighed by Tshombe's conclusion that the Americans were giving up. He played up the victory for all it was worth. He wrote McGhee on October 24, taking credit for having bailed out President Kennedy politically by agreeing to receive his special emissary. Tshombe said that he understood the "grave divergencies of view which divide American opinion" and "how desirous President Kennedy had been to avoid military action . . . against Katanga during the period of American elections." Since Katanga had made such efforts "against its own interests," it wanted formal assurances of support from the United States. Consul Dean termed the letter impudent and suggested that someone had better disabuse Tshombe of his delusions.[112] It was, of course, too late.

The central government, shocked by what appeared to be the abrupt change in American policy, prepared for war. Adoula met with Soviet Ambassador Nemchina to discuss possible Russian assistance in an invasion of Katanga. The UN leadership was contemptuous of the McGhee mission and devised its own plan for military operations against Katanga.[113]

Gullion and his staff worked desperately to discourage the Congolese from accepting the Soviet offer. By late October, the ambassador had reached a point of physical exhaustion but, sensing the disengagement drift in Washington, asked to come home. The seventh floor vetoed the request and gave Williams the responsibility of so informing Gullion.[114]

It was time for "harsh decisions," Schlesinger wrote the President on October 14. U Thant wanted action—probably a military show of force—and his political survival as Secretary-General seemed to depend on it. The State Department was split: the Williams faction supported the UN; the Ball faction wanted out.[115] There could be no doubt that Kennedy was leaning toward disengagement. But on the very evening the President received Schlesinger's memorandum, the CIA informed Bundy of an incredible discovery—Soviet missiles in Cuba. For the next two weeks, the attention of the President and his men was riveted on this most dangerous crisis. All other matters were deferred.

By the time the missile crisis was resolved in late October, Katanga was near war. A UN-Katangese clash on November 2 left two Katangese policemen dead and three wounded. Tshombe blocked a shipment of $1 million worth of UN fuel and supplies, much of which was later pillaged by the gendarmerie. The UN ordered its pilots to repel mercenary-flown bombing squadrons in north Katanga. Then came the most serious development: Nehru indicated that he might be forced to withdraw his entire 5,700-man contingent from the Congo to meet the Chinese threat on India's border.

Responding to this news, the President wrote to Rusk on November 5: "I wish you and George Ball would take a long look as to where we are in the Congo. If the UN effort is going to collapse we should work out some alternatives."[116]

DISENGAGEMENT OR INTERVENTION?

The next day the African Bureau sent the White House a contingency paper, which Rusk qualified with the notation that it did not necessarily represent his final view. There was no mention in the paper of the possible "paths of withdrawal" that the President had requested. The paper instead recommended a series of forceful actions: an airlift of UN troops and weaponry by USAF planes to Elisabethville, full freedom of movement of UN forces in Katanga, the possible dispatch of U.S. fighter aircraft, and the immediate bolstering of the Adoula regime through economic aid and a military training program.[117]

The President took strong exception to the whole thrust of the African Bureau proposal. He said that he did not believe that building up the UN and the Adoula government militarily would cause Tshombe to renounce the secession. Nor did he think that the U.S. could depend on the UN army, given India's threatened withdrawal.[118] The Tunisian contingent was also a question mark, since the Katangese were holding several Tunisian soldiers captive until the entire contingent was repatriated. American military intelligence in the Congo rated the attitude of the UN military commanders as "static, non-flexible, and over-confident."[119] Like many others in Washington, the President doubted that the UN army of 9,625 in Katanga could defeat Tshombe's mercenary-led force of 18,000.

At a White House meeting, Williams charged that the administration had failed to live up to its commitment to support the U Thant Plan. Kennedy brushed this contention aside: ". . . our performance was better than [that of] any European, that we were doing what we could do, and that the problem was that we simply could not carry the whole burden of forcing on Tshombe the settlement that Adoula desired."[120]

Adoula was still in desperate political straits. The Lumumbist (MNC/L) bloc in Parliament was intent on removing the Premier, either constitutionally or otherwise. On November 21, in the wake of strikes and unrest, the government declared martial law over the capital. Four members of Parliament were arrested, including Adoula's own former

Interior Minister, Christophe Gbenye. American intelligence reported that Adoula, with Mobutu's and Nendaka's support, was prepared to disband Parliament and to govern with emergency powers granted by President Kasavubu.

While this action might forestall a radical government from taking power and keep the Russians at arms length, it also carried the risk of further discrediting Adoula in the eyes of the Afro-Asians, whose troops were critical to the operation. Gullion maintained that the only way to preserve Adoula democratically, (i.e., in Parliament) would be to overwhelm Tshombe immediately. To hammer this message home to administration officials, Gullion flew to Washington in mid-November for consultations.

Before Gullion could return to Léopoldville, the Chambre de Députés (the lower house of Parliament) met and presented a motion of censure against Adoula. With the vote still pending, Gullion flew back to his post. To appease the Lumumbists, Adoula released Gbenye and three other members of Parliament from prison a few days before the vote.[121]

Belgian Foreign Minister Spaak and President Kennedy discussed Adoula's dire situation on November 27 and agreed upon a joint communiqué saying that "voluntary discussion and action" had not worked and that Katanga faced "severe economic measures" if progress toward re-unification were not made within "a very short time."[122]

Coming from Kennedy, the statement was surprising, given his skepticism about economic sanctions. Coming from Spaak, however, it was extraordinary, as Belgian public reaction subsequently indicated. The following day, Belgian settlers, shouting "Spaak assassin," stoned their own consulate in Elisabethville. Ambassador MacArthur reported from Brussels that the government might not last the month of December. But Spaak would not back down. On December 11, the Belgian Foreign Minister called Tshombe a "rebel" and said that he was prepared to support the UN even if it resorted to armed force to end Katanga's secession. Kennedy was deeply impressed by Spaak's willingness to put his political survival on the line and ordered a complete reassessment of his own policy.[123]

The President was looking principally to the recommendations of INR (the Bureau of Intelligence and Research) in preparation for the upcoming National Security Council meeting on the Congo. Hilsman and his team of analysts led by the Africanist Robert C. Good produced an exceptionally well reasoned appraisal of the alternatives. Their conclusion was that the Central Government would not tolerate the impasse any longer. If the UN should be forced to withdraw because of American disengagement, the Central Government would turn to the Soviet Union for assistance in its invasion of Katanga. Washington would then be faced with the prospect of having to back Tshombe to stop the Russians. It would be the summer of 1960 all over again, only this time there would be no UN presence to prevent either the spread of the Cold War or the breakdown of relations between the U.S. and black Africa. If we disengaged now, INR concluded, we could be forced into a more dangerous form of intervention later.[124]

The pivotal figure in the debate over Congo policy was George Ball. It was he who had originally convinced Kennedy to take over the leadership of the UN operation in the aftermath of Hammarskjold's death. A year later, it was also he who had led the fight to pull out of the Congo. Now, two days before the National Security Council was to meet, Ball called Bundy: "We either have to fish or cut bait at this point, and fishing in the case involves the willingness to commit American forces . . ." Ball said that after much thought he felt that we had no choice but to resort to force. Ball's about face—which Kaysen for one found extraordinary in the light of his previous opposition—was singularly consequential.[125]

Across the river at the Pentagon, Defense officials followed suit. The Joint Chiefs recommended that the UN be offered a "U.S. military package consisting of one Composite Air Strike Unit with necessary support elements and the requisite base security forces." If this were insufficient to end the secession, more U.S. forces should be committed.[126] Over at State, Secretary Rusk, after some hesitation, threw his support to intervention. "If the UN suffered a reverse because of our withdrawal, we would have it on our hands."[127]

The National Security Council met on December 14. Cleveland and Hilsman argued that the best way to avoid fighting was to demonstrate to Tshombe that he would be crushed if he refused to capitulate. Sending an American fighter squadron to the Congo would convey this message. McNamara wondered what would happen if Tshombe and his mercenary-led forces resisted and the UN were to face a protracted guerrilla conflict. Bowles remarked that he could not imagine the mercenaries getting the best of the Gurkha brigade, particularly since the mercenaries' contract probably stated that they would not fight more than 300 yards from the nearest bar.[128]

The President was not persuaded. Sending American combat forces against noncommunist Katanga would be hard to explain to Congress, the allies, and the American people unless the administration could make a better case for the threat of a communist takeover.[129] Kennedy's skepticism was only deepened by the Pentagon's glowing estimate of the military prospects of U.S. intervention. "The first advice I'm going to give my successor," Kennedy remarked to Newsweek's Ben Bradlee during this period, "is to watch the generals and to avoid the feeling that just because they were military men their opinions on military matters were worth a damn."[130] As in the recent missile crisis, Kennedy called for more deliberations—a thorough review of other options short of intervention—before authorizing an air strike by U.S. jets in the Congo. He scheduled a final NSC meeting for December 17 and asked Stevenson in the meantime to inform the Secretary-General that the U.S. was "willing to intervene, if necessary."

Stevenson's session with U Thant the next day hit a snag. The Secretary-General said that he was appreciative of the "epochal" decision taken by the U.S., but that he could not legally sanction direct American intervention without the UN Security Council's approval. Such a request, of course, would bring a Soviet veto. He proposed that instead of directly intervening, the U.S. simply supply the UN with military equipment and the aircraft.[131]

This was not what Under Secretary Ball wanted to hear. We had tried the UN military build-up route before, he remarked, and it had resulted in a "long, drawn-out, bloody mess" due to UN incompetence and delays. Swift action was the only way to go. It was U.S. jets under U.S. control or nothing. Assistant Secretary Cleveland delivered the message—which had a distinctly Prussian tone to it—to U Thant: If "present ineffective arrangements" continued, the U.S. Congress would cut off appropriations for the Congo operation. If the UN wanted a quick solution to the Katanga problem, a U.S. military unit was the answer. Thant gave in and said that if Adoula gave his OK, the UN would go along.[132]

Thant's ruling solidified the State-Defense-CIA consensus for military intervention. On December 16, the President was presented with an hour-by-hour plan of the diplomatic operation that would accompany the deployment of the jets. On the eve of the NSC meeting, intervention seemed a sure thing.

The National Security Council reconvened on December 17. This time the President was not there to listen. He had definite moves in mind. Cutting discussion short, Kennedy ruled against any immediate intervention, deciding instead to lend the UN the aircraft and material requested earlier by U Thant. To drive the point home to Tshombe, the President also decided that he would send a "military survey mission" to the Congo to assess further UN military needs.[133]

On December 18, the State Department announced that an eight-man military team headed by General Louis W. Truman would be leaving for the Congo immediately. Ambassador Zorin described the mission as "direct subversion" and Tshombe warned that if the UN or the U.S. tried anything, he would "scorch the earth."[134] Once again the position of the European governments was critical. Belgium's Spaak sent word that his government approved of the military mission. The British, as before, took refuge in equivocation. After having signaled his "tentative" support for the UN military build-up, Prime Minister Macmillan raised his usual alibi about trouble in Parliament. Kennedy replied forcefully, pointing out that Adoula's position was desperate; he was a strong anticommunist and must be backed at all costs. Tshombe's intransigence was destroying the chance for a moderate solution. If Adoula failed, the Russians would surely move in. Macmillan reiterated his opposition to more fighting, but in the end was "driven to accept the position that . . . there must be a military operation to overcome Tshombe's resistance and to give strength to Adoula at the centre."[135]

THE FINAL ROUND

During the Christmas holiday the mood in the White House among those monitoring the Congo was gloomy. Although the UN command had an ambitious military plan of operations, code-named Grandslam, Kaysen thought the chances of a quick and military victory were at best 50–50.[136]

On Christmas eve, a UN helicopter was shot down. Roadblocks in and around Elisabethville were erected by the gendarmes, who began firing on a UN outpost. The UN command then activated Phase I of Grandslam. Swedish Saab jets made pre-emptive air strikes on Katangese planes on the ground, destroying several planes and setting fuel dumps afire at the Kolwezi-Kengère airfield. On the ground, UN units attacked key points in Elisabethville. With the gendarmerie breaking ranks and fleeing at every point of encounter, nearly all the city was under UN control by December 29. Tshombe was forced to flee to Southern Rhodesia. UN forces siezed Kipushi on December 30 and UN Officer-in-Charge Gardiner publicly vowed to maintain the drive until all Katanga was subdued. Tshombe meanwhile had flown to Kolwezi, where he warned that he would blow up the dams and sabotage the mines if the UN advance were not stopped. Many in Washington took him at his word.[137]

The President, who was in Palm Beach for the Christmas vacation, telephoned Ball on the evening of December 30 and told him that he wanted the UN command to keep control over its forces in the field. Rusk telephoned Bunche to remind him that the UN's objective was re-integration of Katanga into the Congo—not the annihilation of Tshombe and the conquest of the province. Rusk said he feared that Tshombe might think that he was in a trap and resort to sabotage. Bunche agreed to instruct the UN military commander to cease all action pending further instructions.[138]

Tactical surveillance in Washington was overtaken, however, by developments in the Congo. Indian commander Noronha received Bunche's injunction to halt the advance only after two of his companies had already crossed the Lufira River and had established a bridgehead on the other side. Since the brigade was already straddling the river and was under sporadic fire, Noronha disobeyed the order and continued to advance.[139] Resistance evaporated and the Indians pressed on and took Jadotville unopposed.

The loss of Jadotville was a severe blow to Tshombe's collapsing secessionist regime. Serious dangers remained, however. INR reported that Tshombe's extremist ministers were exerting strong pressures on him to destroy Union Minière's installations and carry on guerrilla activity from the bush. If the fanatical Munongo and extreme anti-European elements took power, attacks on Belgians and intertribal fighting would probably ensue.[140] Most of the Congo hands in Washington were worried at the prospect of sabotage. Bundy wasn't. He told Ball that demolition attempts in World War II had never caused half as much damage as threatened or predicted. Anyway, blown-up dams and factories would only give Edgar Kaiser another government-guaranteed investment opportunity in Africa.[141]

The UN continued its advance on Kolwezi with full American support. In telling contrast to Spaak's extraordinary restraint in the face of bitter opposition, Macmillan once again capitulated to his regressive backbenchers. The British consul in Elisabethville, as he and his predecessor had done in the previous two rounds of fighting, sued for negotiations between Tshombe and the UN, until he himself was ordered out of the country by Adoula.[142] Spaak stayed hitched and Kennedy wrote to thank him for his "great political courage . . . in these very difficult circumstances."[143]

After repulsing half-hearted Katangese resistance, UN troops reached the outskirts of Kolwezi on January 15. A week later, they entered the city without incident and were personally greeted by Tshombe. Sabotage of Union Minière installations was minimal. After two and one-half years, the Katangese secession was over.

The Congo was still a badly fractured society with little claim to nationhood, but it had been spared the consequences of complete disintegration by UN peacekeeping efforts. The UN's diplomats and soldiers had succeeded in separating the superpowers, fending off colonial intervention, and restoring some semblance of unity to the large and regionally disparate country. As Ambassador Stevenson said, it was the UN's finest hour. None of this would have been possible without the leadership of the UN's most powerful member.

Diplomatic victories, Lord Salisbury had once noted, are won by "a series of microscopic advantages: a judicious suggestion here, an opportune civility there, a wise concession at one point and a far-sighted persistence at another . . ." The series of advantages Kennedy achieved in the Congo were not based on the use of power so much as on the restraint of power. It was this that had averted a superpower showdown and had enabled the UN to keep the peace in the Congo. "You were firm in your determination that the Katanga secession be ended," George McGhee wrote the President. "At the same time you sought to prove to the world that every possible peaceful means of solution was tried before forceful means were applied."[144]

The President took time off on a Tuesday afternoon to compose letters of thanks to those who had worked so hard and who had waited so long for the breakthrough that had finally come. The task had been "extraordinarily difficult," he wrote McGhee, and now we were entitled to "a little sense of pride."[145]

6

Quite a Few Chips on a Very Dark Horse

> Whoever you are holding me now in hand . . .
> I give you fair warning before you attempt me further,
> I am not what you supposed, but far different.
>
> Kwame Nkrumah
> quoting Walt Whitman in
> *Ghana: The Autobiography of Kwame Nkrumah*

The leading African figure of Kennedy's day was Kwame Nkrumah of Ghana who had led the Gold Coast colony to independence in 1957. Nkrumah regarded himself as the tribune of Africa's unemancipated and as the chosen agent of "pan-African union."

Washington got its first full view of the magnitude of Nhrumah's ambitions in the Congo crisis. During the summer and fall of 1960, Nkrumah had first championed the assailed Lumumba before vainly trying to save him. By the time Kennedy took office in January 1961, Nkrumah, shocked at Lumumba's demise and furious at the West, was consorting openly with the Communist powers.

Kennedy was determined to win Nkrumah back. His means for doing so would be American financial participation in a vast hydroelectric scheme known as the Volta River Project. For the next three years, Kennedy found himself caught up in the declining fortunes of this unique and troubled personality.

THE END AND THE BEGINNING

"I, KWAME NKRUMAH OF AFRICA," his last will and testament began. That was how he had been introduced to 500,000 Chinese in Beijing's Tienanmen Square in 1961: "Kwame Nkrumah of Africa." The Square had "rocked to the deafening clapping of hands . . . " "Imagine," he had later exclaimed, "a black man hailed at the gates of the Forbidden

City." He could not forget it. Now, as he prepared to visit China again—this time to try to negotiate an end to the Vietnam war—he composed his final will.[1]

He had always thought of himself as Black Africa's liberator. On the occasion of Great Britain's historic grant of independence to the Gold Coast in 1957, Nkrumah had told his people that "the independence of Ghana is meaningless unless it is linked up to the total liberation of the African continent."[2] In the heady days after independence, he had laughingly said that he would never marry a Ghanaian woman because "all of Ghana is my bride." He had eventually married an Egyptian woman (on whom he had never set eyes before her arrival in Ghana) in order to fulfill a prophecy that the son of a black African man and a white African woman would rule all of Africa.[3] For Nkrumah, liberation was only the first step. The next was the unification of the entire continent.

In the years after independence, the idea of African unity became his obsession. The criticism mounted, but Nkrumah was undeterred. "This is *not* an idle dream. It is not impossible. I see it; I feel it; it is real; indeed I am living in it already (emphasis Nkrumah's)."[4] Other African leaders such as Tanganyika's Julius Nyerere and the Ivory Coast's Félix Houphouet-Boigny were not, however. The West, at first disdainful of Nkrumah's pan-Africanism, later grew alarmed at his willingness to use subversion and communist aid in pursuit of his ambition.

Later, when there were attempts on his life, Nkrumah saw the hand of the West at work. Vowing not to become another Lumumba, he sought refuge—and vindication of his pan-Africanist dream—in the East. The Russians gave him what he wanted—the Lenin Peace Prize and military advisors to train his praetorian guard—but no amount of attention from the Kremlin could restore his lost standing at home. The week before his departure for China in February 1966, there were reports of military plots. His aides urged him not to leave the country, but Nkrumah brushed aside their warnings. Perhaps he felt, as Basil Davidson later wrote, "an inner hopelessness" about it all.[5]

The will he composed read like a political testament. Like the "immortal Lenin," Nkrumah wanted to loom even larger in death than he had in life. He charged his executors to "cause my body to be embalmed and preserved," or, if this were not possible, to be cremated "and the ashes scattered throughout the African Continent, in rivers, streams, deserts, savannas . . . "

Neither wish would be granted. On February 24, 1966, while en route to Beijing, Kwame Nkrumah was overthrown. He lived in exile thereafter in Guinea. He would tell visitors who came to the secluded villa outside

Conakry that he was now "Africa's prisoner." The books he wrote during those years railed at the West for having subverted African independence.[6]

Michael Dei-Anang remembered that after he learned that he had cancer, the bitterness seemed to leave him. What remained was regret. He talked sometime of how it all could have been different, of how he might have lived with the West—"a revolutionary socialist among the capitalist states"—if the man to whom he had once pledged "complete kinship" had not died so early.[7]

John Kennedy and Kwame Nkrumah had gotten to know each other through Barbara Ward (whose husband, Robert Jackson, was one of Nkrumah's chief advisors). During the late 1950s when she was living in Accra, she had told Nkrumah about Kennedy—"his intense ambition, his distaste for colonialism . . . " She had likewise provided the senator with a running commentary of Ghana's first two years of independence.[8]

Kennedy's famous Algeria speech (given a few months after Ghana was granted independence) had excited Nkrumah's interest in the prospect of a new generation of American leaders. It was no accident that in his 2,000-word message to Kennedy a few days after his inauguration, Nkrumah said he felt sure that Kennedy would approach "the question of the Congo with the same courage and realism" that he had demonstrated in his stand on Algeria.[9]

THE FIRST YEARS OF INDEPENDENCE

While Kennedy maneuvered to secure the Democratic nomination, Nkrumah struggled to close up the deep divisions in independent Ghana. Although the transition from colony to nation (1951 to 1957) had been relatively bloodless, it had been divisive. Nkrumah's Convention People's Party had drawn much of its popular following from the urban dispossessed —the "verandah boys"—who had rallied to the cry of "Independence Now!" The more conservative United Gold Coast Convention, which favored a less rapid transition, had been electorally overwhelmed by the CPP in 1951, 1954, and again in 1956. Ghana's "men of substance"— the English-educated *haute bourgeoisie*—detested Nkrumah for having usurped their "right" to succeed the British in Ghana. They were few in number but fierce and articulate in their accusations and were openly favored by the British press.[10]

The fact that there was a tribal aspect to Nkrumah's opposition made it a more ominous challenge. Nkrumah's opposition in Ashanti—the former seat of West Africa's last great empire and the location of most of Ghana's mineral and agricultural wealth—was violently provincial.

Under the British, the Ashanti chiefs had retained most of their kingly privileges. Nkrumah's agitation for independence and centralized rule threatened to undo this arrangement. They responded to Nkrumah's resounding electoral victory over their party in 1954 with bombings and terror. There were also violent stirrings among two of Ghana's other major tribes, the Ga and the Ewe. On the eve of independence, the Queen's governor-general in the Gold Coast was obliged to send troops to the Trans-Volta region to put down an Ewe revolt against the new government.

Faced with violent opposition, Nkrumah was soon looking for authoritarian power to maintain order. A year after independence, the Parliament enacted the Preventive Detention Act, which allowed Prime Minister Nkrumah, in effect, to detain any person "acting in a manner prejudicial to the security of the state" for up to five years without due process of law.

Passage of the Preventive Detention Act drew cries of "incipient dictatorship" and "destruction of due process" in the Western press. In a letter to Senator Kennedy, Barbara Ward took a more sympathetic view of Nkrumah's predicament. Ghana "has real security problems and has done much better than many other newly-independent inexperienced governments. Thus it cannot fail to sense a core of hostility and cold superiority in Western reactions."[11]

For all the fanfare surrounding independence, the truth was that Ghana was still in the Gold Coast. The three major instruments of government—the army, the police, and the civil service—were still run by British expatriates. Below them was a stratum of Ghanaian professionals who had been trained and educated in the West and who remained deeply attached to the British mode of rule. After more than a century of colonialism, the British government had grown accustomed to obedience in the realm. When Nkrumah indicated his intent to make Ghana a republic (in effect, to get out from under the thumb of the Queen's governor-general), Her Majesty's government was displeased. Soviet Premier Khrushchev was incredulous: "How can a former colony choose its own course of development if the commanding officers in its army are all colonialists?"[12]

Barbara Ward reported to Kennedy in July 1959 that the British mood on Ghana amounted to a "nagging, carping run of criticism in the British press, aloofness in official reactions, marking time on the Volta project (Ghana's Aswan Dam) and a complete drying up of public capital . . . "[13]

Nkrumah, for his part, was increasingly dissatisfied with British control of the Ghanaian economy. The presence of the huge United Africa Company in Ghana effectively pre-empted the development of an indigenous consumer-goods industry; this was a major cause of the country's chronic balance-of-payments deficit. Mining rents paid by another British company, the Ashanti Gold Fields, Inc., were scarcely above the colonial level; the real wages of Ghanaian miners had not risen since 1938.[14]

The vagaries of the world price of cocoa (which provided Ghana with about 70 percent of its foreign-exchange earnings) put development plans on a precarious base and seemed to necessitate substantial investment in the area of cash-crop diversification. Following British advice, however, Nkrumah had left Ghana's $500 million of reserves, accumulated during the colonial period, in long-term, low-interest British securities; thus this great source of productive investment was unavailable in 1959[15] Political independence, in short, did not mean economic independence.

What Nkrumah could not accomplish in Ghana, he tried to accomplish abroad. His status as Black Africa's pre-eminent leader was unquestioned and his visit to the United States in 1958, which came, significantly, at the conclusion of a long tour of Africa, showed his talent for charming the West. As Africa's emissary, Nkrumah said everything he could to allay Eisenhower administration anxiety over the radical course of events in North Africa and the Middle East. *Time* wrote, "Seldom was a guest from a small country more welcome. The State Department saw the nationalism of his year-old country and the promise of his African leadership as a possible future counter-balance to rampant nationalism spreading from the Mideast."[16] Nkrumah even proposed the creation of a United Nations force led by three Ghanaian battalions to replace American marines in Lebanon.[17]

He cast himself as the West's best friend in Africa, scolding Nasser for his irresponsible declarations, and stating on *Meet the Press* that, "We in Ghana have no fear of communism." The Preventive Detention Act, he said, was only "temporary." As for the spectacle of segregated America, "the racial question has often been exaggerated by those wishing to bring the United States into disrepute."[18]

Anyone in the American government who had read Nkrumah's memoirs, published the previous year, would have had reason to question the sincerity of these remarks. During his ten years as a student in the U.S. during the Great Depression, Nkrumah had lived the wretched life of the American Negro. He had felt the sting of racial humiliation. His 1958 motorcade through Harlem may indeed have been "triumphal." It may even have awakened the "somnolent imagination of the American Negro," as one reporter put it.[19] But it was difficult to say which American memory lay deeper in Nkrumah's mind: that of the Ghanaian Prime Minister standing in the back of a Cadillac waving to the screaming Harlem crowds, or that of the shivering "Negro" of fifteen years before standing on the corner of 125th street in the dead of winter hawking fish.[20]

The prize that he hoped to win by his deference to American sensibilities was U.S. financing of the Volta project—a $600 million enterprise that had been discussed for nearly fifty years. Nkrumah fervently believed in electrification as the essential prerequisite to industrial growth. He had admonished his Western readers in a *Foreign Affairs* article, "We have to modernize. Either we shall do so with the interest and support of the West or we shall be compelled to turn elsewhere . . . "[21] Senator Kennedy, who was then engaged in a major effort to sell the Senate on a long-term aid package for India, was one who took note of Nkrumah's appeal.

The Volta project proposed the construction of a 2,100-ft.-long earthen dam and the creation of a 3,275-square-mile lake. To make the project economically viable, a 100,000-ton aluminum smelter would have to be constructed. The plan was for the smelter to purchase a large share of the generated power on a long-term basis. Sir Robert Jackson's 700-page feasibility report in 1955 concluded that the dam could not be justified without the smelter. He bluntly informed Nkrumah before his trip to the U.S. that the dam and the smelter would have to be built with American dollars, and not British sterling.[22]

At their meeting, President Eisenhower listened favorably to Nkrumah's appeal for American capital. The State Department subsequently offered to pay for half the cost of an engineering assessment and recommended to the Ghanaians that Kaiser Engineers do the study. Kaiser's man in Washington, Chad Calhoun, saw the possibility of publicly guaranteed profit in the enormous project. He was also fascinated by the historic opportunity of applying American engineering and management to Africa's largest hydroelectric scheme. He convinced his boss, Edgar Kaiser, to explore the possibility further by having him meet with Nkrumah in New York.[23] The session at the Waldorf-Astoria went well and the Prime Minister urged Kaiser to visit Ghana. Kaiser accepted—and with visions of pith helmets in his head—asked Nkrumah what he should bring in the way of clothes. "A dinner jacket would be fine" was the reply.[24]

Kaiser's engineers concluded in their 1959 analysis that the Volta project's cost could be scaled down to $300 million without changing its essential character. This made the project a more attractive proposition. Edgar Kaiser was willing to try to form a consortium of aluminum companies to build the smelter. It was now up to Ghana to mobilize its own resources and to obtain sufficient Western capital to make the project a reality. Nkrumah committed $98 million (or half the estimated dam construction cost) to the project. The World Bank's assessment report, however, was discouraging: "the balance of costs and benefits is on the positive side to only a modest extent at best." This meant that without an unconditional endorsement from the U.S., the World Bank would not participate in the Volta project.[25]

In August 1960, President Eisenhower informed Nkrumah that the U.S. intended to provide $30 million to back the project.[26] Within a month, however, Ghana and the U.S. were quarreling bitterly over the Congo. American officials regarded Nkrumah's backing of Lumumba as tantamount to being pro-Soviet. In truth, his conduct was essentially a matter of pan-Africanism.

As far back as 1958, Nkrumah's dream of a "United States of Africa" had begun to take institutional form. He sponsored two conferences in Accra (the Conference of Independent African States and the All-African Peoples Conference), which were brilliant successes and substantially enhanced his continental stature. The Conference of Independent African States established an informal secretariat at the UN and strengthened inter-African collaboration on nonaligned issues. The All-African Peoples Conference, held a few months later, brought together representatives of thirty-six liberation movements. It was "ideally timed to meet the needs of a rebellious continent."[27]

Nkrumah used the conference to reinforce his personal relations with such established nationalists as Kenneth Kaunda (Northern Rhodesia), Jomo Kenyatta (Kenya), and Ahmed Sékou Touré (Guinea). His capital of Accra soon became the mecca of "freedom fighters" from all corners of the continent. Joshua Nkomo (Southern Rhodesia), Holden Roberto (Angola), and Amilcar Cabral (Portuguese Guinea) all began to look to Nkrumah for guidance and financial support to foment rebellion in their home colonies. Patrice Lumumba was one delegate who had gone home determined to press for immediate independence in the Belgian Congo.[28]

In that same crowded year of 1958, Nkrumah also made visits to Egypt and India. In so doing, he laid the foundations of a nonaligned "third force" in international affairs. "It is our belief," he told the Council on Foreign Relations in New York in July, "that international blocs and rivalries exacerbate and do not solve disputes and that we must be free to judge issues on their merits and to look for solutions that are just and peaceful, irrespective of the Powers involved."[29]

In October 1958, Guinea became independent after France's petulant withdrawal. In November, Nkrumah and Guinean President Sékou Touré announced to the world that "Inspired by the example of the thirteen American colonies . . . " Ghana and Guinea were forming the "nucleus of the Union of West African States." "The tide of history is with me,"

Nkrumah excitedly told his aide Michael Dei-Anang. "Nothing will stop me now."[30]

NKRUMAH AND THE CONGO

The sudden emergence of Lumumba as the Congo's most popular leader appeared to give Nkrumah the opportunity to unite Ghana and the Congo. Prior to Congolese independence, Lumumba had discussed the prospect of such a union with his "idol." When order disintegrated in the week after independence, Nkrumah airlifted more than 1,000 troops, as well as medical and administrative personnel, to the Congo in support of the UN peacekeeping operation. Lumumba was grateful. He flew to Ghana on August 8, 1960 to sign a document uniting the Congo and Ghana. It was Nkrumah's finest hour.[31]

But then Lumumba miscalculated. He broke relations with Hammarskjold, and in so doing lost the protection of the UN force against domestic mutiny and international intrigue. When he invited the Russians to intervene, the United States and Belgium moved to eliminate him. In the struggle for power in Léopoldville, Nkrumah repeatedly urged Lumumba to restore relations with the UN before it was too late. On September 5, when President Kasavubu dismissed Lumumba, Nkrumah's own troops (acting under UN orders) prevented the premier from gaining access to the radio station. Lumumba accused Ghana of "treachery." Nkrumah's trump card was lost.

The news of Lumumba's arrest on December 1 put the Ghanaian President into a fury. He bitterly accused the Western powers of subversion and for the first time, turned on Hammarskjold for having stood by and maintaining neutrality: "I am appalled to see that a band of armed men which has prevented the functioning of the elected Parliament of the Congo is being loudly applauded from the rooftops of the Western world . . . "[32]

The Soviets were quick to take advantage of Nkrumah's anger at the West. During the week of December 15, 1960, Ghana received two of an eventual six Ilyushin aircraft from the Soviet Union. Nkrumah welcomed a thirty-four-member Soviet technical-assistance team to discuss $40 million worth of projects.[33] Pointing to Nasser's unhappy experience with the Americans, the Russians suggested that Nkrumah scrap the Volta project in favor of a smaller Soviet-financed dam. Nkrumah told them that he would consider the offer.

Kennedy's election gave Nkrumah hope that there would be a fundamental change in the American attitude. A few days after the inauguration,

Nkrumah appealed to the new president in the strongest manner to act immediately to secure Lumumba's release. The U.S. must not stand by, he wrote, and watch the "crumpling up of democracy in Africa by one of your close military allies—Belgium—in flagrant disregard of the unanimous opinion and sentiment of all those African people who are free to express their views."[34]

British Prime Minister Harold Macmillan received a similar communication from Nkrumah. "If [Lumumba] were to be murdered by his Belgian captors," Nkrumah wrote, "this would have an effect upon relations with the Commonwealth and also with non-African powers whose extent it would be difficult to estimate." The gauntlet was down.[35]

Kennedy's reply of February 2 revealed that the U.S. had decided to do nothing to save Lumumba. The reply so disappointed Nkrumah that he later claimed never even to have received it. Nonetheless, he steadfastly refused to commit Ghanaian troops serving in the UN force in the Congo to the Lumumbist secession in Stanleyville.[36]

The eventual news of Lumumba's murder had a shattering effect on Nkrumah. His belief in the UN and in the process of multilateral compromise was deeply undermined. His doubts about Western intentions drifted toward paranoia and it was not long before he began to see himself as the next victim of Western neocolonialism. In a broadcast to the Ghanaian people, Nkrumah accused the U.S. and other Western countries of "conniving at a brutal and savage colonial war . . . Alas, the architects of this murder are many." A crowd of party activists invaded the U.S. embassy grounds and damaged the chancery. The racial aspect surfaced in brutish fashion. The Ghanaian press featured old photographs of Negro lynchings in the U.S.[37]

Nkrumah invited Soviet President Leonid Brezhnev (then in Guinea) to fly to Accra to confer on the Congo.[38] Nkrumah subsequently summoned the new U.S. ambassador, Francis H. Russell, and handed him a stinging *aide mémoire* in which President Kennedy was personally rebuked. Nkrumah's letter to Kennedy a week later flatly accused the President of bad faith.[39]

Kennedy, who had been in office for less than a month, was taken aback by the fury of the African reaction. On February 17, he had a long conversation with Barbara Ward in which she described in detail the nature of Nkrumah's Congo position. In a letter to the President a few days later, Ward characterized Nkrumah as "tempermental, mercurial, and caught in the shifting sands of the Cold War." She claimed that Nkrumah —like Kennedy—wanted to keep the Cold War out of Africa, to strengthen the UN, and to end the Belgian-supported regime in Katanga. She urged

Kennedy to meet with the Ghanaian President as soon as possible. "If America can keep him neutral and dependent on the United Nations, much is gained. It is worth a risk and could conceivably be a triumph."[40]

Nkrumah was somewhat placated by the news of Ambassador Stevenson's dramatic endorsement of the February 21 Security Council resolution on the Congo (which called for, among other things, an investigation into the death of Lumumba), and by Kennedy's measured and conciliatory response (from Barbara Ward's draft) to Nkrumah's accusations of U.S. complicity with Belgium. "Public rebukes have rarely been effective in international relationships . . . We have tried to be restrained in our public comment about all governments with whose attitude on the Congo we may not be in full agreement."[41]

When Nkrumah let it be known that he would like to visit Washington "to clear up this whole thing," Kennedy proffered an effusive invitation.[42] Nkrumah typically needed more wooing than this. Could Ambassador Stevenson persuade Hammarskjold to issue him an invitation to address the General Assembly? Nkrumah inquired. This was done. Could President Kennedy send a jet to New York to take him to Washington? he asked. That too was arranged. Then Nkrumah indicated that the mid-March date for his meeting with President Kennedy was inopportune— "perhaps we should cancel it." Secretary Rusk sent off a Night Action cable to the embassy in Accra: "The President is anxious not to give Nkrumah any reasonable grounds to feel snubbed . . . "[43] Any date would do.

The Americans were beginning to realize that they had on their hands a man whose need for attention exceeded all other concerns. The CIA's briefing paper may have overstated matters somewhat, but did identify the central trait: "[A] man beginning to slip just a bit and too conceited to see it, a politician to whom the roar of the crowd and the praise of the sycophant are as necessary as the air he breathes . . . [and who] desperately wants a favorable verdict from history."[44]

What the Americans did not seem to realize was that for all his vanity, Nkrumah was a subtle and disarming supplicant. How else could one explain his extraordinary odyssey from the obscure shade of colonialism in a remote village in southwestern Ghana to Balmoral Castle, where he dined, as head of state, with the Queen of England?

Whatever the case, the White House let it be known that inviting Nkrumah to Washington had been "a difficult decision." The prevailing editorial attitude in Washington was grudging at best: "Mr. Kennedy decided that it would be useful to meet Nkrumah since he is rated as the only person in his country [with whom] to do business."[45] The White House received another view from Komla Gbedemah, Nkrumah's pro-

Western finance minister, who was in Washington to see World Bank officials about the Volta project. Gbedemah suggested to Walt Rostow at a midnight meeting at Rostow's home that the President should express "with great directness and force" his concern about Ghana's communist ties.[46] This would not be the last the White House would hear from Mr. Gbedemah.

McGeorge Bundy urged the President to emphasize the personal dimension of his relations with Nkrumah. "I think there ought to be a sharp look at all possible cases in which your own personal authority as the new President may be important. With a leader like Menzies [the Australian prime minister, who had just visited the White House] there is nothing to worry about . . . But with these new-fangled potentates, there is both more to gain and more to lose."[47]

THE NKRUMAH-KENNEDY MEETING

Nkrumah arrived in Washington on March 8 in a downpour. The rain removed whatever drama might have been possible at the greeting. He and the President shook hands and mounted a platform inside a nearby hangar. "The disease of liberty is catching," Kennedy said, quoting Jefferson. "It has been the object of our guest's life to make sure that that disease spreads around the globe."[48] They then motored to the White House.

The formal meeting at the White House went poorly. Nkrumah made a disorderly presentation of his views on the Congo and generally monopolized the conversation without effect. Kennedy emphasized that his leverage with the Europeans on African issues was limited and that he hoped that Nkrumah and other African leaders appreciated this. He also told Nkrumah of his surprise and puzzlement over Sékou Touré's recent letter accusing Kennedy of complicity in the murder of Lumumba. Nkrumah seemed sympathetic, but made no comment. Regarding Congo policy, the two Presidents agreed that Belgian military and paramilitary personnel should be removed, that Congolese military forces should be neutralized, and that the Congolese should be permitted to work out their own political situation free of foreign interference.[49]

Kennedy then escorted Nkrumah upstairs to the family quarters and introduced him to Mrs. Kennedy and daughter Caroline. Nkrumah was delighted with the gesture and returned to the Fish Room to meet the press, beaming at the "wonderful experience." On the plane back to New York, he wrote a warm personal note to Kennedy. He told his aides that he was convinced that the meeting "marked a new era of African-American friendship."[50]

The most positive result of the Nkrumah-Kennedy meeting was to put the Volta project back on track. In the light of Nkrumah's "hostile" Congo stand and his sudden association with the Soviet Union, the Eisenhower administration had frozen the $30 million commitment in September. Thanks to the spirited intercession of Chad Calhoun and Barbara Ward in January 1961, the new administration had re-opened negotiations.[51]

By the first week of February, Ghana had lined up tentative loan commitments from the World Bank ($47 million), the U.S. Development Loan Fund and Export-Import Bank ($37 million), and the British government ($14 million). All loans were conditional on two factors. The first was the signing of an investment agreement between the Ghanaian government and the Volta Aluminum Company (Valco), the Kaiser-headed consortium that would build the $128 million aluminum smelter. The second was the full backing of the U.S. government for the Volta project.

By the time Kennedy took office, the Ghanaian government had already signed the agreement with Valco. The Ghanaian concessions were more than generous. Valco was promised a ten-year tax holiday and a cheap kilowatt rate (2.65 mills) for its purchase of a predetermined amount of Volta Dam power (about $7 million a year). All the alumina to be smelted would be imported from Kaiser's mines in Jamaica; Kaiser would be under no obligation to mine Ghana's own considerable reserves of bauxite.[52]

Edgar Kaiser wanted a major concession from the American side as well, particularly after three of his other partners (Alcoa, Alcan, and Olin Mathieson) withdrew from the Valco consortium. He informed Governor Williams in early January that without a U.S. government guarantee of the Valco investment, he would build no smelter.[53] What Kaiser was seeking was full political risk coverage not only against nationalization, but also against confiscatory taxation and politically inspired labor troubles.

At first, State Department officials balked at the request. In the afterglow of the Nkrumah-Kennedy meeting, however, they were inspired to dig deeper and soon discovered a little-known Development Loan Fund clause that could be stretched to give the guarantee. Treasury Secretary Dillon was not pleased with the idea of doing Kaiser a business favor at taxpayers expense. "What is good for Edgar Kaiser may not be good for the United States," he told George Ball, pointing out that Congress was drafting new foreign aid legislation and might react badly to the provision of special favors.[54]

As Dillon had predicted, Senator Albert Gore (Kennedy's successor as chairman of the Senate African Subcommittee) was indignant. By giving Kaiser such an investment guarantee, the administration would be arranging a "pass-through" to American stockholders in Kaiser Aluminum," he wrote Kennedy. The Senate had previously refused even to contemplate such "tax-forgiveness" treaties. Gore also believed that the administration was giving Kaiser an unfair market advantage over its competitors. The principal beneficiary of the Volta project would not be the people of Ghana, Gore maintained, but the Valco consortium. "Do you really wish to endorse this?" he asked Kennedy.[55]

The President did and gaily announced to Edgar Kaiser, "If they ever take over the plant and we have to make good on the guarantee, both you and I will have to leave the country."[56] In the end, Kaiser got even more than he originally asked for. Through the Export-Import Bank, the U.S. government lent Kaiser $96 million for the smelter; the remaining $32 million of Kaiser investment was to be fully guaranteed.[57] The President then asked State Department Legal Advisor Abram Chayes to take charge of the Volta project negotiations and to bring them to a rapid conclusion.

There were serious problems in Ghana, however. Soviet President Leonid I. Brezhnev had taken advantage of the news of Lumumba's murder to urge Nkrumah to abandon the Western financing in favor of Soviet backing. The majority of Nkrumah's ministers had, in fact, voted in favor of turning the project over to the Russians. The success of the White House meeting had kept the U.S. in the project, but in May, Nkrumah demoted Finance Minister Gbedemah, who had been the leading advocate of U.S. participation. Meanwhile, Washington had begun to receive reports that Ghana was transshipping Soviet arms into the Congo.[58] When Nkrumah rejected outright the loan agreement that Gbedemah had concluded with the World Bank (on the grounds that it was improper for the bank to dictate Ghana's fiscal policy), Bank President Euguene Black asked the White House to step back and reconsider matters.[59]

The President, however, was listening to Barbara Ward, who recommended immediate commitment. "Otherwise, Nkrumah may not be able to resist, after *ten* years deferred, the open cheque book waved under his nose in the Kremlin. Must we have two Aswans?" (emphasis Ward's.)[60] Stevenson, who was on cordial terms with Nkrumah after two visits to Ghana in the late fifties, also said that it was no time to stall. Under Secretary Bowles agreed: "[W]e should get some word on the VOLTA to Nkrumah before he goes to Moscow in July."[61]

Kennedy was persuaded and told Abe Chayes that he wanted to make a commitment. "We know how long it takes a democratic government to make up its mind," he observed to Edgar Kaiser, "but does Nkrumah?"[62]

On June 29, 1961, Kennedy wrote the Ghanaian President: "I am delighted to be able to advise you that all major issues involved in the negotiations for the United States Government's share of the financing of the dam and smelter have now been resolved.[63] Two weeks later, Nkrumah left for a tour of the communist world.

RECONSIDERATION

Nkrumah's purpose in making an extended visit to the East was to give "practical effect" to Ghana's policy of nonalignment which, until this point, had had a decidedly pro-Western orientation.[64] The itinerary alone, however, raised eyebrows in Washington. Nkrumah visited eight Eastern European countries, spent a week in the People's Republic of China, and entered the Soviet Union on three different occasions. He was in the communist world for a total of two months.

What allegiance the Russians could not procure with foreign aid, they made up for in flattery. Brezhnev went everywhere with Nkrumah, extolling his "mastery of the dialectic" while blasting the role of the U.S. and Great Britain in Africa. Khrushchev let it be known that Nkrumah was a candidate for the Lenin Peace Prize and announced that he had invited the Ghanaian President to join him on his summer vacation. Nkrumah, a man who subsisted on personal gestures, was deeply impressed. His tongue loosened: "Had it not been for Russia, the African liberation movement would have suffered the most brutal persecution."[65]

Pravda ran the statement on page 1. The *Evening News* of Accra, exceeding even its own customary level of hyperbole, featured a picture of Nkrumah at Lenin's tomb with the caption: "The true mantle of Leninism has fallen on the shoulders of Dr. Nkrumah." A Russian correspondent in Accra observed, "If Nkrumah succeeds in convincing Ghanaians that what he is doing in this country is Communism, our own cause will be doomed forever."[66]

The Ghanaian delegation was meanwhile making a 10,000-mile tour through the Soviet Union. When Nkrumah evinced admiration after a tour of an atomic reactor, the Russians quickly promised that he would have one. Michael Dei-Anang remembered Soviet officials declaring repeatedly: "Look at us. We were more backward than you thirty years ago." Nkrumah agreed and stated that the Soviet Union was indeed a model to be emulated in Africa's search for political union.[67]

After a month of ardent wooing, the Soviets made their proposition: they would train Ghana's army. Khrushchev had warned Nkrumah that "unless he rid himself of the [English] commanding officers in his army, he would face a threat . . . from internal antidemocratic forces which were gathering strength."[68] Nkrumah accepted the offer and agreed to send 400 Ghanaian military cadets to the Soviet Union for training. News of his decision caused serious concern in London and Washington. Rusk predicted to Kennedy that if Nkrumah went through with his plan, Ghana's British-trained officer corps might try to depose him. In late August, the CIA station in Accra received word of such a conspiracy among senior Ghanaian officers. The plot collapsed after the chief conspirator, Brigadier General Joseph E. Michel, was killed in an airplane crash in Ghana on September 3.[69]

Nkrumah had meanwhile moved on to China, where Mao outdid Khrushchev with a tumultuous greeting at the gates of the Forbidden City. The two leaders signed a Treaty of Friendship and issued a communiqué stating that both Ghana and China supported the "national liberation movement in Asia, Africa and Latin America."[70]

Kennedy was ready to overlook such grandiose behavior provided that Nkrumah tread a genuinely neutralist line at the Conference of Non-Aligned Leaders in Belgrade in early September. After all, he observed to Barbara Ward, hadn't Nehru, Nasser, and Sékou Touré gone through a similar stage? Kennedy was more concerned about Ghana's stand on three issues: the Soviet "troika" proposal (to transform the single position of UN Secreary-General into a triumvirate), recognition of East Germany, and disarmament.

At least in Kennedy's eyes, Nkrumah proceeded to fail on all three counts. He called for a "modified troika" to consist of three Deputy Secretaries-General, one each for the West, the East, and the nonaligned. Kennedy berated the proposal in his address to the General Assembly on September 25, saying, "It would entrench the Cold War in the headquarters of peace." At Belgrade, Nkrumah also called on the great powers to sign a peace treaty recognizing East Germany, a position that Rusk considered procommunist. On arms control, Nkrumah proposed "general and complete disarmament," which the Kennedy administration considered nothing more than a Soviet ploy.[71] Nkrumah did characterize the Soviet resumption of nuclear testing as "a shock to me, as it was to all," but went no further. How could he? Khrushchev was to be his host for a vacation on the Black Sea at the conclusion of the conference.

The proceedings at Belgrade moved Kennedy, in Schlesinger's words, to "great and profane acrimony." Not one leader had censured Khrushchev for his general belligerence and, in particular, for his attack on Hammarskjold and Russia's resumption of above-ground nuclear weapons testing. So much for the nonaligned nations self-defined role as the "conscience of the world." When he learned that Presidents Achmed Sukarno of Indonesia and Modibo Keita of Mali had been dispatched to Washington to carry the Belgrade gospel to him [Nkrumah and Nehru had been sent to Moscow], Kennedy observed, "Khrushchev certainly drew the pick of the litter."[72]

The New Republic detected a note of "injured innocence" in Kennedy's press conference statement that "in the administration of [foreign aid] funds, we should give great attention and consideration to those nations who have our view of the world crisis."[73] Robert Kennedy, the attorney general, who believed that Nkrumah was a "communist," tried to direct his brother's ire against the Volta project.

On September 9, the President asked Secretary Rusk to determine "whether Mr. Nkrumah is going ahead with his plan to send 400 of his troops to the Soviet Union for training."[74] Without answering the question, Rusk managed to recommend a "strong protest" and the need for "confrontation" of Nkrumah by the British as well as to discuss the chances of a right-wing coup against Nkrumah.[75] After further inquiry, the White House discovered that Nkrumah would not be able to send more than twenty cadets to the Soviet Union in the coming year. "The British have already helped knock the number way down," Bundy observed to the President, "but he's a great little fellow."[76]

While Nkrumah was in Belgrade discussing with his nonaligned counterparts how best to provide the world with "moral leadership," Ghana was engulfed by strikes. The immediate cause was the promulgation of a draconian budget designed to raise additional revenue for the government's extensive development plans. In addition to freezing salaries and raising taxes, the budget introduced a compulsory savings scheme in which 5 percent of all wages and salaries (and 10 percent of other kinds of income) would go toward the purchase of nontransferable ten-year National Development Bonds.[77]

Despite the virtual paralysis of his country, Nkrumah elected to remain in Russia. Former Finance Minister Gbedemah (then serving on the three-man presidential commission ruling in Nkrumah's absence) saw his chance to seize power. Gbedemah had no problem in obtaining CIA backing for his conspiracy, but he wanted an official assurance of American support. He approached Ambassador Russell on September 6 and told him of his plans. Would the U.S. support him? Washington gave an unequivocal yes.[78]

Nkrumah returned to Ghana on September 16 and demanded on national radio that striking workers return to their jobs. The next day 3,000 skilled and semi-skilled workers struck in Accra. Railroad and dock workers in Takoradi also ignored the directive and appealed to American, British, Liberian, and Nigerian unions for financial support. Nkrumah thereupon dismissed four of his cabinet ministers (including

Gbedemah), and relieved all 230 British officers of their command positions (including his chief of staff, General H.T.S. Alexander). He warned the strikers for the final time to return to work.[79] This time they obeyed.

On September 25, Radio Moscow announced that the Soviet government was sending a team to Ghana to do a survey of the dam on the Black Volta. A week later there was more discouraging news for the White House. The National Security Agency intercepted a Soviet telex that indicated that the Russians wanted to displace the Americans outright on the Volta project.[80]

The U.S. faced "another Aswan or worse," Kennedy grimly told Kaiser. If he cancelled out, he would lose in Africa. If he went ahead, Congress would rip up his foreign aid bill.[81] The President decided to inform Nkrumah that the United States wanted to reconsider its participation in the Volta project.

Kennedy believed that it had been Eisenhower's cancellation of his offer to finance the Aswan Dam that had driven Nasser into the arms of the Russians and had triggered a succession of events that had brought the superpowers to the brink of nuclear war.[82] In May 1956, Secretary of State John Foster Dulles had been outraged by Nasser's recognition of Communist China and had declared that the issue was whether "nations which play both sides get better treatment than nations which are stalwart." The offer of American financing had been brusquely withdrawn in July; a week later, Nasser had nationalized the Suez Canal and invited in the Russians. When Britain and France (along with Israel) had mounted an invasion of Egypt, the Soviet Union threatened the European nations with a nuclear strike. Eisenhower—who had previously warned the Europeans against trying an invasion—had forced them to withdraw.[83] In Kennedy's view, the cost of Dulles's petulant reaction to Nasser's wish to 'play both sides' had been much too high.

George Ball, who was monitoring cable traffic from Ghana, urged the President to sit tight on the Volta decision; there was a chance that Nkrumah might be overthrown in the next couple of weeks and a "really solid government" would be installed. The State Department also wanted "to see if Gbedemah gets anywhere."[84]

Gbedemah, however, proved to have little aptitude for intrigue. He seemed to want the Americans to do the work for him and spent as much time plotting with the CIA station chief in Accra as he did with other Ghanaian conspirators.[85] Also assisting Gbedemah was the local agent of a New York diamond merchant, Leon Tempelsman and Son. The son, Maurice Tempelsman, was a friend and political supporter of Adlai Stevenson and had a liking for mixing conspiracy with commerce in his African trade.[86] A few days after Nkrumah dismissed him from the

cabinet, Gbedemah sent a letter to Governor Williams detailing those involved in the plot and requesting money.[87] Kennedy was apprized of this
unusual message at Hyannis Port and instructed Bundy not to respond.[88]

Whatever chance Gbedemah may have had of ousting Nkrumah was
lost when Tempelsman's agent in Ghana, Mr. Grosse, called his employer
on an open transatlantic line and "spilled everything," including his assurance to Gbedemah of U.S. support. As U.S. officials feared, the line had
been tapped by Ghanaian security agents.[89]

Washington prepared for the worst. Grosse had apparently compro-
mised "everybody," including the top CIA man in Accra. Bronson Tweedy,
the CIA chief of Africa operations, was summoned to his office on
Saturday to attend to the damage. Ball telephoned Tempelsman and coldly
informed him that Mr. Grosse had been "quite indiscreet" and should
be pulled out.[90]

Nkrumah, who had generally been restrained in his use of the security
apparatus until this point, now struck back. In early October, he ordered
the arrest of forty-eight persons (including three MPs) under the Preventive Detention Act. Ball briefed Bundy on the situation. Gbedemah was
under surveillance and might be arrested and shot. The affair might be
identified as an American plot. Maybe the Ghanaians didn't have a record-
ing of the telephone conversation, Bundy ventured. That was a possibility,
Ball replied. "We might be lucky but we didn't deserve that sort of luck."[91]

On October 31, the Ghanaian Parliament passed a bill requested by
the President to establish special, nonjury courts that could order the death
sentence for political offenses with no right of appeal. In late October,
Gbedemah fled the country.[92]

In December, the Ghanaian government issued a White Paper (prepared by Geoffrey Bing Q.C., Nkrumah's British legal advisor) on the
September strikes and political discontent. It claimed that the conspirators
had received financial aid from "certain expatriate interests" and that these
"interventions" were either undertaken with the "connivance of their own
government" or were actually carried out "in a planned way by governmental agencies which have become so powerful their activities may be
hidden even from officials who are supposed to control them." No names
were mentioned, since London was at the point of deciding whether or not
the Queen should visit Ghana and since Washington was in the process of
reconsidering the Volta project. But the report's implications were unmistakable.[93]

The *Ghanaian Times*, a crude but generally reliable indicator of the
undisguised state of Nkrumah's mind, began railing on a daily basis
against "imperialist crookery" and "capitalist blackmail."[94] British and
American officials were righteously indignant. Commonwealth Secretary

Duncan Sandys flew to Accra to give *Osageyfo* (Great Warrior) Dr. Kwame Nkrumah the royal word about the Queen's visit. A U.S. Senate delegation led by Senator Gore visited Nkrumah and protested about the wave of arrests in Ghana. Nkrumah coldly replied that he always kept an American history book on his desk. "Every young country goes through a period of stress at the beginning. The first task of any government is to maintain order and security."[95]

The Western press matched Ghana's press epithet for epithet, if somewhat less inelegantly. Nkrumah was "Stalinist." He was blaming foreign powers in order to disguise the domestic ills he himself had wrought. American political scientist Henry L. Bretton later expressed the established scholarly view of the "CIA scare": "a most effective foil [by Nkrumah] in preventing consolidation of an internal opposition."[96]

Unfortunately for Ghana and the United States, the truth was more involved than that. Aware of the West's role in eliminating Lumumba, Nkrumah feared that he was next. It was hardly surprising that he struck back at his domestic opposition—which had a history of resorting to violence—and later lashed out publicly against Western intelligence agencies. Volta Dam or not, September 1961 marked the beginning of the end of Nkrumah's relationship with the West.

A year after the troubles of September 1961, there was a serious attempt of Nkrumah's life. This time there was no reason to be silent and the Ghanaian press exploded with accusations against the U.S. and Great Britain. The Ghanaian government severed its intelligence relationship with the British and demanded that two U.S. embassy officers leave Ghana. President Kennedy sent his personal assurance to Nkrumah that the CIA was not "out to get him." By this time, however, too much had already happened.

THE VOLTA DAM DECISION

Nkrumah seemed genuinely upset when he got the news in late September that Kennedy was sending a special mission to Ghana to review American participation in the project. "I must confess," he wrote Kennedy "that it has been with considerable dismay and anguish that I have come to realize that you may now have doubts and concern about the understanding between us which was created during my visit."[97] What followed was a 2,500-word message explaining in detail Ghana's foreign relations and, in particular, Nkrumah's statements while on tour in the communist countries. "I am sure you will continue to recognize and appreciate that we in Africa need to develop in our own way, that we have growing pains and must make our share of mistakes, even as your great country experienced in its growth. We will not necessarily be bound to either the East or the West..."

Nkrumah asked Edgar Kaiser and Chad Clahoun, who were returning to the U.S., to hand-deliver the letter to the President. With his characteristic panache, Nkrumah added a postscript: "Please give my regards and best wishes to Mrs. Kennedy and little Caroline..."

After conferring with the President on October 10, Barbara Ward sent along additional encouragement, emphasizing that the Volta loan would be "phased" and urging him to ask President Léopold Sédar Senghor for his judgment.[98] Kennedy greatly admired the Senegalese poet and philosopher and, during Senghor's visit to Washington, asked him plainly what should be done. Senghor was frank in reply. What Nkrumah needed more than anything else was a psychiatrist, he said, "*et un très bon psychiatrique.*" But all Africa was waiting, Senghor continued, so the only alternative was to go ahead.[99]

Senghor's judgment seemed to make an impression on the President, who later told Kaiser and Calhoun that he had fully recovered from his "fit of pique" at Nkrumah. What he needed now was a "political cover" if he were to proceed. Could Kaiser persuade Nkrumah to send some of the Ghanaian cadets in question to the U.S.? Kaiser said he would do his best, but told the President that his father had called him from Honolulu to ask why he was getting mixed up with that communist Nkrumah? Kennedy laughed and said, "That is exactly what my father has been asking me."[100]

The President asked Bundy to procure a "respectable Republican" to head the review mission to Ghana. "Typical of JFK's administrative methods," Arthur Schlesinger, Jr., wrote in his journal, "if he wanted to veto the project he would have sent Chester Bowles."[101] In any case, this would not be the last time that sending a respectable Republican to do Democratic business would backfire on the President.

Ball came up with the name of Clarence Randall, the steel magnate who had served as Eisenhower's chairman of the Council on Foreign Economic Policy. The President approved. Randall would be accompanied by two pro-Volta project officials, Legal Advisor Chayes and Harry Shooshan, deputy managing director for operation of the Development Loan Fund. The mission would receive loaded marching orders (i.e., to submit a report "which will provide the basis for our proceeding with the project.")[102]

That was not the way it turned out. The Randall mission arrived in Ghana on October 25 and conferred with Nkrumah several times over a four-day period. Nkrumah told them everything they wanted to hear and patiently explained Ghana's rather irregular version of nonalignment.[103]

Sir Robert Jackson, Nkrumah's chief Volta project adviser, who had gathered from his wife, Barbara Ward, that Kennedy was favorably disposed to give the go-ahead, tried to make the decision palatable to the U.S. At Jackson's encouragement, Ghanaian Defense Minister Kofi Baako approached Ambassador Russell with an open-ended request for American military training assistance. Nkrumah issued an order calling for a reexamination of Soviet bloc assistance projects and opened the U.S. Trade Fair in Accra—"a not-too-expensive implementation of his neutral commitment," Russell observed.[104]

Nkrumah excelled at the personal touch. Upon learning that Randall was a bird lover, he insisted that he come to the Flagstaff House gardens for a look at his West African cranes. At their final meeting, Nkrumah presented Randall with a copy of an out-of-print classic, Bannerman's *The Birds of West Africa*.[105]

Neither Nkrumah's indulgence nor Kennedy's instructions, however, proved quite enough to convince Randall to "do the right thing," in Jackson's words. Randall came home and bluntly warned the President that he was putting a lot of American money into a questionable project for the benefit of a "dictator." The administration would appear "soft on Communism" if it proceeded.[106] Ball was appropriately contrite for having suggested Randall in the first place, but now the administration had to deal with the risk that he would go public with his opposition.

The British somehow got wind of Randall's "secret" report and discreetly saved the day.[107] The Queen was scheduled to visit Ghana from November 9 to 20, but several bombs had exploded in the capital in October. ("Someone is trying to give Accra a Parisian look," Interior Minister Kwaku Boateng blithely noted.) The British government tried to discourage the Queen from going, but she insisted. Pleading the Queen's safety, Prime Minister Macmillan wrote Kennedy urging that there be no negative announcement concerning the Volta project—if indeed there were to be one at all. Ambassador Ormsby Gore went one step further and archly told Ball that a leak would place the Queen in "a dangerous position."[108]

The President took the hint and informed Ormsby Gore, "Long live the Queen!" Randall was summoned to the Oval Office and Kennedy got his chance to even the score with his Under Secretary: "George Ball thinks we should go ahead and I am leaning to the fact we shouldn't." But there was the Queen . . ., Kennedy explained. Randall said he understood, and promised the President he would say nothing. He returned to his Winnetka, Illinois home assured that he had done his duty.[109]

The Queen's visit to Ghana was a great success. The Ghanaian press, in its inimitable manner, pronounced her "the greatest socialist monarch in the world."[110] In Washington, carping on Capitol Hill (chiefly from

Senators Gore, Dodd, and Goldwater) died down. Antagonistic press commentary from such journalists as Marguerite Higgins, Clark Mollenhoff, and James Kilpatrick also subsided; for the better part of a month there had simply been no story to tell.

By the end of November, the President was inching toward a decision in Rooseveltian fashion. A group of British African experts came to town and provided the right advice: Ghana was "balancing" between East and West and "must be placed in a neutral category unless pushed in another direction." The foreign policy apparatus also fell into line with the CIA's Office of National Estimates providing a well-argued case for a go-ahead and the State Department submitting a small tome (complete with maps, chronology, and balance sheet) in support of its recommendation.[111]

Macmillan sent another letter to Kennedy, which the President showed to his doubting brother Robert. He warned that the Africans would regard an American withdrawal as an attempt to use financial power to dictate the national policy of independent states. Cancellation might have the same consequences in West Africa as John Foster Dulles's repudiation of Aswan had had in Egypt in 1956.[112]

The National Security Council met on December 5. It was clear from the outset that the President had already made up his mind, and seemed more concerned about ways of justifying the decision. Treasury Secretary Dillon nonetheless made a case on the merits. The essential question was whether Nkrumah was a Castro or a Nasser, Dillon said, and to him Nkrumah was a Castro. That meant we should pull out.[113]

The President asked his secretary, Mrs. Evelyn Lincoln, to bring him a copy of his June 29 letter to Nkrumah. He read the entire text of the letter with dramatic inflection, observing dryly that this seemed a fairly warm letter. He was "gently reminded" by Ball that it had been made warmer at the President's own direction. Kennedy remarked that as far as he could tell, the Secretary of the Treasury and the Attorney General were the only NSC members who opposed the project.

The Attorney General (who had arrived late and was seated behind his brother) had not spoken, the President said, but he could feel the hot breath of his opinion on the back of his neck. At that point, the Attorney General voiced his strong opposition to financing the project. Without responding, the President adjourned the meeting. A week later on December 12, 1961, the United States formally announced its participation in the Volta project.

Prime Minister Macmillan congratulated the President on his decision at their summit meeting in Bermuda. Kennedy replied that gallantry demanded that he match the Queen's "brave contribution" with his own.[114] In a letter to Barbara Ward a few days later, the President put the matter more plainly: "We have put quite a few chips on a very dark horse but I believe the gamble is worthwhile."[115]

RELATIONS IMPROVE

After the decision to stick with the Volta project, the President asked Clarence Randall to return to Accra to inform Nkrumah that the U.S. wanted no more "surprises" in its relations with Ghana. "Aid to under-developed countries," he was instructed to tell Nkrumah, "depends on a yearly appropriation by Congress and can continue only so long as the program has the wholehearted support of the American people . . ." There had been "widespread criticism and alarm over what appears to the American people as an accented trend toward the suppression of civil and political rights in Ghana . . . [and] policies in the international field that coincide with Soviet Bloc positions . . ."[116]

Nkrumah gave categoric assurances to Randall on all matters of U.S. concern. He wrote Kennedy that he would reiterate them in a radio broad-cast to the Ghanaian people and was cabling an advance copy of the broadcast to the President. To the stupefaction of the White House, how-ever, not only did Nkrumah fail to give the assurances promised in the draft of the address, but he proceeded to congratulate the Soviet Union—and not the U.S.—for its role in Ghana's development.[117]

Kennedy was "keenly disappointed and upset." Although he did not hold Ambassador Russell in any way responsible for the embarrassment, he felt that the U.S. lacked the "local muscle" to check the wayward Nkrumah before he went astray. He was convinced that the right man in Accra could make the difference.[118]

The communist powers had their best men in place in Accra. Chinese Foreign Minister Zhou Enlai had sent his most gifted deputy (and later successor) Huang Hua as ambassador to Ghana. Khrushchev's envoy, Mikhail Sytenko, enjoyed what one Western diplomat called, "instant access" to Nkrumah. Now Kennedy decided to send one of his own political collaborators, William P. Mahoney, Jr., to make sure that the U.S. would at least break even politically on its Volta commitment. Mahoney's civil rights background was not lost on Nkrumah, who told the head of the Rockefeller Fund in West Africa that he fully approved of the appointment.[119]

Elsewhere in Africa, Kennedy political appointees were already making headway. In the Congo, Edmund A. Gullion had almost singlehandedly wrought an agreement ending the Katanga secession. In Guinea, former journalist and Stevenson speech writer William Attwood was making the way straight for Sékou Touré's sudden exit from the Soviet embrace. As one Kennedy appointee put it, the ambassadorial strategy in Africa was "stay in close, keep working, and wait for the breaks."[120]

Mahoney's arrival coincided with an easing of political repression in Ghana. In the spring of 1962, Nkrumah declared a "general amnesty" and released 160 persons from prison. From the American standpoint, there were still grounds for concern, of course. Procommunist CPP radicals such as Tawia Adamafio continued to have the upper hand in Flagstaff House (the President's office). There was still no hint of sobriety in the party press on the subject of Nkrumah: "Could there be another prophet in Nazareth? Yes, this day a Messiah is born in Ghana . . ." intoned the *Evening News.* Nkrumah himself continued to harbor suspicions about the West. But for all the radical talk, he was practical enough to ask for the assistance of two World Bank economists in putting the country's external balance into better order. Such requests gave Western representatives some basis for hope, as did the fundamental reality that Ghana was still attached culturally and financially to the West.[121]

In June 1962, Ghana hosted the "World Without the Bomb Conference." Disarmament was something of a crusade among the nonaligned at this time, and the resumption of nuclear testing (first by the Soviet Union and then by the United States) had touched off a chorus of protest in the Third World. "In the name of God and mankind, put an end to the high altitude testing," Nkrumah advised Kennedy on behalf of Africa.[122] The fact that the invitations to the conference coincided with the American resumption of testing meant that Nkrumah would be getting the headlines he so dearly desired once the conference had convened.

The majority of the 100 delegates attending the conference were from the East and, as far as the State Department was concerned, this meant that it was "Soviet sponsored." Ambassador Mahoney disagreed, and set about to organize the Western delegates, chiefly, Sean McBride of Ireland, Lord Kennett of Great Britain, and James Wadsworth of the United States. As a result of the embassy's efforts, the resolutions finally adopted by the conference proved to be considerably less obnoxious than expected.[123]

Such efforts at damage control by Kennedy's men in the field would not be in vain. Four months later, after the discovery of Russian missiles in Cuba, the U.S. would plead its case against the Soviet Union in the courtroom of world opinion before a jury of the nonaligned. The overwhelming verdict would be guilty as charged.

As Arthur Schlesinger, Jr., later wrote, it was during the second week of the missile crisis that African relations assumed vital importance.[124] The only way in which Moscow could defend its Cuban missile installations, short of nuclear war, was to send its bombers and transport planes to relieve the quarantine island. The Russians had no choice but to refuel their aircraft at African airports; the only countries that might grant them access were Ghana and Guinea.

Armed with the photographic blow-ups used with such effect by Ambassador Stevenson before the UN Security Council, Mahoney met with Nkrumah and asked him to deny the Soviet Union all overflight and landing rights in Ghana. Nkrumah acceded categorically to the request, despite the fact that he had signed a major aviation assistance agreement with the Russians only three months earlier.[125] Attwood duplicated this success with Sékou Touré the next day. The strategy of staying in close, working hard, and waiting for the breaks seemed to be paying off.

CONSPIRACY AND SUBVERSION

Despite the Kennedy administration's diplomatic gains in Ghana, a sudden outbreak of political violence in the summer and fall of 1962 left Nkrumah more fearful than ever of Western intentions. On August 1, 1962, he was nearly killed when a would-be assassin threw a grenade at him as he was greeting a group of school children in the small northern town of Kulungugu. Washington professed outrage at subsequent accusations in the Ghanaian press that the West was involved in the attempt.[126] But the record reveals that Nkrumah had reasons for suspecting the worst.

Ghana's neighbor to the east, Togo, had long been a meeting and staging ground for Ghanaian opponents of the Nkrumah regime. The feud between Ghana and Togo had begun in 1956 when a UN plebiscite had permanently split the Ewe tribe in two by giving Ghana sovereign control over British-administered Togoland. The French Togolese believed that the election had been rigged and blamed Nkrumah for having forced the UN's hand. From that point forward, Togo served as a dissident and, at times, terrorist sanctuary for Nkrumah's adversaries.[127]

The Ghanaian government believed that the October 1961 conspiracy to assassinate Nkrumah had originated in the Togolese capital of Lomé. Ghana retaliated six weeks later by sending Togolese commandos, trained and armed in Ghana, across the border to assassinate President Sylvanus Olympio. The commandos nearly succeeded in their operation. The CIA and the State Department agreed that Nkrumah at least had prior knowledge of the operation and probably planned it through his Bureau of African Affairs. The establishment of a commando trainning base for 400 exiled Togolese at Wora Wora, in the Volta Region, was further proof that the Ghanaians were deadly serious about ridding themselves of the Olympio regime.[128]

U.S. ambassador to Togo, Leon Poullada appealed to the State Department to provide U.S. military assistance to protect Olympio. Washington, however, preferred not to "get out in front of the Africans in this matter." President Olympio renewed the appeal through his ambassador in Washington, who asked Secretary Rusk for help in persuading the UN to investigate the attempt. Rusk told the ambassador that the U.S. regarded Ghanaian aggression as intolerable, but made no commitment of assistance in any form.[129]

Washington's ambivalence about protecting Olympio stemmed in good part from its desire to conceal CIA association with Nkrumah's Ghanaian opponents in Lomé. The State Department was concerned that "the residence in Togo of political refugees plotting against Nkrumah might muddy the issue of Togolese security if it were raised in the UN."[130] The CIA's "leadership alternative" in Togo, in short, was not to be exposed. A chance for reconciliation and stability in both Ghana and Togo was thereby tragically lost.

Part of Nkrumah's reason for trying to subvert the pro-Western Olympio was personal: he detested him and held him personally responsible for the October bombings in Accra and the assassination plot in Lomé.[131] Subversion of bourgeois regimes was also part of Nkrumah's pan-Africanist game plan. The State Department reported to the National Security Council that "Ghana's influence, or interference, is felt in all sections of the continent."[132]

The mainspring of Ghanaian subversion was Nkrumah's Bureau of African Affairs, which directed the activities of more than 100 agents in Africa. Through the reports of these agents, Nkrumah had learned of the American role in Lumumba's demise and had later received what Nkrumah's adviser Geoffrey Bing called "incontrovertible evidence" of American involvement in the Lomé conspiracies.[133]

The Bureau of African Affairs also provided ideological and, to a lesser extent, paramilitary training for several hundred "freedom fighters" from all over the continent. Ghana's neighbors were frightened by the bureau's sponsorship of dissidents from their own countries and were nettled by Ghana's transmission of political broadcasts throughout West Africa. The breadth of Nkrumah's ambition was evident in his remarks at the opening of the Kwame Nkrumah Institute of Ideology at Winneba: "I see before my mind's eye a great monolithic party growing up, united and strong, spreading its protective wings over the whole of Africa—from Algiers in the North to Capetown in the South, from Cape Guardafui in the East to Dakar in the West."[134]

At the Heads of State Conference in Lagos (which Nkrumah boycotted), seven of Africa's leaders decided to do something about Ghanaian intervention in their national affairs. They resolved to communicate to

Nkrumah that if he did not stop his subversive activities, they would jointly sever diplomatic relations with Ghana.[135]

Kennedy's meeting with President Olympio added a further twist to U.S. involvement in the Ghana-Togo feud. Kennedy was greatly taken with Olympio's sophistication and strongly pro-Western views and, undoubtedly, took his side in the dispute with Nkrumah. On his return trip to Ghana, Clarence Randall was instructed by the President to exact Nkrumah's word that Ghana would not "resort to subversive, terroristic or other measures designed to interfere in the internal affairs of other African states."[136] In the light of his own information about American activities in Lomé, Nkrumah had reason to wonder about the fairness of such a request.[137]

The feud simmered on until the assassination attempt at Kulungugu. After the grenade explosion, the wounded Nkrumah stood transfixed before the carnage, shaking uncontrollably and saying, "They want to kill me. They want to kill me."[138] Ghanaian security forces later determined that the attacker had escaped into Togo.

The circumstances of the attack suggested an inside job by a handful of Nkrumah's more ambitious subordinates. Even after the arrest of two cabinet ministers and the party secretary, however, the terrorist bombings continued.[139] By late September 1962, the toll of dead and wounded exceeded 300. There was little doubt that Lomé was serving as the base of terrorist operations and, at least in Nkrumah's mind, the reports of meetings between American officials and Gbedemah and Busia revived a fearful specter. In early October, at a meeting in Flagstaff House, Nkrumah, in a desperate tone, reported to aides that the "imperialists" were trying to kill him.[140]

Khrushchev saw his opportunity to capitalize on Nkrumah's fear for his life. He advised the President that the imperialists, "realizing that the ground is slipping from under their feet, are trying to oppose historical changes."[141] A few weeks later, Nkrumah severed Ghana's intelligence and security relationship with the British and called in the Russians to replace them. In November, Khrushchev sent Georgi Rodionov as the new Soviet ambassador to Ghana. Rodionov had previously served as first secretary in the Russian embassy in London during the time that KGB "mole" Harold "Kim" Philby held a senior position in MI-6 (British counter-espionage).[142]

Nkrumah's dread suspicion of Western complicity appeared in broadside form in the daily editorials of the Ghanaian press. Great Britain and the United States were accused of "murderous conspiracy" and the clandestine use of "local bastards" in furtherance of their interests. In reference to his Arizona origins, Ambassador Mahoney was routinely identified as "the cowboy nuclear imperialist." When Mahoney went to

Flagstaff House to protest the press attacks, he found Nkrumah in a "volcanic" mood—deeply disturbed, but willing to issue a formal retraction of the press charges on the basis of his "trust" in President Kennedy.[143]

Kennedy considered the situation serious enough to warrant a full-scale review of U.S.-Ghana relations and, in particular, reconsideration of the phased disbursements of aid for the Volta project. He asked the State Department and the CIA to take "a long hard look" at Ghana and ordered Mahoney home for consultations.[144]

The discovery of missiles in Cuba in mid-October superseded any major reckoning of relations with Ghana. Nkrumah's critical decision to deny landing rights to the Russians during the crisis undoubtedly improved his standing in the White house. Bundy's assistant Carl Kaysen believed that the demise of the radicals and the rehabilitation of the moderates in Ghana, as well as Mahoney's frank relations with Nkrumah, justified continued participation in the Volta project. "At a moment when we have won a significant victory in the world struggle we should show a position of generosity in relation to small neutrals, even those who have been more neutral with respect to the Soviet Union than they have to us."[145]

The CIA, in its fashion, had difficulty in leaving well enough alone. "The United Party of Ghana," one CIA cable from Accra wishfully pronounced, "is organizationally and mentally prepared to assume the reins of government in Ghana should a turn in events make this possible."[146] Agents in London and Lomé continued to consort with the exiled Gbedemah, who told them what they wanted to hear: that Nkrumah had murdered several of his ministers (this was simply erroneous) and was on the brink of "popular collapse." The State Department was ultimately obliged to instruct the embassy in Lomé to pass the word that contacts with Gbedemah and the rest remain covert. For this marginal vindication of common sense, officials at Langley scorned their counterparts at Foggy Bottom as "pro-Nkrumah."[147]

The embassy in Accra saw no basis for operational activity and recommended that "we maintain our presence on a business as usual basis."[148] Ambassador Mahoney was soon to find out, however, what careerists normally prefer to ignore by instinct and what political appointees usually fail to grasp through innocence—that an ambassador is seldom the master of his own house.

The matter concerned Dr. J.B. Danquah, Nkrumah's opponent in the presidential elections of 1960, who had been released from prison a few months after Mahoney's arrival as ambassador. Danquah paid a visit one November day to the embassy to ask Mahoney why the funds his family had been receiving during his imprisonment had been cut off after his release.

This was the first time that Mahoney had heard of the arrangement. After Danquah left, he summoned the CIA chief of station to ask why he had not been advised of the agency's association with Danquah. Dissatisfied with the explanation, Mahoney flew to Washington two days later and personally informed Kennedy about the matter.

The President reacted sharply to the news and told Mahoney that he had sent a letter to all ambassadors in May 1961 making it clear that their authority extended to all phases of embassy decision making. Kennedy then telephoned CIA Director John McCone and told him that he was sending Mahoney over to CIA headquarters and wanted the matter resolved immediately. The understanding that emerged from the meeting at Langley was that "no undertakings of any kind, even remotely involving our situation in Ghana, would either be continued or launched without the ambassador's knowledge and approval."[149]

It appeared, however, that the damage had already been done. A siege mentality had taken hold in Flagstaff House. More than 500 persons were being held in detention as the police continued to search for the terrorist group. The government ordered all foreign consulates outside Accra to be closed immediately. The embassy reported that Nkrumah was now "pathologically obsessed" with the CIA and was passing out copies of Andrew Tully's expose, *CIA: The Inside Story*, on an indiscriminate basis.[150]

On December 7, Ghana openly threatened Togo, warning that if the Togolese government did not repatriate Ghanaian dissidents, "the Government of Ghana will have no alternative but to institute such measures as may be found necessary to protect the safety and security of the State of Ghana and its citizens."[151]

News of worsening relations with Ghana moved Senator Dodd to launch a Senate subcommittee investigation to determine whether U.S. money was aiding another communist state. Professor Kofi Busia (recently of Lomé and other exile staging grounds) provided the testimony Dodd needed: "Ghana is the center for subversive Communist activities in Western Africa." Mahoney appealed to Washington to stall the appearance of the Dodd report, but this, of course, was not possible. Nkrumah found Dodd's wide-ranging accusations galling in the extreme, and the fact that the senator was a senior member of the President's own party was not lost on the Ghanaians.[152]

Nkrumah then called for the expulsion of all Peace Corps volunteers on the grounds that they were, according to the party press, "subversive agents" employed by the CIA. There was no doubt that if the U.S. were forced to pull its Peace Corps contingent out of Ghana, it would also withdraw from the Volta project. One-third of Ghana's secondary schools also stood to be closed if the 300 Peace Corps volunteers departed. After two weeks of nearly hourly discussions with Ghanaian officials, American diplomats persuaded the Ghanaian government to abandon the idea of expulsion, but the mood of trauma remained.[153]

Nkrumah was still convinced that the CIA was conspiring with his opponents in Togo and began to act accordingly. On Christmas Day 1962, two U.S. Agency for International Development employees were detained and questioned at the Ghana-Togo border by Ghanaian Special Branch officers. A few days later, Ghana closed the border to American diplomatic couriers. Another bomb went off in Accra on January 8, 1963. Three days later, the Ministry of Foreign Affairs formally requested that the U.S. withdraw two embassy officials, Cultural Affairs Officer William B. Davis and Regional Medical Officer Dr. Carl C. Nydell. The Ghanaians were convinced that Davis and Nydell were CIA agents involved in the Ghana-Togo arms traffic. Ghanaian police had found Dr. Nydell seated next to a terrorist courier whom they arrested on board a Ghana Airways plane in Accra airport. The terrorist in question had allegedly tried to pass a message to "Nidel" before being taken away.[154]

As American officials in Accra and Washington debated possible responses to the Ghanaian demand, there was tragic news from Lomé. Early Sunday morning on January 13, 1963, President Olympio was murdered by a group of Togolese soldiers. All eyes turned accusingly to Accra. Even Nkrumah's *"frère de combat"* Sékou Touré demanded an international investigation of the murder.[155]

Kennedy seemed to share the same suspicion. When Edgar Kaiser came by the Oval Office on January 23 to discuss the current crisis in U.S.-Ghana relations, the President coldly inquired, "What is this guy— some kind of a nut?"[156] The Volta project was once again on the rocks.

7

Kennedy Against Salazar

> Nationalism does not exist in either Angola or
> Mozambique. You Americans have invented it.
> Portugal will continue its 400 year old effort to
> build a multi-racial society . . .
>
> António de Oliveira Salazar
> (*July 15, 1961*)

> The United States has no intention of abdicating its
> leadership in [the] world-wide movement for inde-
> pendence to any nation committed to systematic
> human oppression.
>
> John F. Kennedy
> (*July 4, 1962*)

At the end of 1960, Portugal was the only colonial regime that had been spared rebellion in its African territories. The Portuguese, who had been the first Europeans to colonize Africa, pointed proudly to the results of their 400-year "civilizing mission." They claimed that the condition of "racial equality" in the *ultramar* (overseas territories) had made political independence unnecessary for their Africans. Just to be sure, Portugal's seventy-two-year-old autocrat, Dr. António de Oliveira Salazar pronounced that no quarter would be given to those who incited "agitation."

When Angola exploded in nationalist violence early in 1961, the Salazar regime resolved not to concede the field but to fight. In so doing, Portugal expected at least unofficial sympathy from its senior NATO partner, the United States, and strict American abstention on condemnatory resolutions that might come before the United Nations.

Kennedy, however, had pledged in 1956 that if a Democratic administration were elected, "we shall no longer abstain in the UN from voting on colonial issues, we shall no longer trade our vote on other such issues for other supposed gains. We shall no longer seek to prevent subjugated peoples from being heard."[1] In the weeks before his assumption of office, he had agreed with Ambassador Stevenson that the U.S. needed a tougher posture at the UN on colonialism. Now the decision of whether to break with Portugal and to call for self-determination in Angola was his.

"A NEW DECLARATION OF INDEPENDENCE"

The struggle to liberate Portuguese Angola began on February 3, 1961 just two weeks after Kennedy's inauguration. Some 200 Africans armed with machetes and clubs attacked the police barracks and military prison in Luanda, the capital of Angola. Portuguese police held off the attackers with machine gun fire, killing thirty-three. The state funeral for the seven white policemen who had also lost their lives in the assault erupted into a bloody melee, with white vigilantes murdering approximately 300 Africans. At the week's end, seven more Africans were shot trying once again to storm the military prison. To the east of Luanda, in the district of Malange, hundreds of rebellious Africans were killed before Portuguese authorities could restore control. The so-called "Kingdom of Silence" was silent no longer.[2]

To the incoming Kennedy administration, the Third World seemed to be disintegrating. "Each day the crises multiply," the President told the nation on January 31. "Each day their solution grows more difficult. Each day we draw nearer the hour of maximum danger." Kennedy listed the countries wracked by civil war and threatened by Soviet subversion: the Congo, Laos, Vietnam, and Cuba. He alluded to Premier Khrushchev's pledge to support "wars of national liberation." "The tide of events has been running out," Kennedy said, "and time has not been our friend."[3]

The President's old friend, British economist Barbara Ward, warned him from Accra that Western influence in Africa was being seriously weakened by "the assumed NATO backing for Portugal . . . The Communists, of course, are busy with the theme that the West doesn't give a damn about the massacre of Africans."[4] At the United Nations, Liberian Ambassador George Padmore formally requested on February 21 that the Security Council deal with the situation in Angola. He said that "five million un-enfranchised and almost forgotten inhabitants of this vast area cannot wait an eternity before achieving the freedom which their brethren to the north have already won."[5] The Soviet Union and the United Arab Republic promptly supported the Liberian request.

After consultations with Harlan Cleveland and Wayne Fredericks, UN Ambassador Adlai Stevenson placed a call to President Kennedy in late February.[6] He asked for the President's permission to support inscription of the Angola issue on the Security Council agenda. Stevenson also proposed that the U.S. cast an affirmative vote on an expected Afro-Asian resolution calling for self-determination in Angola. Kennedy agreed to the inscription request but preferred to reserve judgment on the resolution until he saw the text.[7]

Secretary Rusk instructed the American ambassador in Lisbon, C.

Burke Elbrick, too meet with Premier Salazar. Elbrick was to inform Dr. Salazar that the U.S. would vote in favor of inscription and that Portugal could not expect American support in the forthcoming Security Council debate:

> The United States feels that it would be remiss in its duties as a fellow NATO member of Portugal if it did not point out its conviction that step by step actions are now imperative for the political, economic and social advancement of all the inhabitants of Portuguese African territories toward full self-determination within a realistic timetable.[8]

When Ambassador Elbrick relayed Rusk's message to the Prime Minister, Salazar was incredulous. Why this policy reversal? Elbrick replied that his government was convinced that "Portuguese policies were totally out of step with the political and economic advancement elsewhere in Africa." It was time to adjust to reality.[9]

It was little wonder that Salazar found Washington's sudden decision to reverse policy shocking. For more than a decade, Portugal had been a staunch and esteemed member of the North Atlantic Alliance. In 1951, Portugal had signed a defense treaty with the U.S. that had given the Americans free use of a strategically located air base on the Azores Islands. In the final months of 1960, Washington had agreed to provide the Portuguese navy with two warships and had concluded an accord for arms production in Portugal.[10]

Throughout 1960, the U.S. had helped stave off censorious UN resolutions, put forth by the Afro-Asian nations, aimed at Portugal. In December, for example, Eisenhower had ordered the U.S. representative to the UN to abstain from Resolution 1514, which called for self-determination in dependent territories.[11] Now, barely three months later, the United States was serving notice that the "special relationship" between the U.S. and Portugal had ended. In the days preceding the Security Council vote, Portuguese diplomats in Lisbon and Washington appealed to the American government for reconsideration. They were not alone.

Riding over to the White House with Rusk on March 15 for a National Security Council meeting on NATO, former Secretary of State Dean Acheson saw a copy of the draft telegram instructing Stevenson to cast an affirmative vote in the upcoming inscription issue. Once they arrived at the White House, Acheson waited as the President huddled briefly with Rusk and Deputy Assistant Secretary Woodruff Wallner, before signing the cable. During the NSC meeting, Acheson observed that "some people" were "much too light-hearted about kicking our friends around."

Kennedy encouraged Acheson to say what he had on his mind. "I didn't know you had this view. Talk about it." "It's silly to talk about it," Acheson replied. "You already sent the telegram and we're going to take this step . . . What we are doing is . . . acting for the purpose of appeasing the Afro-Asian group. This is all we accomplish. We accomplish nothing in Angola . . . We will alienate the Portugese. Now, this is not the way to run an alliance."[12]

Late that afternoon, Stevenson cast his vote in support of Liberia's resolution, which called for reform in Angola, progress toward independence, and a UN commission of inquiry into Angola. As expected, the Western majority of the council (Britain, France, Nationalist China, Chile, and Ecuador) supported Portugal's contention that Angola was a domestic matter and accordingly abstained. "I regret to find myself in disagreement," Stevenson said as he rose to explain the American position. He cited Jefferson's creed that governments derive their just powers from the consent of the governed.[13] The Soviet Union joined with the U.S. in voting affirmatively.

Reaction to the vote was emphatic. A Portuguese spokesman said that his government viewed it "with the greatest apprehension," claiming that Portugal had received no advance notice of the way the U.S. would vote. The *Diario da Manha* denounced the vote as "an act of stupidity."[14] But Angolan nationalist Holden Roberto paid tribute to "the new American administration and its young and dynamic chief, John Kennedy," whose acquaintance Roberto had made in 1959.[15] *The New York Times* called the administration's vote "in a very real sense, a new declaration of independence . . ."[16]

Some policy makers from the Truman and Eisenhower administrations were disturbed by Kennedy's decision. In a letter to the President, Acheson observed that the vote had already produced "mischief" and warned him that "one of the great traps in the UN is to allow small nations to maneuver responsible powers into voting on every conceivable issue. We are great enough not to do this . . ."[17] Eisenhower's Under Secretary of State Robert D. Murphy took Stevenson aside to tell him that the spectacle of the U.S. voting with the Soviet Union against her own allies was a "matter of deep concern."[18] Nevertheless, the U.S. voted again with the Afro-Asian majority on April 20 in support of a General Assembly resolution calling for "preparation for independence" in Angola.[19]

While the Security Council deliberated on March 15, Angola exploded into an orgy of bloodletting that signaled the beginning of the protracted nationalist struggle. Holden Roberto's UPA (*União das Populações de Angola*) militants, after filtering over the colony's northern border from the Congo, led uprisings that coincided with isolated outbreaks of violent rampage in the north. African workers beat and chopped their masters to death. Hundreds of Portuguese lost their lives. Portuguese reprisals were uncontrolled and unsparing. Within six months, there were as many as 20,000 African casualties as a result of aerial strafings, mop-up operations, and isolated acts of vengeance. By the end of the year, 150,000 Angolan refugees had fled to the Congo. One Baptist missionary said that all hope of containing the rebellion ended when "the savagery of the Portuguese reaction kicked and scattered the fire until the whole north was ablaze."[20] Meanwhile in Lisbon, Portuguese officers, in touch with the U.S. diplomatic mission, conspired to remove Salazar.

COVERT DESIGNS IN LISBON

By deciding to wage war in defense of Portugal's holdings in Africa, Salazar put his political survival on the line. It was not long before he faced dissension from within the ranks of those who were obliged to fulfill Portugal's military mission in the field. Not unnaturally, the dissenters found sympathy and intermittent support from the Kennedy administration, committed as it was to a change in Portugal's colonial policy.

On February 17, 1961, the Portuguese minister of defense, General Julio Botelho Moniz, informed U.S. Ambassador Elbrick that he and several leading figures in the Salazar regime had decided to force the Prime Minister to liberalize his policies both overseas and at home. Whether or not American intelligence operatives had encouraged Botelho Moniz to approach Elbrick in this fashion is unclear. What is certain is that the Kennedy administration saw an unexpected opportunity to assist in the liberalization of the Portuguese government and took advantage of it.[21]

The relationship between the Defense Minister Botelho Moniz and Ambassador Elbrick during this period was unusually close. They had a three-hour luncheon together on March 6. The fact that Elbrick briefed Botelho Moniz fully about Washington's decision to call for self-determination in the Portuguese African territories one day before he broke the momentous news to Salazar is one indication of their intimacy.[22]

On March 25, Botelho Moniz, his assistant, Major Lemos, General Albuquerque de Freitas (the commander-in-chief of the Air Force), and another unidentified person drafted a letter to Salazar demanding internal reform. They drew attention to the deteriorating situation in the overseas provinces and noted that although terrorism in Angola was instigated in part from the outside, many native Angolans were willing supporters of the conspiracy. The letter to Salazar was polite in tone but menacing in implication: "[W]e are heading for an impossible position where we might be at the mercy of a frontal attack, considering that our forces are dispersed over four continents, without sufficient equipment, and carrying out a suicidal mission from which it may be impossible for us to disentangle ourselves."[23]

The letter was reviewed by eighteen senior generals at a meeting of the High Military Council on March 27. General Camara Pina, the army chief of staff, alone dissented. That evening Botelho Moniz delivered the letter to Salazar and discussed its contents with him for three and one-half hours. The next day, Elbrick lunched with the Defense Minister, who reported to him in the strictest confidence that Salazar had received his critique courteously, but that "it was difficult to fathom his real thoughts." About two weeks later, Salazar announced his proposals for reform, which included abolition of the *indigenato*, a legal and social distinction between civilized and uncivilized African natives.[24]

This was apparently not enough to suit Botelho Moniz. He told Elbrick that if he did not force Salazar's hand, he would become "another revolutionary-minded general without portfolio." The CIA station chief was certain that the Defense Minister had enough backing to move forcibly. Botelho Moniz informed the American embassy that he would ask President Américo Tomás one more time either to neutralize Salazar or to dismiss him from office. If Tomás refused, the armed forces would overthrow Salazar.[25]

Salazar himself was playing for time, as he had done so artfully during previous bouts of dissension in his twenty-nine years in office. He apparently knew that his support in the military had seriously eroded and that the fidelity of the *Guardia Nacional Republicana* and the *Policia International de Defensa de Estado* (PIDE) was in question. Salazar also realized, however, that Botelho Moniz was strongly in favor of a peaceful changeover—the fatal miscalculation for the Defense Minister—and had the sympathy of many in the armed forces but the allegiance of very few.[26]

The frequency of contact between Elbrick and Botelho Moniz had meanwhile focused attention on the American role in the developing crisis. The ambassador was worried that the Portuguese government might establish "that Botelho Moniz and I are directly involved." Already there was a story circulating in Lisbon that the Defense Minister was "plotting with the U.S." On April 13, Botelho Moniz sent word that he would move against Salazar "in a day or two."[27]

But it was already too late. President Tomás, a staunch ally of Salazar, who had told the malcontents, "I won't dismiss the only great statesman of the century after Churchill," informed the Prime Minister on April 12 that a delegation of the Supreme Council for Defense had formally requested that he dismiss him. Salazar moved quickly, alerting the PIDE and the Republican Guard (both of which Botelho Moniz had mistakenly counted in his camp). For a time on the afternoon of April 13, the situation was fluid. Salazar actually had to slip out of his residence at São Bento and take refuge for the night at the headquarters of the Republican Guard. He found an unexpected ally in the former Defense Minister, General Sanchez Costa, who raillied some troops and managed to cut off the Defense ministry's telephone communications.[28]

The conspirators had assembled in the ministry that morning for yet another meeting and had agreed that at 4 P.M. the army would start taking over key positions in the capital. At noon, however, Salazar dismissed Botelho Moniz.[29] Faced with this predicament, Botelho Moniz and his colleagues refused to issue an order for their troops to seize the presidential palace and other strategic points. (The CIA later ascribed his reaction to a failure of nerve.)[30]

Salazar was deeply disturbed by the apparent American role in the conspiracy. Thereafter, he looked upon Kennedy's policy as not only an effort to disband Portugal's empire, but also as a personal vendetta against him. Salazar told André de Staerke, the Belgian ambassador to NATO, for example, that it was America's "brusque and cavalier tactics" that he found so offensive, rather than its policy.[31] For a man of such measured expression as Salazar, these were strong and revealing words. The day after the threatened putsch, the Prime Minister announced that the political and educational reforms in Angola would be postponed. President Kennedy was singled out for personal criticism in a government communiqué.[32]

Salazar emerged from the crisis with new resolution, a stronger grip on the military, and greater support from his people. A Portuguese government official told *The New York Times* correspondent Benjamin Welles that American opposition "has had the reverse effect of making us rally more strongly around Salazar . . ."[33] The attempted coup, which might have saved Portugal and Portuguese Africa thirteen years of war, only made that war all the more inevitable and intense with its failure.

CONFRONTING PORTUGAL: I

If President Kennedy had had any doubts about Soviet intentions, Premier Khrushchev conclusively resolved them at their contentious summit in June 1961. Khrushchev called the Angolan uprising a "sacred" war of national liberation and assured Kennedy that the Soviet Union would actively support the struggle.[34] At the UN, Russian Ambassador Zorin proposed "measures of coercion" against Portugal. The Soviets clearly wanted to pin the stigma of Portuguese colonialism on the U.S. and its NATO allies.

Breaking with Portugal may have marginally neutralized the Soviet propaganda advantage, but it also caused trouble within NATO. The Portuguese complained bitterly about the American position, while the British and French (who themselves were exposed to Afro-Asian attacks over their own colonial policies) indicated distinct unhappiness with Washington. Although the Kennedy administration had decided that "trying to straddle the independence issue" was useless, it would soon find that not straddling it could be equally problematic.[35] The Azores base was perceived as critical to U.S. military security, a fact that gave Salazar considerable leverage over Kennedy and his Angola policy.

At a meeting in Paris in late May, Kennedy discussed the Angola situation with General de Gaulle. As a matter of long-established principle, the General held the UN in the highest disdain (*"ce machin,"* he called it). At the same time, he also realized that the Kennedy administration might elect to call for the independence of France's own colony, Algeria, if he did not defer in some fashion to the American position on Angola.[36] As a result, he was uncharacteristically complaisant. De Gaulle agreed with Kennedy that the Portuguese attitude was inflexible and obsolescent, but pushing Salazar too hard, he thought, might cause a revolution in Portugal and establish a communist state on the Iberian peninsula. Kennedy replied that change in Africa was inexorable and that any attempt to block it would only benefit the communists. The United States had therefore decided to take a progressive position on Angola in the UN. De Gaulle said that he would encourage Salazar toward more constructive policies and promised that, while he could not support the American position, he would not oppose it.[37]

The new assistant secretary of state for African affairs, G. Mennen Williams, for one, was pleased by the President's efforts. "Dear Jack:" he cabled Paris, "Appreciate your vigorous stand on Angola . . ."[38] The President's personal effort with De Gaulle also produced results. A public statement from the Quai d'Orsay (the French Foreign Affairs Ministry) a month later left litttle doubt about the change in French sentiment about the Portuguese presence in Africa: "Nothing could be more mistaken, more tragic than to be guided by concepts and principles which were, perhaps, good in their time but which no longer apply in our time."[39]

In late May, Lord Home, the foreign secretary, paid a visit to Dr. Salazar. Amid the starchy expressions of mutual esteem and fidelity between the members of the oldest alliance (which dated back to 1386) there was the British request: "[I]t is necessary both to name a political goal and to be seen making progress toward it."[40]

Salazar was highly offended by this. Lisbon charged that American "bullying" and "arm-twisting" of European governments had caused

Portugal's diplomatic isolation.[41] There was a good deal of truth to this, but the "shock treatment"—as *The New York Times* called it—did produce positive results. In an interview on May 29, Salazar pledged "important political, social, and economic reforms for the African, mulatto, and white populations of Angola." He indicated his intention to abolish the *indigenato*.[42] Salazar's new foreign minister, Dr. Alberto Franco Nogueira, wrote Rusk that these reforms would "increasingly bring the population into local and administrative life."[43] The condition, however, on which each of these reforms was predicated was military pacification first.

The Portuguese launched a military counteroffensive in Angola at the end of the rainy season in June 1961. "We will hunt the terrorists down like game," a Portuguese air force officer predicted to London *Daily Telegraph* correspondent Richard Beetson. "We have no alternative but extermination."[44] During the next four months (June to October), this prediction was put into effect with deadly success. Equipped with incendiary bombs and napalm, Portuguese bombers set rebel strongholds ablaze while army units sealed off escape routes. Few prisoners were taken or civilians spared. The African death toll climbed above 10,000 (Roberto claimed 25,000). According to the UN, there were more than 125,000 Angolan refugees in the Congo.[45]

After a visit to Angola in August, Williams reported a deliberate campaign to arrest or liquidate literate Africans.[46] Beatings and executions of missionaries by Portuguese settlers continued. The Roman Catholic vicar-general in Angola, Monsignor Manuel J. Mendes das Neves, was imprisoned and brutally beaten by the Portuguese secret police. The new Overseas Minister, Dr. Adriano Moreira, tried to prevent atrocities by white settlers against Africans with little success. As Foreign Minister Franco Nogueira had predicted to the Americans, African resistance would produce a "bloodbath."[47]

ARMS AND THE PORTUGUESE

The American role in this tragedy could not have been more anomalous. On one hand, Portugal was using American planes, napalm, automatic weapons, tanks, and military vehicles supplied under the U.S. Military Assistance Program (MAP) in order to crush the insurgency. On the other, Angolan refugee camps in the Congo were receiving food and medicine from American sources.

When Kennedy read a dispatch in a London newspaper reporting the finding of a "Made in America" mark on part of a bomb dropped on an Angolan village, he expressed concern to Rusk and McNamara. Could the Portuguese be dissuaded from using American equipment in Angola, or would this have "an adverse effect upon the use of the Azores base"?

The Secretary of Defense insisted that the military necessity of access to the Azores bases had to remain pre-eminent. Public pressure on the Portuguese regarding the use of U.S.-supplied equipment in Angola should be avoided. Rusk agreed, noting that a public announcement "would only further infuriate the Portuguese." Governor Williams disagreed. NBC was planning to broadcast an hour-long documentary on September 19 detailing the use of American napalm in Angola. Unless the administration made a public announcement of its arms policy, "many African states [would continue] to believe wrongly that his government had had no objection to the use by the Portuguese of American-supplied arms in Angola."[48]

No public announcement was made, but privately the administration's warnings to the Portuguese grew more stringent. Several commercial licenses to sell arms to Portugal previously granted by the Department of Defense were revoked.[49] A routine disbursement to one of Portugal's NATO divisions (two of which had already been sent to fight in Angola) was slashed. Ambassador Elbrick vigorously protested this decision. The embassy was then instructed to notify the Portuguese government that the U.S. Military Assistance Advisory Group (MAAG) would require "verification" that all military materiel purchased from the U.S. was being used for NATO and nothing else.[50]

The embassy cabled that it had "serious reservations" about such a move. It argued that under the Portuguese-American defense treaty of 1951, the possibility that Portugal might divert MAP-supplied equipment to its overseas territories had been recognized. Under the terms of the treaty, however, Portugal did have to obtain the "prior consent" of the U.S. That such consent would be forthcoming was virtually guaranteed in a secret supplemental exchange of notes made a few months after the signing of the treaty. At that time, the U.S. stated that there was "no doubt" that such consent would be given in the event of an emergency. (Two weeks before the Kennedy administration took office, the Eisenhower administration had reiterated this commitment.) Elbrick argued that if Washington now tried to stop Lisbon from shipping arms to Africa, Salazar would publicly invoke the secret exchange, either to abrogate the defense treaty or to smear the U.S. as the hypocritical arms merchant who was pretending to be otherwise.[51]

The tone of the embassy cable was little short of defiant. In contrast to U.S. efforts, it claimed, the British (who had nominally suspended arms shipments to Portugal) "have used great finesse in meeting a domestic political necessity which is presumably similar to our own."[52] This remark angered the White House. State was instructed to reiterate to Lisbon: "Our actions amount to a complete arms embargo against arms and munitions control items intended for use in Portugal's overseas territories." Elbrick was again instructed to see the foreign minister. With "misgivings," he complied. A frosty reception awaited the ambassador in the Oval Office when he returned to Washington in November for consultations.[53]

Portugal would never return MAP-supplied equipment that had been diverted to Africa, a furious Franco Nogueira told Elbrick. As to future deliveries of arms, he "inquired derisively if we are afraid to have U.S. arms found in Portuguese hands. He wondered if we have the same concern about possible discovery of U.S. arms in terrorists' hands." Portugal had other sources, he warned Elbrick, particularly in the communist bloc. Elbrick reported to Washington that the meeting was "the latest nail in the coffin of U.S.-Portuguese relations."[54]

CONFRONTING PORTUGAL: II

Throughout 1961, pressure from the African states continued to mount. Senegal broke relations with Portugal and the moderate governments of Tunisia and Tanganyika began openly to aid and harbor the insurrectionists. Radical regimes like those of Ghana and Guinea began supplying money and weapons to the nationalist movements. President Kwame Nkrumah spoke for most of Africa when he declared that Portugal represented too slight an asset to the other NATO powers to justify their condoning its colonial policy at the price of risking African enmity. Prime Minister Nehru described the situation in Angola as "horrible almost beyond belief" and called for the UN to impose sanctions against Portugal, a proposal the Soviet Union quickly endorsed.[55]

Working with the Egyptian, Liberian, and Ceylonese representatives at the UN, Stevenson succeeded in getting language in specific regard to the imposition of sanctions deleted from the draft resolution to be presented to the Security Council.[56] Rusk then appealed to Lisbon for an announcement before the vote that Portugal would allow a UN investigating committee to go to Angola. In this way, the U.S. could "buy time" for its ally.[57] The Portuguese reply came in UN Ambassador Vasco Garin's speech, in which he blasted the U.S. and reiterated that Angola was an integral part of metropolitan Portugal; as such, it was not open to UN scrutiny. Portugal, he insisted, was the victim, not the perpetrator, of savagery.[58]

Such statements, Rusk wrote his Portuguese counterpart, Dr. Franco Nogueira, "have not made our moderating task any easier. I sincerely believe, for example, that an indication of willingness to cooperate with the UN subcommittee could have done much to remove the sting from the Council meeting."[59] On June 10, 1961, the U.S. and eight other Security Council members voted affirmatively on a resolution calling on Portugal "to desist forthwith from repressive measures" in Angola. The resolution also authorized an immediate investigation of Portuguese colonial rule by a special five-nation subcommittee. Foreign Minister Nogueira called the resolution a "green-light" for terrorism in Angola.[60]

Addressing the National Assembly on June 30, Salazar attacked the U.S. for allegedly serving the communist policy of subversion and expansion. European governments were losing faith in the U.S., Salazar declared, and he reiterated that Portugal had no intention of complying with the UN resolution calling for a cessation of hostilities.[61]

Kennedy telephoned Rusk and said that the speech should not go unanswered.[62] Ambassador Elbrick accordingly received instructions to see Salazar and express great disappointment in the speech. Time was running out rapidly, Elbrick was instructed to tell Salazar: " . . . we believe that the long-run interests of us all will be adversely affected if political and economic measures are not soon indicated that would respond to this situation."[63]

The American warning hardly registered; a siege mentality had taken hold in Lisbon. Franco Nogueira received Elbrick first and told him that Portugal would go to the bitter end to maintain her overseas territories and that a world war might result. "Would Portugal attempt to drag the whole world down with it because of Angola?" Elbrick asked. Indeed it would, Nogueira replied.[64]

Immediately after his session with Elbrick, Nogueira went to brief Salazar on the nature of the American démarche. Salazar asked the Foreign Minister what he thought of the American request for immediate reform in Angola. Franco Nogueira described it as an ultimatum. He told Salazar that Portugal had to be ready for every contingency—whether armed intervention or economic sanctions. The Foreign Minister cited the landing of American marines in Lebanon in 1958. "Until they do that," Salazar observed, "we won't worry."[65]

As one biographer has put it, beyond Salazar's other qualities—his cold austerity, the "almost anarchical taste for having his own way," the self-ordained and institutionalized role as Portugal's *paterfamilias*—"the overriding memory is that of his massive calm . . . [O]n matters of principle, Salazar would not budge." He had enjoined his collaborators in 1958 when the trouble was just beginning: "Stand firm! Stand firm! That is all that is needed for the storm to subside and for justice to be done to us."[66]

For thirty years, Salazar had ruled Portugal more in the manner of an ascetic headmaster than of the fascist dictator he was supposed to be. "Mine is the dictatorship of professors," the former economics instructor had once said of his regime. He lived the life of a cloistered bachelor among his books and papers and behind an iron curtain of protocol.[67]

Salazar received Elbrick on July 15. He was, as usual, unfailingly courteous, and, as usual, completely unmovable. It was as if, George Ball later recounted, he were "absorbed by a time dimension quite different from our own conveying the strong yet curious impression that he and his whole country were living in more than one century."[68] Even his dress and office décor were strictly nineteenth century—the buttoned-up shoes, the blanketed lap, the crimson velvet Louis XIV chairs. Salazar saw his mission in the light of papal encyclicals from the nineteenth century: the stern pastor of the Portuguese flock.

Reform in Angola, Salazar told Elbrick, had to be slow, in order to protect the native. U.S. activity at the UN only encouraged the "terrorists." Nationalism did not exist in either Angola or Mozambique; the Americans had invented it. Portugal would continue its 400-year-old effort to build a multiracial society in Angola.[69] Kennedy and others in Washington were fond of calling this Salazar's second 500-year plan for Africa.[70] Yet it was one the Prime Minister took very seriously. Towards the end of their meeting, Elbrick presented Washington's trump card— economic aid to the faltering Portuguese economy. If such aid were predicated on Portugal's loss of her overseas territories, Salazar replied, then he was not interested.

The idea of offering Salazar a multimillion-dollar aid package in exchange for granting independence to the African provinces was popular among administration liberals. Ambassador-at-Large Chester Bowles revived the proposal a year and one-half later. The terms of exchange would be $500 million for the granting of independence within five years. Bowles argued that helping Portugal develop into a modern industrial state would engender healthy political change within the country, stop the present drain of its meager resources, and ultimately save it the humiliating experience of a military defeat in Africa.[71]

The problem was that much of this self-interested goodwill was at variance with Portuguese reality. Even with the north of Angola ablaze and 40,000 troops in the field, the province continued to be a financial asset to the metropole—a fact that was often ignored in estimates of how long Portugal could hold out in Angola.[72]

Premier Salazar, moreover, had an enduring distaste for foreign aid and investment, which he regarded as internally disruptive. "Portugal is not for sale," he announced rather archly not long before one more American emissary—this time George Ball—came to Lisbon to offer yet another aid package.[73] There was also the simple fact that Salazar's own political fate was tied to the preservation of the *ancien ordre*. Any massive infusion of aid would almost certainly disrupt his corporatist state, based as it was on a meager, but carefully allocated patrimony. A human problem loomed, as well. In the event of Angolan independence, Salazar would have to deal with a half-million Portuguese refugees in an already crowded metrapole. No amount of foreign aid could make this an acceptable prospect

Paul Sakwa, a gifted young idea man at the CIA, who had also served with distinction in the field, reached a more realistic conclusion: since "an aged potentate like Salazar is not likely to accept the above plan without benefit of a frontal lobotomy," the U.S. should initiate covert contacts with members of the moderate opposition and young, middle-grade officers in the Portuguese armed forces in the interests of succession.[74] As *Le Monde* later observed, there would be no decolonization in Africa until there was revolution in Lisbon.[75]

Reporting to the department in July 1961, Elbrick concluded that since the March exchange Salazar had adopted "a more, rather than less, rigid position." Pressure on the Portuguese only seemed "to stiffen their resistance."[76] Part of the reason for this was that Salazar's political condition, so shaky in April, was by July much restored. He had completely overhauled his government in May and had summoned several talented and experienced men to defend his foreign policy.

Foremost among these was Dr. Pedro Theotónio Pereira, Salazar's trusted partner and touted successor, who had successfully negotiated Portugal's entry into NATO while serving as Portugal's ambassador in Washington during the Truman administration. Salazar now sent him back to Washington to do an even more difficult task.[77] The foreign affairs portfolio went to Dr. Franco Nogueira, a forceful forty-two-year-old diplomat with a doctorate in law, who was fluent in English. As overseas minister, Salazar chose Dr. Adriano Moreira, a politically ambitious thirty-seven year old with "furious energy" and relatively liberal ideas.[78]

Both Franco Nogueira and Moreira proved formidable advocates in Portugal's defense. For Salazar, who had scarcely set foot outside Portugal in thirty years, spoke rarely and poorly in public, and who had little rapport with his fellow heads of state, their selection was a masterstroke. He had always favored promising young men of humble origins (Franco Nogueira's father was a shepherd, Moreira's a policeman). Both were seemingly tireless, traveled constantly, and had excellent relations with the press. In September, 1961, for example, Franco Nogueira went to Harvard University to deliver a full-length defense of Portugal's position.[79] Moreira rallied support among the threatened and restive settlers in the *ultramar*. He made good on Salazar's pledge to abolish the *assimilado* system, thus making all blacks and mulattoes Portuguese citizens, at least as a matter of law. Forced labor was abolished and native land laws were strengthened. Two universities were established during Moreira's tenure, one in Luanda, the other in Lourenço Marques.[80]

Like Salazar, Franco Nogueira took his philosophical cue from António Enes, who had written in 1888 regarding his government's position toward Southern Africa: "We do not refuse to compromise, but the indispensable basis for compromise is the recognition of our historic and present sovereignty."[81] Franco Nogueira's diplomacy blended tactical accommodation with singleminded and aggressive prosecution of Portuguese policy. No one was a better gamesman than he.[82] To gain leverage over the Americans, for example, Franco Nogueira authorized trade with Cuba. (In 1965, he would try to estabilsh diplomatic relations with the People's Republic of China.[83]) He was also an artful player of personalities. He denounced Stevenson and Williams regularly, cultivated Rusk with notable success, and was invited to the Oval Office for a private conference with the President every time he went to Washington.[84] Kennedy, who was thoroughly bored by the pedantic Ambassador Pereira, found Franco Nogueira refreshingly candid and witty.[85]

SHOWDOWN

If Rusk was pliant, Kennedy was not, and in the face of Portuguese intransigence he asked Governor Williams to chair a task force on the Portuguese territories in Africa. The task force grouped representatives from the CIA, Treasury, Defense, the State Department and the White House and was to submit recommendations for action to the President. In mid-July 1961, the task force concluded its deliberations and proposed that the President take the following actions: send an envoy to Lisbon to prevail on Salazar to accept self-determination in Angola; coordinate diplomatic pressure with Britain, France, Brazil, Spain, and the Vatican to bring about a change in Portuguese colonial policy; interdict MAP equipment supplied to Portugal from being diverted to Africa; expand U.S. assistance to Angolan refugees; and develop an educational program for Portuguese Africans.[86]

The Task Force recognized the serious risks inherent in its proposals: possible loss of the Azores and Spanish bases, the conceivable withdrawal of Portuguese military support from NATO in the event of limited or general war over Berlin, and "a major overhaul in U.S. wartime plans."[87]

Not surprisingly, the Pentagon was totally opposed to the task force recommendations. At the White House, Rostow, for one, was skeptical:

" . . . even if Salazar moves," he wrote Kennedy, "he will move too little too late. We should avoid a deep U.S. involvement in inadequate measures . . . The truth is that no one is confident what the risks are . . . We are flying pretty blind on this one."[88] Nonetheless, Kennedy gave the go-ahead, authorizing that all tactical capabilities be brought to bear on Salazar as well as measures to keep the door open with the Angolan nationalists. However abrupt the break with past U.S. policy, the decision was perfectly consistent with Kennedy's own thinking during the previous ten years. In 1956, for example, he had publicly predicted that American support for decolonization "will displease our allies. We will find our policies hailed by extremists, terrorists and saboteurs for whom we could have no sympathy—and condemned by our oldest and most trusted friends who will feel we have deserted them . . . Some will plead for a more cautious course; but halfway measures will not do."[89]

In approving the proposals set forth by the task force on the Portuguese territories, the President affirmed his support for Angolan self-determination. These proposals were promulgated in a National Security Action Memorandum—the highest form of presidential authorization in foreign policy.[90]

By the end of 1961, the diplomatic skirmishes between Portugal and the United States were over; the disputants had entrenched themselves in their respective positions. From this point forward, it would be a test of will, a question of who would prevail—Salazar, who clung to the centuries-old belief that Portugal's integrity as a nation was bound up in its overseas empire, or Kennedy, who sought to align the United States with the future of Africa and who believed that Angolan nationalism could be shaped to moderate ends through peaceful means.

8

Angola or the Azores?

> We must firmly resist Portuguese efforts to link the
> Azores to U.S. policy on Angola . . . (and) take a
> hard-line against the moldy colonialism of Salazar's
> Portugal . . .
>
> Stevenson to Kennedy
> (*April, 1962*)

> If you're going ahead and fight what they're doing in
> Angola, you won't get the extension (of the Azores
> lease). Nobody can get it. I can't—nobody can.
>
> Acheson to Kennedy
> (*April, 1962*)

The whole premise of the administration's policy was that through pressure by the U.S. on both sides—Portuguese and African—an orderly
transition toward independence could be achieved and a full-scale colonial
war that might invite Soviet intervention averted. If such a policy succeeded, U.S. security interests in a united NATO and in access to the
Azores base would be preserved while American standing in Africa and
at the UN would be enhanced. "It would be easy to serve one of these
interests by neglecting the other," Kennedy wrote in July 1962. "Our
object must be to serve them both."[1]

This confidence in being able to have it both ways epitomized Kennedy's response to revolution throughout the Third World. If only the
right would undertake reform and the left accept compromise, the center
would hold. In some trouble spots, this reform-compromise strategy had
worked. U.S. acceptance of the neutralization of Laos had led to a negotiated peace between the Soviet-supported Pathet Lao and the American-
backed Royal Laotian Army. In the Congo, the administration was
shepherding both an uneasy coalition of moderates and radicals in Léopoldville and an even more disparate alliance of governments in New
York in support of the UN peacekeeping operation in Katanga.

As persuaded as the President may have been about the chances for a
peaceful Portuguese withdrawal from Africa, his advisers were not. Personalities as philosophically opposed as Acheson and Stevenson agreed
at least about one thing—that Salazar would never compromise in Angola

so long as Portugal controlled the American lease to the mid-Atlantic Azores base. In response to a question by an American reporter about the prospect for renewal of the lease, Salazar ominously observed: "I would prefer not to answer this question and I would ask you not to put it."[2] In January 1962, Salazar gave the Americans a hint of what was coming if they didn't back down on Angola; Portugal forbade refueling rights on the Azores to USAF plans carrying UN troops or cargo to the Congo.

AID TO THE ANGOLANS

In late April 1961, the National Security Council Special Group authorized covert funding for Angolan nationalist leader Holden Roberto. The moving personality behind the decision was Attorney General Robert F. Kennedy.[3] The slender, bespectacled Roberto had impressed the Americans during his visit to New York in March 1961. Asked whether he was pro-Western or pro-Soviet, Roberto had replied that he was neither. He was only pro-Angolan, but would accept support from wherever he could get it. Roberto was well connected in African circles; he was a long-time ally of Ghana's Kwame Nkrumah, friendly with Algeria's Ben Bella, and—reassuringly—on good terms with the Congo's Joseph Mobutu, the CIA's general-in-waiting in Léopoldville.[4]

The initial size of the retainer, $6,000 a year, was relatively small, but the consequences of the association were not. It ultimately tied the United States in Angola to the political fate of Roberto.[5] Moreover, rumors of the association soon undermined Roberto's own legitimacy among fellow African nationalists. In Lisbon, nothing about the Kennedy administration's Angola policy galled the Portuguese more than CIA support for Roberto. In many ways, nothing was more damaging to the central purpose of American diplomacy than this connection. As Elbrick repeatedly pointed out, persuading Salazar to compromise and to negotiate was impossible when the U.S. was secretly engaged in activities "which the Portuguese consider to strike at the very structure and life of the Portuguese state."[6]

Throughout 1961, the administration pushed ahead with its programs of assistance to Angolan exiles. In July, the President approved the task force's recommendations to give emergency medical and nutritional relief to the 125,000 Angolan refugees in the Congo. The program was small— costing only slightly more than $1 million in its first year—but highly successful. Kennedy also gave the go-ahead to a program that he had advocated as a presidential candidate in August 1960: to bring young Portuguese African exiles to the U.S. and provide them with college educations.[7] By late July 1961, Governor Williams was able to report to the President that food supplies and medical provisions from the U.S. (provided for under Public Law 480) and several charitable sources were adequate to meet the needs of the 125,000 refugees.[8]

However humanitarian in purpose, the relief program was politically consequential. Without foreign assistance, Roberto's UPA would probably have enjoyed less support from the exiled Angola community. The insurgency would have weakened and possibly collapsed. Liberals like Williams argued that, "The fact that most of them [the refugees] identify themselves with the UPA does not diminish their status or make them less deserving . . . "[9] Rusk, Elbrick, and the European Bureau decidedly thought otherwise and there were subsequent efforts to phase out the program.

In late April 1961, pursuant to National Security Action Memorandum 60, the President asked his military adviser, Maxwell D. Taylor, to look into the problem of sixty-one Angolan students formerly studying in Portugal, who had sought asylum in France and Switzerland. Could we bring them to the U.S. and finance their education with Point IV funds? Taylor reported back that the State Department was opposed to the idea: " . . . it might be impolitic for the United States to be associated with their further education . . . " An "indirect (i.e., CIA) method of assistance" would be preferable.[10]

U.S. missions in Africa (mainly those in Léopoldville, Accra, and Dar es Salaam) began offering scholarships to refugee students from the Portuguese territories. The cultural attaché in Accra, William B. Davis, managed to whisk a dozen Angolans from the Kwame Nkrumah Ideological Institute at Winneba and send them to the U.S. A report from a covert source in Léopoldville that 400 Angolans had already left to study in the Soviet Union resulted in a redoubling of efforts. The race was on. In Dar es Salaam, the African-American Institute, with CIA funding, provided university training for exiles from Mozambique at the American University in Beirut and at local secondary schools. Rusk and Elbrick tried to exclude the Mozambicans from the program on the grounds that "the delicate balance" of U.S.-Portuguese relations might be upset. Williams fought the proposed change and won.[11]

For the university education of the refugees in the United States, the State Department negotiated a contract with Lincoln University, which was chosen because of its "fully integrated character, and its long history and competence in dealing with African students."[12] The program was an outstanding success in its first year but struck a raw nerve in Portugal. Franco Nogueira charged that some of the students were UPA partisans. The program was not only "an unfriendly act but a hostile one as well." Another Portuguese official asked Elbrick how the U.S. expected Portugal to improve education in Angola "while at the same time [the U.S.] was training cadres to assume control there."[13] (Elbrick might well have replied that since the illiteracy rate among the native population of Angola was about 99 percent, Portuguese efforts in the educational area had been something less than a total success. Nor was their record as a multiracial society any more exemplary: less than one percent of the African populace had been accorded assimilated status.)

The U.S. embassy in Lisbon said the Lincoln program had "poisoned" U.S.-Portugal relations and should be discontinued.[14] On the eve of the Azores negotiations in June 1962, the seventh floor of the State Department moved to block the renewal of the Lincoln contract. Williams protested. The program had been created "in response to specific Presidential interest. Failure to renew our contract could only be interpreted by the Portuguese as a direct retreat from present policies . . . " The dispute was taken to the President, who decided that the program would continue.[15]

Salazar and his lieutenants were in a white hot fury over American assistance to the exiles. At first, they confined their anger to bitter and accusatory talk about "arming terrorists." Then they retaliated in kind. A few months after the CIA had established its relationship with Roberto, agents of the Portuguese secret police broke into the U.S. consular offices in Luanda and Lourenço Marques and made off with classified and unclassified documents.[16] Foreign Service stationery, apparently stolen in the break-in, was later used to forge an official U.S. document purportedly detailing the extent of U.S. military aid to the UPA. Franco Nogueira brandished this as "incontrovertible proof" of subversion.[17] Rusk summoned Ambassador Pereira and told him that the "titles, names, terminology as well as substance "revealed the document as "an obvious forgery designed to sow dissension between the two governments."[18] The Portuguese remained convinced that the CIA was providing Roberto's guerrillas with weapons—a completely mistaken belief. Nevertheless, the more traditionally minded in Foggy Bottom and at the Pentagon harbored the gravest reservations about the nonmilitary assistance Roberto was receiving from the CIA.

CONSPIRACY IN LISBON

On the Lisbon front, the CIA continued to monitor conspiracies to overthrow Salazar. Columnist C. L. Sulzberger of *The New York Times* thought Portugal ripe for just such a coup. "We should examine possible consequences to the West of a putsch in Lisbon," he suggested on June

14, 1961.[19] A group of forty officers revolted on New Year's Day 1962 and attempted to seize the barracks of the Third Infantry Regiment at Beja. Opposition General Humberto Delgado slipped into the country to lead the uprising. Although the revolt failed, military and civilian uprisings elsewhere in Portugal, particularly in Oporto and Braga, revealed the depth of discontent.

Covert action in support of anti-Salazarist elements continued to be a topic of deliberation in the Kennedy administration. One CIA official thought Salazar should be confronted with an either/or proposition: either accept an eight-year independence plan for Portuguese Africa with a $500-million-aid package as a sweetener, or face a coup by "pro-American officers of a younger generation with whom friendly contact already would have been established."[20] Ambassador Elbrick, however, sent a cautionary message to those who seemed to be licking their chops for covert action: "I assume it is not the policy of the U.S. Government to depose the 'aged dictator' here, particularly if we cannot ensure a successor regime which will cooperate with the U.S. and NATO equally as well as its predecessor."[21]

The Beja revolt, indeed, had revealed two dangers in covert action against Salazar. First, the CIA had evidence of communist penetration of the police and armed forces and believed that the revolt had been planned and directed by the Portuguese Communist Party. In a conversation with Ambassador Pereira in May 1962, Secretary Rusk stated that the Soviet Union had sent clandestine funds and "technicians of unrest" into Portugal.[22] Destabilizing Salazar, in short, might well open the door to a communist takeover.

The second risk was equally menacing. Within six hours of the Beja revolt, Spanish tanks at Mérida were spotted rumbling toward the frontier city of Badajoz. It later became clear that Franco intended to intervene with his crack, American-equipped 11th Division to occupy Lisbon, Oporto, and Coimbra in the event that Salazar was overthrown by a left-wing group. Even the CIA's Sakwa, who advocated subverting Salazar, conceded that Spanish intervention "might produce civil war on the Iberian peninsula."[23]

There was also the compelling prospect that a conservative successor regime to Salazar would continue to pursue a military solution to the African conflict. A CIA estimate sent to the White House concluded: "Though it would probably endeavor to improve Portugal's image by implementing reforms in Angola and Mozambique, it would almost certainly be as firm as Salazar in its determination to hold those territories." In the embassy's view, anything less than predictable (i.e., "a leftist and/or neutralist regime") was dangerous. This attitude precluded everything but association with the bourgeois opposition.[24]

True to form, the CIA station in Lisbon sent roseate reports of the prospects for "a rapid bloodless coup" and "moderate succession" throughout 1962. In July, the station reported that "a shadow cabinet" composed of Marshal Craveiro Lopes as president, Dr. Marcello Caetano as prime minister and Botelho Moniz as defense minister had been formed.[25]

It was a formidable grouping. Lopes was the former president of Portugal (1951–58) and, as the CIA report noted, "has great value in being known abroad . . . [N]o radical action would be forthcoming under any junta he headed." Of equal importance, Lopes's accession would apparently be acceptable to Franco and would not precipitate Spanish intervention. Caetano, an internationally known jurist who had served Salazar in many influential positions, had resigned in protest as rector of the University of Lisbon in 1962 after the police had invaded the university precincts. (He was to succeed the disabled Salazar in 1968.) In addition to Botelho Moniz, the conspirators also had the support of Admiral Ramos Pereira.

In November 1962, the CIA station chief cabled headquarters that Lopes's group was ready "to take action in the near future," possibly by first initiating a revolt in Angola. The conspirators hoped for "immediate U.S. diplomatic recognition and encouragement after they seized power." It may be significant that the state of readiness of these "strong supporters of NATO" coincided with the most disputatious stage of the negotiations over the Azores lease.[26]

Internecine rivalry, however, impeded the conspiracy. Powerful personalities, such as Overseas Minister Moreira (who himself had clandestine pretensions) and General Delgado, who had, in exile, led the struggle against Salazar for four years, were excluded from the plotting. Moreira's exclusion was a particularly costly miscalculation, since his influence in the territories might have tipped the balance in favor of those who wanted to remove Salazar. Such miscalculations, however, were thoroughly in keeping with the record of Botelho Moniz and Lopes as ineffectual conspirators. Caetano, for his part, was opposed to the use of force.[27] As a result, the plot never materialized.

Aligned as it was with the elite opposition, American intelligence was essentially interested in reshuffling—not in changing—the existing order. There was a practical reason for this. After a decade of NATO-induced intimacy, many Portuguese officials were drawing two salaries—one from their own government, the other from the Pentagon or the CIA.

Occasionally, it was three. A former U.S. deputy chief of mission recalled a country team meeting in which the CIA station chief and the army attaché discovered, to their surprise and embarrassment, that a Portuguese bureaucrat in the National Secretariat of Information was on both their payrolls.[28] It was not an unfamiliar story: the more intelligence that was purchased (instead of collected without payment), the less reliable it became. The more people put on the payrolls of the CIA and Pentagon, the more interests these agencies had to protect and the more wishful their assessments became.[29]

As if to demonstrate that Portugal would no longer even pretend to undertake colonial reforms in the provinces, Salazar fired his progressive overseas minister on December 3, 1962 and appointed the highly conservative chief of the Armed Forces General Staff, General Araujo, to the key Defense portfolio. He also reshuffled six cabinet posts, mustering what he regarded as "the strongest and most reliable possible defense-overseas team in anticipation of a worsening situation in Angola and Mozambique." As State Department Intelligence and Research Bureau Director Roger Hilsman concluded in his analysis, if ever there was much hope for "broad colonial reform" in the near future, it ended with this purge.[30]

THE AZORES ISSUE

Salazar was preparing to play his single trump card: the lease on the Azores bases. Foreign Minister Franco Nogueira called his government's game "blackmail."[31] How valuable were the bases from a military standpoint? Acheson contended that the refueling, communications, and anti-submarine bases were "perhaps the single most important [set of bases] we have anywhere."[32] The Azores had been used in a succession of crises: to shuttle Marines to Lebanon in 1958, to ship American troops and equipment to Berlin in the autumn of 1961, and to transport several thousand UN troops to the Congo in 1960 and 1961. The Joint Chiefs of Staff flatly insisted that the bases were indispensable in an emergency build-up of Western forces in Europe or the Middle East.[33] In fiscal 1961, the bases reportedly handled 14,000 aircraft departures—more than forty long-range planes per day.[34] The Lajes airstrip complex also included sophisticated electronic equipment, which was locked into the U.S. early-warning system. (The Azores communications and antisubmarine capabilities would play a key role during the October 1962 Cuban missile crisis.[35]) For these reasons, the President's military advisor, General Maxwell Taylor, believed that the administration had no choice but to yield to Salazar.

The President was clearly uncertain. Governor Williams discussed the question with the President and Ralph Dungan on April 16. Kennedy said that he was "very concerned" about the Azores: "If we lose the Azores, we will lose support for the UN."[36] At the time, the Congress was debating the purchase of a $100 million bond issue for the bankrupt UN. If the bond issue failed to pass, the UN peacekeeping operation in the Congo would have to be terminated, so the administration was determined to effect its passage.

Kennedy wrote Ambassador Stevenson on April 18, 1962 saying that he was most anxious to have Stevenson's views on Azores strategy: "[T]he loss of the Azores will be a most serious situation and these negotiations will have considerable impact in the UN especially in relation to Angola."[37] The lease for the Azores bases was due to expire in six months. McGeorge Bundy described the up-coming session with the Portuguese as "a very tough, hard, serious negotiation and the sooner we get at it the better." So controversial was the issue—with "three sides of the Pentagon and four sides of the Department" expected to submit their recommendations— that Bundy thought it would take the better part of six months for the administration itself to reach agreement on Azores policy.[38] Kennedy also invited Acheson, the author of the original Azores lease and one of the founders of the NATO alliance, to prepare a position paper for the negotiations. By summoning Stevenson and Acheson, the President was asking for the fullest airing of differences regarding his Angola policy. What followed was a furious skirmish that Kennedy himself had difficulty in controlling.

Philosophically, Adlai Stevenson and Dean Acheson were poles apart. Acheson, whom Kennedy described as a man of "intimidating seniority," was hard-line on issues involving Atlantic security. He was openly doubtful about the capacity of Africans to govern themselves.[39] Stevenson, on the other hand, believed that the U.S. had to participate in the historic process of decolonization in Africa and Asia—that was where the Cold War was to be won or lost. Stevenson wrote Kennedy that Africans at the UN "want to know whether . . . we stand for self-determination and human rights and, therefore, the mind of Africa, or whether . . . we give our Azores base and the tracking stations in South Africa priority."[40]

The policy disagreement was sharpened by personal antipathy. Both men were formidable in the area of persuasion, but Stevenson avoided the ad hominem mode. Acheson had never seen fit to suffer fools either gladly or privately and considered Stevenson a prime example. He referred to Stevenson as "the weak man from the Midwest"—the unworthy successor to Harry Truman as head of the Democratic Party during the fifties—and described the U.S. mission to the UN, in a speech to the National Press Club, as the "department of emotion."[41] Stevenson elected to make no public response. He observed to his assistant, Clayton Fritchey, that the whole McCarthy scourge had made Acheson a bitter and vindictive man.[42]

Well before the Angola-Azores debate, Kennedy himself had been stung by Acheson's sharp and wide-ranging tongue. Kennedy asked the former Secretary of State to go to Paris to discuss NATO matters with President de Gaulle. In the course of the meeting, Acheson remarked that he and de Gaulle could at least agree on one point—that U.S. Angola policy made little sense.[43] This angered Kennedy, as Clark Clifford informed Acheson. Acheson graciously sent his regrets to the President: "I continually err in regarding my humor as less mordant and more amusing than the facts warrant. My apologies."[44]

From his outpost in New Delhi, Ambassador John Kenneth Galbraith found the prospect of Acheson's involvement in the Angola-Azores debate disturbing. "I have difficulty in appreciating your use of Dean Acheson," he had earlier written to Kennedy. "He is able. He has established himself politically with the right. But I cannot think he is capable of loyalty. He will be a source of trouble for he wants the policy that serves his ego, not your needs."[45]

Within days of the President's request for their counsel, Stevenson and Acheson were crossing swords at the White House. Never one to use indirection, the imperious Acheson proposed to his former assistant secretary of state, Dean Rusk, that Rusk "obtain the President's support in directing the executive branch to stay out of the debates, or drafting of resolutions, on Angola in the General Assembly."

Stevenson responded to Acheson the next day by suggesting to the President that we "firmly resist Portuguese efforts to link the Azores to U.S. policy on Angola. Rather, we should insist that the Azores base is vital not only to the defense of the United States but to all NATO, including Portugal. We should, therefore, treat it as a NATO matter." Stevenson proposed a scenario for negotiation involving the NATO partners in which we would seek "to take a hard-line against the moldy colonialism of Salazar's Portugal and to make a spirited defense of our anti-colonialist policy."[46]

The embassy in Lisbon found the idea "useless and undoubtedly provocative."[47] Stevenson was insistent: it was time for the administration "to go on the offensive," he told Ball. The notion that any NATO country would deliberately imperil the security of the others was intolerable.[48] Kennedy agreed, and on April 27, Stevenson discussed a joint effort on

Salazar with British Prime Minister Macmillan. Macmillan was sympathetic to Stevenson's argument but felt that he exaggerated British influence with the Portuguese.[49]

The administration also tried to convince the government of Brazil to intercede with Lisbon. During the state visit of Brazilian President João Goulart in April 1962, Kennedy brought up the subject at a meeting in the White House. Brazilian Foreign Minister Francisco San Tiago Dantas, who had publicly stated on a previous occasion that Brazil could be an active agent in transforming Portuguese rule in Africa, told Kennedy that his government might be able to influence Portugal were the U.S. to offer Salazar a large economic package. The President found this proposal agreeable, but said that political concessions from Salazar had to be forthcoming first. Aid would only be given within "a transitional political framework."[50] The prospect of Brazilian intercession seemed to hold some promise until the energetic Dantas resigned as foreign minister the following July.

Regarding the issue of retaining the Azores base, the President "seemed to be moved not by military arguments . . . but by his own sense of the political consequences of losing the Azores." He was exposed politically on the Hill. If there was a crisis in NATO, his Congo policy might become the casualty of a bipartisan attack.[51] The mood of Congress seemed to be strongly against any diminution of Atlantic security. Kennedy's close collaborator, Senate Majority Leader Mike Mansfield, made a scathing attack on the UN. "Vote victories," he said, "have only little relevance to the great and fundamental questions." Mansfield characterized the Security Council as "an arena for staging the wars of violent words," while the General Assembly was "a marketplace for trading votes."[52] U.S. News and World Report ran a cover story on the bankruptcy of the administration's UN policy and said that the President was reconsidering the importance of the American mission to the UN in his overall foreign policy.

Another prominent member of the President's party, Senator Henry M. Jackson, made an even more unsparing attack on UN policy before the National Press Club: "The truth is . . . that the best hope for peace and justice does not lie with the UN. The concept of world opinion has been, I fear, much abused." Jackson blamed Stevenson for "the disproportionate amount of energy" the administration had been expending on UN issues such as Angola. The ambassador to the UN was not "a second Secretary of State," he said, and it was "unfortunate" that he had been given cabinet rank.

Stevenson was highly upset by these speeches and described Jackson's as "the most damaging personal attack he had experienced since coming to the UN." He saw the dark hand of Dean Acheson at work, particularly since two of Acheson's old friends, Joe Alsop and William S. White, were wielding the knife against him. It was a "plot," Stevenson said, part of "a well-coordinated movement going back to Dean Acheson a dozen years ago and deriving its momentum today from the Pentagon, the European division at State, and the Dulles-line diplomats who favor Europe over the new states."[53]

Stevenson also felt that Kennedy was abandoning him; that after his highly effective defense of the UN bond bill, the President was cutting him loose. He called Cleveland and virtually demanded that the President publicly disavow Jackson's speech, deny the stories, and affirm his own confidence in Stevenson. He drafted a message for the President to read at his press conference.[54] Kennedy, however, ignored Stevenson's statement and confined himself to a general defense of his foreign policy. "Adlai Stevenson doesn't have to be protected from Scoop Jackson," he told Schlesinger. He thought that there was no sense in dignifying Jackson; it would be enough to urge his Eastern liberal campaign contributors to squeeze him.[55] (This was done and Jackson fell into line during the UN bond debate.)

The President sent Stevenson a letter of reassurance, but more slights, both real and perceived, followed. The problem was that Stevenson was touchy about criticism and the President, though protective of the ambassador's special status, was impatient with subordinates.[56] During one of Stevenson's occasional absences from New York in June 1962, Kennedy inquired of Schlesinger: "Where the hell is Stevenson? Out in Libertyville doing his income tax?"[57] Stevenson acquired the habit of referring to the President as "Kennedy" or, in moments of exasperation, as "that young man."[58]

As the debate over Angola or the Azores raged back and forth during the summer of 1962, the President grew noticeably more irritable. He wanted the issue resolved, once and for all, and instructed Rusk to wind things up. When he learned that Stevenson had left for a two-week cruise on the Adriatic with *Washington Post* publisher Agnes Meyer, he blew up and sent word for Stevenson to cut the trip short and come home. For good measure, the President's appointments secretary, Kenneth O'Donnell, called Ball to tell him to inform Stevenson that the owner of the yacht Mrs. Meyer had rented was a violator of the Cuban trade embargo. (This slap was unnecessary and accomplished nothing except to offend Stevenson.[59]) Such spats reflected the growing distance between the two men. By July 1962—six months before the Azores lease was to expire—Stevenson's once-central influence with the White House was waning. The effect that this had on the outcome of the Angola-Azores debate was unmistakable.

THE DEBATE INTENSIFIES

In the aftermath of the Jackson-Stevenson flap, the Democratic leadership asked the White House for guidance on Angola policy. But there was none to be given. What had begun as a policy debate was quickly becoming a political brawl. A Republican congressman from Virginia, Porter Hardy, took inspiration from the disarray and launched his own investigation of U.S. Angola policy. He demanded to have classified files from the African Bureau relating to the March 7, 1961 démarche to Salazar. "Damn if I ain't going to blow it up," declared Congressman Hardy.[60] Williams and Legal Adviser Abram Chayes refused. "Never to my knowledge did even the Eisenhower administration permit internal Department policy documents to be scrutinized by Joe McCarthy or his agents," Williams wrote Rusk.[61] Hardy demanded that Chayes be fired. The White House was called in and Ball and others were advised to ignore Hardy—politely.

Much of the ammunition used by Hardy and other congressional critics was being supplied by the New York public relations firm of Selvage and Lee that had been hired by the Portuguese government. The firm retained the services of a motley host of "public opinon makers": retired military officers, John Birch Society activists, black American journalists, supporters of the National States Rights Party, and others. Nearly seventy American reporters were airlifted to Angola for a well-organized glimpse of the colony's "harmonious multiracial society."[62] In the South, the lobby inspired printed racial attacks on Kennedy's "pro-Negro" policy in Africa.[63] On Capitol Hill, Speaker of the House John W. McCormack and nineteen of his colleagues delivered prepared speeches, compliments of Selvage and Lee, in defense of Portugal.[64]

Portugal's propaganda campaign (which ceased operations in 1963 after a Justice Department investigation) succeeded in shifting the momentum of the policy debate against Angola. Administration liberals were put on the defensive and their arguments showed it. "If the Angola policy is discarded to hold on to the Azores," Williams reasoned, "the U.S. might eventually lose bases in Libya, Morocco, and Ethiopia." The Joint Chiefs of Staff rejected this extraordinary claim.[65] Galbraith took another potshot at his favorite target—the Pentagon: "We are trading in our African policy for a few acres of asphalt in the Atlantic."[66] But from Lisbon, Ambassador Elbrick replied that "One cannot airily subtract the Azores base from Portugal's importance to NATO, or vice versa."[67] Why bother, suggested Wayne Fredericks: in case of war, the U.S. could seize the Azores and use them as it wished.[68] Such debating points made little impact on the phalanx of Pentagon bureaucrats whose stake in the Azores was as much occupational as strategic and who were not about to give up a threatened piece of their realm without a fight. *"Iberia Über Alles,"* Galbraith observed in his diary.

Chester Bowles tried one more time to reach the President. "Our African policy has been one of the most successful efforts of your Administration. It has reversed the 1960 tide which was running strongly in a pro-Soviet direction in a number of African countries, won us the friendship and respect of many African leaders, and helped us to stabilize several crises . . . It would be unthinkable to modify an effective policy in a key continent to fit the 18th century views of the Lisbon Government." Like Stevenson, Bowles favored turning the Azores base over to NATO under General Lauris Norstad's command. If Portugal objected, she could take the Azores and leave the Alliance—something which he believed Portugal would never do. "I believe we should take every opportunity to challenge the assumption that our European allies are doing us a favor whenever they provide us with the necessary facilities from which to defend their continent," he wrote.[69]

Had it not been for the sudden chill in U.S.-Soviet relations during that summer of 1962, Kennedy might well have sided with Bowles and the other liberals on the Angola question. Not long after the Bowles memo, however, the CIA sent an urgent report to the President. There was "something new and different" about Soviet operations in Cuba. (Aerial discovery of the nuclear missiles emplacements would come later, in October.)[70] Worse yet for the liberal position, Berlin, which had traumatized the Kennedy administration during its first year, was heating up again, giving the Pentagon added leverage on all policy fronts.

The Joint Chiefs insisted that an airlift on the order of the Berlin airlift of 1948 made the Azores irreplaceable. If the lease were not extended, either Congress would have to appropriate $2 billion to provide the necessary transatlantic jet transport or the Air Force would have to utilize a network of northern bases plagued by bad weather. The Pentagon provided the White House with maps of alternative strategic air routes, each one inadequate.[71]

Doubts about the indispensability of the Azores remained. McNamara's position was that the disposition of the Azores was a political question, not purely a military one, and should be evaluated accordingly. Neither Ralph Dungan nor Bundy's assistant, Carl Kaysen, was particularly impressed by the Pentagon's invocation of military security. They contended that technological developments such as midair refueling would soon make the Azores much less critical than it now was.[72]

The President turned again to Acheson—this time to take charge of the lease negotiations with the Portuguese. Bundy explained to Ball that the former Secretary was "a Portuguese pal." ("A libertarian may properly disapprove of Dr. Salazar," Acheson once wrote, "but I doubt whether Plato would . . . ") He could go over to Lisbon, Bundy thought, and tell Salazar, "Of course you have been treated outrageously but that is not the point."[73]

It was a favorite Kennedy tactic: send a conservative to do a liberal's business, a hard-liner to sell the soft-line. It was also a tactic that had failed on at least two other occasions. Clarence Randall had returned from his mission to Ghana in October 1961 recommending against U.S. participation in the Volta River project. George McGhee's mission to the Congo in September 1962, although it did little to placate the handful of aroused senators on Capitol Hill, had undercut the UN effort and partially discredited Ambassador Gullion. (The most unfortunate exercise of all was to come in 1963, when the President appointed General Lucius Clay and a group of bonded conservatives to head a blue-ribbon panel to investigate foreign aid. They were to give a full airing to conservative skepticism and then, theoretically, support the administration's aid request. The Clay Committee, however, issued a report critical of the administration's aid porgram and, as a result, the congressional budget allocation was slashed by about 25 percent. Kennedy was his own best critic after the aid debacle: "I am so busy protecting my flank from right-wing criticism that I sometimes wonder where I am getting anything done."[74])

When Kennedy asked Acheson to go to Lisbon to get the Portuguese to renew the lease, Acheson agreed provided that the policy was "sensible." Portugal is a devoted and loyal ally, he told the President, "She would like nothing better than to extend this lease. On the other hand, if you're going [to go] ahead and fight what they're doing in Angola, you won't get the extension anyway. Nobody can get it. I can't—nobody can." The President observed that it would be quite "silly" to ask Acheson to do something that he thought government policy was rendering impossible.[75]

The disagreement between Acheson and Kennedy was an old one. The passage of five years and the change of positions had done little to diminish its intensity. Acheson had always regarded Kennedy's Algerian position as unseemly; he had termed the senator's call for the "orderly achievement of Algerian independence" in 1957 as "the supreme touch of naiveté."[76]

CAPITULATION

Rusk intervened at this point and offered to go himself to Lisbon to talk to Salazar. He quickly produced a formula for the decent bureaucratic burial of Angola policy—"the postponement of all discussion and action on Angola pending a settlement of the Azores question."[77]

Kennedy was surprised and rather pleased that Rusk, whose usual instinct was to cooperate on all matters, would take an assertive position on such a controversial question. Stevenson, however, was distrustful of Rusk's sudden interest. To salvage something of Angola policy, the ambassador suggested a new tack for Rusk to propose in Lisbon: the appointment by the UN of an internationally recognized figure as *rapporteur* to investigate, with full Portuguese cooperation, conditions in Angola.[78] Stevenson was confident that he could pry away enough moderate African support in the General Assembly to get the measure passed. Rusk and Kennedy liked the idea and a compromise of sorts was reached.

On June 27, 1962, after a quick tour of the Western European capitals, Secretary Rusk stopped in Lisbon for a twenty-two-hour visit. The next day he conferred with Salazar for two hours, briefing him "on certain of the most sensitive problems of the Atlantic Alliance—the nuclear situation, the East-West problem, and Laos . . ." Here was Rusk at his best—finding the right words to reassure a jilted ally. Salazar seemed grateful "because he felt isolated and left out on such matters."[79] Both Salazar and Franco Nogueira reacted favorably to the rapporteur proposal, particularly when Rusk characterized it as a means to "split the Afro-Asian bloc." For this negligible concession (which later would prove nonexistent), Rusk agreed that the Azores would only be negotiated after a complete review of bilateral relations—"a systematic *tour d'horizon*"—had been completed.[80] This fit nicely into Franco Nogueira's Azores strategy, as would later become apparent.

Prior to Rusk's mission, Ambassador Stevenson had warned the Secretary about edging toward Salazar's line in his talks in Lisbon.

We are sure you will have in mind that accelerated economic and social development will not alone solve fundamental Portuguese problem vis-a-vis her overseas provinces. Acceptance of the principal [sic] of self-determination is key . . . we should take care not to give the Portuguese the impression through politeness that lesser steps will be enough.[81]

The fact was, however, that Rusk had never had much use for the administration's Angola policy. Regarding Portuguese rule in Angola, he had told Foreign Minister Dantas: "The case we believe to be considerably better than is generally known . . . [W]e have had less chance to support Portuguese actions than the facts known to us would justify." To the

Senate Foreign Relations Committee, he declared: "I don't believe the answer to Angola lies in these terrorist groups . . ."[82]

"Politeness" did little to mollify Salazar's position. A few days after Rusk's visit, Salazar described U.S. policy to a *U.S. News and World Report* editor as "diluted and contradictory . . . less favorable to an ally than to an enemy."[83] Whatever may be said about the accuracy of Salazar's charges, they did not constitute much of a tribute to Rusk's mission.

A week later, the Foreign Minister accused Assistant Secretary Williams of having made "a violent attack" against Portugal. The accusation turned out to be specious but more of the same was in the offing. Ambassador Pereira delivered another protest against an imaginary remark Williams had made. "Pray tell, what particularly roused his Excellency's ire?" Williams sarcastically inquired of his counterpart in the European Bureau who had passed the protest along to the seventh floor.[84] Then Lisbon demanded that the Reverend George M. Houser, the director of the American Committee on Africa, and Professor John Marcum be removed immediately from the African Bureau's Advisory Council, on the grounds that they had visited rebel-held Northern Angola. "If they push us around on this one, there is no telling where they will stop," Williams observed to his superiors. But two of Rusk's faithful subordinates, U. Alexis Johnson and George C. McGhee, had been assigned by the Secretary to assume control over Portuguese affairs and the European Bureau had reasserted claim to some of its lost realm. U.S. Angola policy was in full retreat.[85]

Formal capitulation occurred in September, when Washington responded to Lisbon's list of grievances with an *aide mémoire*: "Our efforts . . . are designed not to force Portugal to leave Africa but to encourage measures which we are convinced are necessary to enable her to stay and complete work which she has begun." At the North Atlantic Council meeting in Paris, U.S. Ambassador Thomas K. Finletter was instructed to avoid "political discussion or controversy" on Angola. "We will be remembered as resisting exit at five minutes to twelve," Galbraith concluded.[86]

In September 1962, Rusk instructed both the African Bureau and U.S. mission to the UN to cease all contact with Roberto and all other African nationalists. Williams argued that if this were done, the U.S. would "forfeit the opportunity to influence these leaders and to establish the basis of understanding and cooperation with eventual independent governments." He later charged that Lisbon was using the Azores as "a lever to force us to cease contact with nationalists . . . [W]e have progressively succumbed to Portuguese pressure to a point at which even covert contact with Angolan and Mozambican nationalists is being challenged within the U.S. Government."[87]

Ambassador Galbraith had already taken Rusk to task for his "limited, passive and even slightly apologetic approach to the Portuguese on their default in respect to colonialism."[88] Support for African independence would be agreed upon, Galbraith had cabled Washington in December 1961, "by all who over the years have been singed either in reputation or conscience by too prolonged dalliance with decayed dictators or enfeebled strong men—with Peron, Perez, Batista, Trujillo and most recently, one fears, [with] some in Southeast Asia. So disagreeably lucid has been this lesson that we can only assume that it has been wonderfully well-learned." Rusk had replied: "To the extent your recommendation has any merit, it has been considered and rejected." Stevenson, Williams, Galbraith and the rest of the liberals were simply to be ignored on Angola policy.[89]

During the Azores negotiations, Ambassador Elbrick was able to tell Franco Nogueira that, in order "to accommodate Portugal," all contact with Holden Roberto had ceased.[90] When nationalist Amilcar Cabral of Guinea Bissau sent a message to President Kennedy, word went out to Conakry to ignore him. The Portuguese then demanded that the U.S. mission in Leopoldville prevail on the Congo government to disband the UPA guerrilla camp near Thysville, north of the Angolan border. If not, Lisbon warned, Portugal would have no choice but to sell arms to secessionist Katanga. (In fact, they were already doing so.) The Americans did not comply with this request.[91]

Roberto reacted angrily to the sudden cold shoulder from the Americans. The Kennedy administration's original stand on Angola had been, Roberto wrote the President, "an indication of your country's willingness to cleave to morality and justice at the risk of severe criticism from some local elements and despite adding to the discomfiture of a NATO ally."

"Now, however, the situation is reversed," he contended: ". . . purely humanitarian needs of our refugees and students must be left unattended, help cut off because of pressure from the Department of State . . . Portuguese officials have stated that they have received official assurances that no American assistance will be given to programs for medical relief and rehabilitation of Angolan refugees." He appealed to Kennedy to restore American support for the Angolan cause—"a struggle to which you must certainly still subscribe."[92]

It was ironic that at the very time Roberto was being cut adrift by the Washington leadership, his putative association with the U.S. was also discrediting him among African governments. Roberto had received financial assistance from Nkrumah since 1958. After Lumumba's demise in the Congo, Roberto had fled to Accra, where he appealed to the

Nkrumah regime for full-scale support. "This was the answer I got: the Government of Ghana had given orders that we must not help you because you are in the pay of America."[93] Shortly thereafter, Nkrumah switched his support to the Movimento Popular de Libertação de Angola (MPLA). Support from the Algerian FLN (which had been training some two dozen UPA guerrillas as officers) was also affected by the CIA stigma. By November 1962, the MPLA had also gained the upper hand in terms of support from the FLN.[94]

The Portuguese military was meanwhile engaged in full-time seduction of the American brass. The artful Franco Nogueira hinted strongly to Admiral Lyman Lemnitzer of the Joint Chiefs of Staff that Portugal might grant the U.S. Navy a base at Nacala Bay in northern Mozambique—provided that the present crisis in U.S.-Portuguese relations were resolved. On another occasion, Franco Nogueira asked Admiral Thomas Moorer in Lisbon how he would react to the granting of independence to the Cape Verde islands (another strategically located archipelago under Portuguese rule). "Very negatively," the Admiral replied. Air Force Chief of Staff, General Curtis LeMay, urged the Portuguese Air Secretary, Colonel Kaulza Arriaga, to take Portugal's case to the American public, conceding that he had, of course, no business making political judgments.[95] To gain leverage over the Americans and to forestall any joint action by NATO against them, the Portuguese discussed the possibility of granting Azores access to the French and the West Germans. (France later established a missile-tracking station on Flores Island.) There were also reports that the British lease on their base on Sal Island was under reconsideration.[96]

Threatened with expulsion from the Azores, Washington gave up its efforts to stop Portugal from using NATO arms in its African wars. The administration announced the delivery of thirty Cessna T-37C aircraft, over half of which were paid for by MAP. Officially, these aircraft were supposed to be used for pilot training; in fact, they were being used on reconnaissance sorties. Responding to an apparent policy change, the Pentagon immediately proposed to grant Portugal 24 light tanks, 119 armored personnel carriers, and 60 torpedoes. This request was denied.[97]

The Portuguese brass began feeling the pinch on military supplies. Vice Admiral Roboredo, the Portuguese naval chief of staff, called in the U.S. naval attaché and threw a batch of messages at him in order to dramatize that Portuguese requests were going nowhere. Roboredo was especially upset by the refusal of the Pentagon to give Portugal a license to purchase 20 amphibious rubber boats. He wrote to his old friend, Admiral George W. Anderson, the U.S. chief of naval operations, for help. Anderson took the request straight to the President. It was a minor matter, and Kennedy, eager not to give the outspoken Anderson any cause for another speech, complied. "We should bend over backwards" to avoid harassing the Portuguese, Kennedy advised Bundy.[98]

The granting of his request did not satisfy the Admiral, however. He had developed a reputation as something of an unreconstructed martinet, after having advised McNamara during the Cuban missile crisis that naval strategy was a military, not a civilian, concern.[99] He later wrote Bundy a lengthy memorandum on Angola, inveighing against the "terrorists" and the "destruction of property," while praising the Portuguese. "I, too, have a grave concern for the welfare of the numberless natives in Angola and Mozambique who will suffer immeasurably if external agitators are not contained . . ." In a remarkable stroke of strategic thinking, the Admiral offered a solution to the plight of the Angolans: the provision of naval landing craft to the Portuguese. "I can see in these LCMs a capability to improve considerably Portugal's capacity for guaranteeing the safety of the colonial Africans."[100]

Portugal was subsequently awarded both landing craft and Anderson as the new U.S. ambassador. A disturbed Wayne Fredericks rushed over to the White House to protest the appointment. "I'm sorry," said Ralph Dungan, "but the President just wanted him out of here so badly and sort of figured they deserved each other." This did not prove to be the case, however, as even Franco Nogueira, whose outlook presumably converged with that of the Admiral, found Anderson equally insupportable.[101]

At the UN, Ambassador Stevenson continued to maintain that the U.S. was shipping no offensive arms to Portugal. Few officials in African governments (or in the Pentagon for that matter) believed him. Although Stevenson did not then know it, the disparity between American policy and Portuguese practice was considerable. Monitoring the diversion of arms was practically impossible, particularly since the Portuguese concealed shipments. Two crated RT-33 aircraft, for example, disappeared from the Alverca air base sometime between July 15 and 18, 1962. According to one embassy officer, the U.S. military attachés made little effort to verify such diversions. The Pentagon blandly reported to the White House in July 1963 that since September 1961 the Portuguese had diverted *no* MAP material to Africa.[102]

Rusk's efforts meanwhile to soothe the Portuguese had only emboldened them. Lisbon's "Bill of Complaints Against the United States"— a Rusk concession—pre-empted any renegotiation of the Azores lease. Franco Nogueira used the list to disinter every accusation imaginable— from "Protection and Assistance of Terrorist Chiefs" to the subversive activities of the AFL-CIO. Three months went by. Ambassador Elbrick reported that he had had enough of the Foreign Minister's "marathon of complaints . . . his wearisome hammering at the list."[103]

Rusk tried to get the negotiations off center by proferring another nicety—an invitation to Franco Nogueira to visit Washington. The Foreign Minister arrived in the capital in the middle of the Cuban missile crisis. At a small luncheon Rusk hosted at the State Department, he asked Franco Nogueira if he could make a public statement of support for the U.S. in the missile crisis. The Foreign Minister replied that he would do no such thing. If the U.S. would not come to Portugal's defense in Angola, then Portugal would not stand by the U.S. in the Caribbean.[104]

Kennedy was exasperated with Rusk's tepid performance. He ordered Franco Nogueira to be brought over to the White House even though the ExCom was meeting almost constantly on the missile crisis.[105] In his meeting with Franco Nogueira, Kennedy came straight to the point. "Could Portugal not see its way to proclaiming publicly its acceptance of the principle of self-determination?" The Foreign Minister replied that if Portugal did, Afro-Asians at the UN would call for independence in Angola and Mozanbique by the end of the year—"the African continent would become Communist." Kennedy dismissed this claim: "[I]t was evident from what happened to former French, Belgian, and British territories in Africa that these pressures stemmed from the basic desires of the populations and were not due to any external agency . . ." He warned the Portuguese that "unless farsighted and forward looking policies were adopted to meet these demands, we would run into even greater difficulties." After more desultory discussion, the two parted.[106]

On December 31, 1962, the Azores lease formally expired. No new lease was concluded. Portugal simply agreed to allow the U.S. to use the facilities "on a day-to-day basis."

American temporizing and the President's desire to have it both ways had left the United States with neither Angola nor the Azores. By standing firm, Salazar had forced Kennedy to yield, at least temporarily.

9

Summer and Autumn 1963

> I am seeing again the promise of restoring
> some of our African efforts.
>
> Kennedy to Ball
> (*April, 1963*)

The consistent theme of Kennedy's prepresidential declarations had been that defining African and Asian policy in Cold War terms was self-defeating. "The assumption that American foreign policy is simply a question of the battle against communism is one of the greatest errors we all make in this campaign," he had said in 1956. "The tragic failure of both Republican and Democratic administrations since World War II to comprehend the nature of this [nationalist] revolution . . . has reaped a bitter harvest today."[1] Kennedy had predicted that if America continued to base its policy exclusively on the external Soviet threat and, in so doing, to ignore the internal realities of emerging states, it could expect more Indochinas and Algerias.

As President, however, Kennedy was persuaded early—by Khrushchev's truculence at the summit meeting in Vienna as well as by Soviet intervention in Laos, Vietnam, and the Congo—that his plan to base his foreign policy on internal realities was not possible as long as the Kremlin insisted on exploiting political change in the Third World. For the sake of Soviet containment, therefore, Kennedy stepped back from an African policy based on African merits.

In the Congo, he permitted the CIA to shore up the right wing in case Adoula's center coalition fell prey to the left wing. In Angola, he backed off on the issue of independence in order to preserve U.S. access to the Azores base. In Ghana, he repeatedly ordered reconsideration of the Volta project to counter Nkrumah's overtures to the communist powers. Indeed, the central fact of U.S. African policy during 1961 and 1962 was that the President had not been able to reduce Cold War tensions. It was clear that without a breakthrough in Soviet-American relations, African policy would continue to be a hostage of the Cold War.

The breakthrough came in unexpected form on October 16, 1962 when Soviet missiles were discovered in Cuba. For the next thirteen days, as Khrushchev put it, "the smell of burning hung in the air . . ." Going to the brink of nuclear war forced a new recognition on both sides of the need to work for peace. "It seems to me, Mr. President," Khrushchev wrote Kennedy a month after the missile crisis, "that the time has come now to put an end once and for all to nuclear tests. . . ." Kennedy similarly saw the prospect of disengagement. "That was why we tried to make their setback in Cuba not the kind that would bring about an increase in hostility but perhaps provide for an easing of relations."[2] He saw a fresh possibility of placing African policy on an African—instead of on an anti-Soviet or pro-European—footing.

The decline in Soviet-American bipolarity coincided with fragmentation within the rival alliances. Khrushchev's misadventure in Cuba, in addition to earning Castro's derision, resulted in further alienation between Moscow and Beijing. Mao Zedong plainly accused the Soviet Union of cowardice. Khrushchev replied bitterly that "only madmen" could hope to destroy capitalism by nuclear war.[3]

Cracks began to appear in the Western bloc as well. Eleven weeks after the missile crisis, General de Gaulle blocked British entry into the Common Market and declared that France had no desire to accept American domination in the area of defense. As Arthur M. Schlesinger, Jr., put it, "[I]n two sharp and elegant strokes, he knocked out the economic and military pillars of Atlantic unity."[4]

As the Cold War ebbed and the NATO alliance loosened, Kennedy found more running room in Africa. The European allies had been able to use NATO's traditional commitment to anticommunism as a lever to influence U.S. policy toward Africa. With the beginning of Soviet-American détente and the sudden defection of de Gaulle, however, the maintenance of a common Atlantic front at the cost of African initiatives seemed less compelling. This development was immediately apparent in U.S. African policy.

During his visit to Europe in the summer of 1963, the President acknowledged the reality of national self-interest within the Alliance itself. The Atlantic partnership, he declared, should be an "entity of independent parts, sharing equally both burdens and decisions." There was "no right course or any single final pattern." During the final months of his administration, Kennedy also tried to nudge the American public toward a new recognition of the chance for conciliation with the Soviet Union. It was important that the Russians reconsider their objectives, he said at American University, "but I also believe that we must re-examine our own attitude. . . . If we cannot end now all our differences, at least we can help make the world safe for diversity."[5]

In Africa, the challenge, as always, was to coexist with the forces of nationalism in all their volatility. The collapse of the Katanga secession had brought welcome relief for Washington but no long-term solution for the Congo. Since the nearly bankrupt UN was determined to withdraw its forces, the Kennedy administration faced the prospect of presiding over a second slide into national chaos.

In Ghana, Kennedy had one last chance to reconsider the Volta aid commitment. In the light of Togolese President Olympio's murder in January 1963 and the continuing crusade against the CIA in the Ghanaian press, Nkrumah never looked more dubious. The President feared that the fate of his foreign aid bill might depend on the outcome of the Ghanaian gamble.

In Portuguese Africa, Kennedy's choices were no less uncongenial. In 1963, insurgency began to spread to Mozambique and Portuguese Guinea. Kennedy wondered whether, by having traded his Angola policy for the Azores lease, he had forfeited his chance to bring about a peaceful transition to independent rule—if indeed, that were even possible given the siege mentality in Lisbon.

Despite the complexity of the predicament, Kennedy was encouraged that he could still devise a policy that could satisfy U.S. security concerns and yet meet African needs. The decline of the Cold War had somewhat devalued Atlantic attachments and had widened the President's margin of maneuver.

THE CONGO

The mood in Washington after the fall of Katanga in 1963 was one of relief and pride. Stevenson had told the Security Council in February 1961 that the new administration was convinced that the only way to keep the Cold War out of the Congo was to keep the UN in the Congo. After two years of trying to justify the presence of 20,000 UN troops at American expense, that belief had been substantially vindicated.

Under Secretary Ball told James Reston of *The New York Times* that, "it was a tribute to patience, a victory of diplomacy, a testament to peacekeeping."[6] "There are no uninvited foreign troops, no Communist enclaves, no 'army of liberation', no reason for a single American soldier to die there, no excuse for a Soviet soldier to live there," declared Assistant Secretary Harlan Cleveland.[7]

The feeling of euphoria did not last long, however. Within weeks of

Tshombe's capitulation, units of the ANC (the central government's army) went on a rampage, pillaging and terrorizing villages and finally attacking UN forces. In Léopoldville, Premier Adoula, under constant political assault from the Lumumbists, was clearly on the way out. Mobutu, Nendaka, and the rest of the CIA-supported Binza boys prepared to seize power if Adoula faltered.[8] It looked like 1960 all over again.

The UN, whose mandate in the Congo was to expire on June 30, 1963, had begun the process of withdrawing its forces. President Kennedy tried to slow the withdrawals of UN troops from Katanga (where the ANC rampage had begun) by offering to finance the retention of 2,000 UN troops; but the UN leadership wanted none of it. The peacekeeping operation was driving the UN into deeper debt and disrupting the organization's effectiveness on other international issues. Secretary-General Thant was determined to end the Congo operation. Kennedy was left with Hobson's choice: either to quit the Congo along with the UN, or to stay and assume responsibility for rebuilding the Congo. Kennedy chose to stay.

Staying would mean retraining the ANC—"a major, if not *the* major, threat to internal law and order throughout the period" (emphasis Ernest Lefever's).[9] Without an obedient national army, it was obvious that political order and economic recovery would be impossible in the Congo. Six months before the fall of Katanga, Washington had sent the Pentagon's chief Congo expert, Colonel Michael J.L. Greene, to assess what it would take to transform the ANC from a predatory rabble into an effective fighting force. Greene recommended that the UN coordinate a series of limited bilateral programs to assist the ANC officer corps in forming small territorial units capable of preserving order.[10]

Shortly after the fall of Katanga, the President approved the implementation of the Greene plan. Six western countries (including the U.S., which was to provide $4–6 million annually) agreed to assist the ANC in various phases of military training. Problems began when the Pentagon brass elected to express their reservations about the Greene plan by sending Colonel Greene to Vietnam in the fall of 1962. Thereafter, the White House encountered willful inaction by the Joint Chiefs and general indifference by the Pentagon bureaucracy.

Kennedy's dissatisfaction with the Pentagon's meager contribution to the retraining effort was evident in a meeting in the Oval Office in May 1963. Why had no military equipment arrived in the Congo yet? he asked the two Army officers present. Colonel Gall resorted to procurement talk. The arrival time, he explained to the President, depended on "the programming lead time and availability of equipment." This in turn depended on "production schedules of industry [which] in part were influenced by the amount of money made available to the various services for the procurement of equipment." Kennedy then asked what kinds of equipment we were going to send. The Colonel replied that he didn't know. Exasperated, Kennedy said he would look into the matter himself. "We cannot just go on talking about this program."[11]

The Pentagon was not the only obstacle to the quick implementation of the retraining program. Secretary-General Thant was insistent that there be African representation in the retraining program. Washington agreed, but the Central Government in Léopoldville did not. General Mobutu preferred white officers. (He was later said to have commented in regard to an offer of military advisors from fellow African states, "*Je ne veux pas ces nègres.*") ["I don't want these black men."][12]

African delegations at the UN liked neither the attitude of the ANC command nor the apparition, as one ambassador put it, of "a Western Trojan horse being wheeled into the Congo under UN guise." Sensing trouble, Kennedy decided that the U.S. would seek nothing more than the UN's "endorsement" of the retraining program. Adoula accordingly wrote the Secretary-General asking for his approval of the Greene plan. By this time, Thant was listening solely to his Afro-Asian Congo Advisory Commission. He informed Adoula that the UN would neither coordinate nor endorse the retraining program. Four of the countries that had agreed to participate in the retraining program then withdrew.[13] Thant's decision, perhaps justifiable in light of short-term political pressures, would prove to be a blow to the Congo's prospects for national peace and order.

With the frustration of the multinational retraining program, the Pentagon saw its chance to develop a military assistance program more to its liking. Although Colonel Greene had once warned that trying to Americanize the ANC command was a hopeless proposition, the Pentagon had no interest in tailoring military assistance programs to local needs. It preferred the traditional model.[14]

Mobutu and his chief officers were flown to the United States in a chartered plane and given the Army's high-level massage. They toured Fort Benning and other military installations. Mobutu was highly pleased and impressed. What the Congo needed, he thought, was an American-trained army and he asked President Kennedy for permission to stay in the U.S. to get his own paratroop jump wings.[15]

The ANC rank and file (whose salaries had risen 500 percent between 1960 and 1963) had meanwhile made no noticeable progress in the area of devotion to duty. Reports of atrocity and pillage had become routine. The U.S. mission soon inherited the UN's practice of making large cash payments to Mobutu for the purpose of pacifying his troops. As a secret investigation ordered by the Secretary-General in 1962 revealed,

Mobutu had already diverted several million dollars of this money to his own Swiss bank account. (By 1975, Mobutu's estimated take from U.S. covert sources had reached $150 million).[16]

The failure of the ANC retraining program effectively wiped out whatever hope was left for the Adoula regime. When the Premier formed a new government in March 1963, the Lumumbist Parliament welcomed its installation with a vote of no confidence. The White House believed that the coalition regime could yet be revived if there were a new constitution and new elections. But Adoula was no longer up to the task. Two years of unceasing crisis had taken their toll. Gullion reported that the Premier showed signs of physical exhaustion, nervous anxiety, and dangerously high blood pressure.[17]

As Adoula faltered, Mobutu grew more assertive. When the Léopold-ville police mutinied in May demanding pay raises, Mobutu promptly called out the ANC and crushed the rebellion. The fact that 213 of his soldiers had received paratroop training from Israeli advisers strengthened his hand politically. When Adoula appealed to the UN to postpone the withdrawal of its troops, Mobutu angrily opposed him. The CIA's "safety catch" was being readied.[18]

Then came the benediction. In May 1963, on the occasion of his visit to the United States, Mobutu was accorded full military honors on his arrival and was personally greeted by General Earle G. Wheeler. The Pentagon's William P. Bundy alerted his brother at the White House to the importance of Mobutu's visit. "Although it appears General Mobutu would like to remain apart from politics, his stature and position as Commander-in-Chief of the Army are not likely to allow him to do so." The appended biographic data composed by the Pentagon predicted: "The Army, either as a whole or in part, will of necessity be involved in any violent changes in the composition of the Government of the Congo." A meeting at the White House was arranged.

Mobutu lost no time during his session in the Oval Office in communicating his wishes to President Kennedy. He personally wanted to take parachute training at Fort Benning and to spend two weeks at the Special Warfare School at Fort Bragg. Mobutu said that he had been promised a command aircraft and he wanted it. Kennedy was surprised by the request for the airplane—that was the first he had heard of it—but agreed that the General should have it. "General, if it hadn't been for you," the President said, "the whole thing would have collapsed and the Communists would have taken over." "I do what I am able to do," the General modestly replied. In saying good-bye, Kennedy again thanked Mobutu for his cooperation. There was nobody in the world, the President rather grandly declared, who had done more than the General to maintain freedom against the communists.[19]

Adoula was embarrassed by the gift of the command aircraft to his nominal subordinate. The State Department sought to redress the situation somewhat by instructing Gullion to tell Adoula that he could use the plane too.[20] This could hardly change the impression that, at a time when Adoula was struggling for his political survival, the Americans were grooming a strong man to succeed him.

Gullion had not yet given up on salvaging the fig leaf of popular rule in the Congo. He flew home in early September to push for an extension of the UN peacekeeping operation until June 1964. Sentiment against Gullion's proposal ran high on the seventh floor of the State Department. The attitude of Secretary Rusk and other senior officials was, "Let's call it a success and quit while we're ahead."[21] Stevenson cabled in from New York that getting the UN to agree to an extension was highly improbable.

The President, however, supported the idea and ordered the State Department to mobilize international support for the retention of a 3,000-man contingent in the Congo.[22] Addressing the opening of the eighteenth General Assembly on September 20, 1963, Kennedy told the delegates, "a project undertaken in the excitement of crisis begins to lose its appeal as the problems drag on and the bills pile up . . . I believe that this Assembly should do whatever is necessary to preserve the gains already made and to protect the new nation in its struggle for progress. Let us complete what we have started." He pledged full American material and logistical support for the effort. After the speech, the President met privately with the Secretary-General regarding troop retention.[23]

On October 18, the General Assembly approved the funds necessary for an extension of the UN mandate by a vote of 76 to 11 with 20 abstentions. Adoula wrote Kennedy of his country's gratitude. It was obvious that without Kennedy's intercession, the UN would never have mustered the will to keep the peace in the Congo for another year.[24]

Despite the success of Kennedy's effort in New York, the news from Léopoldville turned from bad to disastrous. When President Kasavubu disbanded Parliament, the Lumumbists reignited their rebellion. Strikes and army mutinies by the left forced the government to declare martial law. Mobutu and Nendaka narrowly escaped assassination at the hands of Lumumbist agents. A Lumumbist government-in-exile was established in Brazzaville by Gaston Soumialot and Christophe Gbenye.[25]

Kennedy followed these events with growing concern. With Adoula now defenseless, he was convinced that emergency retraining of the ANC was the single means left with which to avert civil war. The White House ordered a progress report. The Pentagon, once again, had little to show for itself and blamed the UN for the frustration of the retraining program. The State Department blamed the Belgians for having failed to deliver on their part of the plan. The White House was exasperated: "We feel irreplaceable time is slipping away."[26]

Within weeks of Kennedy's death, a rebellion broke out in Kwilu province and spread quickly to neighboring provinces. The Johnson administration abandoned its support of the center and moved to shore up the right wing. The CIA sent Cuban exile pilots to the Congo to fly sorties against the rebels and began bankrolling a short-lived attempt by Adoula and internal security chief Nendaka to establish a new political party. When the UN withdrew in June 1964, the U.S. and Belgium intervened with arms, airplanes, and military advisors. Mobutu brought Tshombe home from exile to replace Adoula as premier.[27] Munongo was given back his old portfolio as minister of interior, this time on a national basis. His first directive was to execute all rebel prisoners. African leaders as disparate in outlook as Nkrumah and Kenyatta were galled by Tshombe's sudden rehabilitation.

The rebels continued to advance. By mid-summer, they controlled nearly one-third of the country. Desperate to stop the rebels, the Belgians and Americans formed a mercenary force of 700 South Africans, Rhodesians, and Europeans to spearhead a counterattack. David Halberstam observed that hiring South African mercenaries to bring peace to the Congo was like the mayor of New York summoning the Mississippi Highway Patrol to quell riots in Harlem.[28]

In October 1964, the rebel forces took Stanleyville and seized several hundred hostages, many of them missionaries, whom they threatened to execute. When negotiations failed to secure their release, U.S. Air Force C-130s dropped 545 Belgian paratroops on Stanleyville as the mercenary column was converging on the city.

Operation Dragon Rouge, as it was called, was a military success and a political disaster. As historian Rupert Emerson saw it, the "military adventure in the heart of Africa . . . the arrival of the detested mercenary forces of Tshombe . . . the fear and disgust roused among Africans by the Stanleyville affair" all did irreparable damage to the American position in Africa.[29]

Eighteen African states formally accused the United States and Belgium of a flagrant violation of the UN Charter in threatening the peace and security of Africa. Stevenson lost his temper during the Security Council proceedings. "I have served in the United Nations from the day of its inception off and on for seventeen years. But never have I heard such irrational, irresponsible, insulting and repugnant language in these chambers." Stevenson later remarked to Ambassador Godley that it was hard to believe. A year before, Stevenson said, we were regarded as champions of Africa's cause. Now we were as reviled as the Belgians. It was very depressing.[30]

GHANA

The continued visibility of Nkrumah on the international scene stemmed, as usual, from his capacity to inspire headlines in the western press. The murder of Togolese President Olympio on January 13, 1963 had put him back on page one. Nkrumah's notoriety was further enhanced by a report that the Ghana Government intended to try former Foreign Minister Ako Adjei (accused of treason in the Kulungugu attempt on Nkrumah's life) as a CIA agent in the conspiracy trial.[31] With Ghana still demanding the immediate withdrawal of U.S. Embassy officers Dr. Carl C. Nydell and William B. Davis, whom they accused of involvement in anti-regime activity, relations were at an all-time low. President Kennedy knew that if Nkrumah continued his anti-American crusade, he would have no choice but to cut off U.S. financing of the Volta project—the symbol of America's commitment to African economic development. The White House additionally feared that the foreign aid appropriation bill, then before Congress, might well become a casualty of the miscalculation in Ghana.

The President decided that no Volta aid would be disbursed unless Ghana withdrew its demand that Nydell and Davis be removed from the country.[32] Alluding to Nydell, Nkrumah informed Kennedy in late January that the "difficulty we faced was that there was always, and still is, a possibility that those accused in the bomb outrage might in Court disclose their association with him." Kennedy replied immediately. "We have seen no such evidence [of improper behavior] and I have been informed by my officials, who have had a close review of his actions, that there is no basis, other than coincidence, for the belief that he is in any way involved in improper activities."[33] After six weeks of pressure at all levels, the U.S. mission in Accra succeeded in getting the Ghana government to back away from the idea of trying Adjei as an American agent and from its request that Nydell and Davis be withdrawn.

By this time, according to Carl Kaysen, the President was convinced that "damage control" was our only real option in trying to coexist with nonaligned charismatics such as Nasser, Sukarno, and Nkrumah. Public pressure by the U.S. would only produce more *coups de théâtre*. The lesson of the Volta project was that the certain cost of withdrawing had always been higher than the risk of going ahead. With misgivings, the President authorized Volta disbursements to proceed and asked the State Department to provide him henceforth with a monthly review of the situation in Ghana.[34]

Relations in the following months continued in their usual see-saw fashion. Nkrumah was still obsessed with the CIA. In one session with Ambassador Mahoney, Nkrumah spoke of "these people who run around snooping into things. . . . We've got to keep an eye on these people." The ambassador might well have agreed.[35]

Nkrumah's suspicions appeared in more vituperative form in the party press. The *Ghanaian Times* charged that American Negroes were providing the raw material for "subversion and neo-colonial interference in Africa." The *Spark* which had acquired the habit of reprinting editorials from the Soviet press in unattributed form, came to the point more bluntly, claiming that President Kennedy had taken office with the plan to recruit Negroes "for ugly purposes in Africa."[36]

The Americans were beside themselves with indignation. Both Kaiser and Mahoney made visits to Nkrumah to accuse him of bad faith for permitting such abuse. Peace Corps Director Sargent Shriver flew to Accra to inform Nkrumah that President Kennedy had given him direct personal assurance that no one in the Peace Corps was in any way connected with the CIA.[37]

Name calling was not solely the province of the Ghanaians, however. In late January 1963, Attorney General Robert Kennedy charged that Ghana was practicing the same kind of repression as South Africa. Nkrumah was infuriated. "In whatever other ways we may be lagging behind," he wrote President Kennedy, "I think that on the question of racial toleration we have established a standard during our short period of independence which can be regarded as a shining example for the rest of the world."[38] Kennedy thought it better not to respond.

The crude little drama continued. *Newsweek* reported in April 1963 that the CIA "monitored" certain foreign students in the U.S., including Ghanaians. "The hope is that they will be better disposed toward the U.S. than Kwame Nkrumah." This article caused great excitement in Accra and touched off another unusually adjectival round of abuse.[39]

At the heart of the dispute between Ghana and the U.S. was simply a difference of national purpose. As Henry Kissinger wrote, for revolutionaries such as Nkrumah, "the significant reality is the world they are striving to bring about, not the world they are fighting to overcome . . ." As a "revolutionary government," Ghana had committed what power it possessed to the immediate unification of the continent—in some cases, by force. As a major power with established security obligations, the U.S. preferred orderly change in the status quo. Given this broad difference of national purpose, it was not surprising that relations foundered.

At the diplomatic level, nonetheless, there remained some cause for hope. The appointment of Kojo Botsio (a pro-Western member of Nkrumah's old guard) as foreign minister was welcomed by Washington, as was the designation of M.A. Ribeiro as ambassador to the U.S., a post that had been vacant for over six months. When Ribeiro presented his credentials, Kennedy told him that he was following events in Ghana personally and advised the ambassador that "critics of the U.S. decision to undertake heavy commitments in Ghana must be proven wrong."[40]

Some in the State Department thought that the President was overdoing it on Ghana, but Kennedy insisted on personally monitoring the cable traffic from Accra. Little escaped his attention. One morning the Ghana Desk Officer at State received a call from the President asking him for the details about Ghana's problem controlling the capsid, a parasite that was ruining the cocoa crop.[41]

Under the terms of the Volta Master Agreements, construction of the Valco Aluminum plant was scheduled to begin in November 1963. The President wanted to get as clear a picture as possible of Nkrumah's future direction before giving his final approval to the $96-million guarantee of the Kaiser investment. He asked for assessments from the State Department, the CIA, and the U.S. mission in Ghana. The embassy produced an unusual assessment drawn from a series of conversations with Flight Captain Hanna Reitsch, a former test pilot for the Third Reich and intimate of Adolf Hitler, whom Nkrumah had invited to Ghana to train his air force. Miss Reitsch was housed in one of Nkrumah's mansions and, according to Ambassador Mahoney, gave "every appearance of having a deep, platonic attachment to Nkrumah."[42]

The point of the Reitsch assessment was that Nkrumah's outlook on East and West was more a product of personal experience and emotional inclination than of rational calculation. His attachment to Khrushchev— "he treats me like a brother," he said often to Reitsch—stemmed from their vacation together in the Crimea. Mao was Nkrumah's hero. Reitsch believed that Nkrumah's difficulties with the U.S. had less to do with his communist friendships than with his revulsion at the brutalized state of the black man in America. The years in America had left scars. President Kennedy's relative inactivity on civil rights gave Nkrumah no reason to hope for anything better from a white American. Suddenly, however, events in the U.S. gave him reason to change his view.

In May 1963, Birmingham, Alabama, exploded in racial violence.

Whites set off bombs in black neighborhoods and beat up Negroes while
the police stood by. Newspapers across the world featured a photograph
of a snarling police dog lunging at a black woman. Black Africa was
horrified. In June, after ordering the forcible desegregation of the University of Alabama at Tuscaloosa, Kennedy addressed the nation. The time
had come, he declared, for the U.S. to fulfill its promise. If the Negro
could not live a full and free life which all of us want, he said,

> then who among us would be content to have the color of his skin
> changed and stand in his place? Who among us would then be content
> with the counsels of patience and delay? We say to the world and to
> each other that we are the land of the free; do all we mean is that it is
> the land of the free except for the Negroes; that we have no second-
> class citizens except Negroes; that we have no class or caste system, no
> ghettos, no master race except with respect to Negroes?
>
> We face a moral crisis as a country and as a people. It cannot be
> met by repressive police action. It cannot be left to increased demon-
> strations in the streets. It cannot be quieted by token moves to talk. It
> is a time to act. . . . Those who do nothing are inviting shame as well
> as violence. Those who act boldly are recognizing right as well as
> reality.[43]

Nkrumah was deeply moved. He called Michael Dei-Anang into his
office and read passages of Kennedy's speech from the Reuters dispatch,
his voice breaking.[44] He asked Ambassador Mahoney to convey his profound thanks to the President when he was next in Washington. The
United States Information Service Mission procured a film of the speech
and began showing it all over Ghana. The response was thunderous.[45]

A year after the attempt on his life at Kulungugu, Nkrumah had re-
gained a good deal of his former self-confidence. According to the State
Department, he was "more solidly in the saddle than ever." With Olympio's
death, the opposition based in Togo had evaporated. Although the first
meeting of the Organization of African Unity had fallen far short of
Nkrumah's aspiration for "continental union government now!", the
convocation itself was a testament to his soaring vision of a united Africa.[46]
On the economic front, there was also good news. Sir Robert Jackson
reported that work on the Volta Dam was "roaring ahead and is a continuing example of the effectiveness of American Engineering and European construction."[47] Nkrumah had signed into law a Capital Investments
Act to attract foreign capital.

Kennedy watched the steady improvement of relations with gratifica-
tion. In early November 1963, he approved the U.S. government's guarantee of the Kaiser Valco investment. When Mahoney returned home for
consultations in mid-November, the President invited him to come by the

Oval Office for a visit. During their conversation on November 19, they talked about the impact of the civil rights crisis on the President's re-election chances and the administration's first steps to normalize relations with Red China. On Ghana, Mahoney predicted that the President would not regret his decision on the Volta project; that it would prove to be "a lasting boon to Ghana, with or without Nkrumah."[48]

Nkrumah was overcome with emotion at the news of Kennedy's death. He told the Ghanaian people that Africa would always remember Kennedy's "understanding of the grave issues confronting our world. . . ."[49] He had no doubts about who was behind the assassination. When Ambassador Mahoney handed him a copy of the Warren Report a few months later, Nkrumah opened it and pointing to the name of Allen Dulles (a member of the Warren Commission), handed it back to Mahoney saying simply, "whitewash."[50]

Nkrumah himself was once again nearly assassinated in January 1964 when a policeman in the presidential compound opened fire on him. Thereafter, Accra was turned into an armed camp. Russian military advisers were brought in to train the President's guard regiment. Chinese guerrilla instructors were sent to "freedom fighter" camps in the bush to train exiles for warfare in their home countries. In his rare public appearances, Nkrumah would wear a bullet-proof vest beneath his high collared military jacket. Ghana joined with China and the Soviet Union in the summer and fall of 1964 in providing arms to the Congolese insurgents. In protest against U.S. intervention, a crowd of CPP militants invaded the American embassy grounds and tore down the flag. It seemed like the last straw.

For all the political fury in Ghana, work on the Volta Dam proceeded smoothly. In January 1966 the dam was dedicated—a year ahead of schedule. At the dedication ceremony Nkrumah was gracious to those assembled, but it was clear that his mind was elsewhere. He told Mahoney that he wanted to fly to Beijing and Hanoi to put a stop to the Vietnam War. He needed American endorsement of the peace effort. Washington responded that it was not interested in his mediation.[51] The Americans now knew through their covert sources that it was simply a matter of time before the conspirators—chiefly, General J.A. Ankrah, Colonel E.K. Kotoka, and Police Commissioner J.W.K. Harlley—made a move against Nkrumah.[52]

Nkrumah's advisors urged him to postpone the trip to Asia. The rumors of a plot had the ring of authenticity, they said. Nkrumah told his trusted aide, Michael Dei-Anang, that he had never allowed such "small things" to stop him. If he had, where would Ghana be today?[53] He spent the remaining days before the trip in his study reading histories of Vietnam and preparing for his talks with Mao Zedong and Ho Chi Minh. On February 18, 1966, he composed his final will. The following day, he left Ghana for the last time. He was deposed on February 24, 1966.

SOUTHERN AFRICA

In 1963, the African tide turned against Portugal. Every African head of state present at the Organization of African Unity conference in May pledged to support the liberation movements in Portuguese Africa and many agreed to contribute to the OAU's Liberation Committee Fund. Algerian Premier Ben Bella promised to commit 10,000 troops to the Angolan insurgency. With a hard-bitten army of 100,000 at his disposal, Ben Bella's pledge could not be taken lightly; nor could his warning that the U.S. would do itself "much harm" in Africa if it placed the Azores base "ahead of independence in Angola."[54] The collapse of Katanga only lengthened the vulnerable frontier the Portuguese armed forces had to defend. Samuel E. Belk of the NSC staff saw Portugal as no longer "a hard and invincible landlord," but rather "a nation in retreat."[55]

Tanganyikan President Julius Nyerere announced that he would permit guerrilla havens to be established along the Mozambique border. The Adoula government in the Congo formally recognized Holden Roberto's government-in-exile (GRAE). Hostilities in Portuguese Guinea broke into open warfare, with the insurgents using modern Russian weaponry to down Portuguese aircraft. A CIA special report concluded, "The Portuguese military in Angola realize that . . . a long war of attrition is in prospect and that in the long run they cannot win such a war."[56]

In Washington, the Azores lease, while not renewed, was no longer under deliberation; this was significant. The African Bureau found a new ally in its efforts to align the U.S. with the national cause. In April 1963, President Kennedy appointed W. Averell Harriman as under secretary of state for political affairs. Harriman was no Europeanist. He told Ball that the U.S. was jeopardizing its whole position in Africa by trying to appease the Portuguese. Harriman soon issued a memorandum—with Rusk's unhappy clearance—that authorized wider contacts with nationalist leaders in Portuguese Africa and the provision of more educational assistance to exiled Africans.[57]

Mozambiquan nationalist leader Eduardo Mondlane came to Washington in May and openly warned of military action unless Portugal agreed to talks. Rusk and Ball decided that Mondlane would be ignored in order not to offend the Portuguese. When Deputy Assistant Secretary for African Affairs Wayne Fredericks was photographed a few days later speaking with Mondlane on African Freedom Day at Howard University,

European Bureau chief William R. Tyler complained to Rusk. The secretary of state telephoned Fredericks and warned him that such activity could not continue. When Fredericks offered to resign, however, Rusk backed off.[58]

Fredericks then contacted Robert Kennedy to suggest that he meet Mondlane. The attorney general agreed to the idea. As a matter of discretion, Fredericks suggested a neutral meeting place. Perhaps the International Club, or someone's house for dinner? "Bring him to the attorney general's office," Kennedy replied. The visit was a success. Together with Harriman, Kennedy arranged a CIA subsidy for Mondlane's travel costs.[59]

Under Secretary Ball commented testily to Kaysen about the younger Kennedy's lack of judgment. What if Mondlane went public about American largesse, or about his personal acquaintance with the President's brother? Ball laughed at the agency's assurance that everything could be done quietly. Two days later, Harriman hosted a luncheon for Mondlane at his Georgetown home. Harriman was highly impressed by Mondlane and urged Rusk and Ball to meet him. They declined.[60]

New thinking about Portuguese Africa appeared elsewhere in the government. A CIA special report on Angola favored a more even-handed approach toward the rival nationalist groups, the UPA (Roberto's movement) and the MPLA (the communist movement). According to the report, one MPLA faction led by the Party President Angostinho Neto favored "genuine neutrality" and reportedly had expelled several pro-Soviet leaders from the party. The CIA reasoned that both the MPLA and UPA would "probably prefer Western assistance and neither desires a commitment to the Communist world."[61]

In its final months, the Kennedy administration attempted to bring about talks between the nationalist movements, both communist and noncommunist. A State Department circular in July directed that "U.S. policy is not, repeat not, to discourage MPLA (Neto-Andrade faction) move toward the West and not to choose between these two movements."[62]

There was still no sign of compromise from Fortress Portugal, however. Salazar believed increasingly, Elbrick reported, that Portugal had only to hold on in Africa for two or three more years and all would be well. "In their dream world, the Portuguese listen only to those who agree with them, and since that number is dwindling, they are frequently found talking to themselves."[63] Actually, Portugal was not entirely isolated since Salazar had found critical support from Spain and South Africa after a series of high-level talks.

Another sympathetic outsider was Richard M. Nixon, who visited Lisbon in June. During a conversation with the Foreign Minister, the former Vice President expressed the view that independence was "not necessarily the best thing for Africa or the Africans." Franco Nogueira was suitably pleased; the White House was not. Special Assistant Michael Forrestal asked Arthur Schlesinger, Jr., "Isn't there something in the Mann Act covering this?"[64]

Ambassador Stevenson alerted the President in early summer that the Africans were planning a showdown with Portugal before the Security Council. "[I]mportant risks will have to be assumed one way or another," Stevenson predicted. He urged the President to write a "letter of warning" to Salazar and proposed that the simple way to stop the adoption of sanctions language was to support the Africans in condemning Portugal and in recommending an arms embargo.[65]

Ball had another idea. He proposed that Stevenson (who was leaving on a one-week cruise in the Adriatic with Agnes Meyer, owner of the *Washington Post*) drop by Lisbon for a call on Dr. Salazar. Stevenson was dubious; he was practically *persona non grata* in Lisbon. Ball said Salazar needed to know "the facts of life" at the UN. The Under Secretary tried to sell the idea to Bundy in different terms: Salazar was "a lonely man and might respond to a personal touch of this kind . . . " Bundy was dubious. "It was crazy," he said, "as crazy as sending Soapy [Williams]." When Kennedy got wind of the idea, he remarked to Kaysen, "Oh Jesus, George is getting creative again." Stevenson was not asked to go to Lisbon, but the President did insist that he cut his vacation short. How can we deliberate seriously, Kennedy remarked to Ball, when Adlai is off in the Adriatic?[66]

On July 11, 32 African states formally requested a meeting of the Security Council to discuss the Portuguese territories and South Africa. The Joint Chiefs described the African move as "blackmail" and set forth the worst-case contingency regarding the Azores if the administration sided with the Africans. Assistant Secretary Cleveland, who wielded pivotal influence in UN strategy, called for support of a partial arms embargo. Ball agreed, but Elbrick cabled in that any embargo would "infuriate" the Portuguese and jeopardize access to the Azores.[67] It was back to Angola versus the Azores.

On July 18, the President met with Rusk, Stevenson, Cleveland, and other key advisors. Cleveland and Stevenson had already hammered out a draft resolution that they thought the U.S. could support at the Security Council debate, or even introduce. Stevenson said that, in his judgment, the draft resolution would not involve serious risk to the Azores. It would not preserve our present position in Africa either, he thought, but, at least, would not seriously damage it.

The President wondered why we had to take the initiative at all. It would only get us into trouble with the Portuguese. What if we hung back and did nothing, and let nature take its course? He hated, he said, to have the U.S. become the scapegoat. We could not afford to lose the Azores with the test ban treaty coming up. Let us not try to shepherd everyone around. Let the Portuguese foreign minister find out for himself how bad things were. We should not take the lead nor give the impression that we could do much for him—or would do much against him. He asked Stevenson what the probable French attitude would be. Stevenson said that France, as usual, would seek the best of both worlds. Kennedy then said, "Well, let us try that this time."[68]

Stevenson flew back to New York. A few days later, the African states, with the sponsorship of Ghana, Morocco, and the Philippines, submitted a draft resolution to the Security Council. It called for an arms embargo on Portugal and used Chapter VII language (i.e., "a threat to international peace" that might entail Security Council intervention) to describe the situation in Angola. Stevenson and his staff worked furiously over the next three days consulting with the African foreign ministers and the Europeans. Major alterations were made in the text of the draft. Cleveland reported to Rusk "a serious softening of opposition" among the Africans. Ghana's UN ambassador (and later General Assembly president) Alex Quaison-Sackey said, "It was one of the most determined efforts I ever saw" in reference to Stevenson's work.[69] It was also not exactly in keeping with the President's preference for not taking the initiative.

By July 28, Stevenson had put together a draft resolution with Norway that he was confident could dislodge the more extreme Afro-Asian draft. Pressured by Cleveland, Secretary Rusk called Stevenson on the 29th and authorized him to cosponsor the alternative resolution. The next day, the President was informed that Stevenson seemed to have the seven votes necessary for passage. The ambassador had turned tables on his Soviet rival (who had no doubt been relishing the thought of how the U.S. would deal with a sanctions mandate), the radical Africans, and his detractors in Washington.[70]

Kennedy, however, was not pleased with Stevenson's unauthorized efforts. The NSC African specialist informed the President, "the compromise language [of Stevenson] goes substantially beyond what you cleared in conversation with Secretary Rusk."[71] Lord Home interceded with a personal message to Rusk objecting to the American text. He urged that the U.S. abstain on the grounds that a dangerous precedent might be established that would later be applied to Rhodesia. Perhaps getting wind of what was happening, Stevenson asked to come to Washington to plead his case, but the White House discouraged him from doing so.[72]

The day before the Security Council vote, the President met again with his advisers on Portuguese Africa. He characterized Lord Home's letter as "very strong, deserving serious consideration." Perhaps the U.S.

should abstain and let a Chapter 6 permissive resolution pass, Kennedy said. He then asked Ball to telephone Lord Home immediately and to discuss a revised version of the text with him.[73]

After the White House strategy meeting ended, the President telephoned Stevenson and instructed him to abstain from voting for his own compromise resolution. Stevenson was "disgusted" by Kennedy's decision. He compared it to Eisenhower's eleventh-hour order in December 1960 to his ambassador to the UN to abstain from voting on the anticolonial resolution. He suspected—correctly—that Kennedy had allowed the British to influence him unduly.[74]

On the morning of the 31st, the Foreign Office in Lisbon informed Elbrick that "Portugal would hold the United States responsible for the resolution." Just before the vote, Franco Nogueira told the Security Council that his government would pay no attention to the "revolting resolution" whatever the result. The Americans were convinced that Salazar had cleared these sentiments. Stevenson, furious, abstained on the resolution (as he had been instructed) and, after a brief statement of explanation, left the chamber. In the corridor, he ran into Franco Nogueira and a bitter exchange ensued.[75]

When Stevenson reported the incident to Rusk (and there is reason to believe that he dramatized Franco Nogueira's commentary), the Secretary was "shocked." The President "went through the roof" and told Harriman to contact Pereira immediately. "Why he's picked on me to do it, I haven't the least idea," Harriman told Ball.[76]

Kennedy was biding his time on the Angola and Azores question until the nuclear test ban treaty could be concluded in Moscow. He would not permit any other foreign policy matter to jeopardize its achievement.[77] On July 30, he told the nation that "Yesterday, a shaft of light cut through the darkness." The next day, he sent a memorandum to McNamara: " . . . I think we should develop a contingency for the loss of the Azores base." Confidentially (the test ban treaty still had to be ratified by the Senate) Kennedy altered two of his closest friends and advisors that "he was prepared to forego the base rather than permit Portugal to dictate his African policy."[78] Although the President's delaying tactic had greatly disappointed Stevenson and others in the administration, he had not abandoned the idea of an independent Angola.

McNamara had anticipated the move. Two weeks earlier, he had sent Rusk a cost-benefit analysis on the Azores—the sort he often used to pacify the Joint Chiefs. McNamara's memorandum discounted the supposedly decisive strategic considerations and concluded: "I believe the decisions on these issues should be based on general considerations of foreign policy. I hope that you share the views I have expressed."[79]

In August 1963, the administration moved decisively against Portugal and South Africa for their violent denial of African rights. George Ball was sent to Lisbon as the President's emissary to Dr. Salazar. Kennedy made it clear in instructions that there was to be no more linkage of Angola and the Azores. "If Dr. Salazar raises the question of the Azores base, you should indicate our willingness to conclude negotiations on the Azores base within the context of a strong NATO alliance."[80]

In Lisbon, Ball had two long sessions with Dr. Salazar. He asked the Prime Minister to repatriate the American-supplied arms that the Portuguese were using in Africa, particularly the F-86 jets in Portuguese Guinea. He proposed the plan drawn up by the White House for self-determination in the African provinces. These requests were brushed aside by Salazar and Franco Nogueira, who repeated the classic litany of reasons why Portugal had to fight it out in Africa: communism, terrorism, the civilizing mission, etc. Ball cabled Washington that we had been laboring under a misapprehension. Portugal was not being ruled by a single autocrat but by a triumvirate: Salazar, Vasco da Gama, and Prince Henry the Navigator. The Portuguese were living in another century.[81]

After he returned to Washington, Ball composed a 6,000-word letter to Salazar. "I have pondered long over this argument," he wrote, "and I have concluded that the point on which we disagree is as simple as it is basic. You believe time works in your favor; we do not." Salazar's equally long reply had a tired and desperate ring to it, but as usual he was unyielding and spoke of "everything enveloped in the babble of empirical and opportunistic solutions, and the web of false expedients."[82]

In South Africa, the Afrikaners were proving to be as unyielding as the Portuguese to international insistence that they dismantle *apartheid*. The Kennedy administration left no doubt where it stood on the project, "The U.S. abhors . . . *apartheid*," U.S. Ambassador Francis Plimpton told the General Assembly. "How and when the South African Government will abandon its hateful racial policies we cannot know, but abandon, it will." The Afrikaners were highly offended but completely unmoved by the U.S. condemnation. They subsequently enacted an "anti-sabotage" law to ban and imprison hundreds of their opponents. The African governments then introduced a Security Council resolution calling for the imposition of a total arms embargo on South Africa, as well as its expulsion from the UN.[83]

The Kennedy administration could not accept the demand for expulsion. Expelling UN members, the President thought, might start a process that would not be easy to halt. The proposal for an arms embargo involved a thornier choice for the administration.[84] In an *aide mémoire* dated June 15, 1962, the administration had agreed to sell military equipment to South Africa for the started purpose of containing international communist aggression. The South African government, in its concurrent *aide mémoire*, had consented to let the U.S. establish a deep space military tracking station near Pretoria on condition that future South African requests for military equipment be met with "prompt consideration."[85]

There was sharp disagreement within the Administration over how to vote on the resolution. The Pentagon argued that South Africa's contribution to Western security through mutual defense cooperation agreements necessitated an American veto of the resolution. Secretary Rusk favored abstention: "[W]e are not the self-elected gendarmes for the political and social problems of other states," he wrote the President. The South Africans weren't the only ones who had violated human rights.[86] Stevenson, however, believed that it was imperative that the United States do whatever was possible to stem the flow of arms to the South African state. He accordingly urged Kennedy to authorize American support for a partial arms embargo.

Although he feared that trying to impose collective sanctions would cause the UN to do more harm to itself than to South Africa, the President was determined to sever military sales to the South Africans.[87] After the test ban treaty was signed in Moscow, Kennedy ordered Ambassador Stevenson to announce that the U.S. would terminate all sales of arms to South Africa effective January 1, 1964. On August 2, Stevenson informed the Security Council of this decision. The black African governments were deeply gratified and, in the spirit of compromise, withdrew the mandatory provisions from their resolution. On August 7, with full U.S. support, the resolution was adopted by a vote of nine to zero, with Britain and France abstaining.

Regarding Portuguese Africa, Stevenson continued to search for some negotiating formula for talks between the insurgents and the colonialists. John Steinbeck invited the ambassador out to his estate in Sag Harbor, Long Island for a short vacation. Stevenson declined, saying that he had to stay in New York "in time to get ready for the forthcoming African assault in the General Assembly."[88]

Stevenson's efforts in New York and Ball's fence-mending in Lisbon ultimately resulted in a minor breakthrough. In October, the Salazar regime indicated that it would agree to participate in talks with African representatives. The talks opened on October 18 in New York between a Portuguese delegation headed by Franco Nogueira and diplomats from nine African countries.[89]

Always his brother's weathervane, Robert Kennedy wrote Bundy on November 20, 1963 urging that the Standing Group discuss the "policy of the United States toward the individuals and organizations in Mozambique, South Africa, Angola, and Rhodesia . . . " The Attorney General was confident that, "if we could take steps now, either through the CIA and/or making a concerted effort with students and intellectuals, we could head off some of the problems that are undoubtedly going to appear on the horizon in the next year or so."[90]

A month earlier, Ball had written to Salazar in an attempt to explain the American strategy in Africa. American policy, he said, was "inspired not by a narrow self-interest but by an anxiety to preserve the values of our civilization. . . . Experience has amply shown the inexorable strength of the drive for self-determination. It can be frontally opposed only at an excessively high price—and a price that, once paid, tends to go higher."[91]

Several years—and some 100,000 casualties—later, the Nixon administration reached a different conclusion with regard to the role of the United States in Southern Africa. Under National Security Advisor Henry Kissinger, the National Security Council staff developed a statement of policy known as "the Tar-Baby Option." It concluded that "the whites are here to stay and the only way constructive change can come about is through them. There is no hope for the blacks to gain the political rights they seek through violence . . . "[92]

President Nixon stated his preference more plainly. At a White House reception on April 10, 1969 marking the twentieth anniversary of the founding of NATO, he took Portuguese Foreign Minister Franco Nogueira aside. "Just remember," Nixon said, "I'll never do to you what Kennedy did."[93]

10

Conclusion

> The most successful course has been for Western nations to employ measures that buy time for dealing with historical forces—not by blocking the tide but by building canals and conduits to direct its flow. This is not 'resistance' merely to preserve a frozen *status quo* but rather a deliberate attempt to work with the forces of history to assure their constructive issue.
>
> George W. Ball
> to António de Oliveira Salazar
> (*October, 1963*)

Nationalism was the historic force of Kennedy's time; the Cold War his principal legacy as President. The challenge he faced was the one that every American president has faced since World War II: how to deal with nationalist revolution in the arena of the Cold War—either by blocking the nationalist tide to contain communist expansion, or by building canals and conduits through diplomatic means to direct its flow. In nearly every instance of revolutionary upheaval, the U.S. has found itself trying to hold back the tide of nationalism in the name of anticommunism.

Kennedy's African record, however, stands out as an exception to the antinationalist tendency of America in the Third World. Kennedy was convinced, as he had said many times during the 1950s, that nationalism would sweep everything before it—communism as well as colonialism—provided that the U.S., as leader of the West, did everything it could to bring about an orderly transition to nationhood. "African independence must be genuine independence," Kennedy wrote Prime Minister Nehru during the first weeks of his presidency, and "not just a cover for some form of continuing control from the outside."[1]

Henry A. Kissinger described the sort of calculation Kennedy made about the historic pre-eminence of nationalism as the "conjectural element in foreign policy—the need to gear action to an assessment that cannot be proved true when it is made."[2] Kennedy's conjecture that the U.S. could shape the African revolution to orderly ends through peaceful means lay at the heart of his diplomatic efforts in the Congo, Ghana, and Portuguese Angola.

Kennedy arrived in the White House with his own portfolio on Africa.

He brought with him a long-standing, personally held conviction on the colonialism issue. He had also attracted a popular following on the continent. The "eager crowds shouting 'Kennedy, Kennedy' " that Frank Church saw in Africa in December 1960, the "complete kinship" Kwame Nkrumah promised him on inaugural day were all there before he had even begun.

These high expectations clearly gave President Kennedy leverage with Africa's new leaders, but they also created hopes among the Africans that Kennedy was often either unable or unwilling to fulfill. When the Russians sought refueling rights in Ghana and Guinea during the Cuban missile crisis, Kennedy was able to persuade Nkrumah and Sékou Touré to reject the Soviet request. But when Nkrumah sent a personal appeal to Kennedy to intercede to save Lumumba, Kennedy did nothing and both Nkrumah and Sékou Touré were deeply disappointed. The same frustration was evident in Holden Roberto's embittered letter to Kennedy in December 1962 accusing him of abandoning the Angolan nationalists in their hour of need.

The Africans came to appreciate that, despite his endorsement of the nationalist cause and his efforts to reunite the Congo, Kennedy was still a cautious leader. His style, as one American journalist later wrote, was to "make decisions at the margin, committing himself to little and leaving room for escape."[3] David Ormsby Gore, a man who knew Kennedy's mind probably better than anyone else, thought that this cautiousness arose from his wariness of "the fatality of activism" at a time when international events seemed to be beyond the realm of presidential control.[4]

What clearly emerges from the White House record is a man who knew very much what he wanted but who was rarely sure if he could get it. James Reston's conclusion that it was the President's deep knowledge that made him a pessimist evoked Kennedy's own qualified idea of the presidency as a post of "extraordinary powers" and "extraordinary limitations."[5] It is in this ambivalent posture that Kennedy's qualities as a statesman are most apparent: as a decisionmaker, he seemed to be ruled by his sense of "limitations"; as a diplomat, he seemed ready to take full advantage of the "powers" of his presidency.

Kennedy was inclined as a decisionmaker to preserve options, which, in operational fact, usually meant practicing wait-and-see. In the Bay of Pigs crisis, "he didn't say yes and he didn't say no" and disaster followed. "If a President fails or refuses to make a clear-cut decision on long-term policy," George Ball later wrote, "he will have less rather than more freedom to maneuver as events alter the facts and compel further action."[6] In Vietnam, Kennedy steadily increased troop commitments without ever deciding how far he would ultimately go.

In the Congo, however, it was precisely Kennedy's habit of avoiding decisive commitments and taking gradual steps that kept the loose coalition of states supporting the UN operation together. Decisiveness in the form of precipitate military action would have split the tentative alliance and played into either the Soviet Union's or Katanga's hands. Kennedy's insistence on keeping some slack in his decisionmaking gave him the flexibility with which to deal in an extraordinarily fluid environment.

Like Joseph Conrad's Marlow in *Heart of Darkness*, who described Belgium's Congo as an "accursed inheritance to be subdued at the cost of profound anguish and excessive toil," Kennedy feared that the further he traveled into the Congo, the more treacherous would be his path of extrication and the more the U.S. would become part of the problem instead of part of the solution.[7] This was the reason for his successive vetoes of the proposals of the State Department and the Joint Chiefs of Staff for direct U.S. military intervention in the Congo in September 1961 and December 1962. To those who expressed doubts about his policy of supporting the UN peacekeeping operation, the President often quoted Ambassador Stevenson's statement to the Security Council that the only way to keep the Cold War *out* of the Congo was to keep the UN *in* the Congo. The apparition of a more costly and dangerous alternative— deeper American intervention—was essentially what kept Kennedy on the UN path.

He began badly in the Congo, partly because he failed to understand the deadly effect that Kantangese secession had on Congolese nationhood and partly because he felt that Hammarskjold was trying to force his hand. Kennedy dodged the Lumumba affair (although Lumumba had been murdered before Kennedy took the oath of office, word did not leak out until four weeks later) and then dragged his heels when Hammarskjold attempted to use his Security Council mandate to end the Katangese secession.

The irony of Hammarskjold's death was that it impelled the uncertain Kennedy to do exactly what the Secretary-General had tried and failed to do—bring the European powers back into the peacekeeping alliance and force a showdown with Tshombe. The larger purpose of Kennedy's diplomacy then emerged: to build a durable political center around the Adoula coalition. The signature of the Kitona accord—a tribute to Kennedy's skill in combining the threat of war with an offer for peace— seemed to vindicate the initiatives the President had taken. For a brief moment in December 1961, it seemed that the center would hold.

But in 1962, the center collapsed. Adoula's coalition unraveled and Tshombe seemed stronger than ever. Britain defected from the UN operation and the Congress balked at the President's request to refinance the

UN. On the first anniversary of Hammarskjold's death, the UN and Katangese armies were headed for another bloody and inconclusive exchange. The President was again uncertain; in November 1962, he ordered his advisors to "take a long, hard look" at Congo policy. Their conclusion was that abandoning the UN operation now would mean direct American intervention later. Katanga would have to be crushed. Kennedy accordingly ordered that the UN be rearmed. He then secured the backing of Spaak and Macmillan for a military showdown while Ambassador Gullion kept the lid on Léopoldville. Katanga was thereafter overrun by the UN army with negligible loss of life.

For all the exorbitant cost of the operation, the UN had won its greatest victory in peacekeeping and had prevented a Soviet-American confrontation in the heart of Africa. Hammarskjold's "great adventure" had been vindicated and a precedent set. For the Congo, however, the fall of Katanga resulted in only a brief interlude of national unity. But the U.S. had succeeded in buying time for dealing with historic forces—"not by blocking the tide but by building canals and conduits to direct its flow." Kennedy had proven that there could be a creative aspect to containment policy: by addressing the internal origins of the Congo crisis in addition to addressing the external communist threat, the President made containment in the Congo what it never was in Vietnam—a workable and constructive policy that was fundamentally in consonance with nationalist reality.

It was as a diplomat—in the day-to-day travail of tactical maneuver in shifting conditions—that Kennedy exploited the "powers" of his presidency. In the first place, as transcribed telephone conversations reveal, his daily intake of information was considerable. After the Bay of Pigs blunder, the President habitually asked for factual verification of critical reports. To make sure that diplomatic action was not impeded or undone by unauthorized CIA operations, he sent a circular letter in May 1961 to all U.S. ambassadors advising them that their authority extended to all embassy activities. Kennedy's inclination to doubt the word of the specialists and his practice of screening facts were central to the successful outcome of the Cuban missile crisis. One scholar attributed Kennedy's mastery of that crisis to his "having perceived reality with the accuracy of a draftsman."[8]

Although he temporized at times as a decisionmaker, Kennedy could be a bold diplomatic tactician. Ambassador Gullion was to remember a faint voice shouting daily instructions over a military short-wave hookup on how to maneuver Adoula and Tshombe to the negotiating table in December 1961. In September 1963, the President again interceded personally and succeeded in persuading the UN General Assembly and a doubting U Thant to keep the UN army in the Congo for another year.

The President's able use of the personal gesture in Washington complemented his diplomacy in the field. The passage of twenty-eight African heads of state through the White House, intermittent presidential correspondence with a half-dozen African leaders, and the presence of several of Kennedy's acquaintances as ambassadors gave the administration working leverage in Africa.

Kennedy wanted his ambassadors to "stay in close, keep working, and wait for the breaks." The fact that they had his full backing permitted small gains, on occasion, to add up to major breakthroughs. Sékou Touré's sudden exit from the Soviet embrace in 1963 was possible because Kennedy's ambassador, William Attwood, had kept the American door open.[9] In Ghana, ambassadorial legwork kept Nkrumah neutral enough to justify proceeding with U.S. financing of the Volta River project. Africa's support of the American position in the Cuban missile crisis persuaded even some of the President's most stringent critics on Capitol Hill that there were Cold War advantages to be gained in working with African nationalists.

In Portuguese Angola, however, there were no major breakthroughs or even small gains. Salazar, in his medieval fastness, repulsed all overtures and forced Kennedy to make a tactical withdrawal. But the President never let go of his conviction that the future lay with the nationalists. In the final weeks of his administration, he strengthened relations with the Angolans and resolved that he would accept no more of Salazar's blackmail over the Azores. Ball wrote Salazar to explain Kennedy's policy: the U.S. position was not based on "narrow self-interest but on an anxiety to preserve the values of our civilization."[10]

For all of the sound and fury of the Cold War, the President was determined that nationalism would have its place in American foreign policy. "The strongest force in the world is the desire for national independence," Kennedy remarked to Finnish President Urho K. Kekkonen. "That is why I am eager that the United States back nationalist movements even though it embroils us with our friends in Europe . . . "[11] The conviction was an old one. "Nationalism," Kennedy had concluded after his trip through insurgent Asia in 1951, "is the most important international fact of life in the second half of the 20th century."[12]

In the end, the expectations proved far greater than the achievements, the memories far grander than the actual record. But Kennedy did succeed in identifying nationalism as the central reality of his age and in doing what no other American president before or after him has done—establishing a common ground between African ideals and American self-interest in the midst of the Cold War.

Notes

Introduction: Nationalism and the Cold War

1. Quoted in Basil Davidson, *Let Freedom Come, Africa in Modern History* (Boston, 1978), p. 199.

2. Harry S Truman, *Memoirs I: Year of Decisions* (Garden City, 1955), p. 552.

3. David Nunnerly, *President Kennedy and Britain* (New York, 1972), p. 21.

4. Remarks at St. Patrick's Day Dinner, Baltimore, March 16, 1957, Pre-Presidential Papers, John F. Kennedy Library, Waltham, Mass. [hereafter PPP, JFKL].

5. Raymond F. Betts, ed., *The "Scramble" for Africa, Causes and Dimensions of Empire* (Boston, 1966), p. 41.

6. Ibid., pp. 55–60.

7. J.D. Fage, *A History of West Africa* (Cambridge, U.K., 1969), pp. 171–74.

8. A.J. Wills, *An Introduction to the History of Central Africa* (London, 1967), pp. 120–60, 180–81.

9. Quoted in Betts, *The "Scramble" for Africa*, p. xv.

10. Gerald J. Bender, *Angola Under the Portuguese, The Myth and the Reality* (Berkeley, 1978), pp. 59–94.

11. Quoted in Waldemar Nielsen, *The Great Powers and Africa* (New York, 1969), p. 22.

12. Fage, *A History of West Africa*, pp. 175–76.

13. The phrase is Basil Davidson's and the examples are his as well. *Let Freedom Come*, pp. 38–39, 43.

14. Quoted in N. Gordon Levin, Jr., *Woodrow Wilson and World Politics, America's Response to War and Revolution* (New York, 1968), pp. 247–48.

15. E. David Cronen, ed., *The Political Thought of Woodrow Wilson* (New York, 1965), p. 442. Arthur S. Link, *Wilson the Diplomatist* (Baltimore, 1957), pp. 112–13.

16. Jean Lacouture, *Ho Chi Minh: A Political Biography* (New York, 1968), p. 24. J. William Fulbright, "The Truman Doctrine Reconsidered: From Greece to Vietnam," in Charles Gati, ed., *Caging the Bear* (New York, 1974), p. 74.

17. This is Alexander Dallin's characterization, in Zbigniew Brzezinski, ed., *Africa and the Communist World* (Stanford, 1963), p. 9.

18. Link, *Wilson the Diplomat,* p. 104. See also, Arno J. Mayer, *Wilson vs. Lenin, Political Origins of the New Diplomacy, 1917–1918* (New Haven, 1959).

19. Jomo Kenyatta, *Facing Mount Kenya, The Tribal Life of the Gikuyu* (London, 1953). Kofi A. Busia, *The Position of the Chief in the Modern Political System of Ashanti* (Totowa, N.J., 1968).

20. L.H. Ofosu-Appiah, *The Life and Times of J.B. Danquah* (Accra, 1974).

21. Jean-Paul Sartre, "Orphée Noir," in Léopold Sédar Senghor, *Anthologie de la nouvelle poesie nègre et malgache de langue française* (Paris, 1969).

22. Bankole, Timothy, *Kwame Nkrumah* (London, 1955), p. 25.

23. Interview: Michael Dei-Anang, Washington, D.C., 5/16/78.

24. Quoted in James S. Coleman, *Nigeria, Background to Nationalism* (Berkeley, 1958), p. 244.

25. Quoted in Davidson, *Let Freedom Come,* p. 199.

26. Quoted in Gati, *Caging the Bear,* pp. 74–75.

27. Vernon McKay, *Africa in World Politics* (New York, 1963), p. 24.

28. Quoted in Ronald Steel, *Walter Lippmann and the American Century* (Boston, 1980), p. 433.

29. Ibid., p. 428.

30. Ibid., p. 429.

31. Ibid., p. 440.

32. Reprinted in Gati, *Caging of the Bear,* pp. 3–8.

33. Dean Acheson, *Present at the Creation* (New York, 1969), p. 219.

34. Kennan's "X" article is reprinted in Gati, *Caging the Bear,* pp. 9–24.

35. Steel, *Walter Lippmann and the American Century,* p. 444.

36. Richard J. Barnet, *Intervention and the Revolution, the United States and the Third World* (New York, 1968), pp. 214–16.

37. Acheson quoted in Gati, *Caging the Bear,* pp. 76–77.

38. Herbert S. Parmet, *Jack, The Struggles of John F. Kennedy* (New York, 1980), p. 228.

1. The Education of John F. Kennedy

1. Robert J. Donovan, *Tumultuous Years, The Presidency of Harry S Truman, 1949–1953* (New York, 1982), pp. 74–88.

2. Herbert S. Parmet, *Jack, The Struggles of John F. Kennedy* (New York, 1980), p. 210.

3. Donovan, *Tumultuous Years,* p. 30.

4. Advance copy of his report on his trip to the Middle and Far East by Hon. John F. Kennedy, Mutual Broadcasting Network, Nov. 14, 1951, PPP, JFKL.

5. David Halberstam, *The Best and the Brightest* (New York, 1972), p. 119.

6. Report of his trip to the Middle and Far East by Hon. John F. Kennedy, Nov. 14, 1951, PPP, JFKL.

7. Letter to John Foster Dulles, Secretary of State, from Senator John F. Kennedy, May 7, 1953, Senate Files (Indochina), PPP, JFKL.

8. Edited draft of speech regarding an amendment to S. 2128, the Mutual Security Act of 1951; 83rd Congress, 1st Session, Senate Files (Indochina), PPP, JFKL. Kennedy's remarks were drawn in great part from a lengthy speech delivered by Edmund A. Gullion to the Seminar on Southeast Asia at the Foreign Service Institute on March 25, 1953. Gullion concluded his speech with this observation: "The native peoples must be convinced that they have something to fight for before we can safely resign them the burden of defending the free world at the frontier which runs along the Hanoi-Haiphong road." (Secret Security Information, Declassified 2/13/73), PPP, JFKL.

9. Parmet, *Jack*, p. 281.

10. Marvin Kalb and Elie Abel, *Roots of Involvement, The U.S. in Asia, 1784–1971* (New York, 1971), pp. 78–83.

11. Barnet, *Intervention and Revolution*, pp. 224–25.

12. Parmet, *Jack*, p. 282.

13. Quoted in Public Papers of the President, Dwight D. Eisenhower, 1954 (Washington, D.C., 1960), pp. 382–83.

14. Joseph Buttinger, *Vietnam: A Dragon Embattled, Volume II, Vietnam at War* (New York, 1967), pp. 831–34.

15. Quoted in Rupert Emerson, *Africa and United States Policy* (Englewood Cliffs, New Jersey, 1967), p. 23.

16. "The Proper Role of Foreign Policy in the 1956 Campaign," Remarks by Senator John F. Kennedy to the Los Angeles World Affairs Council, Los Angeles, Sept. 21, 1956.

17. Telephone interview: Clayton Fritchey, 5/3/78, Washington, D.C.

18. Gurtov, *The United States Against the Third World*, p. 24.

19. Divine, *Eisenhower and the Cold War*, p. 86.

20. Ibid., pp. 83–88.

21. Quoted in Gurtov, *The United States Against the Third World*, p. 29.

22. "The Choice in Asia—Democratic Development in India," Speech of Hon. John F. Kennedy, U.S. Senate, March 25, 1958, p. 3, PPP, JFKL.

23. Remarks of Senator John F. Kennedy, "American Leadership for Peace," University of Pennsylvania, October 18, 1959, Speech File, PPP, JFKL.

24. John F. Kennedy, "A Democrat Looks at Foreign Policy," *Foreign Affairs*, vol. 36, no. 1, October 1957, p. 53.

25. *The New York Times*, July 3, 1957.

26. "Facing Facts on Algeria," Remarks by Senator John F. Kennedy, United States Senate, July 2, 1957, p. 4, PPP, JFKL. Also *Congressional Record*, July 2, 1957, p. 10788.

27. Quoted in the San Francisco *Examiner*, July 11, 1957.

28. Dulles's remark: Drew Pearson column, undated, Speech File, Algeria, PPP, JFKL. Stevenson's remark: quoted in John Bartlow Martin, *Adlai Stevenson and the World*, p. 415. Acheson's commentary: Dean Acheson, *Power and Diplomacy* (Cambridge, Mass., 1958), pp. 126–27.

29. *Le Figaro*, July 7, 1957, *U.S. News and World Report*, undated clipping, PPP, JFKL. Morice was quoted in *Time*, July 15, 1957, p. 18. See also the *Wall Street Journal*, Aug. 12, for an article on the French effort to launch a propaganda campaign in the United States concerning the Algerian war.

30. Arthur M. Schlesinger, Jr., to John F. Kennedy, Aug. 4, 1957, PPP, JFKL.

31. *The New York Times*, July 6, 1957. Lacoste quoted in an undated clipping in the Algeria Speech File, PPP, JFKL, about the speech Lacoste delivered on July 7, 1957 in Algiers. Kennedy quoted in the Toronto *Globe and Mail*, July 13, 1957.

32. See Speech Files, PPP, JFKL, and also *Lynn* (Mass.) *Republican*, July 23, 1957.

33. *The New York Times*, July 18, 1957. Senator Kennedy replied to accusations of meddling or irresponsibility, "I have always been reluctant to use the Senate floor as a forum for discussion of sensitive foreign policy issues." He claimed he had delayed the speech for a long time in the hope that the (Guy) Mollet government "would make good on its promise for 'liberal' solutions to the worsening crisis." It did not and America continued to follow "a policy of drift," he said. "Ignoring the problem will neither alleviate it nor lessen the inevitability of eventual Algerian independence—and it is my hope that the nationalists in that and other countries will then regard the United States as a friend and not an enemy." John F. Kennedy to H. Allan Sillcox, July 26, 1957, Algeria Speech File, PPP, JFKL.

34. *Time*, Dec. 12, 1957.

35. Chester Bowles to John F. Kennedy, July 23, 1957, PPP, JFKL.

36. Oral History of Dean Acheson [hereinafter OHDA], JFKL.

37. See Kennedy's second address on Algeria in "Facing Facts on Algeria," Speeches of the Hon. John F. Kennedy, July 8, 1957, Algeria Speech File, PPP, JFKL.

38. The article by *Manchester Guardian* Washington correspondent, Alistair Cooke, was printed in the *Toledo Blade*, July 14, 1957. Pierre's letter is in *The New York Times*, July 10, 1957. *L'Express* editor Jean-Jacques Servan-Schreiber, who had written a devastating account of his military service as *Lieutenant en Algérie*, ran the full text of the speech in *L'Express* with Kennedy's picture on the cover. Kennedy thanked Servan-Schreiber: ". . . it took courage for your paper to do this in the face of much violent criticism." John F. Kennedy to Jean-Jacques Servan-Schreiber, Aug. 13, 1957, PPP, JFKL.

39. *Le Monde*, July 10, 1957.

40. Interview: Philip M. Kaiser, July 22, 1977, London. Oral history of Phillip M. Kaiser, JFKL: "He [Senghor] had a warm feeling for this young, vigorous man who'd caught the imagination of the Africans. It all began with the Algeria speech."

41. Schlesinger, *A Thousand Days*, p. 511.

42. Theodore C. Sorensen, *Kennedy*, p. 65.

43. Holden Roberto to John F. Kennedy, Dec. 19, 1962, Angola: National Security Files [hereinafter NSF], JFKL.

44. This list of visitors is culled from the appointment book of Sorensen and the files of Winifred Armstrong.

45. Oral history of Mongi Slim [hereinafter OHMS], JFKL. Telephone interview: Lorna Hahn, April 6, 1976, Washington, D.C.

46. Interview: Winifred Armstrong, Aug. 18, 1977, New York City.

47. OHMS, JFKL.

48. Statement of Senator John F. Kennedy on the Tunisian Incident of February 8, 1958 (Press Release), Algeria File: 1958, PPP, JFKL.

49. Sorensen, *Kennedy*, p. 65. Also see memorandum from Chester Bowles to Senator Kennedy, Nov. 23, 1960, Bowles's message concerns a conversation he had with the French ambassador to the U.S. Hervé Alphand, who told him that de Gaulle was about to act in Algeria along the lines of Kennedy's recommendations of three years earlier. *Promises to Keep: My Years in Public Life* (New York, 1973), p. 230. See also, *Christian Science Monitor*, July 15, 1957.

50. Eric Sevareid, CBS Radio News Analysis, March 18, 1958, File: Eric Sevareid's News Analyses, PPP, JFKL. See also transcript of Kennedy's appearance on "Face the Nation," Feb. 22, 1959.

51. Hilaire du Berrier to John F. Kennedy, May 29, 1958, File: France, PPP, JFKL.

52. Chester Bowles, *Africa's Challenge to America* (Berkeley, 1956).

53. Handwritten notes, "Africa Trip": files, 1955 and 1957, Adlai E. Stevenson Papers, Princeton University [hereinafter AESP, PU]. See also, Martin, *Adlai Stevenson and the World*, pp. 412–13.

54. Martin, *Adlai Stevenson and the World*, p. 414.

55. Adlai E. Stevenson, "The New Africa," *Harper's* magazine, May 1960, p. 54.

56. John F. Kennedy, "A Democrat Looks at Foreign Policy," *Foreign Affairs*, vol. 36, no. 1, Oct. 1957, p. 53.

57. Draft of remarks (edited by JFK) on Flanders Resolution, Senate Files (McCarthy), PPP, JFKL. See also, Burns, *John Kennedy*, ch. 8, "McCarthyism: The Issue That Would Not Die."

58. Ibid., pp. 156–68.

59. Chester Bowles to John F. Kennedy, July 23, 1957, PPP, JFKL.

60. *Time*, July 15, 1957.

61. Interview: Ralph A. Dungan. Sept. 6, 1976, Washington, D.C.

62. Governor Williams's reaction: Oral History of G. Mennen Williams [hereinafter OHGMW], JFKL; Senator Humphrey's reaction: see Humphrey's remarks in "Facing Facts on Algeria," July 2, 1957, PPP, JFKL; Senator Clark's reaction: see Algeria Speech File for his correspondence, PPP, JFKL; Gilbert Harrison's reaction: letter to John F. Kennedy, July 11, 1957; Walter Reuther's reaction: letter to John F. Kennedy, July 6, 1967, PPP, JFKL; William O. Douglas's reaction: letter to John F. Kennedy, July 14, 1961; *The New York Times*, August 3, 1957, PPP, JFKL. *Congressional Record*, Aug. 8, 1957. John F. Kennedy to Reinhold Niebuhr, Aug. 15, 1957. Norman Thomas invited Kennedy to join the Friends of Algeria, which Kennedy declined to do, PPP, JFKL.

63. Leonard I. Carlson to John F. Kennedy, July 29, 1957. PPP, JFKL.

64. Gil Jones to Ralph Dungan, July 18, 1957, Algeria Speech File, PPP, JFKL.

65. William McCormick Blair to Theodore C. Sorensen, Sept. 18, 1957. Algeria Speech File, PPP, JFKL.

66. Theodore C. Sorensen to William McCormick Blair, Oct. 7, 1957. Algeria Speech File, PPP, JFKL.

67. Arthur M. Schlesinger, Jr. to Adlai E. Stevenson, with copy to John F. Kennedy, President's Office Files [hereinafter POF], JFKL.

68. Barbara Ward to the author, May 18, 1977. See also Martin, *Adlai Stevenson and the World*, p. 383.

69. John F. Kennedy to Eleanor Roosevelt, Aug. 26, 1960. Eleanor Roosevelt to Mrs. Albert D. Lasker, Aug. 15, 1960. See also letters of Dec. 11, 1958, and Jan. 22, 1959. All PPP, JFKL.

70. The Advisory Council on Foreign Policy of the Democratic National Committee, "Why We Need Allies and They Need Us To Preserve the Free World," p. 5. PPP, JFKL.

71. Jonathan B. Bingham to John F. Kennedy, May 23, 1960, PPP, JFKL.

72. John F. Kennedy to Barbara Ward, July 9, 1959, File: Foreign Relations, PPP, JFKL.

73. Kennedy's staff did help organize the Senate Foreign Relations Committee's hearings on U.S. policy toward Africa, March 16, 1960. Memorandum to Sen. Kennedy from Winifred Armstrong, Re: Hearings on Africa Report, March 11, 1960, PPP, JFKL.

74. Memo, Ted Sorensen to Sen. Kennedy, Aug. 14, 1959, concerning speech drafts. A representative sampling of the speeches is as follows:
"The United States and Africa: A New Policy for A New Era," Remarks of Senator John F. Kennedy before the Second Annual Conference of the American Society of African Culture, at Waldorf Astoria Hotel, New York City, June 28, 1959.
Remarks of Senator John F. Kennedy, Saint Anselm's College, Manchester, N.H., March 5, 1960.
Remarks of Senator John F. Kennedy, Luncheon in honor of the African Diplomatic Corps, Washington, D.C., June 24, 1960.
See Africa file, PPP, JFKL. Also Harris L. Wofford, Jr., *Of Kennedy and Kings*, pp. 11–99.

75. Ibid.

76. "The United States and Africa: A New Policy for a New Era," June 28, 1959. Kennedy referred to Nixon's report "The Emergence of Africa, Report to the President by Vice-President Nixon on his trip to Africa," White House release, April 7, 1957.

77. "Facing Facts on Algeria," p. 4.

78. See Drew Pearson's column, "The Washington Merry-Go-Round," *Washington Post* and *Times Herald*, July 8, 1957.

79. The *Globe and Mail*, July 13, 1957. *Los Angeles Herald-Express*, July 5, 1957. Also see the *Boston Traveler*, July 8, 1957. Cited in the *Globe and Mail*, July 13, 1957. Also the *Columbus Dispatch*, July 12, 1957. *Los Angeles Herald-Express*, July 5, 1957.

80. Cooke's *Manchester Guardian* column was reprinted in the *Toledo Blade*, July 14, 1957.

81. *Time*, December 12, 1957.

82. Arthur M. Schlesinger, Jr. to John F. Kennedy, Aug. 30, 1960, POF, JFKL. Sorensen (*Kennedy*) and Schlesinger (*A Thousand Days*) concur generally in their assessment of Kennedy's postconvention predicament.

83. Note to Senator Kennedy from Richard Goodwin, Sept. 10, 1960, File: Campaign 1960, PPP, JFKL.

84. Joint appearances of Senator John F. Kennedy and Vice President

Richard M. Nixon, U.S. Senate, Committee on Commerce, "Final Report," 87th cong., 1st sess., pp. 146–65.

85. Remarks of Senator John F. Kennedy, Los Angeles, Nov. 1, 1960. In a letter to Kennedy on May 6, 1958, Wilkins warned Kennedy that he would suffer the same fate in 1960 as Stevenson did in losing the Negro vote in 1956. "Negroes feel uneasy over this apparent entente cordiale between Kennedy of Massachusetts and Griffin, Talmadge, Timmerman, Eastland, et al. of Dixie." Correspondence File, PPP, JFKL.

86. Fifth message from Harriman to Kennedy, from London, Sept. 13, 1960, and Summary of Report on the Congo and West Africa to Senator John F. Kennedy by W. Averell Harriman, POF, JFKL.

87. Notes on Sékou Touré, Briefing papers prepared by Herbert Weiss, Africa File, PPP, JFKL.

88. Press Release, Aug. 23, 1960, United States Senate Committee on Foreign Relations, Statement by Senator J. William Fulbright (includes Fulbright's letter to Secretary Herter; Assistant Secretary Macomber's letter to Fulbright; William X. Scheinman's telegram to Fulbright); see also Final Report of the Committee on Freedom of Communications on the Airlift of Students to Kenya, August 1–November 7, 1960 in Schlesinger edition, *U.S. Foreign Policy*, pp. 868–75.

89. Remarks of Vice President Richard M. Nixon on CBS Television, November 3, 1960.

90. Interview: W.W. Witman III, March 8, 1976, Washington, D.C. Witman, who was the director of the Office of North African Affairs in the State Department, accompanied the Ben Bella entourage to the White House in July 1963.

91. Frank Church (D-Idaho), "Our Overinvolvement in Africa," *Congressional Record*, Feb. 17, 1965, pp. 2869–71.

92. Kwame Nkrumah to John F. Kennedy, Jan. 26, 1961, Ghana: POF, JFKL.

93. Kweku Anyani to John F. Kennedy, Nov. 23, 1960, General Correspondence File: 1960, PPP, JFKL.

2. Eisenhower's Legacy

1. Harold Macmillan, *Pointing the Way* (London, 1972), pp. 264–65.

2. Rupert Emerson, *Africa and United States Policy*, p. 22.

3. Ibid., p. 26.

4. Brzezinski, *Africa and the Communist World*, p. 15.

5. Testimony of C. Burke Elbrick, Review of Foreign Policy: 1958, Hearings, U.S. Senate, Committee on Foreign Relations, 85th Cong., 1st sess., June 3, 1958, p. 18.

6. Divine, *Eisenhower and the Cold War*, pp. 10–11.

7. *The New York Times*, May 21, 1960. *Department of State Bulletin*, June 6, 1960.

8. "U.S. Aid Moves Awaited as Guinea Marks Eighth Month," *Africa*, May 1959, pp. 10–18. The U.S. ambassador, John Howard Morrow, arrived on Aug. 1, 1959.

9. *The New York Times*, April 30, 1959.

10. Ibid., April 30, 1959.

11. For background on the decolonization in the Congo, see Catherine Hoskyns, *The Congo Since Independence, January 1960–December 1961* (London, 1965), pp. 1–84.

12. Ibid., pp. 85–104.

13. *The New York Times*, July 13, 1960, p. 1. Hoskyns, *The Congo Since Independence*, p. 114. U.S. ambassador in the Congo Clare H. Timberlake had also initially urged the dispatch of two companies of U.S. troops to stabilize the situation until the UN force could be gathered and organized. "Analytical Chronology of the Congo Crisis" January 1961, p. 7. This briefing paper [hereinafter Analytical Chronology], was prepared in the African Bureau of the State Department for a restricted number of officials in the incoming Kennedy administration, NSF, JFKL. Lumumba was in Stanleyville when the Congo government made the request to the American ambassador for troops. He subsequently countermanded it. Hoskyns, p. 114.

14. Ernest W. Lefever, *Uncertain Mandate, Politics of the UN Operation* (Baltimore, 1967), p. 12. Security Council Official Records [hereinafter SCOR] 15th Yr. Supplement for July, August, and September, 1960 (S/4382,I), pp. 16–21.

15. Stephen R. Weissman characterizes this outlook as the "from-chaos-to-Communism complex [which] was rooted in the conservatives' lack of sympathy for and lack of experience in the 'new nationalisms' . . . Some feared that instability in the Congo would spread beyond its borders, creating golden opportunities for the Soviet bloc." Stephen R. Weissman, *American Foreign Policy in the Congo, 1960–1964* (Ithaca, 1974), p. 53.

16. Lefever, *Uncertain Mandate*, p. 11.

17. Jules Gérard-Libois, *Katanga Secession* (Madison, 1966), pp. 282–84.

18. Brussels telegram 300 (from the U.S. embassy) quoted in "Analytical Chronology," p. 10, NSF, JFKL. Leotel 125 quoted, ibid., p. 11.

19. Ibid.

20. Leotel 269 (Léopoldville telegram), quoted, ibid., pp. 19–20.

21. National Security Council Minutes, 7/21/61, quoted in Alleged Assassination Plots Involving Foreign Leaders, An Interim Report, United States Senate, Select Committee to Study Governmental Operations with respect to Intelligence Activities, 94th Cong., 1st Sess., Nov. 20, 1975, p. 57. [Hereinafter *Church* Committee Report.]

22. Memorandum of Conversation between Prime Minister Lumumba and Secretary of State Herter, et al., July 27, 1960, quoted in "Analytical Chronology," p. 16.

23. Interview: Thomas Kanza, 5/29/78, Oxford, Eng. During Lumumba's tenure, Kanza served as Congolese minister delegate to the United Nations.

24. Herz, "Some Conclusions," p. 1, NSF, JFKL.

25. Analytical Chronology, p. 14, NSF, JFKL.

26. Herz, "Some Conclusions," p. 1, NSF, JFKL.

27. Interview: Thomas A. Cassilly, Jr., 2/3/78, New York City. Confidential Interview 57 (a member of the White House staff.)

28. Dillon's testimony is quoted in the *Church* Committee Report, p. 53.

29. Pierre de Vos, *Vie et mort de Lumumba* (Paris, 1961), pp. 195–96.

30. Interview: Cassilly.

31. Leotel 545, August 27, 1960, quoted in Analytical Chronology, p. 28, NSF, JFKL.

32. Analytical Chronology, p. 17, NSF, JFKL.

33. Night Action cable [hereinafter NIACT] 282 from Léopoldville quoted, ibid., p. 17.

34. Quoted, ibid., p. 11.

35. Madeleine G. Kalb, "The CIA and Lumumba," in *The New York Times Magazine*, Aug. 21, 1981, p. 34.

36. CIA Cable, Leopoldville to Director, 8/18/60, in *Church* Committee Report, p. 14.

37. National Security Council Minutes, 8/18/60, quoted ibid., p. 58.

38. Special Group Minutes, 8/25/60, quoted in the *Church* Committee Report, p. 60. The Special Group was an interdepartmental working group that authorized and reviewed covert operation overseas. CIA Cable, Dulles to Station Officer, 8/26/60, quoted in the *Church* Committee Report, p. 15. The *Church* Committee concluded: "The chain of events revealed by the documents and testimony is strong enough to permit a reasonable inference that the plot to assassinate Lumumba was authorized by President Eisenhower." p. 51. Both CIA Director Allen Dulles and Robert H. Johnson, an executive member of the NSC, took Eisenhower's statement during the National Security Council meeting to mean assassination. Johnson recalled: ". . . I remember my sense of that moment quite clearly because the President's statement came as a great shock to me." p. 55. CIA Deputy Director of Plans, Richard E. Bissell, Jr., under whose aegis the plot was carried out, claims that he was convinced, based on the Special Group Minutes, that President Eisenhower had authorized the assassination, p. 52. Dulles told the NSC with Eisenhower present on September 21, 1960 (a month after the initial directive) that Lumumba "would remain a grave danger as long as he was not yet disposed of." By this time, Lumumba had already been dismissed from office. Memorandum, 460th NSC meeting, 9/21/60, quoted pp. 52–53. The CIA scientist who carried the poison to Léopoldville told the station officer that the President had authorized the operation, p. 53.

On the other hand, probable participants at the meeting (Deputy Secretary of Defense James Douglas and Assistant Secretary of Defense John N. Irwin II) had no recollection of the meeting, pp. 54–55. Gordon Gray and Andrew Goodpaster, two members of President Eisenhower's staff responsible for National Security Affairs, testified that they had no knowledge of any such order, pp. 64–65. Under Secretary of State C. Douglas Dillon took a neutral position in testifying whether Eisenhower was responsible for the directive, p. 58. According to testimony received by the *Church* Committee, if Eisenhower had made such an authorization, it would probably have been omitted from the minutes or euphemistically alluded to, p. 56.

Bissell's explanation of the etiquette used in such decisions is worth noting: ". . . a good intelligence officer conducts his conversations with the Chief of State in such a way that the Chief of State can never be proved to have explicitly authorized certain kinds of actions." The President is briefed in such a way that he can "plausibly deny" knowledge of what subsequently occurs. Quoted in Open Letter from Bill Moyers to Arthur Schlesinger, Jr., Boston Sunday *Globe*, p. A2, July 31, 1977. *Church* Committee Report, pp. 20–21.

39. Leonard Mosley, *Dulles*, pp. 462–63.

40. I. F. Stone, "At least there is the Promise of Bigness in Kennedy," 18 July 1960, vol. 8, no. 28 in Neil Middleton, ed., *The I. F. Stone's Weekly Reader* (New York, 1974), p. 162.

41. Nathan and Oliver, *United States Foreign Policy and World Order*, pp. 225–26.

42. Ibid., p. 223.

43. Divine, *Eisenhower and the Cold War*, p. 133.

44. Nathan and Oliver, *United States Foreign Policy and World Order*, p. 230.

45. Divine, *Eisenhower and the Cold War*, p. 152.

46. Dillon's testimony is quoted in the *Church* Committee Report, p. 53.

47. The following Foreign Service officers who dealt with and observed Lumumba were interviewed by the author: Clare H. Timberlake; Robinson McIlvaine; Frank C. Carlucci III; Andrew L. Steigman; Thomas A. Cassilly, Jr.: Also Jerome LaVallee, Fitzhugh Green, and Allison Palmer who were serving in the U.S. embassy in Leopoldville at that time. Also Alex Quaison-Sackey (Ghanaian representative to the UN); Brian Urquhart (Ralph Bunche's assistant in Léopoldville), and Baron Robert Rothschild (head of the Mission Technique in Elisabethville and also Belgian Chargé in Léopoldville) were particularly helpful in their appraisals of Lumumba. Among Congolese who may be identified: Cléophas Kamitatu (President of the Léopoldville provincial government in June 1960 and later a minister in the Lumumba government) and Albert Ndele (commissioner of Finance and later governor of the Bank of the Congo).

48. Hoskyns, *The Congo Since Independence*, p. 86.

49. Ibid., pp. 80–81.

50. CIA cable quoted in Kalb, "The CIA and Lumumba," in the *New York Times Magazine*, p. 47.

51. Fifth Message from Harriman to Kennedy, from London, September 13, 1960. Leotel 655, September 11, 1960, Analytical Chronology, p. 36, NSF, JFKL.

52. Ibid., p. 17. See also Herz, "Some Conclusions," January 1961, pp. 1–2, NSF, JFKL.

53. Leotel 440, Analytical Chronology, p. 25, NSF, JFKL.

54. Leotel 494, August 24, 1960 in ibid., p. 31.

55. Weissman, *American Foreign Policy in the Congo*, pp. 53–54.

56. Herz, "Some Conclusions," pp. 1–2, NSF, JFKL. Interview: W. Averell Harriman, 11/12/76, Washington, D.C.

57. Briefing by the Honorable Dean Rusk, Secretary of State, before U.S. Senate, Committee on Foreign Relations, "Briefing on the Congo," (Top Secret/Declassified), February 28, 1961, p. 57.

58. NSC Minutes, 8/18/60, *Church* Committee Report, p. 58.

59. Quoted in Nathan and Oliver, *United States Foreign Policy and World Order*, p. 235.

60. Letter from Oliver Wendell Holmes to Harold J. Laski, July 2, 1947,

Mark DeWolfe Howe, ed., *Holmes-Laski: Letters: The Correspondence of Mr. Justice Holmes and Harold J. Laski*, volume 1 (Harvard, 1953), p. 91.

61. *The New York Times*, August 17, 1960, p. 1, quoted in Weissman, p. 81.

62. U.S. Mission to the UN telegram [hereinafter USUN tel] 517, August 18, 1960, quoted in Analytical Chronology, p. 27, NSF, JFKL.

63. Hoskyns argues that Michel, while radical, was anti-Russian, pp. 188–89. Blouin, while a militant nationalist, lacked any serious policy-making influence, as Weissman points out, pp. 259–61. Djin had been sent to the Congo by Ghanaian President Nkrumah as a messenger. He knew practically nothing about diplomacy and was described by one scholar as "a clever Tammany Hall politician." W. Scott Thompson, *Ghana's Foreign Policy, 1957–66* (Princeton, 1969), p. 122.

64. Analytical Chronology, p. 25, NSF, JFKL. Abako stands for *Alliance des Ba-kongo*.

65. CIA Cable, Director to Leopoldville, 8/26/60, in the *Church* Committee Report, p. 16.

66. Weissman, p. 97.

67. *Church* Committee Report, p. 18.

68. A CIA officer who served in the Brussels embassy from 1958 to 1961 told the author that the station was first advised of Mobutu's relationship with Belgian intelligence early in 1960. Confidential Interview 67. See also Cléophas Kamitatu, *La Grande Mystification du Congo-Kinshaha, Les Crimes de Mobutu* (Paris, 1971), p. 37.

69. Hoskyns, *The Congo Since Independence*, pp. 199–202.

70. Interview: George Ivan Smith, 5/27/78, Lypiatt, England. Ivan Smith was then serving with the UN Civilian Operation in the Congo. He later served as UN representative in Katanga.

71. Hoskyns, *The Congo Since Independence*, pp. 213–17.

72. CIA Cable Leopoldville to Director, 8/24/60 in the *Church* Committee Report, p. 15; Andrew Tully, *C.I.A.–The Inside Story* (New York, 1962), p. 221; Special Group Minutes, 8/25/60, the *Church* Committee Report, p. 50. Lash writes that the Kasavubu coup was "clearly an inspiration of the Belgians with reported backing of the U.S." *Hammarskjold*, p. 246. Regarding the UN role, Weissman states: "Evidence of UN complicity in the Kasavubu coup appears overwhelming," pp. 90–92.

73. Leotel 643, in Analytical Chronology, p. 34, NSF, JFKL.

74. Eisenhower, *Waging Peace*, p. 575. Analytical Chronology, p. 32, NSF, JFKL.

75. Special Group Minutes, 9/8/60, the *Church* Committee Report, p. 62. NSC Minutes, 9/7/60, *Church* Committee Report, p. 62. CIA Cable, Director to Leopoldville, 9/13/60, *Church* Committee Report, p. 17.

76. NSC Minutes, 9/21/60, *Church* Committee Report, p. 62. *The New York Times*, April 26, 1966, p. 30. Tully, *C.I.A.–The Inside Story*, p. 222.

77. Fifth message from Harriman to Kennedy, From London, September 13, 1960, POF, JFKL.

78. USUN tel 1188, Analytical Chronology, p. 47, NSF, JFKL.

79. Lefever, *Uncertain Mandate*, pp. 99–100. *Christian Science Monitor*, September 20, 1960 quoted in Hoskyns, p. 235.

80. Quoted in Waldemar A. Nielsen, *The Great Powers and Africa* (New York, 1969), pp. 274–75.

81. See Kwame Nkrumah, *Challenge of the Congo* (London, 1967).

82. Memorandum of conversation, Subject: President Nkrumah's call on the President, Participants: The President, Secretary of State Herter, General Goodpaster, J.C. Satterthwaite; President Kwame Nkrumah, Ambassador Halm, September 22, 1960, Dwight D. Eisenhower Library.

83. Ibid., Interview: W.M.Q. Halm, 6/18/72, Accra, Ghana.

84. Ibid.

85. Interview: Dei-Anang, who cited the reports of Andrew Djin and N.A. Welbeck. W. Scott Thompson, *Ghana's Foreign Policy: 1957–1966* (Princeton, 1969), pp. 140–43. See also, Nkrumah, *Challenge of the Congo*.

86. Interview: Halm.

87. Speech in full, see Nkrumah, *Challenge of the Congo*, pp. 83–86.

88. *The New York Times*, September 24, 1960. Eisenhower described Nkrumah as having "cut loose with a speech following the Khrushchev line . . ." *Waging Peace*, p. 583. Edgar Kaiser was president of Kaiser Industries, Inc. Kaiser Engineers had done a project feasibility study for the proposed Volta River project. Kaiser was contemplating major participation in the project with U.S. aid backing.

89. Chad F. Calhoun (Executive President, Kaiser Engineers), Responses (written) to questions submitted by author, March 7, 1973. Interview: Satterthwaite.

90. *Washington Post*, September 29, 1960. *The New York Times*, October 17, 1960. The Ghanaian *Daily Graphic* said that Herter's remark was "a rude shock to most of Africa . . . a surprise to millions throughout the world also believe in America's understanding approach to the problems of our time." September 30, 1960.

91. Remarks of Senator John F. Kennedy, Montgomery Blair High, Silver Spring, Md., October 16, 1960, PPP, JFKL.

92. Interviews: Michael Dei-Anang (Principal Secretary, Ministry of External Affairs, 1959–61), 5/16/78, Washington, D.C., Geoffrey Bing (Attorney-General of Ghana, 1957–61, adviser to President Nkrumah, 1961–66), 6/2/76, London, England. Thompson, *Ghana's Foreign Policy*, pp. 164–66.

93. The senior official mentioned served in the African Bureau during this period. Confidential interview 8. U.S. Senate, Hearing held before the Committee on Foreign Relations, National Archives and Records Service [hereinafter NARS], February 6, 1961, pp. 90–95.

94. Analytical Chronology, p. 28, NSF, JFKL.

95. Ibid., p. 53.

96. Speech of Senator John F. Kennedy, Cow Palace, San Francisco, California, November 2, 1960.

97. CIA Cable, Leopoldville to the Director, 9/27/60, *Church* Committee Report, p. 25. CIA Cable, Tweedy to Station Officer, 10/15/60, *Church* Committee Report, p. 31. The Americans were given credit for sabotaging the nearly concluded reconciliation accord between Lumumba and Kasavubu. Weissman, pp. 93–95. Luis Lopez Alvarez, *Lumumba ou l'Afrique frustrée* (Paris, 1964), pp. 116–17.

98. Leotel 962, Analytical Chronology, p. 44, NSF, JFKL.

99. *Church* Committee Report, p. 24, 44–48.

100. Leotel 980, Analytical Chronology, p. 46, NSF, JFKL.

101. Leotel 1078 and Deptel to Rabat in ibid., pp. 46–47.

102. Analytical Chronology, pp. 49–50, NSF, JFKL. Hoskyns, pp. 259–66. Weissman, pp. 106–8.

103. Briefing by the Honorable Dean Rusk, Secretary of State, U.S. Senate, Hearing held before the Committee on Foreign Relations (Top Secret/Declassified), February 28, 1961, pp. 73, 75, NARS.

104. The four governments were: Mobutu's College of Commissioners and Ileo's "paper" government in Léopoldville; Albert Kalonji's "Mining State" in South Kasai; Gizenga's regime in Stanleyville (Orientale); and Tshombe's regime in Elisabethville (Katanga). Calling the Léopoldville government the "Kasavubu-Mobutu regime" is shorthand for a complex and chaotic political situation. Kasavubu, as president and head of state, generally collaborated with Mobutu, as commander of the ANC, in opposing Lumumba and his followers through various coalitions and tactics. See Hoskyns, *The Congo Since Independence*, pp. 197–300.

105. Gérard-Libois, *Katanga Secession*, p. 283.

106. Michel Struelens, *The United Nations in the Congo—or O.N.U.C.— and International Politics* (Brussels, 1976), p. 11.

107. In an interview with the author, Colonel Guy Wéber, former commander of the Katanga Armed Forces, said the months of October and November 1960 were "crucial" in the consolidation of Katangan independence. Interview: 6/10/78, Waterloo, Belgium. Hoskyns, *The Congo Since Independence*, p. 272.

108. Deptel 17, Analytical Chronology, p. 18, NSF, JFKL.

109. Weissman, *American Foreign Policy in the Congo*, p. 76.

110. Leotel 125, cited in Analytical Chronology, p. 12, NSF, JFKL.

111. Confidential Interview No. 27. For an analysis of the secession of Katanga, see Jules Gérard-Libois, *Katanga Secession* (Madison, 1966) and Weissman, *American Foreign Policy in the Congo*, pp. 66–67. During the first months of the secession the Belgian government seconded hundreds of its officers to Katanga, where they organized and advised the gendarmerie. Sabena airlines flew in arms including one shipment of 7 to 9 tons of military material. A "technical mission" (which provided the Tshombe regime with both political counsel and economic aid) was sent to Elisabethville and the several thousand Belgian civil servants in Katanga were advised to remain at their posts. Union Minière de Haut Katanga (UMHK), the giant Belgian mining combine, began paying taxes and a share of its dividends to the government of Katanga. In October, Belgian Prime Minister Eyskens attempted to extend formal recognition to the Tshombe regime but his effort was blocked by the head of the "Mission Téchnique," Baron Robert Rothschild. Confidential Interviews 93 and 107 (both Belgian diplomats).

112. The first citation is from an interview Murphy had with Stephen Weissman, March 1, 1968 quoted in Weissman, *American Foreign Policy in the Congo*, p. 47. See also Robert Murphy, *Diplomat Among Warriors* (Garden City, 1964), pp. 324, 328, 330–38.

113. Lefever, *Uncertain Mandate*, p. 79. Lash, *Hammarskjold*, p. 247.

114. Analytical Chronology, p. 53, NSF, JFKL. CIA Cable, Station Officer to Director, 10/11/60, *Church* Committee Report, p. 42.

115. Analytical Chronology, pp. 52–53, NSF, JFKL. Lash, *Hammarskjold*, p. 248.

116. CIA Cable, Station Officer to Tweedy, 11/14/60, CIA Cable 11/28/60, *Church* Committee Report, pp. 44–48. In November, eleven of Mobutu's officers arrived in Washington to visit the Pentagon and army training camps. *The New York Times*, November 2, 1960, quoted in Weissman, p. 108. Hoskyns, *The Congo Since Independence*, pp. 266–77. Interview: Kanza.

117. Interview: Dei-Anang.

118. Analytical Chronology, pp. 53, 62.

119. Ghana, for example, unveiled its own troika plan one month later.

120. Lefever, *Uncertain Mandate*, p. 163. Those countries that eventually withdrew their contingents from the Congo were: Morocco, Indonesia, Guinea, the United Arab Republic, Ceylon, and Yugoslavia.

121. Analytical Chronology, p. 61, NSF, JFKL.

122. Leotel 1328, Analytical Chronology, p. 57, NSF, JFKL. Deptel 1627 to Leopoldville, Analytical Chronology, p. 70, NSF, JFKL.

123. Analytical Chronology, p. 71, NSF, JFKL. USUN tel 1937, January 9, 1961, ibid., p. 71.

124. According to Lash's account in *Hammarskjold*, p. 256. *The New York Times*, January 18, 1961.

125. Leotel 1508, Analytical Chronology, p. 71, NSF, JFKL.

126. Quoted in Hoskyns, p. 303–4. Analytical Chronology, p. 69, NSF, JFKL.

127. CIA Cable, Leopoldville to Director, 1/12/61, *Church* Committee Report. CIA Cable, Leopoldville to Director, 1/13/61, *Church* Committee Report, p. 49. Rajeshwar Dayal, *Mission for Hammarskjold* (Princeton, 1974), p. 198.

128. Analytical Chronology, p. 69, NSF, JFKL. Leotel 1820 cited in Supplement to the Analytical Chronology [hereinafter Analytical Supplement], XVI, January 20 to March 6, 1961, p. 1. Leotel 1558 cited in Analytical Supplement, p. 1. Analytical Chronology, p. 68, NSF, JFKL. Foreign Minister Bomboko flew to Paris and Brussels to arrange arms deals and to recruit "volunteers."

3. Lumumba's House

1. Thomas Kanza, *The Rise and Fall of Patrice Lumumba, Conflict in the Congo* (Cambridge, 1979), p. 314. Interview: Thomas Kanza, 5/29/78, Oxford, England. While at Harvard University in 1958, Kanza had met Senator Kennedy. He records Lumumba's curiosity about the American presidential campaign in 1960, p. 215.

2. Interview: Harriman, 11/12/76, Washington, D.C.

3. Kanza. *The Rise and Fall of Patrice Lumumba*, pp. 262–64. See also, Urquhart, *Hammarskjold*, p. 318, and Analytical Chronology, p. 33, NSF, JFKL.

4. G. Heinz and H. Donnay, *Lumumba: The Last Fifty Days* (New York, 1969), pp. 20–27. Tshisekedi, an assistant commissioner on the Board of Commissioners, was close to Bomboko and Mobutu, both of whom were on the CIA payroll.

5. Ibid., p. 27.

6. CIA Cable, Tweedy to Station Officer, 10/15/60, CIA Cable, 10/17/60, CIA Cable, Station Officer to Tweedy, 11/14/60. *Church* Committee Report, pp. 32–33.

7. CIA Cable, Station Officer to Tweedy, 11/14/60, *Church* Committee Report, p. 33.

8. Ibid.

9. Kanza, *The Rise and Fall of Patrice Lumumba*, pp. 310–11. The children smuggled were: François, Patrice, and Juliana. Heinz and Donnay, *Patrice Lumumba: Les Derniers Cinquante Jours de Sa Vie* (Brussels, 1966), p. 50.

10. Kanza, *The Rise and Fall of Patrice Lumumba*, p. 312.

11. CIA Cable, Station Officer to Tweedy, 11/14/60, *Church* Committee Report, p. 48.

12. For the best account of the flight, see Heinz and Donnay, *Lumumba*, pp. 44–60. Also Kwame Nkrumah, *Challenge of the Congo* (New York, 1967), pp. 89–92. Nkrumah's remark was quoted by Michael Dei-Anang in interview, 5/16/78, Washington, D.C.

13. CIA Cable, 11/28/60, *Church* Committee Report, p. 48.

14. Quoted in Heinz and Donnay, *Lumumba*, p. 64.

15. Dayal's report to Hammarskjold is quoted, ibid., p. 71.

16. Nkrumah, *Challenge* of the Congo, p. 70.

17. Ibid., p. 96.

18. Interviews: Cléophas Kamitatu, 10/20/71, Paris, and Kanza. Also, Kanza, *The Rise and Fall of Patrice Lumumba*, p. 315.

19. Gizenga's message, dated December 22, 1960, is to be found in Congo File: 1961, Memorandum from Brig. General A.J. Goodpaster from Walter J. Stoessel, February 8, 1961, NSF, JFKL. Kanza's visit with Mrs. Roosevelt is mentioned in Kanza, *The Rise and Fall of Patrice Lumumba*, p. 322. Nkrumah's message to Stevenson is quoted in *Challenge of the Congo*, p. 98.

20. The noted English Africanist, Colin Legum, adjudges the authenticity of the letter as "fairly well established." See his foreword, pp. xxii–xxiii, in Patrice Lumumba, *Congo, My Country* (New York, 1962).

21. Schlesinger, *A Thousand Days*, pp. 156–57. See Clark Clifford's Memorandum of Conversation, Special Correspondence File, POF, JFKL.

22. Eisenhower, *Waging Peace, 1956–1961*, p. 614.

23. This was called the Henderson Plan, after the retiring deputy secretary of state for administration. Interview: William B. Brubeck, 6/16/76, Washington, D.C. See also, Schlesinger, *A Thousand Days*, p. 145.

24. Task Force Report, pp. 40–43, AESP, Princeton University.

25. Interview: Frank C. Carlucci, III, 4/12/78, Langley, Virginia. Carlucci was quoting Norman Warner, first political secretary in the U.S. embassy in Léopoldville.

26. CIA Cable, Leopoldville to Director, 1/13/61, *Church* Committee Report, p. 49.

27. Quoted in Heinz and Donnay, *Lumumba*, p. 195. The message was recorded and released by "Italia Canta."

28. CIA Cable, Leopoldville to Director, 1/13/61, *Church* Committee Report, p. 49.

29. Roger Hilsman, *To Move A Nation: The Politics of Foreign Policy in the Administration of John F. Kennedy* (New York, 1967), p. 233.

30. Analytical Supplement, p. 2. Interview: Harlan Cleveland, 2/12/78, Princeton, N.J. Martin, *Adlai Stevenson and the World*, pp. 598–99. Also Analytical Supplement. *The New York Times* called the Congo crisis the "first test of President Kennedy's foreign policy and Ambassador Stevenson's diplomacy . . . A new impetus and new leadership are necessary to cope with this explosive situation." February 2, 1961.

31. Nkrumah to Kennedy, Accra tel 839, January 25, 1961, POF, JFKL. The President of Guinea, Ahmed Sékou Touré, wrote Kennedy in the same vein, NSF, JFKL.

32. Kennedy to Nkrumah, Undated, edited draft, POF, JFKL.

33. Memorandum for the President from Dean Rusk, February 3, 1961 with enclosure of King Baudoin's letter, POF, JFKL.

34. USUN tel 2011, January 25, 1961, Analytical Supplement, p. 2. NSF, JFKL. John Bartlow Martin, *Adlai Stevenson and the World* (New York, 1977), p. 599. Memorandum for Mr. McGeorge Bundy, The White House, Subject: Comment on the Report of the Commission of Investigation Established under the Terms of General Assembly Resolution 1601 (XV), From: L.D. Battle, November 28, 1961, p. 4, NSF, JFKL.

35. Nehru to Hammarskjold, January 25 and 26, 1961 reported in USUN tel 2010, January 26, 1961 with a cover memorandum from Brigadier General Andrew J. Goodpaster to Walter J. Stoessel, Jr., January 27, 1961, NSF, JFKL.

36. Rajeshwar Dayal, *Mission for Hammarskjold* (Princeton, 1976), pp. 80–149. Heinz and Donnay, *Lumumba*, p. 23.

37. Martin, *Adlai Stevenson and the World*, p. 600. Analytical Supplement, p. 2, NSF, JFKL. Brian Urquhart, *Hammarskjold* (New York, 1972), p. 503.

38. In preparation for the Cabinet meeting Stevenson wrote regarding the Congo: *"Both superpowers should fade out by tacit agreement.* (Stevenson's emphasis)." Notes for the January 26 Cabinet meeting, Congo file, 1961, Box 830, AESP, Princeton University. See also Martin, *Adlai Stevenson and the World*, p. 601.

39. Quoted by Secretary of State Dean Rusk at his news conference of February 6, 1961, p. 2, Dept. of State Press Release, Public Files.

40. Kennedy to Nehru, Deptel to New Delhi 2238, February 18, 1961, NSF, JFKL.

41. Martin, *Adlai Stevenson and the World*, p. 601.

42. Interview: Clare H. Timberlake, 4/10/78, Fort Sumner, MD. Interviews: Martin F. Herz, J. Wayne Fredericks, 11/6/77, New York City.

43. Dayal, *Mission for Hammarskjold*, p. 187.

44. Memorandum for the President from Dean Rusk, Subject: Suggested New United States Policy on the Congo, February 1, 1961. NSF, JFKL. Stevenson's notes on his conversation with Hammarskjold read: Kasa should then ask Ileo to form cabinet and then summon Parliament." Folder: Congo 1961, Box 830, AESP, Princeton University. Martin, *Adlai Stevenson and the*

World, p. 602. The State Department was not sure whether Ileo had a stronger constitutional claim to power than Lumumba or not. But the legitimacy of Kasavubu's caretaker government was, at least, a "defensible position" from the State Department's standpoint. Memorandum from Brig. Gen. A.J. Goodpaster, The White House, Subject: Legal and Constitutional Problems of Kasavubu and Lumumba, From Walter J. Stoessel, Jr. February 1, 1961.

45. Memorandum for the President from Dean Rusk, Subject: Suggested New United States Policy on the Congo, February 1, 1961, NSF, JFKL. See Hoskyns's interpretation of the reasons for U.S. "accommodation" with the Soviet Union in *The Congo Since Independence*, p. 322.

46. Charles de Gaulle, *Memoirs of Hope* (New York, 1971), p. 254. In July 1960, de Gaulle had proposed that the U.S., France, and Britain form a sort of tripartite directorate to act in concert to prevent further deterioration in the Congo and to block communist intervention. Eisenhower was cool to the plan. In January 1961 at a NATO meeting, France argued along with Belgium for the adoption of a joint Western line of action and a firmer policy against the Afro-Asian states favoring Lumumba's cause. Lefever, *Uncertain Mandate*, pp. 114–15.

47. Kennedy to Nkrumah, Deptel 802 to Accra, February 2, 1961. Deptel 899 to Accra, March 1, 1961, NSF, JFKL.

48. Nehru to Hammarskjold, USUN 2010, January 26, 1961, with cover memorandum from Brig. Gen. A.J. Goodpaster to Walter J. Stoessel, Jr. January 27, 1961, NSF, JFKL.

49. Interview: Major General Indar Rikhye, 8/11/78, New York City. General Rikhye, then the military adviser to the Secretary-General, stated that only because of President Kennedy's intercession did Nehru agree to send the Indian battalion.

50. Martin, *Adlai Stevenson and the World*, pp. 605–6. *The New York Times* columnist C.L. Sulzberger predicted that the policy shift away from previously adamant stands had a real chance of success. *The New York Times*, February 6 and 11.

51. Frédéric Vandewalle, *Mille et Quatre Jours, Contes du Zaire et du Shaba* (Unpublished monograph, 13 volumes, 1977), Fascicule 4, p. 54. Heinz and Donnay, *Lumumba*.

52. Martin F. Herz, "Some Conclusions," January 1961, p. 1. Herz also argued: "The repeated assertions that Lumumba would sway Parliament if it were reconvened (even after the payment of vast sums of money to deputies to assure their votes against him), or that he would proceed to take over any cabinet of which he was a member, indicate that Lumumba's charismatic personality far overshadows that of any other leader."

53. U.S. Senate, Hearing held before the Committee on Foreign Relations, February 6, 1961, NARS (declassified).

54. U.S. Senate, Report of Proceedings, Hearing, Committee on Foreign Relations, "Briefing on the Situation in the Congo," February 6, 1961, pp. 77–95, NARS (declassified).

55. State Department Intelligence Report 8403, February 7, 1961 quoted in Analytical Supplement, p. 2, NSF, JFKL.

56. See mandatory review list of NSF: Congo, JFKL. The CIA has declined to declassify the top secret memorandum of their conversations.

57. *Church* Committee Report, pp. 49–50. Heinz and Donnay, *Lumumba*, pp. 101–9.

58. Confidential Interview: 27 (a CIA officer who worked in the Directorate of Plans under Richard Bissell, 1961–63). Devlin was advised on January 14, 1961 that Lumumba would be sent to Bakwanga, (Kasai). This meant certain death. Devlin testified in August, 1975 that, "To the best of my knowledge, neither the Station nor the Embassy had any input in the decision to send him to Katanga . . .", *Church* Committee Report, p. 50. The decision to send Lumumba to Katanga instead of to Kasai, however, was made at the last minute, so it is not at all surprising that Devlin, like his Belgian counterparts, knew nothing about it in advance. The change in location does not change the fact that the decision "at the summit" to deliver Lumumba into the hands of his enemies was made by men (Mobutu, Bomboko, Kazadi, Nendaka et al.) in the pay of and receiving constant counsel from the CIA station. Interview: Paul Sakwa, 5/2/78, Washington, D.C.

59. Quoted in the *Church* Committee Report, p. 51.

60. Schlesinger, *A Thousand Days*, p. 282.

61. Miss Ward saw the President on February 7 before his meeting with President Nkrumah and later lunched with him, Mr. and Mrs. John Kenneth Galbraith and Washington hostess Florence Mahoney on February 18. Talk at the luncheon centered on the Congo. Galbraith, while certain in his convictions about what had to be done, was "handicapped by my uncertainty as to whether Katanga was the province and Mobutu the man, or vice versa." J.K. Galbraith, *Ambassador's Journal* (New York, 1969), p. 32. Miss Ward drafted a letter dated February 17 for President Kennedy to President Nkrumah on the Congo, NSF, JFKL.

62. Memorandum for the Secretary of State from McGeorge Bundy, February 13, 1961, NSF, JFKL. Interview: Dayal. The UN special representative met with the younger Kennedy while the latter was in Léopoldville. Edward Kennedy later delivered a speech in Hull, Massachusetts in which he criticized Belgium for allowing its nationals to return to the Congo, *The New York Times*, March 20, 1961, p. 2.

63. Kennedy to Nkrumah, Deptel 802 to Accra, February 2, 1961, NSF, JFKL.

64. Deptel 2069 to New Delhi, February 2, 1961, NSF, JFKL.

65. Kennedy to Nkrumah, Deptel 802 to Accra, February 2, 1961, NSF, JFKL. Interview: Martin F. Herz, 3/21/78, Washington, D.C. Stevenson's notes from a conversation with Hammarskjold read: "Would not exclude possibility of Lumumba." Box 830, Congo Folder, AESP, Princeton University. The following who were interviewed by the author all stated that no serious consideration was ever given to rehabilitating Lumumba or requesting his immediate release from prison: Dean Rusk, 5/3/78, Athens, Georgia; Harlan Cleveland, 2/12/78, Princeton, N.J.; McGeorge Bundy, 3/21/78, New York City; Ralph A. Dungan, 9/6/76, Washington, D.C.; Joseph J. Sisco, 4/14/78, Washington, D.C.; J. Wayne Fredericks, 1/21/78, New York, N.Y.; Samuel E. Belk, III, 4/3/78, Washington, D.C.

66. U.S. Senate, Report of Proceedings, Hearing, Committee on Foreign Relations, "Briefing on the Congo," February 6, 1961, pp. 77–95, NARS.

67. Williams described Timberlake's behavior during this period as "dis-

loyal." Weissman, *American Foreign Relations in the Congo*, p. 140. Interviews: Timberlake, Fredericks.

68. The *Washington Post*, February 3, 1961, p. 1. See also *The New York Times*, February 7, 1961.

69. U.S. Senate Hearings, Committee on Foreign Relations, February 6, 1961, p. 78, NARS.

70. Analytical Supplement, p. 8.

71. Analytical Supplement, p. 4.

72. Leotel 1105 in Analytical Supplement, p. 4.

73. *The New York Times*, February 4, 1961. Jane Stolle, "Gamble in the Congo," *The Nation*, February 18, 1961, pp. 5–7.

74. Heinz and Donnay, *Lumumba*, pp. 112–66.

75. This photograph appears on the book's cover.

76. Lewis Hoffacker, "Reflections on the Katanga Case: British and Other Connections." Remarks at the Center for British Studies, University of Texas, October 7, 1977 (Unpublished), p. 27.

77. Quoted in Kanza, *The Rise and Fall of Patrice Lumumba*, pp. 327–28.

78. This is one of several rumors regarding the disposition of Lumumba's corpse. It is indicative of the popular superstition that has grown up around Lumumba. See also, Heinz and Donnay, *Lumumba*, pp. 167–75.

79. Kanza, *The Rise and Fall of Patrice Lumumba*, p. 328.

80. Jean-Paul Sartre, Foreword, to Jean Van Lierde, ed., *Lumumba Speaks, The Speeches and Writings of Patrice Lumumba, 1958–1961* (Boston, 1972), p. 51.

81. Leonard Mosely, *Dulles* (New York, 1978), p. 463.

82. Quoted in the *Church* Committee Report, p. 51.

83. Open letter from John Stockwell to Admiral Stansfield Turner, printed in the *International Herald-Tribune*, Paris, April 25, 1977, p. 2. Shortly after the announcement of Lumumba's death, Interior Minister Cyrille Adoula flew to Elisabethville to determine how Lumumba and his companions had escaped. It was a curious visit that had the appearance of political cover, as if the Léopoldville regime was trying to support the alibi of the Katangan Interior Minister, Godefroid Munongo. See Frédéric Vandewalle, *Mille et Quatre Jours, Contes du Zaire et du Shaba* (Unpublished, 13 volumes: 1975–1977), Fascicule 4, p. 136.

84. Analytical Supplement, March 11, 1961, p. 5. The fact that Lumumba was transferred to Katanga and killed on January 17—two days before the Kennedy inauguration—would seem to indicate that the new policy had no influence on his death. However, members of the incoming administration had met informally and unofficially before January 17 and it was common knowledge within the government that a new policy was in the offing. One CIA official (then serving in the Directorate of Operations) dated his awareness that there would be a rapprochement with the Afro-Asians and support for UN neutralization at "mid-January 1961—in any case, before JFK took office." Confidential Interview 31.

85. Headlines quoted in Lumumba, *Congo, My Country*, p. xxvi.

86. *Observer* Foreign News Service, February 15, 1961, quoted in ibid., p. xxvi.

87. Dayal, *Mission for Hammarskjold*, p. 205. The reference to Easter time

is apparently an elliptical allusion to Lumumba's martyrdom—a status to which Hammarskjold may not have believed Lumumba was entitled.

88. Kennedy refers to this letter in his talks with President Nkrumah, Summary Record of Conversation, Participants: The President et al.; President Kwame Nkrumah et al. The White House, March 8, 1961, p. 3. Hammarskjold told Stevenson that Sékou Touré had sent him a "go to hell" message accusing the Secretary-General of personal complicity in the murder, NSF, JFKL. Martin, *Adlai Stevenson and the Third World*, p. 610.

89. Nkrumah, *Challenge of the Congo*, pp. 131–32.

90. Accra tel 918, February 18, 1961. Analytical Chronology, p. 19, NSF, JFKL.

91. *The New York Times*, February 16, 1961.

92. Charles P. Howard, Sr. "What Price Kasavubu?" *The Nation*, March 18, 1961, pp. 231–32.

93. *The New York Times*, February 17, 1961.

94. Aimé Césaire, *Jeune Afrique*, February 1961 quoted by Legum in Lumumba, *Congo, My Country*, p. xxviii.

95. Hoskyns, *The Congo Since Independence*, p. 323.

96. Martin, *Adlai Stevenson and the World*, p. 611–13.

97. Draft Statement dated 2/15/61, NSF, JFKL. Kennedy's statement in Public Papers of the Presidents, John F. Kennedy, 1961 (Washington: 1962), p. 92. *The New York Times*, February 16, 1961.

98. See Stevenson's remarks before the Security Council on February 18, 1961, Untitled. Congo File, AESP, Princeton University.

99. Deptel to Cairo 3328, February 17, 1961, NSF, JFKL.

100. *The New York Times*, February 17, 20, 1961. The *Christian Science Monitor*, February 28, 1961. Weissman, *American Foreign Policy in the Congo*, p. 142. The *Times* reported that even in the event of a breakdown in UN control, President Kennedy would be "reluctant to intervene." Ambassador Timberlake however, later unilaterally ordered up the Task Force after it had left Congolese waters.

101. Memorandum for Ralph A. Dungan, March 11, 1961, Analytical Supplement, pp. 5–6. Dayal, *Mission for Hammarskjold*, p. 199.

102. Dayal, *Mission for Hammarskjold*, p. 198.

103. Urquhart, *Hammarskjold*, p. 516.

104. Lettre de M. Tshombe à M. Dayal (datée du 22 Fevrier 1961) in Heinz and Donnay, *Lumumba*, p. 188.

105. Notes, Adlai E. Stevenson, February 17, Folder: Congo, 1961, AESP, Princeton University. Hoskyns, *The Congo Since Independence*, pp. 328–32. *United Nations Review*, March 1961, pp. 6–11.

106. See Memorandum to Henry Tasca from G. Mennen Williams, Subject: Kohler Memo, February 18, 1961, G. Mennen Williams Papers [hereinafter GMWP], National Archives.

107. The Herz memorandum went on to state: "For we know that at the very time when we are calling upon the UN to seal off Gizenga from the outside world, the separatist Tshombe is receiving Belgian and other aid including white 'volunteer' troops. It can be predicted that this contradiction, if not resolved, will involve the United States in the most serious difficulties with

African countries." Herz, "Some Conclusions," p. 37. See also, Memorandum to Mr. Penfield from Martin F. Herz, March 9, 1961, NSF, JFKL.

108. Memorandum for Mr. Bundy from Walt W. Rostow, February 15, 1961, NSF, JFKL.

109. Kennedy to Nehru, Deptel 2238 to New Delhi, February 18, 1961, NSF, JFKL. The same message was sent to Prime Minister Balewa of Nigeria and to President Tubman of Liberia. Martin, *Adlai Stevenson and the World*, p. 612.

110. Interview: Cleveland. Also Martin, *Adlai Stevenson and the Third World*, p. 613.

111. Hoskyns, *The Congo Since Independence*, p. 333. Stevenson noted in the course of the deliberations: "3 Power res.[olution] prevents *entry* of arms. This P[aragraph] also auth. SYG [Secretary-General] to *neutralize* aircraft, weapons to prevent their use against UN, Congo, or civ. pop." (emphasis Stevenson's). If the USSR had vetoed the resolution, Stevenson was ready to request an emergency session of the General Assembly "within 24 hours." Handwritten notes, Congo, 1961, Box 830, AESP, Princeton University.

112. Interviews: Cleveland, Sisco.

113. Martin, *Adlai Stevenson and the World*, p. 613. The President made the remark to John Steele.

114. Leotel 1805, Elisabethville 549, quoted in Analytical Supplement, p. 9. See also, Dayal, *Mission for Hammarskjold*, p. 212.

115. Analytical Chronology, p. 28, NSF, JFKL. *The New York Times*, February 27 and 28, 1961.

116. Leotel 1805, Elisabethville 549, quoted in Analytical Supplement, p. 9.

117. See Schlesinger, *Robert F. Kennedy and His Times* (Boston, 1978), pp. 468–98.

118. Interview: Fredericks. Timberlake, "First Year of Independence in the Congo: Events and Issues," pp. 132–33 quoted in Weissman, *American Foreign Policy in the Congo*, p. 146. *The New York Times*, April 18, p. 1. Analytical Chronology, p. 21, NSF, JFKL. Report of the Congo Task Force, p. 7. NSF, JFKL.

119. Memorandum for the President from Dean Rusk, Subject: The Congo, August 3, 1961, NSF, JFKL.

120. Schlesinger's characterization in *A Thousand Days*, p. 469.

121. See Chapter 5. In Laos, the administration tried "to steer a course between intervention and retreat and end up somehow with neutralization." In the Dominican Republic, the intention was much the same. In Italy, Kennedy's support for the Christian Democrat *apertura a sinistra* (opening to the left) was also indicative of his tolerance for strongly nationalist governments with radical elements in them. Schlesinger, *A Thousand Days*, pp. 310, 801.

122. Confidential interview 12 (a political officer in the U.S. embassy in Léopoldville).

123. "Belgium's Third Thoughts on the Congo," *Africa* 1961, no. 12, June 9, 1961, p. 5.

124. Lefever, *Uncertain Mandate*, p. 100.

125. Confidential Interview 53 (A member of the U.S. mission in the Congo.) Interview: Cassilly.

126. Vandewalle, *Mille et Quatre Jours, Contes du Zaire et du Shaba*, Fascicule 7, pp. 351–52. Interview: Cassilly.

127. *The New York Times*, April 18, 1961. Congo Chronology, p. 21, NSF, JFKL.

128. Report of the Congo Task Force, p. 1, NSF, JFKL.

129. Brown was a formidable anticolonialist who had worked closely with the CIA in establishing contact with nationalist movements in Tunisia and Algeria. He served as Lumumba's interpreter at the All-African Peoples Conference in Accra in 1958. Interview: Irving Brown, 4/27/77, Paris; Interview: Paul Sakwa, 5/2/78, Washington, D.C. (Sakwa was a CIA agent working in the Brussels embassy on covert labor operations.)

130. Welensky, *Welensky's 4000 Days*, pp. 221–22. Memorandum for the President from Dean Rusk, Subject: The Congo, August 3, 1961, NSF, JFKL.

131. Chronology of Events Leading to the Change of Orders of Task Force 88, The White House, Undated (during the week of March 5, 1961), NSF, JFKL.

132. Interview: Belk. Belk was on the NSC staff covering the Congo (along with Rostow and Dungan) for Bundy. He had formerly been an assistant to CIA Director Dulles.

133. Memorandum for the Secretary of State, Secretary of Defense, from John F. Kennedy, March 5, 1961, NSF, JFKL. The date on the memorandum is probably a mistake since the events in question took place on Sunday afternoon (Washington time) on March 5.

134. Chronology of Events Leading to the Change of Orders of Task Force 88, The White House, Undated, NSF, JFKL.

135. Note to McGeorge Bundy from Bromley K. Smith, March 3, 1961, NSF, JFKL.

136. Leotel 1835, March 2, 1961, NSF, JFKL.

137. Interviews: Timberlake, Fredericks.

138. Interview: Dungan.

139. *The New York Times*, February 20 and 22, 1961, p. 2. Lefever, *Uncertain Mandate*, p. 118. Hoskyns, *The Congo Since Independence*, p. 386. The Fouga Magister, although a training aircraft, could be used (and later was) for combat purposes. It seats two, has a maximum speed of 400 mph., and can carry 4 rockets, 2 110-lb. bombs, and two machine guns. Confidential Interview 31 (A CIA officer in DP); Interview: William H. Brubeck, 10/24/76, Washington, D.C. In interviews with the author, two Belgian officials, Colonel Guy Wéber and Colonel Frédéric Vandewalle both doubted the CIA connection.

140. Confidential interview 31. One authoritative account states that it was widely believed that Mr. Doyle, the CIA base chief in Elisabethville, had "positions concerning the Tshombe regime [that] were said to differ from those of the consul Canup." Jules Gérard-Libois, *Katanga Secession* (Madison, 1966), p. 184. Based on conversations with the CIA's Richard Bissell, Leonard Mosely reports in his biography on Dulles: "The CIA was helping the Belgians to promote a breakaway province in Katanga . . ." p. 462. One indication of the CIA's change in outlook is the fact that CIA base chief Doyle looked with apprehension on the appointment of Colonel Roger Trinquier to a command-

ing position in the Katangan armed forces. Vandewalle, *Mille et Quatre Jours,* Fascicule 4, p. 93.

141. Nkrumah to Kennedy, February 22, 1961, p. 3, POF, JFKL.

142. Kennedy to Nkrumah, February 28, Deptel 891 to Accra, POF, JFKL.

143. Nkrumah to Kennedy, February 22, 1961, POF, JFKL.

144. Department of State Press Release 174, March 30, 1961, State Department Press Office Files. Memorandum from C.P. Cabell to C.V. Clifton, Subject: "Seven Seas Airlines," February 18, 1961, (Top Secret/Classified), NSF, JFKL.

145. John D. Marks and Victor Marchetti, *The CIA And the Cult of Intelligence* (New York, 1974), p. 340.

146. Hammarskjold to Stevenson, E 2447 from New York, March 13, 1961, NSF, JFKL.

147. Ibid.

148. *The New York Times,* March 10, 1961. Leotel 2003, March 13, 1961, NSF, JFKL. U.S. Senate, Subcommittee on African Affairs of the Committee on Foreign Relations, Report on the Congo, July 20, 1962, p. 69. Urquhart, *Hammarskjold,* p. 512. The CIA station in Léopoldville reported in late April that meetings had taken place between Indian representatives and the Lumumbiste Jeunesse Congolaise Nationaliste. CIA TDCS Information Report, 3/472, 342, 4/22/61 (Secret/Classified), NSF, JFKL.

149. Dayal's history contains an extraordinary portrait of Hammarskjold. The interview with Edward R. Murrow was done in 1954 and is quoted in Dayal, *Mission for Hammarskjold,* p. 299.

150. Memorandum for the Acting Secretary, From: Harlan Cleveland, Subject: Dayal, March 20, 1961, NSF, JFKL.

151. Memorandum to U — Mr. Bowles, From: AF-G. Mennen Williams, Subject: Proposed U.S. Action in the Congo Situation, April 21, 1961, GMWP, National Archives.

152. Report of the Congo Task Force and Steering Committee Activities, Undated, NSF, JFKL. Memorandum for the Secretary, From: S/P—George C. McGhee, Subject: Congo—Meeting with the President, March 3, 1961, NSF, JFKL. Interview: George C. McGhee, 5/2/78, Washington, D.C. McGhee was at this time director of policy planning at the State Department. In November, 1961, he would become Under Secretary of State for Political Affairs.

153. Memorandum of Conversation with Prime Minister Nehru, Dean Rusk, Subject: Congo, New Delhi, March 30, 1961, NSF, JFKL.

154. *The New York Times,* April 4, 1961. *New York Herald-Tribune,* April 6, 1961.

155. Memorandum for the Acting Secretary, From: Harlan Cleveland, Subject: Dayal, March 20, 1961. Cleveland telephoned the results of the meeting to the President, NSF, JFKL. The *Times* headline read: "UN Chief Keeps Dayal in Congo: Defies Kasavubu. Hammarskjold Will Extend Indian's Tenure as Long as Nehru Will Permit." March 20, 1961, p. 1.

156. Dayal, *Mission for Hammarskjold,* p. 259.

157. Urquhart, *Hammarskjold,* pp. 517–18. See also, Briefing by the Honorable Dean Rusk, Secretary of State, U.S. Senate, Committee on Foreign Relations, February 28, 1961, p. 22, pp. 59–60.

158. Interviews: Rusk, Godley, Edmund A. Gullion, 9/24/76, Medford, Massachusetts. *Newsweek*, "Periscope," June 5, 1961.

159. *The New York Times*, May 26, 1961, p. 1. Urquhart, *Hammarskjold*, pp. 517–18.

160. O'Brien, *To Katanga and Back*, pp. 63–64.

161. In his biography of Hammarskjold, Brian Urquhart, who himself served in the Congo for the UN, wrote that, "The accusations against Dayal were grossly exaggerated and fanciful. It was said that he was arrogant and high-handed and did not sympathize sufficiently with the Congolese . . . Hammarskjold shared the unanimous view of Dayal's Secretariat colleagues that he was an immensely able, high-minded, and dedicated man of rare integrity and courage. Dayal's plight was largely the result of his having served loyally and unswervingly the Secretary-General's directives and policies, and Hammarskjold was determined to support him to the ultimate possible limit." Urquhart, *Hammarskjold*, p. 517. In testimony before the Senate Foreign Relations Committee, Timberlake departed rather revealingly from his antagonistic view of Dayal. The Special Representative's problem, Timberlake explained, was that he had been forced to deal with a government that had "usurped authority." U.S. Senate, Subcommittee on African Affairs of the Committee on Foreign Relations, Report on the Congo, July 20, 1962, p. 69. Dayal to Bowles, May 30, 1961, Box 275, Chester Bowles Papers, Yale University.

162. Williams's letter cited in volume 2, Report on the Congo, Subcommittee on African Affairs, July 20, 1962, Testimony of Clare H. Timberlake, U.S. Senate, Hearing held before the Subcommittee on African Affairs, volume 2, Briefing on the Congo Situation, January 22, 1961, pp. 98–101. Thomas J. Dodd, "Congo: The Untold Story," *National Review*, August 28, 1962, pp. 136–43.

163. Report of Philip M. Klutznick (U.S. representative to the General Assembly), Visit to the Congo (Leopoldville), August 6 to 11, inclusive, p. 7, NSF, JFKL.

164. Ibid. Kennedy's inquiry came on December 13, 1961 during fighting between UN forces and Katangan mercenaries and gendarmes. To: AFC—Sheldon Vance, From: AF—G. Mennen Williams, Subject: The Congo, December 13, 1961; Memorandum for McGeorge Bundy, From: L.D. Battle, Subject: Visit of Dr. Linner, March 13, 1962, NSF, JFKL. The President received Dr. Linner on March 14, 1962.

165. Confidential Interviews 58, 116, 130 (all UN officials that served in the Congo).

166. Hoskyns, *The Congo Since Independence*, pp. 374, 377

167. Memorandum to the President from Chester Bowles, May 18, 1961, NSF, JFKL.

168. de Gaulle, *Memoirs of Hope*, p. 255.

169. Memorandum for the President from McGeorge Bundy, June 10, 1961. National Security Action Memorandum 120, NSF, JFKL. Confidential Interview 18 (a member of the National Security Council staff.)

170. *The New York Times*, April 26, 1966.

171. O'Brien, *To Katanga and Back*, p. 189 quoted in Weissman, *American Foreign Policy in the Congo*, p. 149.

172. Hoskyns, *The Congo Since Independence*, p. 376.

173. Kennedy's message to Rusk is referred to in Memorandum for the President from Dean Rusk, Subject: The Congo, August 3, 1961. U.S. Senate, Hearing held before the Committee on Foreign Relations, Briefing on the World Situation by Secretary Rusk, September 20, 1961, p. 4, NARS (declassified).

174. Interviews: Godley, Fredericks, Carlucci, Rusk, McGhee, Cassilly, Sheldon B. Vance, 4/9/78, Washington, D.C.

175. Weissman's account, p. 150, drawn from U.S. Senate, Committee on the Judiciary, *Visa Procedures of the Department of State*: Hearings held before the Subcommittee to Investigate the Administration of the Internal Security Act and Other Internal Security Laws, Committee Print, 87th cong., 2nd Sess., 1962, pp. 31–39, 207–11, 288–94. Thomas J. Dodd, "Congo: The Untold Story," *National Review*, August 28, 1962, pp. 136–43. Interview: Michel Struelens, 4/23/78, Washington, D.C.; Interview: Sheldon B. Vance. Letter from Fred Dutton, Assistant Secretary of State for Congressional Affairs, to Thomas J. Dodd, quoting Williams, March 3, 1962, GMWP, National Archives.

176. Confidential Interview 108 (a Foreign Service Officer in the embassy); Confidential Interview 57 (a CIA officer).

177. Weissman, *American Foreign Policy in the Congo*, p. 151.

178. Vandewalle, *Mille et Quatre Jours*, Fasc. 5, p. 553. *The New York Times*, July 28, 1961, p. 6. U.S. Senate, Subcommittee on African Affairs of the Committee on Foreign Relations, Briefing by G. Mennen Williams, vol. 3, January 24, 1962, p. 140. Report of Philip M. Klutznick, p. 8.

179. *The New York Times*, July 28, 1961.

180. *The New York Times*, April 26, 1966.

181. Ibid. "Money and shiny American automobiles, furnished through the logistical wizardry of Langley, are said to have been the deciding factors in the vote that brought Mr. Adoula to power."

182. Weissman, *American Foreign Policy in the Congo*, p. 151. Mobutu's threat to seize power had a telling effect on the parliamentarians according to Ambassador Thomas Kanza. Interview: Kanza.

183. U.S. Senate, Hearing held before the Committee on Foreign Relations, Briefing by the Secretary of State, Dean Rusk, December 20, 1961. In interview, Rusk had no recollection of events surrounding the selection of Adoula as prime minister at Louvanium. McGeorge Bundy declined comment. Katangan Information representative Michel Struelens later claimed that Tshombe had been betrayed by the "fait accompli" of Adoula's selection. He blamed the UN (particularly Linner) and the U.S. embassy. Michel Struelens, *The UN in the Congo*, pp. 149–75. Memorandum for the President from Dean Rusk, August 3, 1961, NSF, JFKL.

184. "Elements of our Congo Policy," Address by the Hon. George W. Ball before the Town Hall, Los Angeles, California, December 19, 1961, reprinted pamphlet from the Bureau of Public Affairs, p. 9.

185. Memorandum for the President from W.W. Rostow, Subject: The Congo, August 4, 1961. Memorandum for the President from Dean Rusk, August 3, 1961, NSF, JFKL.

186. Interview: Albert Ndele, 6/21/78, Washington, D.C. Ndele was the governor of the Bank of the Congo.

187. *The New York Times*, August 23, 1961.

4. Engagement in Katanga

1. Neal Ascherson, *The King Incorporated, Leopold II in the Age of Trusts* (New York, 1964), pp. 129–32. President Arthur encouraged recognition of the International Congo Association in his annual message to the Congress on December 4, 1883. The joint resolution of the U.S. Congress was adopted on February 25, 1884. Then-professor Woodrow Wilson described Arthur as "a non-entity with side-whiskers."

2. See S. G. Millin, *Rhodes* (London, 1952), pp. 180–276.

3. Ascherson, *The King Incorporated*, pp. 165–62.

4. The imperial constellation of trusts in Katanga may be confusing. Léopold and the directors of the Belgian conglomerate Société Générale formed the Compagnie du Katanga in 1891 to assist the King with his enterprise in Katanga. To raise more capital, the Comité Special du Katanga (CSK) was set up by the Congo Free State and the Compagnie du Katanga in 1900. The final stage of the interlocking chain of trusts was Union Minière du Haut Katanga.

5. Sir Roger Casement estimated that the population of the Congo had fallen by three million in fifteen years. In addition to Leopold's system of forced labor, a major reason for the decline in population was the sleeping sickness epidemic that swept through the Congo at the turn of the century. Ascherson, *The King Incorporated*, pp. 250–54.

6. From *Heart of Darkness*, quoted in Frederick R. Carl, *Joseph Conrad: The Three Lives* (New York, 1979), p. 287.

7. John Ruskin, 1819–1900, was an author and critic who gave several lectures at Oxford during Rhodes's matriculation. The quotation is drawn from the following passage:

Will you youths of England make your country again a royal throne of Kings, a sceptred isle, for all the world a source of light, a centre of peace . . . This is what England must do or perish. She must found colonies as fast and as far as she is able, . . . seizing any piece of fruitful wasteground she can set her foot on . . ." in Millin, *Rhodes*, p. 29.

8. The origins of the scheme are well described in Ascherson, *The King Incorporated*, pp. 263–67.

9. See Centre de Recherche et d'Information Socio-Politiques [hereinafter CRISP], *Morphologie des Groupes Financiers*, deuxième edition (1966), pp. 176–81. Gérard-Libois, *Katanga Secession*, pp. 320–25.

10. Union Minière was capitalized at 8 billion francs; its assets totalled 20 billion francs. CRISP, *Morphologie des Groupes Financiers*, pp. 176–81. Ritchie Calder, "Shinkolobwe: Key to the Congo," *Nation*, February 25, 1961, pp. 163–65. See also Smith Hempstone, *Rebels, Mercenaries, and Dividends, The Katanga Story* (New York, 1962), pp. 43–67.

11. Léopold is quoted in Guy Burrows, *The Land of the Pygmies* (London, 1898), p. 286. Casement is quoted in Karl, *Joseph Conrad: The Three Lives*, pp. 552–53.

12. Although primary education for Congolese was among the best in the colonial Africa, there were only 26 university graduates among the native

population at the time of independence. Hoskyns, *The Congo Since Independence*, p. 13.

13. Gérard-Libois, *Katanga Secession*, p. 56 and 278.

14. Léopoldville telegram 1328 cited in Analytical Chronology, p. 59, NSF, JFKL. Interviews: Rothschild, Wéber.

15. O'Brien, *To Katanga and Back*, pp. 209–14. Also Hempstone, *Rebels, Mercenaries, and Dividends*, pp. 68–88.

16. *La Libre Belgique*, September 12, 1960 quoted in Gérard-Libois, *Katanga Secession*, pp. 124–25.

17. George Ivan Smith, "Along the Edge of Peace," The Boyer Lectures, 1964, p. 7.

18. Interviews: Harriman, McGhee.

19. Analytical Chronology, p. 54 (citing Elisabethville 260), NSF, JFKL.

20. Interview: Wéber. David Halberstam, *The Making of a Quagmire*, pp. 11–12.

21. Interview: Kanza.

22. The attack was a total disaster: The troops massacred several hundred people and had to be withdrawn. Hoskyns, *The Congo Since Independence*, pp. 173–80, 189–91.

23. Martin, *Adlai Stevenson and the World*, p. 599.

24. This is one of several theories regarding the circumstances of Lumumba's murder. See Nkrumah, *Challenge of the Congo*, p. 119–33. Heinz and Donnay, *Lumumba: The Last Fifty Days*, pp. 129–51. Munongo was clearly involved in Lumumba's transfer and execution. Whether or not he was actually present at the time of Lumumba's death, however, is uncertain.

25. It appears that Hammarskjold had no idea about Linner's collaboration. Interviews: Urquhart, Dayal, Smith, and Indar Rikhye (Hammarskjold's military advisor).

26. By May 1961, the United States Air Force had airlifted 20,460 troops plus 5,953 tons of cargo and equipment into the Congo, and 6,229 troops and 327 tons of equipment out of the Congo. The U.S. Navy had sealifted 5,096 UN troops into the Congo and 2,655 troops out. By May 1961, direct U.S. assistance included: 400 tons of flour, 651 tons of famine-relief supplies, 12 H–19 helicopters, 4 L–20 aircraft, 10 C–47 aircraft, 6 H–13 helicopters, 5 C–119 aircraft, 20 jeeps, 50 tons of field communications equipment, 525,000 rations, and 480,000 rounds of ammunition. Chronology, pp. 22–23, NSF, JFKL. Report on the Congo Task Force and Steering Activities, p. 1, NSF, JFKL.

27. Hammarskjold's speech was delivered on August 21, 1961 and is quoted in Urquhart, *Hammarskjold*, pp. 545–46.

28. Concerning the UN role in disarmament negotiations, Kennedy—to Stevenson's shock—dismissed the idea as "propaganda." Martin, *Adlai Stevenson and the World*, p. 653.

29. Confidential Interview 4 (a special assistant to the President). Also Telcon, Bundy/Ball, 8/22/61.

30. Quoted in Urquhart, *Hammarskjold*, p. 32.

31. Lash, *Dag Hammarskjold*, pp. 270–72.

32. "Décolonisateur" and "la route sacrée" are the characterization of

former French Foreign Minister, Maurice Couve de Murville in interview. 5/21/77, Paris. Concerning France's invasion of Tunisia, see Urquhart, *Hammarskjold*, pp. 534–35.

33. Interview: Rothschild. Barton Rothschild served as Spaak's principal private secretary. See also, Paul-Henri Spaak, *The Continuing Battle, Memoirs of a European: 1936–1966* (New York, 1971), pp. 360–61.

34. Interviews: Lord Home (then foreign secretary), 5/20/77, London; Lord Harlech (then ambassador to the U.S.) 5/10/77, London. See also, Arthur L. Gavshon, *The Mysterious Death of Dag Hammarskjold* (New York, 1962), p. 130. Dayal characterized Hammarskjold as "hostage to the West." Interview: Dayal.

35. Hammarskjold, *Markings*, p. 271.

36. Letter from Dag Hammarskjold to George Ivan Smith, May 26, 1956. Private files of George Ivan Smith.

37. *"Visages tendus, fraternité ménacé, amitié si forte et si pudique des hommes entre eux, ce sont les vraies richesses puisqu'elles sont périssables."* Albert Camus, *Le Mythe de Sisyphe* (Paris, 1942), p. 120.

I am grateful to George Ivan Smith, Brian Urquhart and Rajeshwar Dayal for their commentary about Hammarskjold. The parallel in both imagery and philosophical discussion between Hammarskjold's *Markings* and Camus's *Le Mythe de Sisyphe* is quite remarkable. In April 1961, for example, Hammarskjold wrote a poem in his journal:

> Asked if I have the courage
> To go on to the end,
> I answer Yes without
> A second thought.

Hammarskjold, *Markings*, p. 206.

During the same period, Hammarskjold wrote in his journal:

> I came to a time and place where I realized that the way leads to a triumph which is a catastrophe . . . that the only elevation possible to men lies in the depth of humiliation. After that the word 'courage' lost its meaning, since nothing could be taken from me.

Hammarskjold, *Markings*, p. 205.

38. O'Brien, *To Katanga and Back*, p. 66. Interview: Satterthwaite.

39. In his memoirs, Spaak describes O'Brien as "maladroit and interfering." *The Continuing Battle*, p. 364. Urquhart is slightly more sympathetic. *Hammarskjold*, pp. 568–85.

40. Hoskyns, *The Congo Since Independence*, p. 391.

41. Quoted in Gérard-Libois, *Katanga Secession*, pp. 124–25.

42. Hoskyns, *The Congo Since Independence*, p. 401.

43. Analytical Supplement, March 11, 1961, pp. 9–10, NSF, JFKL.

44. USUN tel 1014, February 19, 1961.

45. Brussels tel 1200, January 4, 1962, NSF, JFKL.

46. Hammarskjold, *Markings*, (Entry June 8, 1961), p. 210.

47. Interview: Gullion. Concerning Hammarskjold's sense of martyrdom, see *Markings* (Entry June 18, 1961):

> He will come out
> Between two warders
> Lean and sunburnt . . .
> He will take off his jacket
> And, with shirt torn open
> Stand up against the wall
> To be executed.
>
> He has not betrayed us.
> He will meet his end
> Without weakness
> When I feel anxious,
> It is not for him.
> Do I fear a compulsion in me
> To be so destroyed?
> Or is there someone
> In the depths of my being
> Waiting for permission
> To pull the trigger?

48. Spaak, *The Continuing Battle*, pp. 362–63. 145 out of 200 Belgian NCOs had been withdrawn from Katanga.

49. This account is drawn from: Urquhart, *Hammarskjold*, pp. 566–89; Hoskyns, *The Congo Since Independence*, pp. 417–35; O'Brien, *To Katanga and Back*, p. 219–88; Gérard-Libois, *Katanga Secession*, pp. 218–32.

50. Urquhart, *Hammarskjold*, p. 575.

51. Interview: Fredericks. Schlesinger, *A Thousand Days*, p. 531.

52. Rusk's comment about Mao's China quoted in Steel, *Walter Lippmann and The American Century*, p. 466. For an example of the Rusk Congo memoranda, see: Memorandum for the President, From: Dean Rusk, Subject: Next Steps in the Congo, November 11, 1961, NSF, JFKL. Interviews: Kaysen and Dungan. Galbraith to Kennedy (confirmed in letter to author, November 1, 1982).

53. Memorandum for the President, From: W.W.R., Subject: The Congo, August 4, 1961. Memorandum for Mr. Bundy and Mr. Rostow, From: Samuel E. Belk, Subject, The Congo, September 26, 1961. *The New York Times*, September 26, 1961. The President was once moved to remark, "Walt, you're the only man I know who can write faster that I can read." Interview: Kaysen. Halberstam also records the observation in *The Best and the Brightest*, p. 158.

54. Telcon, Ball/Rostow, 9/23/61.

55. Urquhart, *Hammarskjold*, p. 580.

56. Urquhart, *Hammarskjold*, pp. 538–40, 575–77.

57. Ibid., p. 582.

58. O'Brien mentions the "Riches-Lansdowne representations" of which the American démarche of September 17th in Léopoldville was very much a part. *To Katanga and Back*, p. 287.

59. The *Albertina*, it was later thought, flew two sides of a triangle first due east from Léopoldville to Lake Tanganyika and then south skirting the Congolese border, toward Ndola. Urquhart, *Hammarskjold*, p. 588.

60. Message from Sir Roy Welensky to President Moise Tshombe, October 10, 1961, reproduced in Vandewalle, *Mille et Quatre Jours*, Fascicule 6, Document 175.

The UN Investigation Commission on the crash reached no firm conclusion on its cause. It found no evidence of sabotage or foul play. The fact that the airplane was on its normal approach to the airport and had been a few feet too low to clear the treetops on the rising ground beneath it appeared incontrovertible. The first person to arrive on the scene of the crash nearly fifteen hours later was the U.S. air attaché, Colonel Benjamin Matlick. On the basis of his flying experience, Matlick concluded that due to the fact that the *Albertina* had been descending on a constant angle before impact and had cut a long curving swathe through the forest, either a malfunctioning altimeter or pilot error was to blame. Others believed that foul play was involved. George Ivan Smith, for example, pointed out to the author that mercenaries were known to be living in and working out of the Ndola area, an assertion that O'Brien subscribes to. Contrary to Sir Roy Welensky's denial that the Fouga was landing at Ndola airport and the assertion of the Belgian pilot that a night attack on the *Albertina* was "a logistic and physical impossibility" for the Fouga (which had no night-flying equipment), the Fouga was indeed refueling at Ndola and Kipushi airfields during the September fighting. Ivan Smith believed that mercenaries "talked down" Hammarskjold's plane with either the threat of being fired on by a cannon on the ground or being attacked by the Fouga. Certainly, the fact that neither the air traffic controller at Ndola (who presumably had established radio contact with the *Albertina* prior to its landing) nor Rhodesian authorities made any effort to locate the Secretary-General's plane after nothing was heard from it seems highly curious. Subsequently, Lord Lansdowne's aircraft (which was waiting for the *Albertina* to land before taking off) was instructed to take off. The airport's lights were then turned off and the airport shut down although the *Albertina* was still unaccounted for. See Urquhart, *Hammarskjold*, pp. 588–89, 592–93, Gavshon, *The Mysterious Death of Dag Hammarskjold*, O'Brien, *To Katanga and Back*, pp. 286–88. Interview: Ivan Smith. Before assuming his UN post in Katanga, Ivan Smith did a private inquiry into the crash. Urquhart discounted the conspiracy interpretation as "sheer fantasy." Interview: Urquhart.

61. Memorandum for: 10—Mr. Wallner, From: The Joint Chiefs of Staff, Subject: Rules of Engagement, September 19, 1961. Interviews: Paul Nitze, 5/3/78, Roslyn, Va.; General Michael J. Greene, 4/4/78, Washington, D.C. General Maxwell Taylor was opposed to the order.

62. Schlesinger, *A Thousand Days*, p. 316.

63. Interview: Kaysen.

64. National Security Action Memorandum 97, To: Secretary of State, From: McGeorge Bundy, Subject: The Use of U.S. Fighter Aircraft in the Congo, September 19, 1961, NSF, JFKL.

65. "Means and Ends in the Congo," *Africa 1961*, Sept.–Oct. 1961, pp. 4–5.

66. Telcon: Adlai Stevenson, George Ball, Harlan Cleveland, George McGhee, December 15, 1962. Memorandum for the Under Secretary, From:

Harlan Cleveland, December 16, 1962, Subject: Report of Conversation with Secretary-General U Thant on the Congo, U Thant revealed Menon's démarche to the Americans in December 1962.

67. Confidential Interview 117 (a UN official serving in the secretariat). Urquhart reports, on the contrary, that Hammarskjold considered U Thant as a possible successor, *Hammarskjold*, p. 592.

68. The *Indian Express* is quoted in Urquhart, *Hammarskjold*, p. 591. Nkrumah to Kennedy, Accra tel 839, January 25, 1961, POF, JFKL.

69. Interviews: Carlucci, Fredericks. Memorandum for the President, From: G. Mennen Williams, Subject: Situation in the Congo and Present U.S. Actions, September 25, 1961, NSF, JFKL.

70. Interview: William R. Tyler, 11/15/76, Washington, D.C. Interview: MacArthur. Brussels Telegram 1200, January 4, 1962, NSF, JFKL. Memorandum for the President, From: G. Mennen Williams, Situation in the Congo and Present Actions, September 25, 1961, NSF, JFKL.

71. Steel, *Walter Lippmann and the American Century*, p. 523.

72. Interview: Gullion.

73. See Dodd's speeches cited by Weissman, *American Foreign Policy in the Congo*, p. 159 in Visa Procedures, pp. 345–74; see also the Congressional Record, September 16, pp. 19883–88 and September 19, pp. 20195–97, and September 21, pp. 20607–15. *The New York Times*, September 17, 1961, p. 1 and September 19, 1961, p. 14. U.S. Senate, Committee on Foreign Relations, Hearings held before the Subcommittee on African Affairs, Report on the Congo, vol. 6, Feb. 26, 1962, p. 288, 435; vol. 2, pp. 113–14, Jan. 22, 1962.

74. Interviews: Dungan, Chayes, Wofford, Thomson. Concerning the demotion of Bowles see Memorandum for the President, Subject: Your Conversation with Chester Bowles, From: Arthur Schlesinger, Jr., July 12, 1961 and Memorandum for the President, From: Harris Wofford, July 17, 1961, POF, JFKL. See, Chester Bowles, *Promises to Keep, My Years in Public Life*, pp. 342–67. The actual shake-up did not take place until late November.

75. See National Security Action Memorandum 120, To: George Ball, From McGeorge Bundy, December 17, 1961, NSF, JFKL.

76. Interview: Brubeck.

77. Notes for the Record, December 5, 1961, McGeorge Bundy (memorandum of discussion concerning the Volta River project), NSF, JFKL.

78. Halberstam, *The Best and the Brightest*, p. 173.

79. Schlesinger, *A Thousand Days*, p. 505.

80. Telcon, Ball/Bundy, November 28, 1961 (discussing the events of September).

81. Memorandum for the President, From: George W. Ball, Subject: U.S. Policy Toward the Congo, September 23, 1961, NSF, JFKL.

82. See Advance Copy of Report on his Trip to the Middle and Far East by the Hon. John F. Kennedy over the Mutual Broadcasting Network From Station WOR, New York, New York, November 14, 1951. The Indochina speech is contained in *John Fitzgerald Kennedy, A Compilation of His Speeches*, Remarks of Senator John F. Kennedy on June 30 and July 1, 1953, pp. 252–63. See edited draft of speech regarding amendments to S. 2128, the Mutual Security Act of 1951, 83rd Congress, 1st Session.

83. This is Jacqueline Kennedy's characterization of remarks made by the

President over dinner: "Last night we had dinner alone, talking about Ed Gullion and what a wonderful man he is . . . how he was put in the deep freeze for eight years . . ." *Newsweek*, January 1, 1962, p. 31.

84. Telcon Ball/The President, March 4, 1963.

85. Kennedy to Macmillan, June 1, 1962, Deptel 6425 to London, June 2, 1962, NSF, JFKL.

86. Schlesinger, *A Thousand Days*, p. 531. Gullion gave Adoula a set of Lincoln's speeches. Oral History of Edmund A. Gullion [hereinafter OHEAG], JFKL.

87. Memorandum for the President, From: George W. Ball, Subject: U.S. Policy Toward the Congo, September 23, 1961, NSF, JFKL.

88. Interview: Harriman.

89. Memorandum for Mr. Rostow, From: Samuel E. Belk, Subject: The Economic Situation in the Congo, August 23, 1961, NSF, JFKL.

90. Schlesinger, *A Thousand Days*, pp. 705–6.

91. Report of Philip M. Klutznick, Visit to the Congo (Leo), August 6 to 11 incl., p. 10, NSF, JFKL.

92. Thomas J. Dodd to Adlai E. Stevenson, November 8, 1961, AESP, Princeton University. Weissman, *American Foreign Policy in the Congo*, pp. 159–60. Department of State for the Press, For Background Only, November 10, 1961 with note from Bromley K. Smith to Bundy, NSF, JFKL.

93. In June 1956 Representative Dodd singlehandedly managed to raise the House military assistance appropriation for Guatemala by $15 million. During 1957 and 1958, Dodd was paid over $65,000 by the Guatemalan government and successfully lobbied for aid to the Trujillo regime in the Dominican Republic. Although he was not in the Congress during part of this period (he ran unsuccessfully for the Senate in 1957), a pattern had been estabished that would re-emerge during his senatorial tenure: sponsorship of right-wing, anticommunist regimes. On June 23, 1967 the Senate formally censured Dodd for "misuse of political funds" to promote overseas business dealings. Herbert Krosney, "Senator Dodd: Portrait in Contrasts," *The Nation*, June 23, 1962, pp. 547–52. See letter of Katherine Welsh to the editor, *The New Republic*, January 29, 1962 quoting Appendix VI to the Report of the Attorney General on the Administration of Foreign Agents Registration Act June 1960. "The Lobby Network," *The New Republic*, July 16, 1962, p. 7.

94. Telcon: Ball/The President, October 31, 1961. Memorandum for the President, From: George W. Ball, Subject: Draft Press Statement on the Congo, October 31, 1961, NSF, JFKL. Hoskyns, *The Congo Since Independence*, p. 439. Memorandum for McGeorge Bundy, From: L.D. Battle, Subject: Status Report on the Congo, November 2,1961, NSF, JFKL.

95. Hoskyns, *The Congo Since Independence*, p. 441.

96. *The New York Times*, November 1, 1961, p. 10. Interview: Cassilly. Vandewalle, *Mille et Quatre Jours*, Fasc. 6, pp. 602–3.

97. Memorandum to Maurice Tempelsman, From: George H. Wittman, Subject: Current Congo Situation, November 9, 1961 (sent to Adlai Stevenson on November 9, 1961), AESP, Princeton University. Memorandum from Wittman to Tempelsman, November 9, 1961. Interview: Albert Ndele (governor of the Bank of the Congo and member of the Binza group).

98. Notes from the National Security Files, JFKL.

99. Telcon. Ball/The President. November 8, 1961. Memorandum for Mr. McGeorge Bundy, The White House, Subject: Your memorandum of August 2 on the Congo, From: L.D. Battle, August 10, 1961, NSF, JFKL. Memorandum for the President, From: Chester V. Clifton (concerning a CIA inquiry into possible UN support of Gizenga forces with UN aircraft), NSF, JFKL. The *London Daily Telegraph*, story cited in U.S. Senate, Hearings held before the Subcommittee on African Affairs of the Committee on Foreign Relations, Report on the Congo, vol. 6, pp. 333–34. What had actually happened was that two UN officials, Conor O'Brien and George Ivan Smith, had flown to Kivu to try to dissuade Gizenga's troops from entering Albertville. They succeeded at considerable risk to their own lives. See George Ivan Smith, "Along the Edge of Peace—Recollections of an International Civil Servant," Australian Broadcasting Commission, The Boyer Lectures of 1964, pp. 27–29.

100. Memorandum for the President, From: Dean Rusk, Subject: Congo Policy, November 11, 1961.

101. Dayal, *Mission for Hammarskjold*, p. 315. Memorandum from Wittman to Tempelsman, November 9, 1961. Hoskyns, *The Congo Since Independence*, pp. 460–61. Leotel 1409, March 6, 1962.

102. Telcons: Ball/The President, October 31, 1961, November 3, 1961; Ball/Alexis Johnson, November 3, 1961; Ball/Bundy, November 4, 1961; Ambassador Martin/Ball, November 3, 1961. David McKillop, the African expert at the U.S. embassy in Brussels, was sent to Geneva to prepare Harriman. Interview: Harriman.

103. Martin, *Adlai Stevenson and the World*, p. 681. Memorandum for Mr. Bundy and Mr. Rostow, From: Samuel E. Belk, Subject: The Congo, September 26, 1961, NSF, JFKL. Memorandum for Mr. Bundy and Mr. Rostow, From: Samuel E. Belk, Subject: The Congo, October 4, 1961, NSF, JFKL.

104. Memorandum for the President, From: The Acting Secretary, Subject: Your Conversations with Nehru, November 3, 1961, Bowles Papers, Yale University. Arthur Krock Papers, Box 1, Book 3, Notes, Conversations with JFK, November 8, 1961, Princeton University. The Indian Government, through Defense Minister Krishna Menon, had urged the Secretary-General to accept Soviet military assistance to conquer Katanga.

105. Interview: Rusk. Spaak, *Combats Inacheves*, p. 383.

106. Memorandum for Mr. McGeorge Bundy, From: L.D. Battle, Subject: Report on Additional Pressure Against Tshombe Resulting from Spaak Visit, November 25, 1961, NSF, JFKL.

107. Memorandum for the President, From: Dean Rusk, Subject: Congo Policy, November 11, 1961, NSF, JFKL.

108. Telegram from Tshombe to Kennedy, Elisabethville 1415, November 15, 1961, NSF, JFKL.

109. Report for Mr. McGeorge Bundy, From: L.D. Battle, Subject: Comment on the Report of the Commission of Investigation Established under the Terms of General Assembly Resolution 1601 (XV), November 28, 1961, NSF, JFKL.

110. Letter from Stevenson to Dodd, November 24, 1961, AESP, Princeton University. Stevenson's handwritten notes in response to Zorin's vetoes. Stevenson Papers. Chronology, pp. 29–30, NSF, JFKL. Report on the United Nations:

1961, pp. 82–84. Resolution adopted by the Security Council at its 982nd Meeting on November 24, 1961 S/5002. Senator Dodd attributed the U.S. vote to Stevenson's need not to let Bomboko go away empty-handed from the Security Council meeting. Dodd, "Congo: The Untold Story," *National Review*, August 28, 1962.

111. Contel 678 from Eville, December 1, 1961, NSF, JFKL. The senator also reported to Kennedy that Tshombe had distributed 30,000 rifles from secret caches to the populace and that Katanga's air force had roughly two dozen aircraft, including several jets. Both these reports were inaccurate. See Dodd's top secret cable to Kennedy: Unnumbered contel from Luanda, December 1, 1961, NSF, JFKL.

112. Memorandum for the President, From: Dean Rusk, Subject: Congo Policy, November 11, 1961, NSF, JFKL. Memorandum for the President, From: WWR, Subject: The Congo, October 10, 1961, NSF, JFKL.

113. OHEAG, JFKL.

114. "The Beating of UN Leaders in Elisabethville on November 28," African Bureau, Department of State, December 13, 1961. Vandewalle, *Mille et Quatre Jours*, Fasc. 7, pp. 110–11. Interviews: Urquhart, Ivan Smith, Hoffacker.

115. Contel Unnumbered from Luanda, For President Kennedy From Codel Dodd, December 1, 1961, NSF, JFKL.

116. Interviews: Vandewalle, Ivan Smith. To: The Under Secretary, From: G. Mennen Williams, Subject: Current Situation in the Congo, December 6, 1961, GMWP, National Archives.

117. USUN 1995, December 6, 1961.

118. Memorandum to the Under Secretary, From: G. Mennen Williams, Subject: Current Situation in the Congo, December 6, 1961. Chronology, p. 31, NSF, JFKL.

119. UN Press Services, Note No. 2483, January 19, 1962, pp. 6–8, Report of George Ivan Smith, UN Officer in Charge. See also Cleveland's testimony in U.S. Senate, Hearing held before the Subcommittee on African Affairs of the Committee on Foreign Relations, Briefing on the Congo Situation, February 2, 1962, p. 235, NARS. The Prince Léopold hospital, the Saint Jean church, and the Saint Boniface school were damaged by Indian mortars. Vandewalle, *Mille et Quatre Jours*, Fascicule 7, p. 151.

120. Contel from Eville 1603, January 1 and 2, 1962, NSF, JFKL. CIA Telegram from Eville, Information Report, [hereinafter TDCS], December 18, 1961, NSF, JFKL. Contel from Eville 941, December 18, 1961 cited in Brussels tel 1200, January 4, 1962, NSF, JFKL. After the fighting was over, Hoffacker and the other Western consuls agreed to put the pressure on the UN to remove the Ethiopians from inhabited areas. Vandewalle, *Mille et Quatre Jours*, Fascicule 7, p. 227.

121. UN Press Services, Note No. 2483, 19 January 1962, Report of George Ivan Smith, UN Officer-in-Charge. Confidential Interview 112 (a senior UN official who served in Katanga). See Document 205, A. 47, Etat du Katanga, Services de la Présidence, Arrete No. II/2, January 3, 1962, repro-duced in Vandewalle, *Mille et Quatre Jours*.

122. Brussels tel 1067, December 13, 1961, NSF, JFKL.

123. Vandewalle, *Mille et Quatre Jours*, Fascicule 7, p. 203. Contel from

Salisbury, December 15, 1961, NSF, JFKL. Hilsman, *To Move A Nation*, p. 255.

124. Telcons (quoting the President's instructions): Bundy/Ball, December 13, 1961; Stevenson/Ball, December 13, 1961. Telcon: Stevenson/Ball, December 13, 1961. Cleveland hammered out the specific military objectives of the UN forces with the UN command and made it clear that the President would not buy a general mopping-up operation. Telcons (2): Ball/Cleveland, December 14, 1961.

125. National Security Action Memorandum 120, To: George Ball, From: McGeorge Bundy, Subject: Intelligence on Operations in the Congo, December 17, 1961, NSF, JFKL. Telcon: Ball/The President, December 11, 1961. Interview: Dungan, February 10, 1973, Princeton, New Jersey. Paris Secto 9, December 11, 1961, NSF, JFKL. Hilsman, *To Move a Nation*, p. 255. Telcon: Ambassador Scheyven/Hartman, December 13, 1961.

126. Telcon: The President/Secretary Rusk/Acting Secretary Ball, December 13, 1961, The White House, NSF, JFKL. Regarding the President's remark about the Volta Dam, Macmillan had interceded with Kennedy two weeks before via telephone to urge him to give the go-ahead on American participation in the $250 million Volta River project in Ghana. Deptel Tosec 35, December 13, 1961, NSF, JFKL. Telcon: Wallner/Ball, December 11, 1961. Telcon: Ball/Bundy, December 14, 1961.

127. Interviews: Home, Harlech. Telcon: Bundy/Ball, December 13, 1961. Telcon: Ball/Stevenson, December 13, 1961. See also Kennedy's instructions to Williams, To: AFC-Sheldon Vance, From: AF-G. Mennen Williams, Subject: The Congo, December 13, 1961, GMWP, NARS. Deptel to Léopoldville, December 13, 1961, NSF, JFKL.

128. Denis Healey, "Britain and Katanga," The *New Leader*, December 25, 1961, pp. 6–7. Alistair Burnet, "The Katanga Fumble," *The New Republic*, December 25, 1961, p. 8. Andrew Boyd, "Katanga: Britain's Dixie," *The Nation*, January 20, 1962, pp. 48–50. Interviews: Home, Harlech, Rusk, Bruce.

129. Interview: Harlech.

130. Telcon: Ball/Stevenson, December 13, 1961, Telcons (2): Bundy/Ball, December 14, 1961.

131. U.S. Senate, Hearing held before the Committee of Foreign Relations, Briefing by Secretary Rusk, December 20, 1961, pp. 35–36, 42–48.

132. Weissman, *American Foreign Policy in the Congo*, pp. 168–9.

133. Telegram From: President of Katanga, To: Mr. Dean Rusk, December 13, 1961, Control 9427, NSF, JFKL.

134. The Elements of Our Congo Policy by George W. Ball, Under Secretary of State, Department of State Pamphlet, Bureau of Public Affairs, From an address delivered by Under Secretary Ball before the Town Hall in Los Angeles, California, December 19, 1961, p. 17. Telcon: Bromley Smith/Ball, December 21, 1961. Telcon: Ball/Orville Dryfoos, December 21, 1961, Telcon: Bundy/Ball, December 14, 1961.

135. Deptel 708 to Caracas, December 16, 1961. Letter from Dwight D. Eisenhower to John F. Kennedy, December 16, 1961, POF, JFKL. The Republican endorsements came in the course of testimony in favor of the UN Bond Issue. Nixon's article opposing the administration's support for the UN

operation appeared in the New York *Herald Tribune* on December 14, 1961. Interview: McGhee.

136. Telegram from Tshombe to Kennedy, December 14, 1961, NSF, JFKL.

137. Leotel 1515 from Gullion, December 14, 1961, NSF, JFKL. Telcon: Stevenson/Ball, December 15, 1961. Deptel 1028 to Léopoldville, December 14, 1961, NSF, JFKL. Deptel 1029 to Léopoldville, December 15, 1961, NSF, JFKL. Telcon: Ball/Gilpatric, December 14, 1961.

138. Telcon: Bundy/Ball, December 14, 1961.

139. Telcons: Ball/The President, December 14, 1961, Ball/Bundy, December 14, 1961, Ball/Stevenson, December 14, 1961. Telcon: Stevenson/Ball, December 4, 1961. U Thant also opposed the idea of a mediation. One year later, when U.S. officials were urging the Secretary-General to accept an American fighter squadron for Round III, Thant remarked: "If you would have let us alone last December we would have finished it up that last time." Telcon: Stevenson/Ball/Cleveland/McGhee, December 15, 1962.

140. Deptel 1017 to Léopoldville, December 13, 1961, OHEAG, JFKL.

141. Letter from Alan G. Kirk to McGeorge Bundy, December 14, 1961, NSF, JFKL. It appears from at least one source that the Robiliart demarche did not succeed. See letter from Adlai E. Stevenson to E. van der Straeten, December 12, 1961, AESP, Princeton University. M. van der Straeten was a top officer in Société Générale, the parent corporation of Union Minière.

142. Deptel 1049 to Léopoldville, NIACT, December 15, 1961. Leotel 1556, December 17, 1961, NSF, JFKL. Press Statement on Congo, Department Circular 1128, December 15, 1961, NSF, JFKL. See the account of the Kitona meeting in Norman Cousins, "Report from the Congo," The *Saturday Review*, February 3, 1962, p. 34. Telcon: Bundy/Ball, December 15, 1961.

143. OHEAG, JFKL. Instructions quoted in Leotels 1489 and 1525, December 14, 1961, NSF, JFKL. Telcon: Salinger/Ball, December 15, 1961.

144. Leotel 1525, December 14, 1961. Leotels 1511, December 15, 1543, December 16, and 1547, December 17, 1961, NSF, JFKL.

145. Incoming Message from Captain Shepard, aide to JFK, to Bundy, December 17, 1961, NSF, JFKL. From the President to Under Secretary Ball, No. 171515Z, December 17, 1961, NSF, JFKL.

146. Contel from Salisbury for Hoffacker, December 18, 1961. Leotel 1622, December 21, 1961, NSF, JFKL. See the account of René Clemens (Tshombe's chief political adviser) of the Kitona meeting in Vandewalle, *Mille et Quatre Jours*, Document 200, A 23 "La Conférence de Kitona," December 26, 1961.

147. Deptel 1068 to Léopoldville for Ambassador Gullion, December 19, 1961, NSF, JFKL. The account of the Kitona Conference is based on Gullion's report to Secretary Rusk, Deptel Tosec 19 to Paris, December 21, 1961 and OHEAG, JFKL. The Kitona Conference was not without comical and bizarre aspects. Something of a hypochondriac, Tshombe at one point declared that his blood was getting thick and begged Gullion to fly him to Brazzaville. Mwinda, one of Tshombe's advisers, who according to Gullion was drunk all the time, advised Tom Mwimba, the minister of justice in the Central government and a Baluba: "I am heir to the Emperor of Katanga. You are my slave. Were I emperor now I would have your head off." Leotel 1622, December 21,

1961. During the talks, the negotiators received a report that an ANC company of presumably Gizengist affiliation was heading for Kitona with the intention of attacking. U.S. air attaché Matlick went up in the *Columbine* for a reconnaissance check and found that the column was nowhere in sight. Interview: Green.

148. Deptel Tosec 16 to Bermuda from Ball for President and Secretary, December 21, 1961. Letter to the President from Edmund A. Gullion, December 21, 1961, NSF, JFKL.

149. Interview: Harlech.

150. Gullion to Kennedy, December 21, 1961, NSF, JFKL.

151. Kennedy to McGhee, January 22, 1963, NSF, JFKL.

5. A Little Sense of Pride

1. Memorandum for the President, From: George Ball, Acting Secretary, Subject: Letter to Ambassador Bruce regarding Talks with the British and Belgians on the Congo, May 13, 1962, with draft letter attached, NSF, JFKL.

2. Deptel 1147 from Brussels, December 27, 1961. Spaak to Tshombe, December 23, 1961, cited in Vandewalle, *Mille et Quatre Jours*, Fasc. 8, Telex 625, Document 198, Annex 21.

3. Pierre Wigny to Moise Tshombe, October 26, 1961 cited in Vandewalle, *Mille et Quatre Jours*, Fasc. 6, Document 178, Annex 72. Marcel Dubuisson to Moise Tshombe, October 26, 1961, Quatre Fasc. 6, Annex 73. Interviews: Rothschild, Vandewalle, MacArthur, Cleveland.

4. Brussels 1206, January 4, 1962. Letter from G. Mennen Williams to Clay L. Cochran, January 30, 1962, GWMP, NARS. Congo Legislation re Katanga Companies, Department of State, NSF, JFKL.

5. Deptels to Brussels 1536 (December 21, 1961), 1540 (December 22), 1547 (December 22). Congo Legislation re Katanga Companies, Department of State, Deptel to Léopoldville 1098, December 22, 1961, NSF, JFKL.

6. Interview: Bundy. The President was also personally acquainted with Kirk, who had gotten the twenty-three-year-old Kennedy a commission in the Navy in 1940. Arthur M. Schlesinger, Jr., *Robert Kennedy and His Times*, p. 40. Adlai E. Stevenson to Maurice Tempelsman, January 4, 1962, AESP, Princeton University. Interview: MacArthur. Deptel 1147 to Brussels, December 27, 1961, Deptel to Brussels, December 28, 1961, NSF, JFKL. *The New York Times*, January 2, 1962.

7. Brussels 1691, March 13, 1962, NSF, JFKL.

8. Deptels to Leo 1662 and 1708, January 2 and 5, 1962, NSF, JFKL.

9. Memorandum of Conversation, Subject: Katanga, February 5, 1962, Participants: The President, the Secretary of State, the Under Secretary, Assistant Secretary Williams, Assistant Secretary Cleveland, Ambassador Gullion, Mr. Glenn, Prime Minister Adoula, M. Ambroise Eleo, Minister of Economy, M. Mario Cardoso, Chief Delegate to the UN, M. Julien Kasongo, M. Emmanuel Kimbimbi, NSF, JFKL.

10. Congo Legislation re Katanga Companies, Department of State, Undated (probably June 1962), NSF, JFKL. Gérard-Libois, *Katanga Secession*, p. 206.

11. Deptel 3505 to London, December 28, 1961, NSF, JFKL.

12. *The New York Times*, January 1, p. 1, January 10, pp. 1 and 6, January 11, p. 6. G. Mennen Williams to Sir Roy Welensky, January 10, 1962, GMWP, NARS.

13. Gérard-Libois, *Katanga Secession*, pp. 56–58. Interview: Colonel Wéber. Leopoldville 2552, April 10, 1962, Deptel 3505 to London, December 28, 1961, NSF, JFKL.

14. Bermuda Memorandum of Conversation, p. 2, Deptel to Leopoldville 1160, 12/28/61, NSF, JFKL. Harold Macmillan, *At the End of the Day*, p. 146. Interviews: Home, Ormsby Gore.

15. Deptel 1281 to Léopoldville. January 17, 1961. Deptel 3505 to London, December 28, 1961, NSF, JFKL. Hoffacker "Reflections on the Katanga Case: The British and Other Connections," p. 18. Deptel 3505. Current Intelligence Memorandum, Subject: Prospects for New Fighting in Southern Katanga, February 12, 1962, 0150/62, CIA, NSF, JFKL. Interviews: Home, Ormsby Gore, Cleveland.

16. USUN 3551, April 26, 1961 (for disclosure by Macmillan's private secretary), NSK, JFKL. Interview: Home. Macmillan's account of the Congo crisis reflects his sympathy for Tshombe who, he writes, "not unnaturally enjoyed the moral support of Welensky" and who "with no unnatural suspicion, was unwilling to integrate his gendarmerie—the only effective native force—with that of the Central Government which was still in disorder." He also mentions the observations of cynics who alleged that the U.S. wanted economic sanctions because the effect of a boycott would benefit American corporations since most of the world's copper not in Africa was in American hands. Macmillan, *At the End of the Day*, p. 280–82. Russell Warren Howe, the African correspondent of the *Washington Post*, described the Katanga lobby in Great Britain as follows: "A noisy and articulate Right exists in Britain whose loyalties to investments in South African mines or Rhodesian tobacco, or simply to the foible of a 'white race,' are much greater than to Crown and Flag . . . This fringe group has, however, little effect on Conservative Party policy—although it contributed to the swing in Macmillan's Congo policy of 1960–62, when copper shares replaced the UN as a votive force." *The African Revolt* (New York, 1966), p. 244.

17. Telcon: Ball/Stevenson, 4/27/62.

18. McGeorge Bundy to the President, 5/26/62, Week-end Reading, Hyannis Port, NSF, JFKL.

19. Telcon: Bundy/Ball, 4/30/62.

20. London 4204, May 15, 1962; 4205, May 15; 4225, May 16; 4223, May 16. The account of the London talks is drawn from ibid. See Spaak's report on the talks in Belext 194 to Consubel Eville, May 19, 1962, in Vandewalle, *Mille et Quatre Jours*, Fasc. 7, Document 234, A. 58. Ormsby Gore's characterization of Lord Dundee is set forth in Bundy's note to the President, see note 18 above.

21. McGeorge Bundy to the President, 5/26/62, Week-end Reading, Hyannis Port, with Macmillan's letter enclosed dated May 25, 1962, NSF, JFKL. Interview: Ormsby Gore.

22. John F. Kennedy to Harold Macmillan, June 1, 1962, Deptel 6425 to London, June 2, 1962, NSF, JFKL.

23. U.S. Senate, Hearing held before the Committee on Foreign Relations, Briefing by Secretary Rusk, December 20, 1961, (Executive session/declassified), p. 45, NARS. U.S. Senate, Hearing held before the Subcommittee on African Affairs of the Committee on Foreign Relations, vol. 1, Briefing on the Congo Situation, January 18, 1962, (Executive session/declassified), pp. 29–30.

24. Special Report No. 53: U.S. Policy on Military Assistance to the Congo Government, December 12, 1961. Memorandum for the President, From: Dean Rusk, Subject: Congo Policy, November 11, 1961, NSF, JFKL. Weissman, *American Foreign Policy in the Congo*, p. 205. Telcons: Wallner/Ball, 11/11/61, Vance/Ball, 11/10/61, 11/12/61. Interviews: Allison Palmer (the consular officer who was summoned to N'djili airport because the CIA's incoming group of Cuban pilots had no visas); Indar Rikhye (then military adviser to the Secretary-General). Memorandum for Mr. McGeorge Bundy, From: L.D. Battle, Subject: United States Assistance to Adoula against Gizenga, November 17, 1961, p. 2, NSF, JFKL.

25. Gullion to Kennedy, December 21, 1961, NSF, JFKL.

26. Memorandum for the President, From: Adlai E. Stevenson, Undated, Subject: Message from Leopoldville, Memorandum for Mr. McGeorge Bundy, The White House, From: L.D. Battle, November 17, 1961 with enclosed memorandum, Subject: Congo: United States Assistance to Adoula Against Gizenga, p. 3. Memorandum for the President, November 11, 1961. Leotel 1916, January 27, 1962, NSF, JFKL. Stevenson explained U.S. strategy to the director of Société Générale as: "The universal hope of getting Gizenga under control and Orientale re-integrated is to deal with Tshombe first . . ." Adlai E. Stevenson to E. Van der Straeten, December 12, 1961, AESP, Princeton University. Hoskyns reports that Gizenga had been formally stripped of his immunity prior to his incarceration. *The Congo Since Independence*, p. 459. This is incorrect.

27. Deptel to Léopoldville 1252, January 12, 1962. Leotel 1817, January 15, 1962, NSF, JFKL.

28. Leotel 2909, January 25, 1962, NSF, JFKL. *The New York Times*, January 28, 1962, p. 16.

29. USUN 2556, January 26, 1962, NSF, JFKL. The Soviet Union had been pressing for a Security Council meeting on the Congo, ostensibly to discuss the UN's failure to remove the mercenaries from Katanga. The Americans thought the real reason for the request was to discuss Gizenga. Stevenson moved quickly in a series of consultations to block it. He asked the Security Council president, Sir Patrick Dean, to postpone the meeting. On January 30, the Security Council met in response to the Soviet request and voted to adjourn before adopting the agenda. USUN 2556 and 2570, January 25, 1962, NSF, JFKL. Report on the United Nations, p. 89.

30. Leotel 1867, January 19, 1962. Deptel to Léopoldville 1924, January 14, 1962. Deptel to Léopoldville 1297, January 21, 1962, NSF, JFKL.

31. Leotel 1896, January 25, 1962. Leotel 2167, February 24, 1962, NSF, JFKL.

32. Leotel 1753, January 7, 1962. Deptel to Leo 1264, January 13, 1962, Leotel 1807, January 13, 1962, NSF, JFKL.

33. *The New York Times*, January 21, 1962, Sec. 4, p. 3, cited in Weiss-

man, p. 207. Vandewalle, *Mille et Quatre Jours*, Fasc. 8, p. 398. Memorandum, To: The Secretary, From: AF—G. Mennen Williams. Subject: Adoula at the UN, January 15, 1962, GMWP, NARS.

34. Leotel 1814, January 30, 1962, NSF, JFKL. *The New York Times*, February 13, 1962.

35. *The New York Times*, February 6, 1962.

36. USUN tel 2649, February 4, 1962, NSF, JFKL. Interview: Rothschild.

37. OHEAG, JFKL. *The New York Times*, February 6, 1962.

38. Memorandum of Working Luncheon, From: G. Mennen Williams: Subject: Congo-Katanga, February 13, 1962, Participants: The Vice President, the Secretary of State, the Under Secretary, the Under Secretary for Political Affairs, the Assistant Secretary for Congressional Affairs, the Assistant Secretary for African Affairs, Senators Aiken, Gore, Sparkman, Tower, Mansfield, Humphrey, Lausche, Church, GMWP, NARS.

39. John F. Kennedy to Cyrille Adoula, April 26, 1962, NSF, JFKL.

40. *The New York Times*, January 16 and February 20, 1962, p. 34. Deptel to Leo, January 26, 1962. Leotel 1951, January 30, 1962. USUN 2818, January 26, 1962, NSF, JFKL. Interviews: McGhee, Chayes. Memorandum to the Secretary, From: AF—G. Mennen Williams, Subject: Proposed Tshombe Visit to the United States, February 16, 1962, GWMP, NARS.

41. Interview: Struelens. *The New York Times*, February 22, 1962, p. 9, February 25, p. 29. Vandewalle, *Mille et Quatre Jours*, Fasc. 8, p. 432.

42. Memorandum to the Secretary, From: AF—G. Mennen Williams, Subject: Proposed Tshombe Visit to the United States, February 16, 1962, GMWP, NARS.

43. Leotel 1951, January 30, 1962, NSF, JFKL.

44. Interview: Chayes. U.S. Senate, Hearing held before the Subcommittee on African Affairs, Committee on Foreign Relations, January 31, 1962. Report on the Congo, vol. 4, p. 170.

45. *The New York Times*, February 22 and 25, 1962.

46. Interview: Gullion.

47. Leotel 1999, February 3, 1962, NSF, JFKL. *The New York Times*, February 16, 1962.

48. Schlesinger, *A Thousand Days*, p. 532.

49. Memorandum for Mr. Dungan, Subject: Activities of Michael (sic) Struelens in the United States, From: Samuel E. Belk, March 6, 1962, NSF, JFKL. Interview: Rothschild.

50. Eisenhower asked Rusk for help in drafting a reply to Tshombe (who had sent an appeal to Eisenhower to mediate the conflict) telling him he must re-integrate Katanga without delay. Rusk to Eisenhower, October 3, 1962 in response to Eisenhower's letter to Rusk, September 28, 1962, GWMP, NARS. *The New York Times*, January 27, p. 4. *New York Herald-Tribune*, March 22, 1962, AESP, Princeton University. Weissman, *American Foreign Policy in the Congo*, p. 172. "At Tshombe's Disposal," *The New Republic*, January 8, 1962, vol. 148, no. 2, pp. 3–4.

51. Editorial, *Chicago Daily News* reprinted from the *New York Herald-Tribune*, January 9, 1962.

52. Telcon: Woodward/Ball, 12/6/61. *The New York Times*, January 4,

1962, p. 1. Vandewalle, *Mille et Quatre Jours*, Fasc. 5, Document 193, A 11. Telecon: Dutton/Ball, 1/4/62.

53. Deptel to Brussels 2302 et al., March 3, 1962. Vandewalle, *Mille et Quatre Jours*, Fasc. 8, p. 487 (citing a telex from Struelens to Tshombe). Brussels 568, October 8, 1962, Deptel to Eville 357, October 5, 1962.

54. Brussels 1606, March 4, 1962. London tel 1947, March 5, 1962, NSF, JFKL. *The New York Times*, March 10, 1962, p. 3.

55. Former Deputy Assistant Secretary of State Rowan was quoted in the *Register Guard* (Eugene, Ore. October 31, 1975): "The State Department had regular access to Struelens' bank records and knew on whom he was spending his substantial expense account. Furthermore, there were daily reports on what Struelens and Tshombe had said to each other via telex. I assumed—correctly —that someone in our government was monitoring that telex." Confidential interview 18. In interview, Struelens also claimed that the FBI had broken into his offices.

56. Schlesinger, *Robert Kennedy and His Times*, p. 272. Confidential interview 18 (a high official in the State Department during the Kennedy Administration).

57. Telcon: Bundy/Ball, 8/9/62.

58. Telcon: The President/Ball, 3/28/62.

59. Telcon: Ball/Bundy, 4/13/62, Ball/Stevenson, 4/16/62.

60. *The New York Times Magazine*, January 14, 1962, AESP clipping, Princeton University. Martin, *Adlai Stevenson and the World*, p. 697.

61. Walter Lippmann, "The Sickness of the UN," Today and Tomorrow column, AESP clipping, undated, Princeton University. Eleanor Roosevelt wrote a supportive column in the *New York Post*, March 22, 1961, p. 3. *The New York Times*, February 7, 1962, p. 8, February 10, p. 3.

62. Philip Geyelin, *Lyndon B. Johnson and the World* (New York: 1966), p. 38. David Halberstam, *The Best and the Brightest*, p. 292. Halberstam writes: 'Even Tshombe—Johnson was a not-so-secret admirer of Tshombe, who, after all, alone among those Africans, was willing to say he liked us and disliked the Communists."

63. Interview: Cleveland. Telcon: Bundy/Ball, 8/21/62.

64. Weissman, *American Foreign Policy in the Congo*, p. 177. Memorandum to Governor Stevenson from Clayton Fritchey, January 30, 1962, AESP, Princeton University. Rowland Evans, Jr., "How to Handle Congress," *New York Herald-Tribune*, April 18, 1962, sec. 2, p. 2.

65. Elisabethville 1223, February 22, 1962. CIA Information Report 3/497,012, December 22, 1961, Subject: Varied Katangan Reactions to Adoula/Tshombe Agreement. Léopoldville 1989, February 22, 1962, 2229, March 4, 1961. American officials, both in Washington and in the Congo, did not rate the chances of success for the Adoula-Tshombe talks very highly. Eville 1342, 1343, March 15, 1962, Keo 2231, March 15, 1962. Memorandum to Mr. McGhee, From: INR-Thomas C. Hughes, Subject: Prospects for Adoula-Tshombe Negotiations, March 4, 1962, NSF, JFKL.

66. O'Brien, *To Katanga and Back*, p. 121. Clemens's strategy was set forth in a paper written for Tshombe in late June. Delay equalled success, Clements wrote the Katangese President. The State Department "will be

paralyzed [by] the bond vote in the House." The UN would be unable to finance the operation any longer. Katanga should seek, the Belgian professor wrote, "neither a rupture nor an accord applying the policy of Kitona." *Note sur la position actuelle*, Clemens à Tshombe, June 28, 1962, in Vandewalle, *Mille et Quatre Jours*, Fasc 9, pp. 748–50.

67. Halberstam, "Congo Talks Fail", *Review of the Week*, IV, July 9, 1962, p. 4. USUN 4157, June 30, 1962, NSF, JFKL. *Report on the UN:* 1962, pp. 74–75.

68. *The New York Times*, July 17, p. 4, July 18, 1962, p. 3. G. Mennen Williams to Edmund A. Gullion, July 6, 1962.

69. Memorandum to the Secretary, From: INR—Roger Hilsman, Subject: Policy Alternatives in the Congo, RAF-29, March 29, 1962, NSF, JFKL.

70. Vandewalle, *Mille et Quatre Jours*, Fasc. 8, p. 221. Halberstam, *The Making of a Quagmire*, p. 19.

71. *The New York Times*, July 20, 1962, p. 4, July 21, p. 1.

72. Interviews: Cleveland, Gullion. Williams's cables from Europe reporting on his consultations are Paris 180, July 11, 1962, London 243, July 17, 1962, NSF, JFKL. To Ralph Dungan's dismay, the details of the White House meeting on the Congo were leaked to reporter Max Frankel of *The New York Times* whose story appeared the next day. Ball promised Dungan that he would summon Cleveland and Williams to the seventh floor and "chew them out." Telcon, Ball/Dungan, 7/26/62.

73. Kennedy's single condition for approving the sanctions proposal was that Adoula make a major concession in the re-integration process. This he did on July 28 when he announced the principles of a federal constitution he was prepared to accept. Ball called it "a crucial concession to Tshombe's demands for local autonomy . . . made with considerable risk to Adoula's domestic political position." Memorandum for the President, From: George Ball, August 3, 1962, NSF, JFKL. Phase I of the Proposal for National Reconciliation called for: the immediate sharing of tax revenues and foreign-exchange earnings between the Central Government and the provinces; reunification of the currency; re-integration of the armed forces; closing of provincial "foreign offices" and withdrawal of representatives from abroad; a general political amnesty; freedom of movement of UN personnel throughout the Congo, representation of Conakat (Tshombe's party) in the national government; submission of a federal constitution to the Parliament. To demonstrate to Tshombe the determination of the UN and other powers to achieve prompt re-integration, the particpating governments would undertake several measures. They would issue public statements calling for an end to the Katangan secession. Duties on goods exported from Belgium to the Congo would be collected at Antwerp to the benefit of the Central Government. An "impact shipment" of U.S. military equipment for the ANC would be made if Tshombe did not comply with the terms of the plan, etc. During Phase II, Tshombe would be presented the proposal and given ten days in which to respond. If he indicated any intent to refuse or delay, he would be warned that Katanga faced a boycott of its copper exports and eventually the application of more stringent measures (i.e., withdrawal of Belgian technicians, UN prohibition of air traffic, petroleum exports, and an economic blockade). During Phase III the government of the Congo would call for a boycott on purchases of Katangan copper. Belgium

had pledged its support for such action even though it imported about 75 percent of Katanga's copper and thus stood to suffer the most. Britain refused to join in this action and France remained noncommittal. If the first three steps had no effect on terminating the secession, the UN would consult with the other participating governments to consider an economic blockade of all Katanga's exports and imports. Memorandum for the President, From: George Ball, Subject: Proposed Action on the Congo, August 3, 1962, NSF, JFKL.

74. *Aide Mémoire* from Lord Home, Undated (referred to in another document as August 8, 1962). Memorandum for Mr. McGeorge Bundy From: William H. Brubeck, Subject: Current Status of Proposed Action on the Congo, August 11, 1962, NSF, JFKL. *Pravda*, September 3, 1962 quoted in Vandewalle, *Mille et Quatre Jours*, Fasc. 10, p. 74.

75. Vandewalle, *Mille et Quatre Jours*, Fasc. 10, p. 74.

76. Current Intelligence Memorandum, Subject: Katanga Air Force, Office of Current Intelligence, No. 2425/62, Central Intelligence Agency, September 29, 1962, NSF, JFKL.

77. Macmillan, *At the End of the Day*, p. 282. Telcon: Bundy/Ball 8/30/62.

78. Telcons: Ball/Kaysen 9/28/62, 10/4/62, Ball/Bundy 9/18/62, Bruce/Ball 9/18/62, Tyler/Ball 9/26/62, Ormsby Gore/Ball 9/27/62. Contrary to Kennedy's impression, Home *did* attempt to press Tshombe to cooperate with the UN plan. Tel. 1070, received by Tshombe from Rhodesia, September 30, 1962, as cited in Vandewalle, *Mille et Quatre Jours*, Document 290, A 46.

79. Telcon: Bundy/Ball 8/10/62. Vandewalle reports that in September 1962 two high-ranking representatives of Tanganyika Concessions met with Tshombe at Kitwe and told him that Lord Home had a "large participation" in the company. *Mille et Quatre Jours*, Fasc. 10, p. 75. In interview with the author, Home declined comment.

80. Interviews: Bundy, Kaysen, Dungan. Schlesinger, *A Thousand Days*, p. 533.

81. Telcons: Dungan/Ball 7/20/62, 8/3/62.

82. Research Memorandum to the Secretary, From: INR—Roger Hilsman, RAF–51, August 31, 1962, NSF, JFKL.

83. Smith Hempstone, *Rebels, Mercenaries, and Dividends, The Katanga Story* (New York, 1962).

84. M. Tshombe, President de l'État du Katanga à Monsieur le Senateur Thomas J. Dodd, September 7, 1962, as cited in Vandewalle, *Mille et Quatre Jour*, Doc. 280, A 19–23. See Vandewalle's three memoranda to Tshombe, Information Diplomatiques, "Résumé de la politique étrangère américaine au Congo," Secret, July 9 and 13, 1962, Docs. 251, 252, 253, 254, A 31–34.

85. Telcons: Cleveland/Ball 5/4/62, Bundy/Dungan/Ball 8/14/62.

86. Halberstam's article was printed in *The New York Times*, July 28, 1962 and referred to in Telcon: The President/Ball 7/24/62.

87. Schlesinger, *A Thousand Days*, pp. 506–8, 701–23. Regarding the Peruvian crisis, Schlesinger states that JFK said he did not regret the decision to suspend relations with the Peruvian junta. In interview, Ambassador James I. Loeb, Jr., told the author that Kennedy was unhappy with him (Loeb) for putting him in the position of making the announcement. Interview: Loeb 12/8/76, New York City. Regarding Vietnam, Kennedy was particularly

haunted by a warning from General Douglas MacArthur on the hopelessness
of winning a war in Vietnam. "The chickens are coming home to roost [from
the Eisenhower years] and you are in the chicken coop." Schlesinger cites
General James M. Gavin's comment: "Having discussed military affairs with
him [and] in detail for fifteen years, I know he was totally opposed to the
introduction of combat troops in Southeast Asia."

88. Memorandum for the Record, Subject: Meeting with the President on
the Congo, October 21, 1962, 4 p.m., Carl Kaysen, Present: Messrs. George
McGhee, G. Mennen Williams, Wayne Fredericks, Harlan Cleveland, G.
McMurtrie Godley, State; Fowler Hamilton, Edmond Hutchinson, AID; Frank
Sloan, Colonel M.J.L. Greene; Mr. Kaysen.

89. Telcons: Ball/Dungan 9/28/62, Ball/Chayes 9/29/62.

90. Telcon: Bundy/Ball 8/10/62. Memorandum for the President, Subject:
U.S. Contact with Tshombe in Geneva, August 9, 1962, NSF, JFKL. Interview:
Harriman.

91. Telcon: Dungan/Ball 8/16/62, Tyler/Ball 8/16/62.

92. Telcon: The President/Ball 9/21/62.

93. Telcon: Kaysen/Ball 10/8/62. Interviews: Harriman, Tyler, McGhee,
MacArthur, Kaysen. Ambassador MacArthur made no effort to conceal his
reservations about U.S. policy or his antipathy for Gullion. In a meeting
(conducted in French) with Michel Isralson, a Belgian banker, MacArthur said
the UN action in September 1961 was "condamnable sans réserve" and that
the December fighting had gone beyond its objective. This was hardly Washington's position. MacArthur also pointed out that Gullion had been instructed
not "to meddle in" ("imiscer") political questions. Note établie après l'entretien
du 3 décembre de Mr. Isralson avec Mr. l'ambassadeur des États-Unis, Son
Excéllence D. MacArthur II, Vandewalle, *Mille et Quatre Jours*, pp. 209–310.

94. Telcon: Bundy/Ball/Dungan 8/14/62. Telcon: McGhee/Ball 5/27/62.

95. Rusk had cabled Chargé Godley instructing him to take whatever
measures to prevent Gizenga from being selected premier. Interview: Cassilly,
Carlucci, and Godley.

96. See, for example, Address by Hon. G. Mennen Williams, First Friday
Club of Roseville, Roseville, Michigan, November 2, 1962, Dept. of State
Press Release 762; Address by Hon. G. Mennen Williams at the opening of
African House at Northwestern University, Evanston, Ill. Documents from the
files of the Council on Foreign Relations. Letter from G. Mennen Williams to
John Oakes, Editor, *The New York Times*, congratulating him on *Times*'s
editorial of August 22, 1962 entitled 'Showdown for Tshombe." GMWP, NARS.

97. Telcon: Bundy/Ball/Dungan 8/14/62. Interviews: Vance, Carlucci.
For a vivid example of a "horror paper" see Memorandum to the Secretary,
From: AF—G. Mennen Williams, Subject: Cuba, the Africans and the Congo,
October 29, 1962, GMWP, NARS. In the memo, Williams argued that since
African countries had sided with the U.S. during the missile crisis (some did;
some didn't) and forbidden Soviet air transit Africa to Cuba (this related only
to Ghana and Guinea, which refused to give the USSR landing rights for their
Ilyushin bombers), the U.S. should look favorably on their interest in preserving the Congo as one. According to Williams, the Africans could not help but
contrast America's decisive action during the October crisis with the failure
of the U.S. to live up to its commitments to support the UN plan.

98. This account of Hoffacker's dissent is based on thirteen interviews with officials serving in the Congo or stateside at the time. Also Vandewalle, *Mille et Quatre Jours*, Fasc. 10, p. 102. Tshombe, Struelens, Clemens, Dodd, and Vandewalle all regarded Hoffacker as "*un homme raisonnable.*" Gullion's nickname was "*le vilain.*" See also, Hoffacker, "Reflections on the Katanga Case: British and Other Connections" (Unpublished paper).

99. President/Ball 8/21/62.

100. Hoffacker, "Reflections on the Katanga Case: British and Other Connections," p. 28. Telecons: Dungan/Ball 8/23/62, Bundy/Ball 8/23/62, President/Ball 9/21/62.

101. Ibid.

102. Memorandum of Conversation, Subject: Letter from Senator Dodd to Tshombe, Participants: G. McMurtrie Godley, AFC, Lewis Hoffacker, American Consul, Senator Dodd, David Martin, Special Assistant to the Senator, August 24, 1962. Letter from Dodd to Tshombe, August 24, 1962. Copy of letter in POF, Dodd folder, JFKL. Also in GMWP, NARS. Dodd to Kennedy, August 17, 1962, POF, JFKL. Interview: Struelens. Dodd, "Congo: The Untold Story," *National Review*, August 28, 1962, pp. 136–44. Telcons: Ball/Dungan 8/24/62, 9/5/62.

103. Confidential interview 67 (a high-ranking officer in the embassy). Leotel 480, August 28, 1962 cited in telcon Bundy/Ball 8/29/62. Vandewalle, *Mille et Quatre Jours*, Fasc. 9, pp. 987–88. Telcons: Bundy/Ball 8/29/62, Stevenson/Ball 8/29/62, Dungan/Ball 8/28/62. Interview: Carlucci.

104. Telcon: Gullion (Léopoldville)/Ball 8/25/62.

105. Telcon: Stevenson/Ball 8/29/62. Telcons: President/Ball 9/21/62, Kaysen/Ball 9/21/62.

106. Ambabelege tel, September 29, 1962 quoted in Vandewalle, *Mille et Quatre Jours*, p. 104. Ball wanted instructions to be sent to Léopoldville telling Gullion that he was not to go to Elisabethville with McGhee. Kennedy vetoed that proposal suggesting instead that Hoffacker accompany McGhee. Telcons: Dungan/Ball 9/28/62, Williams/Ball 9/28/62.

107. Thomas A. Cassilly, Jr., showed the author a photograph of the banner. Interviews: McGhee, Fredericks, Godley, Gullion. OHEAG, JFKL.

108. Entretien entre Mr. MacGhee (sic) et M. le Président, 4, octobre 1962, Doc. 295, A. 56 in Vandewalle, *Mille et Quatre Jours*, Fasc. 10. Tshombe sent a copy of this memorandum of conversation to McGhee, who thanked him in return. Leotel 930, October 16, 1962, NSF, JFKL.

109. Elisabethville 559, October 8, 1962. Leotel 845 from McGhee, October 8, 1962. Leotel 832, October 8, 1962. Elisabethville 55 for Secretary from McGhee, October 7, 1962, NSF, JFKL.

110. Deptel 560 for Ambassador from Acting Secretary, October 8, 1962, NSF, JFKL.

111. Memorandum for the President, From: George C. McGhee, Subject: Mission to the Congo, September 25–October 19, 1962, accompanied by Mr. Wayne Fredericks, October 22, 1962, NSF, JFKL. Report on the UN: 1962, pp. 80Z83. Vandewalle, *Mille et Quatre Jours*, Fasc. 10, pp. 145–58.

112. Letter from Tshombe to McGhee, October 24, 1962 telexed through CIA channels dated October 25, 1962, NSF, JFKL. The chastened McGhee had already realized that he had been taken in and had written Tshombe on

October 9: "I am greatly concerned over the lack of progress . . . Continued delay or insistence on pulling back of forces to their former cantonment . . . can only lead to a frustration of the spirit of cooperation which I believe we had established . . ." Léopoldville 846, October 9, 1962, NSF, JFKL.

113. Memorandum to the Secretary, From AF—G. Mennen Williams, Subject: Approval of the Congolese Army Retraining Program, October 8, 1962, GMWP, NARS. *The New York Times,* October 23, p. 1, October 27, p. 2, November 7, p. 8. Leotel, October 27, 1962. Kennedy was "seriously concerned" about the military aid offers of Soviet Ambassador Nemchina. Memorandum of Conversation, October 22, 1962, Subject: Political Events in the Congo, Participants: Mr. Samuel Belk, White House, Mr. Jason Sendwe, Vice Prime Minister, Central Congolese Government, Frank Carlucci, OIC— Congo Political Affairs, NSF, JFKL.

114. Letter from G. Mennen Williams to Edmund A. Gullion, October 23, 1962. In the message, Williams cites reports of Fredericks that Gullion was near the point of exhaustion, GMWP, NARS.

115. Memorandum for the President, From: Arthur M. Schlesinger, Jr., October 13, 1962, NSF, JFKL.

116. Memorandum for the Secretary of State, From: Carl Kaysen, November 1, 1962. Memorandum for the Secretary of State, From: John F. Kennedy, November 5, 1962, NSF, JFKL.

117. Message to the President, From: Carl Kaysen, Proposed Contingency Plan for the Congo (from the State Department), November 7, 1962, NSF, JFKL.

118. Memorandum for the Record, Carl Kaysen, November 8, 1962, Subject: Meeting with the President on the Congo, November 7, 1962 at 4 p.m., Cabinet Room, Present: Secretary Rusk, Under Secretary Ball, Under Secretary McGhee, Assistant Secretary Williams, Assistant Secretary Cleveland, Deputy Assistant Secretary Fredericks, NSF, JFKL.

119. Léopoldville 2669, April 23, 1962, NSF, JFKL. Hilsman, *To Move a Nation,* p. 263. *The New York Times,* November 6, p. 3, November 7, p. 8, November 9, p. 4.

120. Memorandum for the Record, Subject: Meeting with the President on the Congo, October 31, 1962, 4 p.m. Carl Kaysen, Present: Messrs. McGhee, Williams, Fredericks, Cleveland, Godley, State; Hamilton, Hutchinson, AID; Col. Greene, Defense; Mr. Kaysen. See also, Memorandum for the President, From: George C. McGhee, Subject: Congo, October 31, 1962, NSF, JFKL.

121. *The New York Times,* November 22, 1962, p. 1, November 24, p. 1. Proposed Contingency Plan for the Congo, Message from Carl Kaysen to the President, November 7, 1962, NSF, JFKL.

122. *The New York Times,* November 28, 1962, p. 1. Spaak, *Combats Inachevés,* p. 255. Memorandum to the Secretary, From: AF—G. Mennen Williams, Discussion with Bomboko this Morning, November 26, 1962, GMWP, NARS.

123. Vandewalle, *Mille et Quatre Jours,* Fasc. 11, pp. 349–50. Sorensen, *Kennedy,* p. 638.

124. Telcons, Bundy/Ball 12/12/62, 12/14/62, Kaysen, Ball 12/14/62, Gilpatric/Ball 12/14/62. Memorandum to the Under Secretary, From: INR,

Roger Hilsman. Subject: The Congo: An Appraisal of Alternatives, December 11, 1962. Memorandum for the President, From: Chester Bowles, The Congo Crisis, December 12, 1962 with cover letter to the President, Chester Bowles Papers, Yale University.

125. Telcon: Ball/Bundy 12/12/62.

126. Memorandum for the Secretary of Defense, From: Curtis E. LeMay, Acting Chairman, JCS, Subject: Congo Developments, December 11, 1962. Letter (top secret) to George W. Ball from William P. Bundy attached, December 11, 1962, NSF, JFKL.

127. Memorandum for the President, Subject: New Policy on the Congo, December 12, 1962, From: Harlan Cleveland, NSF, JFKL.

128. This account of the December 14, 1962 is pieced together from interviews with Cleveland, Kaysen, Belk as well as Sorensen's account, *Kennedy*, p. 638. Also Chester Bowles oral histories at the JFK Library and at the Columbia University Oral History Project.

129. Sorensen, *Kennedy*, p. 638.

130. Benjamin Bradlee, *Conversations with Kennedy*, p. 112.

131. Stevenson's meeting is recounted in Martin, *Adlai Stevenson and the World*, p. 750. Martin incorrectly reports that there was only one meeting between U.S. and UN officials. They were in fact, two: the first on December 15 between Stevenson, Bunche, and Thant; the second on December 16 between Stevenson, Cleveland, and Thant.

132. Telcons, The President/Ball 12/15/62, Stevenson/Cleveland/McGhee/Ball 12/15/62. Memorandum for the Under Secretary, From: IO— Harlan Cleveland, Subject: Report of Conversation Secretary-General U Thant on the Congo, December 16, 1962, NSF, JFKL. Telcon, Kaysen/Ball 12/15/62.

133. Operating Plan for the Congo, Department of State, received by the National Security Council December 17, 1962, NSF, JFKL. Sorensen, *Kennedy*, p. 638. Congo Scenario, Undated (probably December 17). Memorandum for the President, From: Carl Kaysen, Subject: Congo Issues, December 17, 1962, NSF, JFKL. Thant's request was for 10 American planes (6 F-86s and 4 Mustangs), 32 army trucks, 6 armored cars, and a Bailey bridging unit.

134. *The New York Times*, December 19, p. 1, December 22, p. 1. Vandewalle, *Mille et Quatre Jours*, Fasc. 11, p. 437, 451.

135. Congo Scenario, Department of State, Undated (probably December 17), NSF, JFKL. Macmillan, *At the End of the Day*, p. 283.

136. Memorandum for the President, From: Carl Kaysen, Subject: Congo Issues, November 17, 1962, NSF, JFKL. Schlesinger, *A Thousand Days*, p. 533.

137. Martin, *Adlai Stevenson and the World*, p. 751. Hilsman, *To Move A Nation*, p. 268.

138. Telcon, Rusk/Ball 12/30/63. Martin, *Adlai Stevenson and the World*, p. 751.

139. Memorandum to the Secretary, From: IO—Harlan Cleveland, Subject: Current Developments in the Congo, 4 January 1963. Telcon, Ball/McGhee 1/2/53. Cable from Kaysen, From General McHugh for the President, Congo Situation Report, January 2, 1962, NSF, JFKL.

140. Memorandum to the Secretary, From: INR—Thomas Hughes, Intelligence Note: Policy Alternatices if Tshombe Fails to Return to Elisabeth-

ville, January 4, 1962. Memorandum to the Secretary, From: Thomas L. Hughes, Intelligence Note: Tshombe's Position After Fall of Jadotville, January 3, 1963. Current Intelligence Memorandum, OCI, Subject: The Consequences of Tshombe's Removal from Katanga, OCI No. 2431/63, 3 January 1963, NSF, JFKL.

141. Hilsman, *To Move a Nation*, p. 270. *Report on the United Nations*, 7963, p. 73. Telcon, Ball/Bundy 1/4/62.

142. Vandewalle, *Mille et Quatre Jours*, Fasc. 11, p. 567.

143. Letter from John F. Kennedy to Paul-Henri Spaak, January 11, 1963 in Deptel 21 to Brussels, January 12, 1963, NSF, JFKL.

144. McGhee to Kennedy, January 22, 1963, NSF, JFKL.

145. Kennedy to McGhee, January 21, 1963, NSF, JFKL.

6. Quite a Few Chips on a Very Dark Horse

1. The will of February 18, 1966 is reprinted in T. Peter Omari, *Kwame Nkrumah, The Anatomy of an African Dictatorship* (New York, 1970), pp. 219–20. *Xinhua*, August 14, 1961 describes the scene in Beijing. See W. Scott Thompson, *Ghana's Foreign Policy, 1957–1966*, p. 177. Interviews: Michael Dei-Anang (head of Nkrumah's African Affairs Secretariat, 1961–66), Washington, D.C., 5/16/78; Erica Powell (Nkrumah's personal secretary, 1954–65), Saltash, England, 7/2/77.

2. Kwame Nkrumah, *Axioms* (London, 1965), Midnight Pronouncement of Independence at Polo Ground, Accra, March 5–6, 1957, p. 52.

3. Jean Lacouture, *The Demigods, Charismatic Leadership in the Third World* (New York, 1970), pp. 258–59.

4. Nkrumah, New Year's Message, 1963, *Axioms*, p. 60.

5. Basil Davidson, *Black Star: A View of the Life and Times of Kwame Nkrumah* (London, 1973), p. 202. See also Thompson, *Ghana's Foreign Policy*, pp. 410–12, and Dei-Anang, *The Administration of Ghana's Foreign Relations, 1957–1965: A Personal Memoir* (London, 1975), p. 62.

6. Interviews: Alex Quaison-Sackey (Permanent Representative of Ghana to the United Nations, 1959–1965; Foreign Minister, 1965–1966), Washington, D.C., 4/18/77; Dei-Anang. See Nkrumah, *Dark Days in Ghana* (New York, 1968), *Challenge of the Congo* (New York, 1967).

7. Interview: Dei-Anang.

8. Barbara Ward to the author, August 31, 1977. See also Oral history of Barbara Ward, JFKL. Robert Raymond, *Black Star in the Wind* (London, 1960), p. 280.

9. Nkrumah to Kennedy, Accra tel 839, January 25, 1961, POF, JFKL.

10. This account of political developments in the Gold Coast 1951 to 1957 is drawn from Dennis Austin, *Politics in Ghana, 1946–1960* (London, 1964). See also Geoffrey Bing, *Reap the Whirlwind* (London, 1970), pp. 85–97. Davidson, *Black Star*, pp. 67–157.

11. Barbara Ward to John F. Kennedy, August 4, 1959, PPP, JFKL. See also, Henry L. Bretton, *The Rise and Fall of Kwame Nkrumah* (New York, 1966), pp. 41–63.

12. Khrushchev communicated as much to Nkrumah. Strobe Talbott (editor

and translator), *Khrushchev Remembers, The Last Testament* (Boston, 1974), p. 334.

13. Ward to Kennedy, August 4, 1959, PPP, JFKL.

14. Bob Fitch and Mary Oppenheimer, *Ghana: End of an Illusion* (New York, 1966), pp. 86–89.

15. Ibid., pp. 82–86.

16. *Time*, August 4, 1958, p. 14 quoted in Thompson, *Ghana's Foreign Policy*, p. 44.

17. Ibid., p. 44.

18. Ibid., p. 43.

19. Interview: Robert Jackson, New York City, 2/4/78. Thompson, *Ghana's Foreign Policy*, p. 43.

20. In his autobiography, Nkrumah recounted one such racial incident during his time in America. Upon entering a whites-only refreshment room in Baltimore, he had been informed, "The place for you, my man, is the spitoon outside." He remembered, "I was so shocked that I could not move." *Ghana: The Autobiography of Kwame Nkrumah* (London, 1957).

21. Nkrumah, 'Africa Prospect," *Foreign Affairs*, vol. 37, no. 1, p. 53.

22. Interview: Jackson. Thompson, *Ghana's Foreign Policy*, p. 43.

23. Chad Calhoun to the author, March 7, 1973.

24. Philip Seikman, "Edgar Kaiser's Gamble in Africa," *Fortune*, November 1961, p. 199.

25. Ibid., p. 204. Also, Calhoun to the author, p. 6.

26. The Volta River project (a paper submitted by the State Department to the National Security Council, December 5, 1961) [hereinafter VRP], appendix, p. 2.

27. Thompson, *Ghana's Foreign Policy*, pp. 58–67.

28. Interview: Irving Brown (the head of AFL-CIO operations in Europe and Africa during this period), Paris, 4/27/77. Brown acted as Lumumba's interpreter during the conference.

29. Nkrumah, speech to the Council on Foreign Relations, *Axioms*, p. 65.

30. Interview: Dei-Anang.

31. Nkrumah, *Challenge of the Congo*, pp. 28–34.

32. Ibid., p. 75.

33. CIA Weekly Review Article of 27 October 1960 and "Ghana's Neutralism Increasingly Favorable to a Communist World," February 18, 1961, POF, JFKL.

34. Nkrumah to Kennedy, Accra tel. 826, January 25, 1961, POF, JFKL.

35. Nkrumah to Macmillan, February 24, 1961, *Challenge of the Congo*, p. 103.

36. Drew Pearson, "Lost Letters Snarl Diplomacy," *Washington Post*, March 14, 1961. H.T.S. Alexander, *African Tightrope, My Years as Nkrumah's Chief of Staff* (London, 1969), pp. 99–100. Nkrumah, *Challenge of the Congo*, p. 104.

37. The broadcast is quoted extensively in Nkrumah, *Challenge of the Congo*, p. 132. Accra tel 940, February 15, 1961.

38. Brezhnev subsequently arrived in Accra on February 18, 1961 and conferred with Nkrumah at length. Accra tel. 1018, February 24, 1961, NSF, JFKL.

39. Accra tel. 959, February 16, 1961. Nkrumah to Kennedy, February 23, 1961, Accra tel. 1015, NSF, JFKL.

40. Barbara Ward to John F. Kennedy, February 21, 1961, Private Papers of Chad F. Calhoun [hereinafter CFCP], J. K. Galbraith describes the White House luncheon on February 15 before the Ward-Kennedy meeting. *Ambassador's Journal* (Boston, 1969), pp. 32–33. See also Memorandum for the President of the United States, From: Frederick Dutton, February 28, 1961, NSF, JFKL. Oral history of Barbara Ward, JFKL.

41. Kennedy to Nkrumah, Department tel. 891, February 28, 1961.

42. Kennedy wrote: "I wish to extend to you my warmest thanks . . . I am delighted to know that you will be coming . . . I look forward with keenest anticipation to making your acquaintance . . ." Ibid.

43. Department tel 899, March 1, 1961, NSF, JFKL.

44. CIA Briefing Paper (for the President), "Kwame Nkrumah," Undated, pp. 3–4, NSF, JFKL.

45. Quoted in *The New Republic*, "Nkrumah's Visit," March 13, 1961.

46. Memorandum to the President, From: WWR, Subject: Interview with Finance Minister K.A. Gbedemah of Ghana, March 4, 1961, POF, JFKL.

47. Memorandum for the President, From: McGeorge Bundy, March 4, 1961, NSF, JFKL.

48. Remarks of welcome to President Nkrumah of Ghana at the Washington National Airport, March 8, 1961. *Public Papers of the Presidents, John F. Kennedy*, 1961, p. 160.

49. Summary Record of Conversation, Visit of President Kwame Nkrumah of Ghana, White House, March 8, 1961, POF, JFKL.

50. Remarks on Introducing President Nkrumah to the Press, March 8, 1961, *Public Papers of the Presidents*, pp. 160–61. Schlesinger, *A Thousand Days*, p. 527. *Washington Post*, March 14, 1961.

51. Memorandum for the President of the United States, From: Chad F. Calhoun, Subject: Ghana—President Kwame Nkrumah, March 7, 1961, CFCP.

52. Seikman, "Kaiser's Gamble in Africa," *Forture*, November 1961, page 206.

53. Memorandum of Conference, January 7, 1961, Lloyd N. Cutler, Andre Mayer of Lazard Frères and George Woods of First Boston Bank also attended the meeting, CFCP.

54. Telcons, Dillon/Ball August 30 and September 16, 1961.

55. Senator Gore explained his contentions that government financing of Valco would result in an unfair market advantage as follows. "Kaiser, by shipping alumina from the United States, where there are ample smeltering and extrusion facilities, to Ghana, thence to Europe as aluminum, will have a distinct competitive advantage over U.S. producers by virtue of a low power rate, in addition to its possibly decisive advantage in access to the Common Market," Albert Gore to John F. Kennedy. November 13, 1961, POF, JFKL. See Committee on Foreign Relations, *Study Mission to Africa*, September-October 1961, Reports of Senators Albert Gore, Phillip A. Hart and Maurine B. Neuberger, 87th cong., 1st sess., 1962. Also Testimony by Senator Gore before the Senate on the Volta River project in Ghana, *Congressional Record*, February 2, 1962, pp. 1979–82.

56. File Memo (Chad Calhoun), Volta/Valco/Ghana Meeting with President Kennedy, October 13, 1961, CFCP, JFKL.

57. The Volta River Project (State Department Paper submitted to the National Security Council), December 5, 1961.

58. Through a covert source in Flagstaff House, the embassy learned of Brezhnev's offer and its consideration by Nkrumah's cabinet. Accra tels. 978 and 1006, February 18 and 22, 1961, NSF, JFKL.

59. Accra tel. 1006, February 22, 1961. Memorandum for Mr. Rostow, From: Samuel E. Belk, Subject: Background on Nickey Kaldor/Ghana, July 18, 1961, NSF, JFKL. Telcon: Ball/Black 2/25/61.

60. Telcon: The President/Ball 4/14/61. Barbara Ward to Walt W. Rostow, May 4, 1961, POF, JFKL.

61. Chester Bowles to Walt Rostow, June 27, 1961, Chester Bowles Papers, Yale University.

62. Telcon: Ball/The President 6/21/61.

63. Letter to President Nkrumah of Ghana, June 29, *Public Papers of the Presidents, John F. Kennedy, 1961*, p. 274.

64. Interview: Dei-Anang. Thompson discusses this point in *Ghana's Foreign Policy*, pp. 169–77.

65. Nkrumah's speech was delivered on July 24, 1961 in Moscow. Memorandum to George Ball, From: G. Mennen William, September 19, 1961, CFC, JFKL. *Times* (of London), August 1, 1961.

66. Quoted in Colin Legum, "Is Ghana Going Communist?" O.F.N.S., October 2, 1961, Bowles Papers, Yale University.

67. Interview: Dei-Anang. Thompson, *Ghana's Foreign Policy*, pp. 173–77.

68. Talbott, ed. and trans., *Khrushchev Remembers*, p. 335.

69. Accra tel. 286, August 28, 1961. Memorandum for the President, From: Dean Rusk, Subject: President Nkrumah Orders the Training of 400 Ghanaian Military Cadets in the USSR, September 11, 1961, NSF, JFKL.

70. The communiqué dated August 19, 1961, is quoted in Memorandum to George Ball, September 19, 1961, CFC, JFKL.

71. Ambassador George F. Kennan provided a more dispassionate critique of the Ghanaian position. Belgrade tel. 368, September 2, 1961, NSF, JFKL. See also Ghanaian Foreign Minister Ako Adjei's conference with Secretary Rusk, Memorandum to the Secretary, From: Assistant Secretary G. Mennen Williams, September 15, 1961, KMWP, National Archives.

72. Schlesinger, *A Thousand Days*, p. 481.

73. *The New Republic*, vol. 145, no. 16, October 16, 1961.

74. National Security Action Memorandum 89, September 16, 1961, NSF, JFKL.

75. Memorandum for the President, From: Dean Rusk, Subject: President Nkrumah Orders the Training of 400 Ghanaian Military Cadets in the USSR, September 11, 1961, NSF, JFKL. Rusk, at this point, believed Nkrumah should be confronted with the fact that "we have no sympathy for pro-communism." The Volta project should be postponed indefinitely. Telcon: Chayes/Ball 9/5/61.

76. Memorandum for the President, From: WWR, Subject: Nkrumah's Plans to Send 400 Cadets to the USSR for Training, September 13, 1961.

Index of Weekend Papers, September 15–18, 1961, Hyannis Port (prepared by McGeorge Bundy), NSF, JFKL.

77. Austin, *Politics in Ghana*, pp. 400–2. *The New York Times*, September 1, 1961. Fitch and Oppenheimer, *Ghana: End of an Illusion*, pp. 102–3.

78. To: The Secretary; From: INR—Roger Hilsman, Intelligence Note: Internal Dissension in Ghana, September 6, 1961, NSF, JFKL. Interview: Francis H. Russell, 4/27/73, Medford, Mass.

79. Memorandum to: Acting Secretary, From: INR—Roger Hilsman, Intelligence Note: Nkrumah Removes British Officers from Ghana Army Command, NSF, JFKL.

80. *The New York Times*, September 26, 1961. Telcon: Bundy/Ball 10/6/61. Moscow tel. 1063, September 28, 1961, NSF, JFKL.

81. File Memorandum to Edgar Kaiser, From: Chad Calhoun, October 11, 1961, CFC.

82. Interviews: Bundy, Dungan. Ward.

83. Robert A. Divine, *Eisenhower and the Cold War* (New York, 1981), pp. 79–88. Melvin Gurtov, *The United States Against the Third World, Antinationalism and Intervention* (New York, 1974), pp. 23–27.

84. Telcons: Ball/The President 9/21/61, Ball/Alex Johnson 9/23/61.

85. Confidential interviews: 26 (a Ghanaian CIA operative and fellow Ewe of Gbedemah's); 32 (a senior CIA officer in the U.S. embassy).

86. Tempelsman was also deeply involved, both commercially and politically, in the Congo. See Richard D. Mahoney, *United States Policy toward the Congo, 1960–1963*, Chapter VII, "Financial Connections." Unpublished Ph.D. dissertation. The Johns Hopkins University School of Advanced International Studies, November, 1980.

87. Memorandum for the President, From: WWR, September 24, 1961 (sent to Hyannis Port), NSF, JFKL.

88. Confidential interview 4 (a senior member of the National Security Council staff).

89. Telcons: Ball/Bundy; Ball/Fredericks 9/29/61. Former Ghanaian Attorney General and legal adviser to Nkrumah, Geoffrey Bing confirmed the existence of the tap. Letter to the author, July 1, 1976.

90. Telcon: Ball/Tempelsman 9/29/61.

91. Telcon: Ball/Bundy 9/29/61.

92. Austin, *Politics in Ghana*, p. 406. *Facts on File: Ghana* (New York, 1971), pp. 73–75. Gbedemah kept in contact with U.S. officials after he fled Ghana. He flew to New York in November to see Tempelsman and sent Eugene Black a letter that the World Bank President forwarded to Ball. Telcon: Black/Ball 11/1/61, 11/22/61.

93. Accra tel. 885, December 10, 1961. The White Paper also accused leading oppositionist Dr. Kofi A. Busia of planning to set up a "government-in-exile" in Lomé, Togo with the aid of $130,000 supplied by "commercial interests in Ghana." *Times* (of London), December 11, 1961.

94. Dei-Anang, Jackson, and Erica Powell agreed on this point in interview.

95. Accra tel. 841, October 19, 1961, NSF, JFKL.

96. Bretton, *The Rise and Fall of Kwame Nkrumah*, p. 57. The *Economist* thought that overwrought criticism of Nkrumah in the West might turn Ghana into "the enemy that it is not." October 7, 1961.

97. Osagyefo Dr. Kwame Nkrumah to President John F. Kennedy, 29 September 1961, NSF, JFKL.

98. Barbara Ward to John F. Kennedy, October 10, 1961, POF, JFKL. See also Ward's oral history at the JFKL.

99. Oral history of Philip M. Kaiser (then ambassador to Senegal and Mauritania), JFKL. Interview: Kaiser (telephone) 4/28/77, London.

100. File Memorandum to Edgar Kaiser, From: Chad Calhoun, October 13, 1961, CFC.

101. Schlesinger, *A Thousand Days*, p. 528.

102. Memorandum for the President, From: George W. Ball, Subject: Clarence B. Randall and Mission to Ghana, October 18, 1961, NSF, JFKL. Telcon: Bundy/Ball 10/18/61. Kennedy wrote Prime Minister Macmillan on October 19, 1961 (Deptel 2144):

> I think I can safely report to you privately that our expectation is that unless the situation on the ground is very different from what we now believe, the Randall Committee will recommend that we should proceed with the Volta River Project. On balance, our current estimate is that the dangers of not proceeding exceed those of going ahead . . . There does remain a real possibility that my decision will go the other way, but I can assure you of prompt warning if that should be the case.

103. Accra tel. 755, October 26, 1961, NSF, JFKL.

104. Accra tel. 840, November 15, 1961, NSF, JFKL.

105. Interview: Jackson.

106. Summary of Volta Project Documents, Undated, Prepared by White House Staff, NSF, JFKL.

107. According to Jackson, he was told that Randall's draft report was seen in his London hotel room by British agents when Randall was enroute to Washington on his return trip.

108. Telcons: Bundy/Ball 11/4/61, 11/8/61. Telcon: Ball/Ormsby Gore 11/8/61. Commonwealth Sandys returned to Accra for a second visit to ascertain the degree of risk for the Queen. Interview: Jackson. *Le Monde*, November 15, 1961. *Economist*, November 18, 1961.

109. Telcon: Bundy/Ball 11/4/61.

110. Quoted in the *Times* (of London), November 21, 1961.

111. CIA, ONE, Memorandum for the Director, Subject: Likely Consequences of Various U.S. Courses of Action on the Volta Dam, 16 November 1961, NSF, JFKL.

112. Schlesinger, *A Thousand Days*, p. 528. Kennedy's reply to Macmillan in Deptel to London 3285, December 15, 1961, NSF, JFKL.

113. Notes for Record, NSC Meeting on Volta Dam, December 5, 1961, McGeorge Bundy, December 18, 1961, NSF, JFKL.

114. Harold Macmillan, *At the End of the Day* (London, 1976), p. 148.

115. John F. Kennedy to Barbara Ward, December 28, 1961, POF, JFKL.

116. Contained in Deptel 939 to Accra, December 14, 1961. Kennedy informed Prime Minister Macmillan that he sought assurances from Nkrumah "which would permit us to have greater confidence in the future course of Ghana." Deptel 3285 to London, December 15, 1961, NSF, JFKL.

117. Nkrumah to Kennedy, December 20, 1961. Deptel 985 to Accra, December 21, 1961. Deptel 995 to Accra, December 22, 1961, NSF, JFKL.

118. Interview: Kaysen. Bundy to Dungan (note), December 29, 1961, NSF, JFKL. The relationship between Nkrumah and Russell had become negative. In a conversation with U.S. Peace Corps Director George Carter on April 2, 1962, Nkrumah pointed to Russell as an example of an "American [who] cannot respect the African and treat him as an equal because the American has no respect for the black man." Accra tel. April 13, 1962, NSF, JFKL.

119. Mahoney, who was leader of Arizona's delegation to the Democratic National Convention, had led the fight to desegregate Arizona's public schools in 1953—a year before the Brown decision. Airgram 214 from Accra, April 17, 1962, NSF, JFKL. Kennedy advised the new ambassador that he would either be, "a success or a failure over there. Nothing in between." Oral history of William P. Mahoney [hereinafter OHWPM], JFKL.

120. Schlesinger, A Thousand Days, pp. 520–38.

121. Accra tel. 1813, June 27, 1962, NSF, JFKL.

122. Accra tel. 38, July 10, 1962, NSF JFKL. Nkrumah invited General Eisenhower, Walter Lippmann, and Ralph Bunche among others to the conference.

123. Accra tel. 1724, June 15, 1962. Accra tel. 3, July 2, 1962, NSF, JFKL.

124. Schlesinger, A Thousand Days, p. 745.

125. Accra tels. 696, 697, October 26, 1962, OHWMP, JFKL. Memorandum for McGeorge Bundy, From: W.H. Brubeck, Subject: Recent Events in Ghana, October 27, 1962, NSF, JFKL.

126. Accra tel. 180, August 3, 1962. Accra tel. 434, September 17, 1962, NSF, JFKL.

127. Austin, Politics in Ghana, pp. 310–12. Thompson, Ghana's Foreign Policy, pp. 83–86.

128. Accra tel. 940, December 8, 1961. Accra tel. 947, December 10, 1961, NSF, JFKL. To: AFW—Mr. C. Vaughn Ferguson, From: RAF—Robert C. Good, Subject: Preliminary Analysis of Reported Assassination Plot in Togo, December 8, 1961, GMWP, NARS.

129. Lomé 45, December 1, 1961. Deptel 50 to Lome, October 23, 1961. CA-574 to Lome, December 2, 1961, NS, JFKL.

130. CA-574, December 2, 1961, NSF, JFKL.

131. Thompson, Ghana's Foreign Policy, pp. 308–16. Accra tel. 147, December 10, 1961, NSF, JFKL.

132. Memorandum for Mr. McGeorge Bundy, From: L.D. Battle, Subject: Ghanaian Subversion in Africa (13 pages), February 12, 1962, NSF, JFKL.

133. Ibid., Bing to the author, July 1, 1976.

134. Nkrumah quoted in Memorandum for Mr. McGeorge Bundy, From: L.D. Battle, February 12, 1962, p. 4, NSF, JFKL.

135. Ibid., p. 12–13.

136. Deptel 939 to Accra, December 14, 1961. Three weeks after the Ghanaian-supported commando attack on his life, U.S. Ambassador Poullada asked Olympio for his opinion of the Volta project decision. Olympio replied that he was in favor of anything that brought long-term benefits to Africans "irrespective of temporary aberrations of some African leaders." He added that

he was particularly impressed that Kennedy had made the decision on the basis of economic soundness rather than political expediency. Lomé tel. 163, December 22, 1961, NSF, JFKL.

137. Interviews: J.W.K. Harlley (then commissioner of Police in Ghana), 7/17/72, Accra, Ghana. Dei-Anang.

138. Accra tel. 180, August 3, 1962, NSF, JFKL.

139. Those arrested were Ako Adjei (foreign minister), Tawia Adamafio (minister of information), and H.H. Coffie-Crabbe (executive secretary of the CPP).

140. CIA Information Report, "Appraisal of Nkrumah's Mental State," August 31, 1962, NSF, JFKL.

141. Quoted in "Nkrumah—Whose Hand?" *Africa 1962*, August 24, 1962.

142. The supposition of some American and British officials was that Rodionov was a high-ranking KGB officer. Confidential interview 23, (a former CIA station chief in Accra); Robert Jackson.

143. *The Ghanaian Times*, September 17, 162. *Evening News* (of Accra), August 11, 1962. Accra tel. 508, September 22, 1962. Regarding the cause of the press attacks, the embassy feared that 'Nkrumah may suspect or at least fear USG involvement or cooperation with his bitterest opponents." Accra tel. 738, December 4, 1962, NSF, JFKL.

144. Memorandum for the Secretary of State, From: The President, October 6, 1962, Memorandum for McGeorge Bundy, Subject: Appointment with the President for William P. Mahoney, Jr., United States Ambassador to Ghana, October 10, 1962, NSF, JFKL.

145. Memorandum for the President, From: Carl Kaysen, October 29, 1962, NSF, JFKL.

146. CIA Information Report, Subject: United Party Plans for Taking Over Ghana Government, November 30, 1962, NSF, JFKL.

147. In May 1963, the CIA's regard for Gbedemah had somewhat dimmed: "[H]e seems to lack essential leadership qualities and to have only a small following in Ghana . . ." As for the United Party leaders, "it is unlikely that they will ever be regarded as an effective alternative to the Nkrumah government." CIA Special Report, 'Domestic Opposition to Ghana's Nkrumah," OCI No. 0281/633, 24 May 1963, NSF, JFKL. Telcon: Rusk/Ball 10/11/61. Gbedemah's allegation is reported in Deptel 193 to Acra, October 3, 1962. See also London tel. 1417, October 4, 1962, NSF, JFKL.

148. The embassy recommended that, "We do everything we can to avoid being drawn into this drama . . . We do not want opinion here or elsewhere in Africa to hold us responsible for Nkrumah's troubles or his collapse." Accra tel. 736, December 2, 1962, NSF, JFKL.

149. This account is drawn from OHWPM, JFKL and William P. Mahoney, Jr. to the author, July 21, 1977. Dr. J.B. Danquah, properly called the "father of his country," was a man of great intellect and character. See L.H. Ofosu-Appiah, *The Life and Times of J.B. Danquah* (Accra, 1974).

On May 29, 1961, Kennedy had sent a letter to all U.S. chiefs of mission overseas:

You are in charge of the entire United States diplomatic position, and I shall expect you to supervise all of its operations. The mission includes not only the personnel of the Department of State and the Foreign Service, but also the representatives of all other United States agencies which have programs or activities in [name of country]. I shall give you full support and backing in carrying out your assignment.

Quoted in David Wise, *The Invisible Government*, p. 268–69.

150. Accra tel 837, January 8, 1963. Briefing Paper for the President, U.S. Ghana Relations, December 12, 1962, NSF, JFKL.

151. Thompson, *Ghana's Foreign Policy*, p. 310.

152. *Ghanaian Times* columnist H.M. Basner asked: "Is it possible that he [Busia] imagines he will convince the American Congress to afford him aid and support at that section of the Central Intelligence Agency which is not engaged in Cuba, Berlin, India and South Vietnam?" December 4, 1962.

153. See exchange of letters between Nkrumah and Mahoney, Accra tel. 1714, November 21, 1962, NSF, JFKL. The *Spark*'s March 15, 1963 issue was entitled, "The Secret War of the CIA. The Killer at Your Door." Accra tel. (Topec) 70, December 5, 1962.

154. Accra tel. 995, February 1, 1963. Memorandum for Mr. McGeorge Bundy, Subject: Relations with Ghana, From: W.H. Brubeck, January 18, 1963. CIA OCI Report, "Ghana-U.S. Relations," February 27, 1963, NSF, JFKL.

155. The evidence of Ghanaian involvement in the murder is circumstantial, but extensive. See Memorandum for Mr. McGeorge Bundy from: W.H. Brubeck, Subject: Possible U.S. Courses of Action in Ghana, February 1, 1963, NSF, JFKL. Thompson, *Ghana's Foreign Policy*, pp. 311–15.

156. 6 PM Meeting with President Kennedy, (Calhoun notes), Present: President Kennedy, Carl Kaysen, Edgar Kaiser, Chad Calhoun, January 23, 1963, CFCP.

7. Kennedy Against Salazar

1. "Colonialism and American Foreign Policy," Remarks by Senator John F. Kennedy, Town Hall Luncheon, Los Angeles, California, April 13, 1956, p. 3, PPP, Speech file, JFKL.

2. John Marcum, *The Angolan Revolution*, vol. 1 (1950–1962), pp. 126–130. *Hispanic-American Review*, March 1961, pp. 109–110. "The Kingdom of Silence, The Truth About Africa's Most Oppressed Colony," *Harper's*, May 1961, pp. 29–37. The article was published anonymously.

3. John F. Kennedy, *Public Papers: 1961* (Washington: 1962), pp. 22–23.

4. Barbara Ward to Walt Rostow, June 2, 1961, NSF, JFKL.

5. *The New York Times*, February 22, 1961.

6. Interview: Harlan Cleveland, 2/12/78, Princeton, New Jersey. Cleveland was the assistant secretary of State for International Organization Affairs. Interview: J. Wayne Fredericks, 11/6/77, New York City. Fredericks was the deputy assistant secretary of state for African Affairs.

7. Handwritten notes of Adlai Stevenson concerning conversation with President Kennedy, Undated, AESP, Princeton University. Report for the President, From: Frederick Dutton, United States Mission to the United Nations, February 24, 1961.

8. Deptel 1703 to Lisbon, March 3, 1961, NSF, Countries: Angola, JFKL.

9. Lisbon tel. 388, March 7, 1961, NSF, JFKL. Interview: C. Burke Elbrick, 10/23/76, Washington, D.C.

10. Arslan Humbaraci and Nicole Muchnik, *Portugal's African Wars*, p. 178. William Minter, *Portuguese Africa and the West*.

11. Hugh Kay, *Salazar and Modern Portugal*, pp. 186–87.

12. OHDA, Interviewer: Lucius D. Battle, April 27, 1964, JFKL.

13. *Report on the United Nations: 1961*, pp. 48–49.

14. *The New York Times*, March 17, 1961. Regarding the Portuguese contention that they received no advance notice, see State Department Background Briefing by Under Secretary Chester Bowles, April 25, 1961, pp. E 30–31, Bowles Papers, Yale University.

15. Marcum, *The Angolan Revolution*, p. 182.

16. *The New York Times*, March 17, 1961.

17. Dean Acheson to John F. Kennedy, March 3, 1961, POF, JFKL.

18. John Bartlow Martin, *Adlai Stevenson and the World*, p. 617.

19. UN General Assembly 1603 (–V), April 20, 1961, Arthur M. Schlesinger, Jr., Papers, JFKL.

20. Kay, *Salazar and Modern Portugal*, p. 228. Marcum, *The Angolan Revolution*, 145.

21. Lisbon 508, February 17, 1961, referred to in Lisbon 558, March 4, 1961, NSF, JFKL. In interview, Elbrick stated that he could not "completely discount the possibility of a deep-down operation." A CIA officers who was then serving in the Lisbon mission, observed that "we came pretty close," but declined to comment in greater detail. Confidential interview 17. A member of the National Security Council staff stated that the White House was highly interested in a change of regime but that, in his view, was as far as it went. Confidential interview 3.

22. Lisbon 564, March 6, 1961, Lisbon 558, March 4, Deptel 472 to Lisbon, March 4, 1961, NSF, JFKL.

23. Lisbon 684, March 28, 1961, Foreign Service Dispatch 391, May 4, 1961 with attached translation of letter, NSF, JFKL.

24. Lisbon 684, March 28, 1961, Lisbon 693, March 29, 1961, NSF, JFKL. *The New York Times*, April 16, 1961.

25. Lisbon 729, April 9, 1962, NSF, JFKL.

26. Interview: Alberto Franco Nogueira, 5/11/78, London, England. Kay, *Salazar and Modern Portugal*, p. 388.

27. Lisbon 748, April 13, 1961, NSF, JFKL. Salazar, for one, thought they were involved. Interview: Franco Nogueira.

28. Lisbon 758 (ref. 751), April 14, 1961. "Report on Portugal," *Atlantic Monthly*, October 1961, vol. 208, no. 4, pp. 33–36.

29. Kay, *Salazar and Modern Portugal*, p. 388.

30. Current Intelligence Memorandum, "The Situation in Portugal," OCI No. 1269/62, 6 May 1962, Central Intelligence Agency, NSF, JFKL.

31. Lisbon 1136, June 4, 1962, NSF, JFKL. Interview: Franco Nogueira.

32. *The New York Times*, April 16, 1961. *Hispanic-American Review*, 1961, pp. 287–88.

33. Benjamin Welles, "Salazar in Trouble," *Atlantic Monthly*, August, 1962, pp. 47–62.

34. Khrushchev's remark is cited in Report of the Presidential Task Force on the Portuguese Territories [hereinafter Task Force Report], July 12, 1961, pp. 40–41, NSF, JFKL.

35. Status Report on Portuguese Africa, Department of State, 5/24/61, NSF, JFKL.

36. Interview: Hervé Alphand, 4/22/77, Paris, France. M. Alphand was the French ambassador to the United States. He stated in an interview that an American announcement of support for Algerian independence was "the last thing we wanted to hear." Acheson to Kennedy, mentioning the danger to France of any American call for self-determination in Algeria, 3/21/61, POF, JFKL. Memorandum for the President, From: McGeorge Bundy, Subject: Specific answers to your questions of March 29th, May 29, 1961, NSF, JFKL.

37. Arthur Schlesinger, Jr., *A Thousand Days*, p. 328 (paperback edition). Kennedy had less success in prevailing on Dutch Foreign Minister Joseph Luns to pressure Salazar. The Dutch government was still smarting over America's refusal to support their position on Dutch New Guinea. *Atlantic Monthly*, June 1961, vol. 207, no. 6, pp. 5–6.

38. Williams to Kennedy, June 7, 1961. GMWP, National Archives.

39. Task Force Report, July 4, 1961, p. 4, NSF, JFKL.

40. *The New York Times*, May 26, 1961. The *Diario de Noticias* commented: "Lord Home came primarily . . . to offer the good offices and compliments of Great Britain upon the beginning of the dissolution of the Portuguese empire . . ." quoted in *Hispanic-American Review*, July 1961, p. 386.

41. This was a constant complaint: See Lisbon 53, July 12, 1963 and Lisbon 56, July 16, 1963, NSF, JFKL.

42. *The New York Times*, June 11, 1961, May 31, 1961.

43. Franco Nogueira to Rusk, June 2, 1961 cited in Task Force Report, July 12, 1961, Appendix A, Chronology of U.S. Actions, p. 3, NSF, JFKL.

44. Quoted in Kay, *Salazar and Modern Portugal*, p. 229.

45. Marcum, *The Angolan Revolution*, pp. 142–47.

46. Contel from Lourenço Marques 25, August 16, 1961, For Secretary from Williams, NSF, JFKL.

47. *The New York Times*, May 19, 1961. The *Washington Post* story concerning the beating on the Roman Catholic cleric is cited in the *Hispanic-American Review*, p. 195. Lisbon 998, June 8, 1961, NSF, JFKL.

48. Kennedy's memorandum of August 21, 1961 is quoted in Memorandum for the President, From: Robert S. McNamara, Subject: Portuguese Use of Military Equipment in Angola, August 25, 1961. Memorandum for the President, From: Dean Rusk, Subject: Restriction of Arms Shipments to Portugal and its Territories, August 29, 1961, NSF, JFKL. Memorandum to the Secretary, From: AF—G. Mennen Williams, Subject: Public Disclosure of our Arms Policy towards Portugal, September 11, 1961, GWMP, National Archives.

49. This was done pursuant to the National Security Action Memorandum 60 directive.

50. Lisbon 935, May 24, 1961, 1068, June 21, 1961: Deptel to Lisbon 809, June 14, 1961, NSF, JFKL.

51. Lisbon 84, August 3, 1961. The secret supplemental exchange of notes concerning "prior consent" in McNamara's memorandum to the President, August 25, 1961, NSF, JFKL.

52. Ibid. For an analysis of British policy, see *Angola: Views of a Revolt* and, in particular, Basil Davidson's chapter.

53. Lisbon 240, August 16, 1961, NSF, JFKL. Interviews: Fredericks, Elbrick. Unnumbered Deptel to Lisbon, August 11, 1961, NSF, JFKL.

54. Lisbon 240, August 16, 1961.

55. *Hispanic-American Review*, XV, p. 476. *The New York Times*, June 7, 1961.

56. Deptel 2406, June 7, 1961, London 4994, June 8, 1961, Deptel 2362 to USUN, June 1, 1961, NSF, JFKL.

57. Rusk to Franco Nogueira, May 25, 1961 (contained in Deptel 728 to Lisbon) and June 7, 1961 cited in Task Force Report, July 12, 1961, Appendix A, p. 3, NSF, JFKL, and in Deptel 2406 to Lisbon, June 7, 1961.

58. *The New York Times*, June 8, 1961.

59. Rusk to Franco Nogueira, Deptel 774 to Lisbon, June 7, 1961, NSF, JFKL.

60. Report on the United Nations: 1961, p. 50. Lisbon 998, June 8, 1961, NSF, JFKL.

61. *The New York Times*, July 1, 1961.

62. Interview: Samuel E. Belk III, 4/3/78, Washington, D.C. Belk was the National Security Council Staff's specialist on Angola policy.

63. Deptel 17 to Lisbon, July 6, 1961, NSF, JFKL.

64. Lisbon 51, July 11, 1961, NSF, JFKL.

65. Interview: Franco Nogueira.

66. Kay, *Salazar and Modern Portugal*, p. 79, 429. Benjamin Welles, "Salazar in Trouble," *Atlantic Monthly*, August 1962, pp. 57–62.

67. Ibid.

68. George Ball, *The Discipline of Power*, p. 246. Interview: Dean Rusk, 5/3/78, Athens, Georgia. Rusk expressed a view of Salazar similar to Ball's.

69. Lisbon 73, July 15, 1961.

70. Interview: Carl Kaysen, 2/24/77, Cambridge, Massachusetts.

71. Memorandum for the Secretary, From: Chester Bowles, Subject: Proposal for a Breakthrough in U.S.-Portuguese Relations in Regard to Africa, January 10, 1963. The figure of $500 million is not mentioned in the Bowles memorandum but was the amount under discussion. The figure is mentioned in Memorandum from Paul Sakwa, Subject: U.S. Policy Towards Portugal, 17 January 1962, NSF, JFKL. Sakwa was an assistant to Richard M. Bissell, Jr., the deputy director of plans at the CIA.

72. The Economics Effects on Portugal of the Angolan Military Operations, S-1101, October 25, 1963 with cover note from William H. Brubeck to McGeorge Bundy, NSF, JFKL.

73. Visit of the Under Secretary to Lisbon, August 29–30, 1963, Portugal— Ball-Salazar Meeting, August 26, 1963, NSF, JFKL. Salazar's speech is printed in full in John Marcum, *The Angolan Revolution*, vol. II, appendix I, pp. 284–97. Ball, *The Discipline of Power*, p. 247.

74. Memorandum from Paul Sakwa, Subject: U.S. Policy Towards Portugal, 17 January 1962, NSF, JFKL. Sakwa's proposal was considered by the National Security Council staff.

75. *Le Monde*, September 17, 1963, cited in Kay, *Salazar and Modern*

Portugal, p. 400. The article in *Le Monde* stated that this was the perception at the UN and one that was probably accurate.

76. Lisbon 73, July 15, 1961, NSF, JFKL.

77. The fifty-eight-year-old Pereira (who held a doctorate degree in actuarial calculus from the University of Zurich) was the chief architect of Salazar's *Estado Novo* and had served in many sensitive positions, including as Salazar's special agent to Franco during the Spanish Civil War. Biographical Sketch, Pedro Theotónio Pereira, For the President's meeting with the Ambassador, Undated, Department of State, see also Pereira's oral history [hereinafter OHPTP], at the JFKL.

78. Kay, *Salazar and Modern Portugal*, pp. 237–38.

79. This speech is reproduced in Franco Nogueira's book, *The Third World*.

80. Kay, *Salazar and Modern Portugal*, pp. 237–38, p. 446.

81. The Enes quote appears as the epigraph of *The Third World*.

82. Interview: Elbrick. The ambassador describes Franco Nogueira's "gamesmanship" in Lisbon 1129, May 31, 1962, NSF, JFKL.

83. Lisbon 969, April 16, 1962, NSF, JFKL. Interview: Franco Nogueira.

84. Lisbon 66, 67, 81, 93, July 23, 24, 26, 31, 1963. Deptels 44 and 45, July 28, 1963, NSF, JFKL. Confidential interview 11 (an American diplomat).

85. Interview: Belk. Franco Nogueira also thought that Kennedy was unimpressed by Pereira. Kennedy did appreciate the ambassador's sailing skills. See OHPTP, JFKL. Welles, "Salazar in Trouble," *Atlantic Monthly*, August 1962, p. 62. Galbraith, *Ambassador's Journal*, p. 283.

86. Report of the Chairman of the Task Force on Portuguese Territories in Africa ,July 4, 1961, NSF, JFKL. Recommendations for Action, Presidential Task Force on Portuguese Territories in Africa, July 12, 1961, NSF, JFKL. Memorandum for Mr. Bundy and Mr. Rostow, Subject: Planning Group Meeting on Angola, July 11, 1961, From: Samuel E. Belk, July 10, 1961.

87. Recommendations for Action, Task Force Report, July 12, 1961, NSF, JFKL.

88. Memorandum for the President, From: WWR, Subject: Background Briefing for Your Meeting on July 14 with the Secretary of State and the Secretary of Defense on the Angola Problem, July 14, 1961, NSF, JFKL.

89. "Colonialism and American Foreign Policy," Remarks by Senator John F. Kennedy, Town Hall Luncheon, Los Angeles, California, April 13, 1956, p. 3, PPP, Speech file, JFKL.

90. National Security Action Memorandum 60. Memorandum for Mr. U. Alexis Johnson, Deputy Under Secretary of State, Subject: Additional Guidance Relating to the Portuguese Territories in Africa, From: McGeorge Bundy, July 28, 1961, NSF, JFKL.

8. Angola or the Azores?

1. Draft letter to Mr. Acheson, July 14, 1961, with handwritten annotation: "Sec. of State, He is handling." NSF, JFKL.

2. Gene Farmer, "Dictator on the Defensive," *Life*, May 4, 1962, p. 1105. Lisbon 789, January 29, 1962, NSF, JFKL.

3. Confidential Interviews, 8 and 23. (A staff member of the National

Security Council and a CIA officer serving under Bronson Tweedy in the Africa Division.)

4. Marcum, *The Angolan Revolution*. Thompson, *Ghana's Foreign Policy*.

5. Memorandum for the Secretary from George W. Ball, Subject: Proposal Regarding Holden Roberto, March 17, 1964.

6. Lisbon 825, February 13, 1962, NSF, JFKL.

7. To: CU—Mr. Battle, From: AF—G. Mennen Williams, Subject: Renewal of the Lincoln University Contract, June 22, 1962, GMWP.

8. Chairman's Report of Actions Taken (pursuant to NSAM 60), Department of State, Operations Center, July 31, 1961, p. 3, NSF, JFKL. Martin, *Adlai Stevenson and His World*, p. 232, 261.

9. To: SCA—Abba P. Schwartz, From: AF—G. Mennen Williams, Subject: Angolan Refugee Medical Program, October 25, 1962, NSF, JFKL. G. Mennen Williams to Henry Clinton Reed (American Consul General in Lourenço Marques), October 25, 1962, GWMP, NARS.

10. Memorandum for Mr. Samuel E. Belk, July 9, 1961. Memorandum for the President, From: Maxwell D. Taylor, Subject: Angolese Students in France and Switzerland, July 21, 1961, NSF, JFKL.

11. Lisbon 844, February 22, 1962, NSF, JFKL. G. Mennen Williams to C. Burke Elbrick, May 31, 1962. Memorandum to the Secretary, From: G. Mennen Williams, Subject: "Review of AAI Program for Mozambican Students," October 3, 1962. See also G. Mennen Williams to William Leonhart (U.S. ambassador to Tanganyika), November 8, 1962, GWMP, NARS.

12. G. Mennen Williams to William H. Taft III (U.S. consul in Luanda), April 5, 1962, GMWP, NARS.

13. Lisbon 777, January 25, 1962. Lisbon 830, February 15, 1962, NSF, JFKL.

14. Lisbon 830, February 15, 1962, NSF, JFKL. G. Mennen Williams to William H. Taft III, April 5, 1962, GMWP, NARS.

15. To: CU—Mr. Battle, From: G. Mennen Williams, Subject: Renewal of Lincoln University Contract, June 22, 1962, GMWP, NARS archives. Interviews: Kaysen, Fredericks.

16. Lisbon 121, July 21, 1962, NSF, JFKL.

17. Lisbon 840, February 21, 1962, NSF, JFKL.

18. ET 863, March 2, 1962, Deptel 693 to Lisbon, March 9, 1962, NSF, JFKL.

19. *The New York Times*, June 14, 1961.

20. Memorandum from Paul Sakwa, U.S. Policy Toward Portugal, 17 January 1962, NSF, JFKL.

21. Lisbon 617, December 8, 1961, NSF, JFKL.

22. Bilateral Matters, Participants: Ambassador Pereira, The Secretary, William R. Tyler, Frederick R. Starrs, July 18, 1962, NSF, JFKL.

23. Sakwa Memorandum, 17 January 1962, NSF, JFKL. Welles, "Salazar in Trouble," *Atlantic Monthly*, August 1962, pp. 57–62. "Our Spanish Landlord," editorial in the *Nation*, September 23, 1963, p. 2.

24. Office of National Estimates, Subject: Significance of Portuguese and Spanish Colonial Problems for the U.S., Central Intelligence Agency, 11 July 1963, Lisbon A-465, March 6, 1963, NSF, JFKL.

25. Current Intelligence Memorandum, Subject: The Situation in Portugal, Office of Current Intelligence, CIA, 6 May 1962. CIA Memorandum, Subject: Factions of the Portuguese Opposition and the Possibility of Anti-Regime Action, 14 June 1962, TDCS-3/514, 496. CIA Memorandum, Subject: Shadow Cabinet of Portuguese Moderate Opposition Group, 26 July 1962, TDCS-3/650, 876, NSF, JFKL.

26. CIA Memorandum, Subject: Anti-Regime Activity, 21 November 1962, TDCS-3/529, 102, NSF, JFKL.

27. See CIA Memorandum of 14 June 1962. Lopes was reportedly involved in the plot of Botelho Moniz to overthrow Salazar in April 1961.

28. Confidential Interview 28.

29. There was nothing new in the problem of a diminishing tradeoff between covert activity and reliable intelligence reporting. In a report to President Eisenhower in 1956, David K. E. Bruce and Robert Lovett of the President's Board of Consultants on Foreign Intelligence Activities had condemned, "the increased mingling in the internal affairs of other nations of bright, highly graded young men who must be doing something all the time to justify their reason for being . . . Busy, moneyed, and privileged, [the CIA] likes its 'King Making' responsibility [the intrigue is fascinating—considerable self-satisfaction, sometimes with applause, derives from 'successes'—no charge is made for 'failures'—and the whole business is very much simpler than collecting covert intelligence on the USSR through the usual CIA methods!]." Quoted in Schlesinger, *Robert Kennedy and His Times*, p. 455.

30. Moreira was fired ostensibly for sacking the Governor-General of Angola, General Venancio Deslandes. Memorandum for the Secretary, From: INR—Roger Hilsman, Intelligence Note: Portuguese Cabinet Reshuffle, December 3, 1962. Airgram A-228, December 7, 1962, NSF, JFKL.

31. Lisbon 789, January 20, 1962, NSF, JFKL.

32. Dean Acheson, "Fifty Years After," *Yale Review*, vol. 51 (Autumn 1961), p. 9. Marcum incorrectly cites this as from the *Yale Law Review* in *The Angolan Revolution*, p. 272.

33. Memorandum to the Secretary of Defense, From: Maxwell D. Taylor, July 10, 1963, NSF, JFKL.

34. Marcum, *The Angolan Revolution*, p. 273.

35. Interview: Admiral George W. Anderson, 4/7/78, Washington, D.C.

36. Memorandum to Wayne Fredericks, From: G. Mennen Williams, Subject: Angola and Rhodesia, April 16, 1962, GMWP, NARS.

37. Kennedy to Stevenson, April 18, 1962, AESP, Princeton University.

38. Telcon: Bundy/Ball 3/16/62.

39. Letter from John F. Kennedy to W. P. Kennard, Yale Club of Montclair, N.J., POF, JFKL. Acheson, *Power and Diplomacy*.

40. Stevenson to Kennedy, June 26, 1963, NSF, JFKL.

41. Interview: George W. Springsteen, Jr., 6/20/78, Rosslyn, Virginia. Springsteen was one of Ball's assistants.

42. Acheson addressed the Press Club on April 25, 1961 in Washington after his trip to Europe. In the speech, he also made disparaging remarks about the President and Secretary Rusk, See POF, Acheson file, JFKL.

43. Interview: Clayton Fritchey, 5/3/78, Washington, D.C. (telephone).

Fritchey was Stevenson's press aide and adviser at the UN. Paris, tel. 4522, April 20, 1961.

44. Dean Acheson to John F. Kennedy, March 18, 1961.

45. Galbraith to Kennedy, July 11, 1961, POF, JFKL.

46. Martin, *Adlai Stevenson and the World*, p. 703.

47. Lisbon 906, March 20, 1962.

48. Telcon: Stevenson/Ball 4/24/62.

49. Telcon: Stevenson/Ball 4/27/62.

50. Memorandum for the Assistant Secretary of State for African Affairs; the Deputy Assistant Secretary of State for European Affairs, Subject: Angola and Brazil, From: Arthur Schlesinger, Jr. April 15, 1962. See also, Memoranda of Conversation, Subject: Angola, Participants: Dean Rusk, San Tiago Dantas, et al., April 3, 4, and 12, 1962, NSF, JFKL. Interview: Lincoln Gordon, 11/16/76, Washington, D.C. Gordon was U.S. ambassador to Brazil.

51. Martin, *Adlai Stevenson and the World*, p. 697.

52. Ibid., p. 697.

53. Ibid., p. 697. See White's article in *Harper's*, March 1962, pp. 100–4.

54. Suggested Reply to a Press Conference Question on Senator Jackson's speech, Final draft of two, Notation: Mr. Cleveland is sending the following to Mr. Ball for the President, March 21, 1962, AESP, Princeton University.

55. Martin, *Adlai Stevenson and the World*, p. 697.

56. Interviews: Abram Chayes, 4/20/77, Cambridge, Mass.; Ralph A. Dungan, 9/6/76, Washington, D.C.; and Harlan Cleveland, 2/12/78, Princeton, N.J. These individuals were particularly helpful in providing commentary about the Kennedy-Stevenson relationship.

57. Martin, *Adlai Stevenson and the World*, p. 703.

58. Oral history of Philip M. Klutznick, JFKL.

59. Telcons: Stevenson/Ball 6/29/63, 7/9/63. Bundy/Ball 7/5/63. Interview: Kaysen. Telcon: The President/Ball 7/15/63. Martin, *Adlai Stevenson and the World*, p. 764.

60. Telcons: Porter Hardy/Ball 1/26/62, 1/29/62.

61. Memorandum to the Secretary, Mr. Ball, Mr. McGhee, From: G. Mennen Williams, Subject: Porter Hardy Committee Inquiry Into Angola Policy, January 26, 1962, GMWP, NARS.

62. The public-relations effort was capitalized at $500,000. Memorandum for McGeorge Bundy, From: L.D. Battle, Subject: Selvage and Lee, September 28, 1961. Daniel M. Friedenburg, *The New Republic*, April 2, 1962, pp. 9–12.

63. The *News and Courier* (Charleston, S.C.) is an example: "In America —particularly in the South—the Negro's drive for equality is supported by the Kennedys at the point of a bayonet. In Africa, the Negro's drive to subjugate the white people is underwritten with American money by the Kennedy administration."

64. Representative Thomas P. O'Neill, Jr., led the effort. See, "Friendly Relations Between Portugal and the United States—A Victory for Freedom," October 5, 1962.

65 Memorandum for Wayne Fredericks, From: G. Mennen Williams, Subject: Angola and Rhodesia, April 16, 1962. Williams made the same argument in a letter to the Secretary of State, Williams to Rusk, April 16, 1962.

Memorandum to G—Mr. Johnson, From: AF—G. Mennen Williams, Subject: JCS Evaluation of North African Attitudes on Portugal and South Africa, July 17, 1963, GMWP, NARS.

66. Schlesinger, *A Thousand Days*, p. 519.

67. Lisbon 617, December 8, 1962, NSF, JFKL.

68. Interview: Fredericks. This view is similar to the conclusion reached by the interagency Planning Group, which argued *inter alia*: ". . . should the Portuguese demand our ouster, it is recommended that we simply temporize . . ."

69. Memorandum to the President, From Chester Bowles, Subject: The Azores, June 4, 1962 with cover letter to McGeorge Bundy, June 5, 1962, Chester Bowles Papers, Yale University. A-2023 from Paris, April 27, 1962, NSF, JFKL.

70. Schlesinger, *A Thousand Days*, pp. 725–32.

71. Chilcote, "Angola or the Azores?" *The New Republic*, pp. 21–22. North Atlantic Route Patterns; Southern Atlantic Route Patterns; Polar Route Patterns, Department of Defense.

72. Interviews: Kaysen and Dungan.

73. Telcon, Bundy/Ball, 3/17/62. Acheson is quoted in Farmer, "Dictator on the Defensive," *Life*, May 4, 1962.

74. Schlesinger, *A Thousand Days*, pp. 549–52.

75. OHDA, JFKL. McGeorge Bundy was also at the meeting.

76. Acheson, *Power and Diplomacy*, pp. 126–27.

77. Memorandum for the President, From: Dean Rusk, May 23, 1962, NSF, JFKL. See also Memorandum to AF—Robert C. Foulon, From: AF— G. Mennen Williams, Subject: Recommended Memorandum to Mr. Rostow, November 9, 1962, GMWP, NARS. Interview: Kaysen.

78. Deptel to Lisbon 58, August 2, 1962. Deptel to USUN 670, September 17, 1962. Deptel 1491 to USUN, December 4, 1962, NSF, JFKL.

79. This is taken from Rusk's description of his talks with Salazar in a meeting with Ambassador Pereira in Washington. Bilateral Matters, Participants: The Ambassador of Portugal, The Secretary, William R. Tyler, and Francis R. Starrs, July 18, 1962, NSF JFKL. See also, U.S. Senate, Hearing held before Committee on Foreign Relations, Briefing by Secretary of State Dean Rusk, July 3, 1962, NARS.

80. Ibid.

81. USUN 4049 for Secretary from Ambassador, June 19, 1962, NSF, JFKL.

82. Bilateral Matters, July 18, 1962, NSF, JFKL. U.S. Senate, Hearing held before Committee on Foreign Relations, Rusk Briefing, July 3, 1962, p. 58.

83. Interview with Portugal's Prime Minister, Dr. António de Oliveira Salazar, *U.S. News and World Report*, July 9, 1962, pp. 78–81.

84. Memorandum to EUR—Mr. Tyler, From: AF—G. Mennen Williams, Subject: Angola, June 18, 1962, GMWP, NARS.

85. Lisbon 182, August 30, 1962. Memorandum to G—Mr. Johnson, From: AF—G. Mennen Williams, Subject: John Marcum and George Houser of the American Committee on Africa, September 4, 1962, GMWP, NARS.

86. Memorandum for the President, From the Acting Secretary George Ball, Subject: U.S.-Portuguese Relations, September 29, 1962 with attached

aide mémoire. Deptel 398 to Paris, September 25, 1962. New Delhi 1611, December 5, 1961, NSF, JFKL.

87. Memorandum for the Acting Secretary, From: AF—G. Mennen Williams, Subject: Portuguese Negotiations, September 28, 1962, NSF, JFKL. Memorandum to the Secretary, From: AF—G. Mennen Williams, November 11, 1962, GMWP, NARS.

88. New Delhi 1808, December 18, 1961, NSF, JFKL.

89. New Delhi 1611, December 5, 1961, NSF, JFKL. John Kenneth Galbraith, *Ambassador's Journal*, p. 294.

90. Airgram CA-4145 to Lisbon, October 19, 1962, NSF, JFKL.

91. Lisbon 178, August 29, 1962, NSF, JFKL. Rusk brought up this matter with Franco Nogueira in Paris in December 1962, Lisbon 438, December 12, 1962. Katanga secessionist leader, Moise Tshombe, made a secret mission to Lisbon to confer with Dr. Salazar. Interview: Franco Nogueira.

92. Holden Roberto to John F. Kennedy, December 19, 1962, POF, JFKL.

93. OAU: Cairo-1964 Verbatims, African Heads of State Group, 21 July 1964, pp. 28–30, cited in W. Scott Thompson, *Ghana's Foreign Policy 1957–1966*, pp. 233–25.

94. Marcum, *The Angolan Revolution*, pp. 255–56.

95. Interview: Franco Nogueira. Lemnitzer declared on May 6, 1963: "Portuguese soldiers, while fighting for the defense of principles, are defending land, raw materials, and bases, which are indispensable not only for the defense of Europe, but for the whole Western world." Minter, *Portuguese Africa and the West*, p. 107. Memorandum of Conversation, Lisbon, March 16, 1962, Participants: Secretary of Air, Col. Kaulza Arriaga, General Mira Delgado, Chief of Staff, Portuguese Air Force, General Curtis LeMay, Chief of Staff, USAF, Theodore A. Xanthaky, Couselor of the Embassy, March 15, 1962, NSF, JFKL.

96. Memorandum for McGeorge Bundy, The White House, From: E. S. Little, Subject: Reported French and West German Interest in the Azores, July 30, 1962. Deptel to London 587, July 27, 1962, NSF, JFKL.

97. Humbaraci and Muchnik, *Portugal's African Wars*, p. 189. Data on Military Assistance, July 17, NSF, JFKL.

98. Naval Message from ALUSNA (Lisbon) to Chief of Naval Operations, C-145, July 11, 1963. To Mr. Bundy, Message From the President, July 7, 1963, NSF, JFKL.

99. Interview: Paul Nitze, 5/2/78, Rosslyn, Virginia. Nitze was assistant secretary of defense for International Security Affairs. Interviews: Dungan, Kaysen.

100. Memorandum for Mr. McGeorge Bundy, From: George W. Anderson, Chief of Naval Operations, Subject: Sale of Military Equipment to Portugal, 20 July 1963, NSF, JFKL. *The New York Times*, September 26, 1963.

101. Interviews: Fredericks, Dungan, Cleveland, Blue, Franco Nogueira. Woodruff Wallner, the deputy assistant secretary of state for International Organization Affairs, was slated to succeed Elbrick in Lisbon. Said Wallner to Cleveland upon hearing the news of Anderson's selection, "I am standing by for notification of assignment to command an aircraft carrier."

102. Marcum writes: ". . . almost no one took very seriously Washington's assertions that it was not helping Lisbon materially in its military campaign to wipe out African nationalism." p. 275. Interview: William L. Blue, 4/5/78, Washington, D.C. Blue was the deputy chief of mission in Lisbon at that time. Data on Military Assistance for Portugal (as of June 1963 prepared by OASD/ISA, 17 July 1963), NSF, JFKL.

103. Lisbon 140, August 17, 1962, Lisbon 145, August 20, 1962, Lisbon 398, December 3, 1962, NSF JFKL.

104. Interview: Franco Nogueira Rusk. Memorandum to the President, From: Dean Rusk, Subject: Meeting with Portuguese Foreign Minister, October 24, 1962, NSF, JFKL.

105. Interviews: Kaysen, Dungan, Komer.

106. Memorandum of Conversation, U.S.-Portuguese Relations, Participants: The President, Alberto Franco Nogueira, Foreign Minister of Portugal, Dr. Theotonio Pereira, C. Burke Elbrick, William R. Tyler, October 24, 1962, NSF, JFKL.

9. Summer and Autumn 1963

1. "The Proper Role of Foreign Policy in the 1956 Campaign," Remarks by Senator John F. Kennedy to the Los Angeles World Affairs Council, Los Angeles, California, Sept. 21, 1956, PPP, Speech File, JFKL.

2. Schlesinger reports that the missile crisis produced "a qualitative change" in Kennedy's outlook. A Thousand Days, pp. 769, 815, 818.

3. Ibid., p. 826.

4. Ibid., p. 769.

5. Ibid., p. 822.

6. Telcon: Ball/Reston, 1/23/61.

7. Department of State Press Release No. 34, July 17, 1963.

8. Memorandum to the Secretary, From: George S. Downey, Jr. (RAF-33), Subject: UN Troop Withdrawal From Southern Katanga May Result in Renewed Violence, July 25, 1963, NSF, JFKL. Report on the United Nations, 1963, p. 76. CIA Special Report, Office of Current Intelligence, The Congo Economy OCI No. 0284/63A, 14 June 1963. Memorandum for Mr. McGeorge Bundy, The White House, Subject: Retraining and Modernization of the Congolese National Army (ANC), From: Benjamin H. Read, October 9, 1963. Untitled State Department Memorandum, March 21, 1963, NSF, JFKL.

9. Lefever, Uncertain Mandate, p. 9.

10. Memorandum for Mr. McGeorge Bundy, From: Ralph A. Dungan, February 9, 1962 reflecting the President's own unhappiness with the ANC retraining program, NSF, JFKL. Interview: Brigadier General (ret.) Michael J.L. Greene, 3/30/78, Washington, D.C. Lefever, Uncertain Mandate, p. 69.

11. Memorandum of Conversation, Subject: Retraining of the Congolese National Army, Participants: The President; Governor G. Mennen Williams, Colonel W. Gall—U.S. Army; Major Romaneski—U.S. Army; General Mobutu—Commander in Chief, Congolese National Army, Mr. Cardoso, Chargé D'Affaires, Congolese Embassy, May 31, 1963, NSF, JFKL.

12. Memorandum to the Secretary, From: INR—Thomas L. Hughes,

RAF-14, Subject: The West at a New Congo Crossroads, April 19, 1963, NSF, JFKL. Weissman, *American Foreign Policy in the Congo*, p. 214.

13. Memorandum for the President, From: Carl Kaysen, March 25, 1963, NSF, JFKL.

14. A White House meeting in late 1962 was illustrative of the lack of attention the retraining program was receiving. When the President turned to Colonel Greene to ask his opinion about a particular matter, Under Secretary of Defense Roswell Gilpatric jotted down a note and passed it to Governor Williams. "Who is Col. Greene?" Williams replied, "He is and has been your representative in the Congo for the past 2½ years." Interview: Greene.

15. Memorandum of Conversation, 'Retraining of the Congolese National Army," May 31, 1963, NSF, JFKL.

16. Interview: General Indar Rikhye (Hammarskjold's military adviser). The estimate, regarding the total amount of CIA payments to Mobutu, is that of Roger Morris, who was the African specialist on the National Security Council during the Nixon administration. See, "Our Man Mobutu," *The New Republic*, May 7, 1977.

17. Memorandum for Mr. McGeorge Bundy, From: Benjamin H. Read, Subject: Talking Paper for the President's Meeting with Prime Minister Adoula of the Congo (Leopoldville), October 4, 1963. Memorandum to the Secretary, From: AF—G. Mennen Williams, Subject: Talking Points for Call on You by Prime Minister Adoula of the Congo, October 10, 1963. Memorandum for the President, From: CK, Subject: Your Congo Meeting at 4 P.M., March 25, 1963, NSF, JFKL. Interview: Gullion.

18. Memorandum to the Secretary, From: AG—G. Mennen Williams, Subject: Congo (L); Information Memorandum, November 8, 1963, NSF, JFKL. Telcon: Bundy/Ball, 11/10/63.

19. Memorandum for Mr. McGeorge Bundy, From: William P. Bundy, Deputy Assistant Secretary of Defense for International Security Affairs, May 16, 1963, Subject: Presidential Meeting with Major General Mobutu, Commander-in-Chief, CNA. Biographic Data—Republic of Congo, April 29, 1963, NSF, JFKL. The memorandum of conversation (May 31, 1963) reports that the President said that "he knew about" Mobutu's interest in having a command aircraft. Carl Kaysen met with the President after his session with Mobutu and related to the author his recollection of the President's surprise.

20. Interview: Gullion, Godley.

21. Interview: Cleveland. Memorandum to the Secretary, From: AF—G. Mennen Williams, Subject: Policy regarding which Ambassador Gullion is Returning on Consultation, August 13, 1963, GMWP, NARS archives.

22. Memorandum for the Secretary of State (from the President), September 6, 1963. See Cleveland's aide mémoire to Bunche in USUN 922, September 20, 1963, NSF, JFKL.

23. President Kennedy's Address to the General Assembly, September 20, 1963, AESP, Princeton University.

24. Cyrille Adoula to John F. Kennedy, October 4, 1963, POF, JFKL. OHEAG, JFKL.

25. Memorandum for the Secretary, From: AF—G. Mennen Williams, Subject: Information Report—The Internal Situation in the Congo, October 18,

1963, GMWP, NARS. CIA Current Intelligence Memorandum, Subject: The Situation in the Congo, OCT No. 2378/63, October 29, 1963, NSF, JFKL.

26. Memorandum for the President, From: Carl Kaysen, April 11, 1963, NSF, JFKL. Memorandum for the Secretary, From: AF—G. Mennen Williams, Subject: Status Report on the Congo Information Memorandum, May 13, 1963, GMWP, NARS. Memorandum for Mr. McGeorge Bundy, The White House, Subject: Retraining and Modernization of the Congolese National Army (ANC), From: Benjamin H. Read, October 9, 1963, NSF, JFKL.

27. Weissman, "CIA in the Congo and Angola," in René Lemarchand, *American Policy toward the Southern Africa, The Stakes and the Stance*, pp. 391–92. The new party was called the *Rassemblement des Démocrats du Congo* (Radeco). Crawford Young, *Politics in the Congo*, p. 381, Interview: Godley.

28. Halberstam, *The Making of a Quagmire*, p. 322.

29. Rupert Emerson, *Africa and United States Policy*, p. 69.

30. Richard J. Walton, *Adlai Stevenson, The Remnants of Power*, p. 89. Interview: Godley.

31. Accra tel. 962, January 23, 1962, NSF, JFKL.

32. 6 P.M. Meeting with President Kennedy, Chad Calhoun notes for the record, January 23, 1963, CFCP.

33. Nkrumah to Kennedy, January 31, 1963. Kennedy to Nkrumah, February 7, 1963, NSF, JFKL.

34. Interview: Kaysen. Telcon: Kaysen/Ball 4/9/63.

35. Accra tel. 995, February 1, 1963, NSF, JFKL.

36. When Mahoney wrote President Nkrumah to protest against the *Ghanaian Times* attack, Nkrumah replied that if the U.S. didn't like the press criticism, it could pull the entire contingent out. Accra tel. 1714, March 21, 1963. Accra tel. 1118, March 15, 1963, Accra tel. 1211, April 14, 1961, NSF, JFKL.

37. Accra tel. 1247, April 26, 1963, NSF, JFKL.

38. Nkrumah to Kennedy, January 31, 1963, NSF, JFKL. See also, Memorandum to J.W. Fredericks, From: G.M. Williams, Meeting with Attorney General, February 1, 1963, GMWP, NARS.

39. *Newsweek*, April 22, 1963. Accra tel. 1231, April 29, 1963, NSF, JFKL.

40. Henry Kissinger, *American Foreign Policy* (New York, 1969) p. 39. Deptel to Accra, April 26, 1963, NSF, JFKL.

41. Schlesinger, *A Thousand Days*, p. 529. Interview: Ball.

42. Memorandum for Honorable G. Mennen Williams, From: Carl Kaysen, June 20, 1963. Current Intelligence Memorandum, Ghana-U.S. Relations, "OCT, CIA, February 27, 1963. Memorandum for Mr. McGeorge Bundy, From: W.H. Brubeck, Subject: Possible United States Courses of Action in Ghana, February 1, 1963. A-71 (from Accra), Evaluation of Nkrumah's Personality and attitude by Miss Hannah Reitsch, August 3, 1963, NSF, JFKL.

43. Sorensen, *Kennedy*, p. 495.

44. Interview: Dei-Anang.

45. President Kennedy was informed of Nkrumah's reiteration of thanks

for the stand on civil rights in Week-end Reading (Hyannis Port), September 21–22, 1963. Oral history, W.P. Mahoney, JFKL.

46. Memorandum for the President, From: William H. Brubeck, October 30, 1963, NSF, JFKL. Thompson, *Ghana's Foreign Policy*, pp. 322–56.

47. To A.E.S. (Ambassador Stevenson), From: Robert Jackson, 8 June 1963, AESP, Princeton University.

48. Memorandum of Conversation, Subject: Ghana, Participants: The President, Ambassador William P. Mahoney, November 19, 1963. See also, Note to the President from Mrs. Lincoln. Memorandum for Mr. McGeorge Bundy, From: Benjamin H. Read, Subject: Appointment with the President for William P. Mahoney, Jr., American Ambassador to Ghana, November 19, 1963, NSF, JFKL. Oral history of William P. Mahoney, JFKL.

49. Quoted in G. Mennen Williams, *Africa for the Africans* (Grand Rapids; 1969), pp. 160–61.

50. William P. Mahoney, Jr., "Nkrumah in Retrospect," The *Review of Politics*, vol. 30, no. 2, April 1968.

51. OHWPM, JFKL. Dei-Anang, *The Administration of Ghana's Foreign Relations: 1957–1965*, pp. 53–54.

52. The conspiracy that led to the February 24, 1966 coup d'état began in the summer of 1965. The CIA station monitored the conspiracy via periodic reports from J.W.K. Harlley. Although Ambassador Mahoney (who had kept a tight rein on CIA activities after the fall 1961 incident with Dr. Danquah) left Ghana for good in June 1965 (and was replaced by Franklin Williams in December 1965), interviews conducted by the author did not reveal that the CIA station operationally contributed to the coup. Interviews: Howard Bain (CIA station chief in Accra, 1963–66), 8/17/77, Washington, D.C.; John W. Foley, Jr., (Chargé d'Affaires, June–December 1965), 10/14/76, Washington, D.C.; Franklin Williams, 2/18/73, New York City; J.W.K. Harlley. The major objective of the CIA in the aftermath of the coup was to procure intelligence from the Chinese, Russian, and North Vietnamese missions in Ghana as well as to recruit personnel from those embassies. Journalist Seymour Hersh, on the other hand, has contended that the CIA's role in the coup was determinative. *The New York Times*, May 9, 1978.

53. Interview: Dei-Anang.

54. Memorandum for McGeorge Bundy, From: B.H. Read, Subject: Council of Minister's Meeting, OAU, August 1, 1963. Deptel to Lisbon 400, February 18, 1963, NSF, JFKL. Rusk did not take the pledge seriously—an accurate supposition for the most part. Marcum, *The Angolan Revolution*, vol. II, p. 76.

55. Memorandum for Mr. Dungan, From: Samuel E. Belk, Subject: Portuguese Africa, January 9, 1962, NSF, JFKL.

56. "Now the Portuguese have something to yell about," Ball told Bundy after one Portuguese plane was downed in Portuguese Guinea. Lisbon 47, July 11, 1963. Telcon, Bundy/Ball, 3/16/63. Special Report, Office of Current Intelligence, "The Angolan Rebellion and White Unrest," CIA, OCI No. 0274/63B, 5 April 1963, NSF, JFKL.

57. Telcon: Ball/Harriman, 7/31/63. Harriman remembered meeting Salazar consequent to organizing the Marshall plan. In an interview with the author, Harriman described Salazar as having "no interest in improving the

lives of his people through education or welfare services. He dealt with human beings like one would deal with livestock."

58. Interviews: Fredericks, Tyler

59. Interview: Fredericks. A similar account of the incident is in Schlesinger, *Robert Kennedy and His Times*, p. 562.

60. Telcons, Ball/Kaysen, 5/9/63, 5/10/63. Interviews: Harriman, Ball, Fredericks.

61. Special Report, Office of Current Intelligence, "The Angolan Rebellion and White Unrest," CIA, OCI No. 0274/63B, 5 April 1963. See also Memorandum to the Secretary, From: INR—Thomas L. Hughes, Subject: Prospects for Angolan Nationalist Movement, RAF–51, November 5, 1963, NSF, JFKL.

62. Circular 92, July 17, 1962, NSF, JFKL.

63. Lisbon tel. 868, May 20, 1963, NSF, JFKL.

64. A-642 from Lisbon, Memorandum of Conversation, Participants: Alberto Franco Nogueira, Richard M. Nixon, William L. Blue, June 15, 1963. Note from Michael Forrestal to Arthur Schlesinger, Jr., undated, Schlesinger Papers, JFKL.

65. Stevenson to Kennedy, June 26, 1963, NSF, JFKL. Lisbon 761, April 10, 1963, USUN 3717, April 10, 1963, Deptel to USUN 2572, April 11, 1963. Draft of Letter to Salazar, Deptel 22 to London, June 26, 1962. Memorandum for the President from Carl Kaysen, July 4, 1963, NSF, JFKL.

66. Telcons, Stevenson/Ball, 6/29/63, 7/9/63. Bundy/Ball, 7/5/63. Interview: Kaysen. Telcon, The President/Ball, 7/15/63. Martin, *Adlai Stevenson and the World*, p. 764.

67. Memorandum for the Secretary of Defense, From: Maxwell D. Taylor, Chairman, Joint Chiefs of Staff, July 10, 1963. Deptel 42 to Lisbon, Operational Immediate, July 15, 1963. Lisbon 66, July 16, 1963, NSF, JFKL. Cleveland met with the President to plot strategy on July 15. Kennedy had earlier met with several of his advisers and State Department officials on July 13. He repeatedly expressed doubts about supporting a resolution that would call for an arms embargo. Memorandum for the President, Subject: U.S. Strategy in the UN Security Countil re Portuguese Territories, From: George W. Ball, July 13, 1963, NSF, JFKL.

68. Martin, *Adlai Stevenson and the World*, pp. 766–67. Schlesinger, *A Thousand Days*, p. 538. Kennedy's instructions to Stevenson are set forth in Deptel 168 to USUN, July 19, 1963, NSF, JFKL.

69. USUN 208, July 23, 1963, NSF, JFKL. *Report on the UN: 1963*. pp. 55–56. USUN 282, July 29, 1963. UN Security Council, Res. S/5372, 26 July 1963 and S/5380, 31 July 1963 with Stevenson's handwritten alterations in the drafts, AESP, Princeton University. Interview Quaison-Sackey. Quaison-Sackey was later Nkrumah's foreign minister. Rusk used the word "brilliant" to describe Stevenson's work at the General Assembly plenary session on Angola the previous February. Deptel 2020 from Secretary, February 3, 1963, ASEP, Princeton University. Memorandum to the Secretary, From: IO— Harlan Cleveland, Subject: Next Steps in Security Council on Question of Portuguese Territories, July 26, 1963, NSF, JFKL.

70. Telcons, Ball/Cleveland, July 29, 1963, July 27, 1963.

71. Memorandum for the President, From: William H. Brubeck, Subject: Portuguese African Problem, July 30, 1963, NSF, JFKL.

72. Telcon, Ball/Ormsby Gore, July 26, 1963. Telcon, Ball/Cleveland/Bundy, July 30, 1963.

73. Memorandum for the Record, Meeting with the President on Portuguese Africa, Tuesday, July 30, 1963, 11:00 A.M. William H. Brubeck, NSF, JFKL.

74. Martin, *Adlai Stevenson and the World*, p. 768. Telcon, Cleveland/Ball, 7/31/63.

75. Memorandum of Conversation, Subject: Security Council Resolution on Portugal, Participants: Ambassador C. Burke Elbrick, Francis E. Meloy, Jr., July 31, 1963. USUN 309, July 31, 1963, NSF, JFKL. Talk with Nogueira in New York, Participants: Ambassador Yost and Harlan Cleveland, July 31, 1963. In a letter to the author (December 5, 1977) Franco Nogueira stated that Stevenson's version of what happened was exaggerated. According to the foreign minister, the Portuguese had information that Stevenson had in his possession a CIA report stating that Portugal was indeed giving autonomy to its African citizens.

76. Telcon, Ball/Cleveland, 7/31/63, Telcon, Ball/Harriman, 7/31/63. Memorandum of telephone conversation, Pereira/Harriman, 7/31/63, for Mr. Bundy.

77. This was the impression of both McGeorge Bundy and Lord Harlech (David Ormsby Gore) in interviews. It is also consistent with Kennedy's own observation at the July 18th meeting about the Security Council debate.

78. Memorandum for Secretary McNamara from John F. Kennedy, July 31, 1963, NSF, JFKL. Sorenson, *Kennedy*, p. 538. He also indicated his intentions to Ambassador Ormsby Gore.

79. Quoted in Schlesinger, *Robert Kennedy and His Times*, p. 561, McNamara's reply of August 14, 1963 has been exempted from declassification, NSF, JFKL.

80. Mr. Ball's Instructions for His Mission to Portugal, undated, NSF, JFKL. Telcon, Bundy/Ball, 8/22/63. The European Bureau suggested that Ball soft-pedal Angola policy in his talks with Salazar. Bundy rejected this idea outright. The notion that "by some fairly gentle talk you can persuade Salazar to do some fairly gentle things and that these gentle things will lead the Africans to be gentle just doesn't seem like the real world to me." The European Bureau's paper is dated August 21, 1963 and entitled Visit of the Under Secretary to Lisbon, August 29–30, 1963, NSF, JFKL.

81. Meeting with the President on Under Secretary Ball's Debriefing Meeting on his Lisbon's Meetings with Salazar, September 9, 1963. Talking Points Paper for the President's meeting with Foreign Minister Franco Nogueira on November 7, 1963, NSF, JFKL. Interview: Ball. See also, *The Discipline of Power*, pp. 246–48.

82. Ball to Salazar, October 21, 1963, p. 12. Salazar to Ball, February 24, 1964, p. 10, NSF, JFKL.

83. Memorandum for the President, From: George W. Ball, Subject: U.S. Policy Regarding Portuguese Territories and Apartheid in South Africa, 7/13/63, NSF, JFKL.

84. Schlesinger, *A Thousand Days*, pp. 535–36.

85. Ball memorandum to the President, 7/13/63, NSF, JFKL.

86. Martin, *Adlai Stevenson and the World*, p. 763.

87. Schlesinger, *A Thousand Days*, pp. 535–36.

88. Stevenson to John Steinbeck, August 15, 1963, AESP, Princeton University.

89. USUN tel. 1817, November 7, 1963, NSF, JFKL.

90. Memorandum to Bundy quoted in Schlesinger, *Robert Kennedy and His Times*, p. 562.

91. Ball to Salazar, October 21, 1963, NSF, JFKL.

92. National Security Study Memorandum 39, quoted in Ernest Harsch and Tony Thomas, *Angola, The Hidden History of Washington's War*, pp. 22–23.

93. Interview: Franco Nogueira.

10. Conclusion

1. Deptel 2238 to New Delhi, February 18, 1961, NSF, JFKL.

2. Henry A. Kissinger, *American Foreign Policy, Three Essays* (Washington, D.C., 1969), p. 14.

3. Joseph Kraft, *Profiles in Power*, (New York, 1966), p. 6.

4. Interview: Ormsby Gore.

5. James Reston, *Sketches in the Sand* (New York, 1967), p. 472. Theodore Sorensen, *Decision-Making in the White House*, Foreword by John F. Kennedy (New York, 1963), p. xi.

6. George W. Ball, *Diplomacy for a Crowded World* (Boston, 1976), p. 61.

7. Joseph Conrad, *Heart of Darkness* (Garden City, 1924), p. 95.

8. Thomas Halper, *Foreign Policy Crises, Appearance and Reality in Decisionmaking*, (Columbus, Ohio, 1971), p. 188.

9. See Attwood's account of his tenure in Guinea in *The Reds and the Blacks, A Personal Adventure* (New York, 1967).

10. Ball to Salazar, October 21, 1963.

11. Quoted in Schlesinger, *A Thousand Days*, p. 515.

12. Edited draft of Report on Trip to Middle and Far East, November 3, 1951, PPP, JFKL.

Bibliography

ACRONYMS AND ABBREVIATIONS

Archival Collections

AESP	Adlai E. Stevenson Papers
CBP	Chester Bowles Papers
CFCP	Chad F. Calhoun Papers
CRISP	Centre de Recherches et d'Information Socio-Politiques
GMWP	G. Mennen Williams Papers
JFKL	John F. Kennedy Presidential Library
NSF	National Security Files (JFKL)
POF	President's Office Files (JFKL)
PPP	Pre-Presidential Papers (JFKL)
NARS	National Archives and Records Service
SCOR	Security Council Official Records

Documents

Deptel State Department telegram
Leotel, Accra tel., etc. Embassy telegram
Memcon Memorandum of Conversation
NIACT Night Action telegram
TDCS CIA Information Report telegram
Telcon Transcribed telephone conversation

U.S. Government Agencies and Bureaus

AF	Bureau of African Affairs (State Department)
CIA	Central Intelligence Agency
DOD	Department of Defense
EUR	Bureau of European Affairs (State Department)
INR	Bureau of Intelligence and Research (State Department)
NSC	National Security Council (White House)
ONE	Office of National Estimates (CIA)
USUN	United States Mission to the United Nations

Political Parties

ABAKO	Alliance des Ba-Kongo (Kasavubu's party)
CONAKAT	Rassemblement Katangais (Tshombe's party)

MNC/L	Mouvement National Congolais/Lumumba (Lumumba's party)
PSA	Parti Solidaire Africain (Gizenga's party)
CPP	Convention People's Party (Nkrumah's party)
UP	United Party (Danquah's and Busia's party)
UPA	Uniao das Populações de Angola (Roberto's party, later reconstituted as the FNLA)
MPLA	Movimento Popular de Libertação de Angola (Neto's party)
FLN	Front de Libération Nationale (Algerian liberation movement)

Miscellaneous

ANC	Armée Nationale Congolaise (the Congolese national army)
NATO	North Atlantic Treaty Organization
ONUC	Organisation des Nations Unies au Congo (UN peacekeeping operation in the Congo)

UNPUBLISHED SOURCES

Private Collections

George W. Ball Papers: Princeton, New Jersey
Chad F. Calhoun Papers: Palm Springs, California
Alberto Franco Nogueira Papers: London, England
George Ivan Smith Papers: Lypiatt, England

Public Collections

Bibliotheque de la Ministère des Affaires Étrangères: Brussels, Belgium
    Public Diplomatic Records
British Public Record Office: Kew Garden, England
    Records of the Foreign Office
Columbia University, Oral History Collection: New York, New York
    Chester Bowles
Dwight D. Eisenhower Presidential Library: Abilene, Kansas
John F. Kennedy Presidential Library: Waltham, Massachusetts
    National Security Files, Pre-Presidential Papers, President's Office Files,
    Speech Files
    Chad C. Calhoun Papers
    Arthur M. Schlesinger, Jr., Papers

Oral Histories

Dean Acheson
Chester Bowles
Edmund A. Gullion
Phillip M. Kaiser
William P. Mahoney
Pedro Theotónio Pereira
Mongi Slim
Barbara Ward
G. Mennen Williams

National Archives: Washington, D.C.
G. Mennen Williams Papers, Senate Foreign Relations
Meetings Transcripts (declassified executive sessions), 1961–63
Princeton University, Seeley Mudd Manuscript Library: Princeton, New
Jersey Adlai E. Stevenson Papers
Yale University, Sterling Memorial Library: New Haven, Connecticut
Chester Bowles Papers
U.S. Department of State, Bureau of Public Affairs: Washington, D.C.
Public Files

Unpublished Monographs

Hoffacker, Lewis. "Reflections on the Katanga Case: British and Other
Connections," Remarks at the Center for British Studies, University of
Texas, October 7, 1977.
Smith, George Ivan. "Along the Edge of Peace—Recollections of an Inter-
national Civil Servant," Australian Broadcasting Commission, The Boyer
Lectures of 1964.
Vandewalle, Frédéric, *Mille et Quatre Jours, Contes du Zaire et du Shaba.*
(13 Vols.)

Government Documents

U.S. Congress, Senate, Committee on Foreign Relations, *Study Mission to
Africa*, September-October 1961. Reports of Senators Albert Gore, Philip
A. Hart and Maurine B. Neuberger, 87th Cong., 1st Session.
U.S. Congress, House of Representatives, Foreign Affairs Committee.
"U.N. Operations in the Congo." Hearings. 87th Cong., 1st Session 1961.
U.S. Congress, House of Representatives, Foreign Affairs Committee
Africa Subcommittee. "Immediate and Future Problems in the Congo."
Hearings. 88th Cong., 1st Session, 1963.
U.S. Congress, Senate, Committee on Foreign Relations, Hearings. 88th
Cong., 1st Session, 1963.
U.S. Congress, House of Representatives. Foreign Affairs Committee.
"United Nations Use of Peacekeeping Forces in the Middle East, the
Congo and Cyprus." 89th Cong., 2nd Session, 1966.
U.S. Department of State. "U.S. Participation in the U.N.," Reports by the
President to the Congress, for the years 1960, 1961, 1962, and 1963.

United Nations Documents

Records of the Security Council meetings on the Congo and the Portuguese
territories, SCOR, 15th through 17th years.
Records of the General Assembly meetings on the Congo and the Portu-
guese territories, GAOR, 15th through 16th sessions.
First and Second Progress Reports to the Secretary-General from his
Special Representative in the Congo, Ambassador Rajeshwar Dayal
(S/4531, Sept. 21, 1960, A/4557, November 2, 1960).
Report on the Investigation into Lumumba's Death (A/4964, Nov. 11,
1961).
Report on the Investigation into Hammarskjold's Death (A/5069, March
20, 1962).

Summary Chronology of United Nations Actions Relating to the Congo (June 30, 1950–December 31, 1962).

General Assembly, Report of the Special Committee on Territories under Portuguese Administration (A/5160, August 15, 1962).

PUBLISHED SOURCES

Books

GENERAL

Acheson, Dean. *Present at the Creation: My Years in the State Department.* New York: 1969.

Attwood, William. *The Reds and the Blacks, A Personal Adventure.* New York: 1967.

Ball, George W. *The Discipline of Power.* Boston: 1968.

————. *Diplomacy for a Crowded World.* Boston: 1976.

————. *The Past Has Another Pattern, Memoirs.* New York: 1982.

Barnet, Richard J. *Intervention and Revolution, The United States and the Third World.* New York: 1968.

Betts, Raymond F. *The "Scramble" for Africa, Causes and Dimensions of Empire.* Boston: 1966.

Bowles, Chester. *Africa's Challenge to America.* Berkeley: 1956.

Bowles, Chester. *Promises to Keep, My Years in Public Life.* New York: 1974.

Brzezinski, Zbigniew, ed. *Africa and the Communist World.* Stanford: 1963.

Burns, James MacGregor. *John Kennedy: A Political Profile.* New York: 1961.

Conrad, Joseph. *Heart of Darkness.* Garden City: 1924.

Cronen, E. David, ed. *The Political Thought of Woodrow Wilson.* New York: 1965.

Dallek, Robert. *Franklin D. Roosevelt and American Foreign Policy, 1932–1945.* New York: 1979.

Davidson, Basil. *Let Freedom Come, Africa in Modern History.* Boston: 1978.

de Gaulle, Charles. *Memoirs of Hope.* New York: 1971.

Divine, Robert A. *Eisenhower and the Cold War.* New York: 1981.

Donavan, Robert J. *Tumultuous Years, The Presidency of Harry S Truman, 1949–1953.* New York: 1982.

Eisenhower, Dwight D. *Mandate for Change, 1953–1956.* Garden City: 1963.

————. *Waging Peace, 1956–1961.* Garden City: 1965.

Emerson, Rupert. *Africa and United States Policy.* Englewood Cliffs: 1967.

Fage, J.D. *A History of West Africa.* Cambridge, U.K.: 1969.

Fairlie, Henry. *The Kennedy Promise.* New York: 1973.

Friedland, Robert and Rosberg, Carl, eds. *African Socialism.* London: 1964.

Galbraith, J.K. *Ambassador's Journal.* Boston: 1969.

Gati, Charles, ed. *Caging the Bear.* New York: 1974.

Halberstam, David. *The Making of A Quagmire.* New York: 1964.

———. *The Best and the Brightest.* New York: 1972.

Halper, Thomas. *Foreign Policy Crises, Appearance and Reality in Decisionmaking.* Columbus, Ohio: 1971.

Hilsman, Roger. *To Move A Nation.* Garden City: 1967.

Hammarskjold, Dag. *Markings.* Westminster, MD: 1964.

Hovet, Thomas Jr. *Africa in the United Nations.* London: 1963.

Kennedy, John F. *The Strategy of Peace.* New York: 1961.

———. *Public Papers: 1961–63.* 3 Vols. Washington: 1961–63.

Kissinger, Henry A. *American Foreign Policy.* New York: 1969.

Kraft, Joseph. *Profiles in Power.* New York: 1966.

Lacouture, Jean. *Ho Chi Minh. A Political Biography.* New York: 1968.

Lash, Joseph P. *Hammarskjold: Custodian of the Brushfire Peace.* New York: 1961.

Legum, Colin. *Pan-Africanism.* London: 1965.

Levin, N. Gordon Jr. *Woodrow Wilson and World Politics, America's Response to War and Revolution.* New York: 1968.

Link, Arthur F. *Wilson the Diplomatist.* Baltimore: 1957.

Macmillan, Harold. *Pointing the Way.* London: 1972.

———. *At the End of the Day.* London: 1976.

Marks, John D. and Marchetti, Victor. *The CIA and the Cult of Intelligence.* New York: 1974.

Martin, John Bartlow. *Adlai Stevenson and the World, The Life of Adlai E. Stevenson.* New York: 1978.

McKay, Vernon. *Africa in World Politics.* New York: 1963.

Middleton, Neil, ed. *The I.F. Stone's Weekly Reader.* New York: 1974.

Miroff, Bruce. *Pragmatic Illusions, The Presidential Politics of John F. Kennedy.* New York: 1976.

Nielsen, Waldemar. *The Great Powers and Africa.* New York: 1969.

Nunnerly, David. *President Kennedy and Britain.* New York: 1972.

Parmet, Herbert S. *Jack, The Struggles of John F. Kennedy.* New York: 1980.

———. *The Presidency of John F. Kennedy.* New York: 1983.

Reston, James. *Sketches in the Sand.* New York: 1967.

Schlesinger, Arthur M. Jr. *A Thousand Days, John F. Kennedy in the White House.* New York: 1983.

———. *Robert F. Kennedy and His Times* ? ? ? ?

Sorensen, Theodore. *Decision-Making in the White House,* Foreword by John F. Kennedy. New York: 1963.

———. *Kennedy.* New York: 1966.

Spaak, Paul-Henri. *The Continuing Battle, Memoirs of a European: 1936–1966.* New York: 1971.

Steel, Ronald. *Walter Lippmann and the American Century.* Boston: 1980.

Talbott, Strobe, ed. and trans. *Khrushchev Remembers, The Last Testament.* Boston: 1974.

Truman, Harry S. *Memoirs I: Year of Decisions.* Garden City: 1955.

Tully, Andrew. *CIA, The Inside Story.* New York: 1962.

Urquhart, Brian. *Hammarskjold.* New York: 1972.

Walton, Richard J. *Cold War and Counterrevolution: The Foreign Policy of John F. Kennedy*. New York: 1972.
————. *Adlai Stevenson, The Remnants of Power*. New York: 1974.
Williams, G. Mennen. *Africa for the Africans*. Grand Rapids: 1969.
Wills, A.J. *An Introduction to the History of Central Africa*. London: 1967.

THE CONGO

Ascherson, Neal. *The King Incorporated: Leopold II in the Age of Trusts*. New York: 1964.
Borri, Michel. *Nous ces Affreux (dossier secret de l'ex-congo belge)*. Paris: 1962.
Bowett, D.W. *United Nations Forces: A Legal Study*. New York: 1964.
Burns, Arthur Lee and Nina Heathcote. *Peace-keeping by U.N. Forces: From Suez to the Congo*. New York: 1963.
Carl, Frederick R. *Joseph Conrad: The Three Lives*. New York: 1979.
CRISP. *Morphologie des Groupes Financiers*. Brussels: 1966.
Davister, Pierre. *Katanga: enjeu du monde!* Brussels: 1960.
Dayal, Rajeshwar. *Mission for Hammarskjold*. Princeton: 1974.
de Vos, Pierre. *Vie et Mort de Lumumba*. Paris: 1961:
Gérard-Libois, J. and Verhaegen, Benoit, eds. Dossiers du CRISP (Centre de Recherches et Information Socio-Politiques), *Congo 1960, 1961, 1962, 1963*. Brussels: 1961–1964.
Gérard-Libois, Jules. *Katanga Secession*. Madison: 1966.
Heinz, G. and Donnay, H. *Lumumba: The Last Fifty Days*. New York: 1969.
Hempstone, Smith. *Rebels, Mercenaries and Dividends: The Katanga Story*. New York: 1962.
Hoskyns, Catherine. *The Congo Since Independence, January 1960–December 1961*. London: 1965.
Kanza, Thomas. *Congo 196?*. Brussels: 1962.
Kanza, Thomas. *The Rise and Fall of Patrice Lumumba, Conflict in the Congo*. Cambridge: 1979.
Kitchen, Helen (ed.). *Congo Story*. New York: 1967.
Lumumba, Patrice. *Congo, My Country*. New York: 1962.
Lefever, Ernest W. *Uncertain Mandate, Politics of the UN Operation*. Baltimore: 1967.
Legum, Colin. *Congo Disaster*. Baltimore: 1961.
Millin, S.G. *Rhodes*. London: 1952.
Monheim, Francis. *Mobutu, l'homme Seul*. Brussels: 1962.
O'Brien, Conor Cruise. *To Katanga and Back, A UN Case History*. New York: 1962.
Struelens, Michel. *The United Nations in the Congo—or O.N.U.C.—and International Politics*. Brussels: 1976.
Trinquier, Roger et al. *Notre Guerre au Katanga*. Paris: 1963.
Weissman, Stephen R. *American Foreign Policy in the Congo, 1960–1964*. Ithaca: 1974.
Welensky, Roy. *Welensky's 4000 Days*. London: 1964.
Young, Crawford. *Politics in the Congo*. Princeton: 1965.

GHANA

Alexander, H.T. *African Tightrope*. New York: 1966.

Apter, David. *Ghana in Transition*. New York: 1963.

Austin, Dennis. *Politics in Ghana, 1946–1960*. London: 1964.

Bing, Geoffrey. *Reap the Whirlwind*. London: 1970.

Bretton, Henry L. *The Rise and Fall of Kwame Nkrumah, A Study of Personal Rule in Africa*. New York: 1966.

Davidson, Basil. *Black Star: A View of the Life and Times of Kwame Nkrumah*. London: 1973.

Dei-Anang, Michael. *The Administration of Ghana's Foreign Relations, 1957–1965: A Personal Memoir*. London: 1975.

Facts on File: Ghana. New York: 1971.

Lacouture, Jean. *The Demigods, Charismatic Leadership in the Third World*. New York: 1970.

Nkrumah, Kwame. *The Autobiography of Kwame Nkrumah*. Edinburgh: 1957.

————. *I Speak of Freedom*. London: 1961.

————. *Africa Must Unite*. London: 1963.

————. *Neo-Colonialism, The Last Stage of Imperialism*. London: 1965.

————. *Challenge of the Congo*. New York: 1967.

————. *Dark Days in Ghana*. New York: 1968.

Ofosu-Appiah, L.H. *The Life and Times of J.B. Danquah*. Accra: 1974.

Omari, T. Peter. *Kwame Nkrumah, The Anatomy of an African Dictatorship*. New York: 1970.

Thompson, W. Scott. *Ghana's Foreign Policy, 1957–1966: Diplomacy, Ideology, and the New State*. Princeton: 1969.

PORTUGAL AND ANGOLA

Abshire, David M. and Samuels, Michael A., eds. *Portuguese Africa: A Handbook*. New York: 1969.

Bender, Gerald J. *Angola Under the Portuguese, The Myth and the Reality*. Berkeley: 1978.

Chilcote, Ronald. *Portuguese Africa*. Englewood Cliffs: 1969.

Davidson, Basil. *In the Eye of the Storm: Angola's People*. Garden City: 1972.

Ehnmark, Anders and Wastberg, Per. *Angola and Mozambique: The Case Against Portugal*. London: 1963.

Franco Nogueira, Alberto. *The United Nations and Portugal: A Case Study in Anti-Colonialism*. London: 1963.

————. *The Third World*. London: 1967.

Galvão, Henrique. *Santa Maria: My Crusade for Portugal*. Cleveland: 1961.

Humbaraci, Arslan and Muchnik, Nicole. *Portugal's African Wars*. New York: 1971.

Kay, Hugh. *Salazar and Modern Portugal*. New York: 1970.

Marcum, John. *The Angolan Revolution (Vol. 1): The Anatomy of an Explosion (1950–1962)*. Cambridge, MA: 1969.

Marques, A.H. de Oliveira. *History of Portugal*, 2 vols. New York: 1972.

Moreira, Adriano. *Portugal's Stand in Africa*. New York: 1962.

Rodrigues, Jose Honório. *Brazil and Africa.* Berkeley: 1965.
Wheeler, Douglas L. and Pelissier, René. *Angola.* New York: 1971.

Articles

THE CONGO

"At Tshombe's Disposal," *The New Republic.* Vol. 148 (January 8, 1962), pp. 3–4.
Boyd, Andrew. "Britain's Dixie," *The Nation*, January 20, 1962, pp. 48–50.
Burnet, Alistair. "The Katanga Fumble," *The New Republic*, December 25, 1961, p. 8.
Cousins, Norman. "Report from the Congo," *Saturday Review*, February 3, 1962, pp. 31–36.
Dodd, Thomas J. "Congo: The Untold Story," *National Review*, vol. 13 August 28, 1962, pp. 136–144.
Good, Robert C. "The Congo Crisis: A Study of Postcolonial Politics," in Laurence W. Martin (ed.), *Neutralism and Nonalignment.* New York: 1962.
Gullion, Edmund A. "Crisis Management: Lessons from the Congo," *Crises and Concepts in International Affairs* (April 1965), pp. 49–63.
Healey, Denis. "Britain and Katanga," *The New Leader*, December 25, 1961, pp. 6–7.
Hoffman, Stanley. "In Search of a Thread: The UN in the Congo Labyrinth," *International Organization*, vol. 16 Spring 1962, pp. 331–61.
Lemarchand, René. "The Limits of Self-Determination: The Case of the Katanga Secession," *The American Political Science Review*, vol. 56 (1962), pp. 404–16.
Schacter, Oscar. "Dag Hammarskjold and the Relation of Law to Politics," *The American Journal of International Law*, vol. 56, January, 1962, pp. 1–8.
Van den Haag, Ernest. "The Lesson of the Congo," *National Review*, vol. 16 (September 8, 1964), pp. 771–73, 785.
Wigny, Pierre. "Belgium and the Congo," *International Affairs*, vol. 37 (July 1961).

GHANA

Mahoney, William R., Jr. "Nkrumah in Retrospect," *Review of Politics*, vol. 30, No. 2 (April 1968).
Nkrumah, Kwame. "Africa Prospect," *Foreign Affairs*, vol. 37, No. 4.
Seikman, Philip. "Edgar Kaiser's Gamble in Africa," *Fortune*, November 1961.

PORTUGAL AND ANGOLA

Acheson, Dean. "Fifty Years Later," *Yale Review*, vol. 51, Autumn 1961.
Chilcote, Ronald. "Angola or the Azores?" *The New Republic*, May 18, 1962.
Duffy, James. "Portugal in Africa," *Foreign Affairs*, vol. 39 (April 1961), pp. 481–493.
Farmer, Gene. "Dictator on the Defensive," *Life*, May 4, 1962.

Friedenberg, Daniel M. "Public Relations for Portugal: The Angola Story as Told by Selvage and Lee," *The New Republic*, April 2, 1962, pp. 9–12.

Interview with Portugal's Prime Minister, Dr. António de Oliveira Salazar, *U.S. News and World Report*, July 9, 1962, pp. 78–81.

Pereira, Pedro Theotónio. "Wars of 'Liberation' in Africa: What They Mean," *U.S. News and World Report*. October 30, 1961, pp. 74–76.

Welles, Benjamin. "Salazar in Trouble," *Atlantic Monthly*, August, 1962, pp. 57–62.

Newspapers and Periodicals

UNITED STATES

The New York Times
Washington Post
The New Republic
Foreign Affairs
Nation
Africa Report
Hispanic-American Review

EUROPE

Le Monde (Paris)
Jeune Afrique (Paris)
Présence Africaine (Paris)
Courrier Hebdomodaire (Brussels)
La Libre Belgique (Brussels)
West Africa (London)
Economist (London)
Africa Confidential (London)
The Observer (London)
The Times (London)

AFRICA

Présence Congolaise (Léopoldville)
Spark (Accra)
Ghanaian Times (Accra)
Evening News (Accra)

Index